Physicalism and Its Discontents

Physicalism, a topic that has been central to philosophy of mind and metaphysics in recent years, is the philosophical view that everything in the space-time world is ultimately physical. The physicalist will claim that all facts about the mind and the mental are physical facts and deny the existence of mental events and states insofar as these are thought of as independent of physical things, events, and states.

This collection of new essays offers a series of "state-of-the-art" perspectives on this important doctrine and brings new depth and breadth to the philosophical debate. A group of distinguished philosophers, comprising both physicalists and their critics, consider a wide range of issues including the historical genesis and present justification of physicalism; its metaphysical presuppositions and methodological role; its implications for mental causation; and the account it provides of consciousness.

Carl Gillett is Assistant Professor of Philosophy at Illinois Wesleyan University.

Barry Loewer is Professor of Philosophy at Rutgers University.

Physicalism and Its Discontents

Edited by

CARL GILLETT
Illinois Wesleyan University

BARRY LOEWER
Rutgers University

CAMBRIDGE
UNIVERSITY PRESS

CAMBRIDGE UNIVERSITY PRESS
Cambridge, New York, Melbourne, Madrid, Cape Town, Singapore, São Paulo

Cambridge University Press
The Edinburgh Building, Cambridge CB2 8RU, UK

Published in the United States of America by Cambridge University Press, New York

www.cambridge.org
Information on this title: www.cambridge.org/9780521801751

First published 2001
This digitally printed version 2007

A catalogue record for this publication is available from the British Library

Library of Congress Cataloguing in Publication data

Physicalism and its discontents / edited by Carl Gillett, Barry Loewer.
p. cm.
Includes bibliographical references and index.
Contents: The rise of physicalism / David Papineau – From physics to physicalism
/ Barry Loewer – Sufficiency claims and physicalism, a formulation / D. Gene Witmer
– Realization and mental causation / Sydney Shoemaker – Physicalism and psychology, a
plea for a substantive philosophy of mind / Georges Rey – Davidson and non-reductive
materialism, a tale of two cultures / Howard Robinson – Substance physicalism / Noa
Latham – Possibility, physical and metaphysical / Stephen Leeds – The roots of
reductionism / Scott Sturgeon – The significance of emergence / Tim Crane – The
methodological role of physicalism, a minimal skepticism / Carl Gillett – Physicalism,
empiricism, and positivism / Gary Gates – Mental causation and consciousness, the two
mind-body problems for the physicalist / Jaegwon Kim – How not to solve the mind-
body problem / Colin McGinn – Deconstructing New Wave materialism / Terence
Horgan and John Tienson – In defence of New Wave materialism, a response to
Horgan and Tienson / Brian McLaughlin – Physicalism unfalsified, Chalmer's
inconclusive conceivability argument / Andrew Melnyk.
1. Materialism. 2. Philosophy of mind. I. Gillett, Carl, 1967– II. Loewer, Barry.
B825 .P49 2001
146'.3–dc21 00-065155

ISBN 978-0-521-80175-1 hardback
ISBN 978-0-521-04212-3 paperback

Contents

Part III   Physicalism and Consciousness: A Continuing Dialectic

Arguments for Pessimism

Optimistic Rejoinders

Contributors

TIM CRANE is a Reader at University College, London.

GARY GATES is an Assistant Professor at Brown University.

CARL GILLETT is an Assistant Professor at Illinois Wesleyan University.

TERENCE HORGAN is a Professor at the University of Memphis.

JAEGWON KIM is a Professor at Brown University.

NOA LATHAM is an Assistant Professor at Barnard College, Columbia University.

STEPHEN LEEDS is an Associate Professor at the University of Colorado, Boulder.

BARRY LOEWER is a Professor at Rutgers, The State University of New Jersey, New Brunswick.

COLIN MCGINN is a Professor at Rutgers, The State University of New Jersey, New Brunswick.

BRIAN P. MCLAUGHLIN is a Professor at Rutgers, The State University of New Jersey, New Brunswick.

ANDREW MELNYK is an Assistant Professor at the University of Missouri, Columbia.

DAVID PAPINEAU is a Professor at Kings College, London.

GEORGES REY is a Professor at the University of Maryland, College Park.

HOWARD ROBINSON is Head of the Department at Liverpool University and Soros Professor of Philosophy at Eovtos Lorand University.

SYDNEY SHOEMAKER is a Professor at Cornell University.

SCOTT STURGEON is a Lecturer at Birkbeck College, London.

JOHN TIENSON is a Professor at the University of Memphis.

D. GENE WITMER is an Assistant Professor at the University of Florida.

Preface

Every era has its weltanschauung and in much contemporary philosophy the doctrine of 'physicalism' plays this role. Such foundational assumptions exert considerable influence by subtly configuring philosophical debates, problems, and projects, though the precise nature of these assumptions is often hard to clearly discern. Happily, however, philosophers have recently begun to subject physicalism to sustained scrutiny, both positive and negative. Exactly how the doctrine of physicalism should be formulated, what its significance is, and whether it has a justification, in addition to a range of other issues, have all recently been discussed.

We believe such attention is intellectually a very healthy development. There are always parts of the reigning weltanschauung that it would be productive to discard and those that ought to be retained. But this process of critically evaluating various assumptions only proceeds in lockstep with the illumination of their natures. The present anthology was conceived with these thoughts in mind and the chapters that follow all seek to further the project of critically illuminating various aspects of physicalism and its implications. Though we shall let the authors speak for themselves, and the variety of their concerns precludes easy summary, it may help the reader to have a general guide to the volume's contents. The largest section, "Part 1, Physicalism," comprises chapters generally sympathetic to the doctrine of physicalism. Among the work they undertake, is that of articulating the historical genesis and present justification of physicalism; its most adequate formulation; modal status; and its implications for mental causation and the special sciences. A range of more or less critical chapters comprise the next section, "Part 2, Physicalist Discontents," and take as their focus the metaphysical presuppositions of physicalism, its methodological role and ultimate significance. The chapters of the final section, "Part 3, Physicalism and Consciousness: A Continuing Dialectic," consider one of the primary issues associated with physicalism: its implications for consciousness. The section's first half, "Arguments for Pessimism," collects chapters arguing for skepticism about various physicalist accounts of consciousness; while the chapters of the second half, "Optimistic Rejoinders," argue that such pessimistic arguments are misplaced.

We would like to thank a number of people for their help and advice with this volume. In particular, we are grateful to Terry Moore and our editors at Cambridge University Press, for their patient help and encouragement. We would also like to thank David Rehagen and Ben Haines for their help in formatting, editing, and proofreading the contents of the volume.

Part I

Physicalism

1

The Rise of Physicalism

DAVID PAPINEAU

No one could seriously, rationally suppose that the existence of antibiotics or electric lights or rockets to the moon disproves ... mind-body dualism.

Stephen R.L. Clark (1996)

Introduction

In this chapter I want to discuss the way in which physical science has come to claim a particular kind of hegemony over other subjects in the second half of this century. This claim to hegemony is generally known by the name of *physicalism*. In this chapter I shall try to understand why this doctrine has come to prominence in recent decades. By placing this doctrine in a historical context, we will be better able to appreciate its strengths and weaknesses.

As a preliminary, note that contemporary physicalism is an ontological rather than a methodological doctrine. It claims that everything[1] is physically constituted, not that everything should be studied by the methods used in physical science. This emphasis on ontology rather than methodology marks a striking contrast with the 'unity of science' doctrines prevalent among logical positivists in the first half of the century. The logical positivists were much exercised by the question of whether the different branches of science, from physics to psychology, should all use the same method of controlled observation and systematic generalization. They paid little or no attention to the question of whether everything is made of the same physical stuff.

By contrast, physicalism, as it is understood today, has no direct methodological implications. Some physicalists uphold the view that all sciences should use the "positivist" methods of observation and generalization. But as many would deny this. You can be a physicalist about biology, say, and yet deny that biology is concerned with laws, or a physicalist about sociology, and yet insist that sociology should use the method of empathetic verstehen rather than third-person observation.

This methodological liberalism goes with the fact that the ontological claims of fin-de-siècle physicalism are often carefully nuanced. If physicalism simply meant type-type physical reduction, of the kind classically characterized in Ernst Nagel's *The Structure of Science* (1961), then methodological unity of science would arguably follow, in principle at least, from physicalism. But physicalism today clothes itself in various subtler shades. We have physical supervenience, physical realization, token-token physical identity, and so on. These more sophisticated doctrines leave plenty of room for different sciences to be studied in different ways.

But I am already drifting away from the main subject of this chapter. My concern here is not to distinguish the different species of physicalism, though I shall touch on this in passing later, but to try to understand the reasons for physicalism of any kind. Why have so many analytic philosophers in the second half of the twentieth century suddenly become persuaded that everything is physical?

Fashions and Arguments

It certainly wasn't always so. Perhaps the easiest way to highlight the recent shift in thinking about physicalism is to recall a once-heated mid-century debate about the status of psychological explanation. In contemporary terms, this debate was about the scientificity of 'folk psychology.' On the one side were those, like Carl Hempel and A.J. Ayer, who argued that 'reasons are causes.' By this they meant that psychological explanations are underpinned by empirical generalizations, implicit in everyday thought, which link psychological states such as belief and desire to subsequent behavior. Opposed to Hempel and Ayer were thinkers such as William Dray, and Peter Winch, who argued that the links between reason and action are "logical" or "meaningful," not empirical (Hempel [1942]; Ayer [1969]; Dray [1957]; Winch [1958]).

In one respect this old debate is still up to date. It concerned the question of whether everyday psychological thinking is suitable for incorporation in a scientific psychology – whether folk psychology is a 'proto-science,' as it is sometimes put – and this question is still very much a live issue. But at another level the old debate is now quite outmoded. This is because the participants in the old debate showed little or no interest in the question of how the mind relates to the brain. They wanted to know whether there are testable, empirical laws linking mental states to behavior. But they seemed to see no connection between this issue and the question of the relation of mental states to brain states.

Nowadays, by contrast, everybody has a view on this latter question. Indeed nearly all analytic philosophers in this area, including those who side with Dray and Winch against the scientificity of commonsense psychology, now accept that the mind is in some way constitutively connected with the brain. (Thus consider Donald Davidson. He is the modern champion of the Dray-Winch view that the explanatory links between reason and action are a *sui generis* matter of rational understanding, not scientific law. Yet he made his name by arguing that, even so, 'reasons *are* causes.' In effect, his contribution was to show how the Dray-Winch methodological denial of psychological *laws* could be combined with a physicalist commitment to mind-brain *constitution* (Davidson [1963]).)

This transformation of the old 'reasons and causes' debate happened very quickly. Until the 1950s the issue was purely about lawlike patterns. The issue of mind-brain identity was not on the agenda. Then suddenly, in the 1950s and 1960s, a whole stream of philosophers came out in favor of physicalism. First there were Herbert Feigl and the Australian central state materialists, and they were followed in short order by Donald Davidson, David Lewis, and functional state theorists such as Hilary Putnam. While the old 'reasons and causes' issue continued to be debated, from now on this debate took place within the larger context of physicalist assumptions about the mind-brain relation (Feigl [1958]; Place [1956]; Smart [1959]; Armstrong [1968]; Davidson [1963], [1970]; Lewis [1966]; Putnam [1960]).

Why exactly did physicalism come to prominence in this way in the 1950s and 1960s? Those antipathetic to physicalism sometimes like to suggest that the emergence of physicalism is essentially a matter of fashion. On this view, the rise of physicalism testifies to nothing except the increasing prestige of physical science in the modern weltanschauung. We have become dazzled by the gleaming status of the physical sciences, so the thought goes, and so foolishly try to make our philosophy in its image. (Thus Stephen Clark says, in the sentence immediately following the quote at the beginning of this chapter: "But such achievements [antibiotics, lights, rockets] lend authority to 'science', and science . . . is linked in the public mind with atheistic materialism.")

I think this attitude largely underestimates the significance of contemporary physicalism. What is more, it doesn't really answer the question about physicalism's sudden emergence. It is not as if the prestige of physics suddenly had a big boost in the middle of the twentieth century. I would say that physics has been pretty prestigious for about 300 years, with occasional ups and downs. Yet the philosophical physicalism we are concerned with is a distinctively late twentieth-century phenomenon.

In this chapter I want to offer a different suggestion. My explanation for the rise of physicalism will be that it follows from an argument, or rather a family of arguments, the crucial premise of which was not available, at least to philosophers, until relatively recently. This is because this crucial premise is an empirical claim, and the evidence for it has only become clear-cut over the last century. Prior to that, this premise was not upheld by scientific theory, and so was unavailable as a basis for philosophical argument.

If this explanation is right, it casts a different light on physicalist views. Physicalism has been pressed on philosophers, not by fad or fashion, but by a newly available line of argument. In saying this, I do not want to suggest that the argument for physicalism is uncontroversial, or that the crucial premise I shall focus on is incontrovertible. But I do want to urge that physicalism deserves to be taken seriously, and that those who want to oppose it have an obligation to show where the argument in its favor goes wrong.

Of course, there are those, such as Stephen Clark, who think that "no one could seriously, rationally suppose" that empirical considerations could possibly yield a disproof of mind-body dualism. I shall not explicitly engage with this attitude in what follows, but shall merely invite those who find it plausible to consider the matter again at the end of this chapter. Of course, to repeat a point just made, the empirically based arguments in favor of physicalism are not incontestable. But, even so, it scarcely follows that you have to be unserious or irrational to suppose that they in fact succeed in establishing physicalism. Indeed it is my contention in this chapter that a number of the most influential of late twentieth-century analytic philosophers have supposed just that.

Phenomenalism and Physicalism

Before I give my own explanation for the rise of physicalism, in terms of the new availability of an empirical argument, let me quickly consider an alternative possible explanation, namely, that the rise of physicalism is simply the other side of the demise of phenomenalism.

No doubt there is something to this thought. Phenomenalism was the dominant metaphysical view among logical positivists and other scientifically minded analytic philosophers in the first half of this century. And there certainly isn't much room within phenomenalism to be a physicalist. If you think that everything, including physical stuff, is logically constituted out of mental items such as sense data, then you would seem already to have ruled out the thought that mental items are in turn constituted by physical items.

Even so, I don't think this is a sufficient explanation for the rise of physicalism. For one thing, the rejection of phenomenalism doesn't yet explain the acceptance of physicalism. After all, you can deny phenomenalism without embracing physicalism. Indeed a significant number of contemporary philosophers do exactly that. These philosophers reject phenomenalism, but see no reason to privilege the physical among the different categories of things that exist, and so do not agree that everything is physically constituted.

Apart from this, there is the question of why phenomenalism died in the first place. This is, of course, a big subject, and any full answer would have to mention Wittgenstein's private language argument and Sellars's attack on givens. But I suspect that just as influential as these was the empirical argument for physicalism I am about to discuss. It is a simple argument, from uncomplicated empirical premises, and phenomenalists would have been as well placed to appreciate its force as anybody else. If there is anything to this suggestion, then it wasn't so much that physicalism happened to fill the space created when phenomenalism left the stage. Rather the argument for physicalism was itself partially responsible for the overthrow of phenomenalism.

It is high time I described this empirically based argument for physicalism. It is simple enough in outline. The crucial empirical premise is *the completeness of physics*, by which I mean that all physical effects are due to physical causes. And the argument is then simply that, if all physical effects are due to physical causes, then anything that has a physical effect must itself be physical.

The important point, for our purposes, is that the premise here, the completeness of physics, is a doctrine with a history. It was not always widely accepted. In particular, it was only after some decades of the present century that it became part of scientifically educated common sense. This in turn was because evidence favoring this thesis did not start to emerge until the mid-nineteenth century and did not become generally persuasive until much later. Once the thesis was widely accepted, however, its implications were obvious, and nearly all philosophers with some acquaintance with modern physical science became physicalists.

In the rest of this chapter I shall proceed as follows. First, in the next two sections I shall get a bit clearer about what the completeness of physics says, and how different philosophers have used it to argue for physicalism. In the following sections I then shall examine the history of this thesis, and in particular the reasons why it has come to be widely accepted nowadays, even though it wasn't always.

The Completeness of Physics and the Argument for Physicalism

Let me start by formulating a more precise version of the thesis of the completeness of physics:

> All physical effects are fully determined[2] by law by prior physical occurrences.

Note first that this thesis does not yet assert physicalism. Physicalism is the doctrine that everything, including prima facie, nonphysical stuff, is physical. But the completeness of physics doesn't itself say anything about nonphysical things. It is purely a doctrine about the structure of the physical realm. It says that, if you start with some physical effect, then you will never have to leave the realm of the physical to find a fully sufficient cause for that effect.[3]

If we want to get from the completeness of physics itself to the imperialist physicalist conclusion that *everything* is physical, we need an argument. However, the general shape of such an argument is not hard to find. As I put it in the last section, if the completeness of physics is right, and all physical effects are due to physical causes, then anything *that has a physical effect* must itself be physical. Or, to put it the other way around, if the completeness of physics is right, then there is no room left for anything nonphysical to make a difference to physical effects, so anything that does make such a difference must itself be physical.

Some version of this line of thought underlies the writings of all the philosophers who started arguing for physicalism in the 1950s and 1960s. Thus, for example, consider Smart's thought that we should identify mental states with brain states, for otherwise those mental states would be 'nomological danglers' that play no role in the explanation of behavior. Similarly, reflect on Armstrong's and Lewis's argument that, because mental states are picked out by their causal roles, including their roles as causes of behavior, and because we know that physical states play these roles, mental states must be identical with those physical states. Or, again, consider Davidson's argument that, because the only laws governing behavior are those connecting behavior with physical antecedents, mental events can only be causes of behavior if they are identical with those physical antecedents.

There is much to say about these arguments, and I shall say some of it in the following text. But the point I want to make here is that none of these arguments would seem even slightly plausible without the assumption of the completeness of physics. To see this, imagine that the completeness of physics were not true, and that some physical effects (the movements of arms, perhaps, or the firings of the motor neurons that instigate those movements) were not determined by law by prior physical causes at all, but by *sui generis* nonphysical mental causes, such as decisions, say, or exercises of will, or perhaps just pains. Then (1) contra Smart, mental states wouldn't be "nomological danglers," but directly efficacious in the production of behavior; (2) contra Armstrong and Lewis, it wouldn't necessarily be physical states that played the causal roles by which we pick out mental states, but quite possibly the *sui generis* mental states themselves; and (3) contra Davidson, it wouldn't be true that the only laws governing behavior are those connecting behavior with physical antecedents, because there would also be laws connecting behavior with mental antecedents.[4]

Comments on the Causal Argument for Physicalism

The interesting historical question, to which I shall turn shortly, is why these completeness-of-physics-based arguments started appearing when they did. But first it will be useful to clear away a bit of philosophical undergrowth. Those readers who are more interested in history than philosophical niceties may wish to skip ahead to the next section.

There are significant differences between the completeness-based arguments put forward by Smart, Armstrong, Lewis, Davidson, and other physicalist writers. However, rather than getting entangled in detailed comparisons, let us focus on one canonical form of this argument, which I shall call the 'causal argument' (Crane [1995]; Sturgeon [1998]). This will enable me to make some general structural points.

Premise 1 (the completeness of physics):

All physical effects are fully determined by law by prior physical occurrences.

Premise 2 (causal influence):

All mental occurrences have physical effects.[5]

Premise 3 (no universal overdetermination):

The physical effects of mental causes are not all overdetermined.

Conclusion:

Mental occurrences must be identical with physical occurrences.

Some comments:

(1) *The Ontology of Causes.* The force of this causal argument is extremely sensitive to how you think about causation. If, just as Donald Davidson (1980), you think of the relata of causation as events and think of events in turn as basic particulars, then the argument concludes only that mental and physical descriptions pick out the same *events*, not that there is any constitutive relationship between mental and physical *properties*. On the other hand, if you think of the relata of causation as

instantiations of properties, or more generally as facts (Mellor [1995]), then the argument promises to establish the stronger conclusion that mental properties are identical with physical ones. Because the stronger version is the more interesting, and because facts in any case seem to me the better candidates for the relata of causation, I shall read the argument in this way henceforth.

(2) *Accepting Overdetermination.* The causal argument seems pretty clearly valid.[6] So those who reject the conclusion must reject one of the three premises. All three moves are found in the literature. The status of premise 1, the completeness of physics, will occupy most of what follows. This leaves premises 2 and 3. Let us first consider rejecting premise 3, the premise of no universal overdetermination.

To reject this premise is to accept that the physical effects of mental causes are always overdetermined. This 'belt and braces' view is defended by Gabriel Segal and Elliott Sober (1991) and D.H. Mellor (1995, pp. 103–5). In response to the worry that this view seems to imply that your arm would still have moved even if you hadn't felt a pain (because your C-fibers would still have fired, say), these philosophers argue that the distinct mental and physical causes may themselves be strongly counterfactually dependent. Still, this then raises the question of *why* such causes should always be so counterfactually dependent, if they are genuinely distinct. Possible causal mechanisms underpinning this dependence can be imagined, but there seems to me no good reason to believe in them.

(3) *Epiphenomenalism and Preestablished Harmony.* What about premise 2? The possibility of denying this premise is familiar enough, under the guise of 'epiphenomenalism' or 'preestablished harmony.' If you are prepared to accept that mental states do not have physical effects, and are indeed 'nomological danglers' with respect to the causation of behavior, then the previously mentioned argument for physicalism will not move you, for you will not embrace its second premise. I leave it to readers to decide whether this denial of the efficacy of the mental is a price worth paying to avoid physicalism.[7]

While we are on this point, it is worth noting that one of the most popular versions of physicalism, namely, functionalism, is arguably a closet version of epiphenomenalism. By functionalism I mean the view that identifies a mental state with a 'second-order state,' that is, the state-of-having-some-state-that-plays-a-certain-role, rather than with the first-order physical state that actually plays that role. Because the second-order mental state cannot be *identified* with the first-order physical state (rather, it is 'realized' by it), it is not clear that it can be deemed to cause what that first-order state causes, such as items of behavior. So functionalism threatens the epiphenomenalist denial of premise 2, the claim that mental states have physical effects.

The recognition of this difficulty has put functionalism under some pressure recently. One option is to turn away from functionalism and insist that mental states are first-order states after all, and so strictly identical with physical states (Lewis [1980]). This option in effect upholds a strong version of premise 2, and allows it to argue for the full identity of mental with physical properties. Another option is to read 'causation' generously in premise 2, so as to allow that second-order states 'cause' what their realizers cause. Taken this way, the causal argument then yields the weaker conclusion that mental states must be physically realized second-order states (for, if they weren't at least this, the completeness of physics wouldn't allow them to 'cause' behavior even in the weaker sense). (For more on this issue, see Papineau [1998].)

(4) *Noncausal Realms.* This discussion of epiphenomenalism shows that the causal argument for physicalism only applies to nonphysical occurrences that *do* have physical effects. Without premise 2, there is no argument, because it is only on the assumption that the nonphysical occurrences in question are *not* 'causal danglers' that we need to identify them with something physical.

This shows that there are limits to this form of argument for physicalism. At the beginning of this chapter I characterized physicalism as the doctrine that 'everything is physically constituted.' However, this ambitious claim outstrips anything that can be delivered by the causal argument. For the causal argument has no grip on putative realms of reality that are outside the causal realm altogether, and so a fortiori don't have physical effects. I particularly have in mind here the realms of mathematics, and of moral and other values. While some philosophers have supposed that mathematical or moral facts do have physical effects, this is not the normal way to think about them. And, if we do deny that moral or mathematical facts have physical effects, then our causal argument will provide no basis for identifying them with physical facts.[8]

I myself think that this limitation to the causal argument constitutes a genuine boundary to the proper ambitions of physicalism. I think that physicalism is best formulated, not as the claim that everything is physical, but as the significantly weaker claim that everything that interacts causally with the physical world is physical. This leaves it open that there may be noncausal realms of reality that are not physically constituted, such as the realm of moral worth, or of beauty, or of mathematical objects.

Of course, there may be other problems with such nonphysical realms. For example, it is not clear how we may come by knowledge of such realms, if they can have no physical effects on our sense organs. But these further arguments are by no means clear-cut, and there is no obvious reason why they should be accepted by everybody who accepts the causal argument. Because of this, I shall use 'physicalism' in the rest of this chapter specifically for the doctrine that everything with causal powers is physical, whatever may be true of noncausal realms.

(5) *What is "Physics"?* In a moment I shall turn to the history of the completeness of physics. But first we need to address a terminological issue, one that may have been worrying readers for some time. How exactly is *physics* to be understood in this context of the causal argument? An awkward dilemma may seem to face anyone trying to defend the crucial first premise, the completeness of physics. If we take *physics* to mean the subject matter currently studied in departments of physics, discussed in physics journals, and so on, then it seems pretty obvious that physics is not complete. The track record of attempts to list *all* the fundamental forces and particles responsible for physical effects is not good, and it seems highly likely that future physics will identify new categories of physical cause. On the other hand, if we mean, by *physics*, the subject matter of such future scientific theories, then we seem to be in no position to assess its completeness, because we don't yet know what it is.

This difficulty is more apparent than real. If you want to use the causal argument, it isn't crucial that you know exactly what a complete physics would include. Much more important is to know what it won't include. Suppose, for example, that you have an initial idea of what you mean by *mental* (the sentient, say, or the intentional, or perhaps just whatever events occur specifically in the heads of intelligent beings). And suppose now that you understand *physical* as simply meaning *nonmental*. Then, provided we can be confident that the "physical" in this sense is complete, that is, that every nonmental effect is fully determined by *nonmental* antecedents (in the sense of antecedents that *can* be identified without using mental categories), then we can conclude that all mental states must be identical with something nonmental (otherwise mental states couldn't have nonmental effects). This understanding of *physical* as *nonmental* might seem a lot weaker than most pretheoretical understandings, but note that it is just what we need for philosophical purposes, because it still generates the worthwhile conclusion that the mental must be identical with the nonmental – given, that is, that we are entitled to assume that the nonmental is complete.

The same point applies if we want to apply the causal argument to chemical, biological, or economic states. As long as we can be confident that all nonchemical effects are fully caused by nonchemical (nonbiological, noneconomic . . .) states, then we can conclude that all chemical (biological, economic . . .) states must be identical with something non-chemical (nonbiological, noneconomic . . .).

We might not know enough about physics to know exactly what physics does include. But as long as we are confident that it excludes such-and-such special categories, then we can use the causal argument to conclude that these special categories are in fact identical with other kinds. I shall suppose this indirect understanding of *physics* in what follows: it should simply be understood as that set of properties that can be specified without appeal to whichever special vocabularies (mental, biological, . . .) we are interested in. Correspondingly, the completeness of physics will be the doctrine that such nonspecial effects are always fully accounted for by nonspecial causes (cf. Papineau and Spurrett [1998]).

Descartes and Leibniz

Let us now concentrate on the history of the completeness of physics. The important question, as we have just seen, is whether any nonspecial effects are produced by *sui generis* special causes. True, the exact content of this question will be relative to which special categories we are interested in, for the reasons just explained. Still, we can take it for the moment that we are interested in a relatively strong version of the completeness of physics, and in particular one that would rule out *sui generis* mental and biological causes, let alone economic, social, or other even more special causes.

When I first became interested in the causal argument a few years ago, I recognized that there were many points where it could be queried. However, I assumed that the completeness premise was quite uncontentious. Surely, I thought, everybody agrees that the movements of matter, such as the movements of molecules in your arm, can in principle always be fully accounted for in terms of prior physical causes, such as physical activity in your nerves, which in turn is due to physical activity in your brain, . . . and so on.

To my surprise, I discovered that some people didn't agree. They didn't see why some physical occurrences, in our brains perhaps, shouldn't have irreducibly mental causes. My first response, when presented with this thought, was to attribute it to an insufficient education in the physical sciences. Sometimes I went so far as to communicate this diagnosis to those who disagreed with me. However, when they then asked me, not unreasonably, to show them where the completeness of physics is written down in the physics textbooks, I found myself somewhat embarrassed. Once I was forced to defend it, I realized that the completeness of physics is by no means self-evident. Indeed further reading has led me to realize, far from being self-evident, it is an issue on which the post-Galilean scientific tradition has changed its mind several times.

My original thought was that the completeness of physics would follow from the fact that physics can be formulated in terms of conservation laws. If the laws of mechanics tell us that important physical quantities are conserved regardless of what happens, then doesn't it follow that the later states of physical systems are always fully determined by their earlier physical states?

Not necessarily. It depends on what conservation laws you are committed to. Consider Descartes's mechanics. This incorporated the conservation of what Descartes called 'quantity of motion,' by which he meant mass times speed. That is, Descartes held that the total mass times speed of any collection of bodies is guaranteed to remain constant, whatever happens to them. However, this alone does not guarantee that physics is complete. In particular, it does not rule out the possibility of physical effects that are due to irreducibly mental causes.

This is because Descartes's *quantity of motion* is a nondirectional (scalar) quantity, defined in terms of speed, as opposed to the directional (vectorial) Newtonian notion of linear *momentum*, defined in terms of velocity. Because of this, the *direction* of a body's motion can be altered without altering its quantity of motion. As Roger Woolhouse explains the point, in an excellent discussion of the relevance of seventeenth-century mechanics to the mind-brain issue (1985), a car rounding a corner at constant speed conserves its 'quantity of motion,' but not its momentum.

This creates room for *sui generis* mental causes to alter the *direction* of a body's motion without violating Descartes's conservation principle. Descartes's conservation principle does mean that, if one physical body starts going faster, this must be due to another physical body going slower. But his principle doesn't require that, if a physical body changes direction, this need result from any other physical body changing direction. Even if the change of direction results from an irreducibly mental cause, the quantity of motion of the moving body remains constant.

According to Leibniz, Descartes exploited this loophole to explain how the mind could affect the brain. As Leibniz tells the story, Descartes believed that the mind nudges moving particles of matter in the pineal gland, causing them to swerve without losing speed, like the car going round the corner. This then explained how the mind could affect the brain without violating the conservation of 'quantity of motion' (Leibniz [1898] [1696], p. 327).

Now, there is little evidence that Descartes actually saw things this way, nor indeed that he was particularly worried about how the laws of physics can be squared with mind-brain interaction. Still, whatever the truth of Leibniz's account of Cartesian theory, his next point deserves our attention. For Leibniz proceeds from his analysis of Descartes to the first-order assertion that the *correct* conservation laws, unlike Descartes's conservation of quantity of motion, *cannot* in fact be squared with mind-body interaction.

Leibniz's conservation laws were in fact a great improvement on Descartes's. In place of Descartes's conservation of 'quantity of motion,' Leibniz upheld both the conservation of linear *momentum* and the conservation of kinetic *energy*. These two laws led him to the correct analysis of impacts between moving bodies, a topic on which Descartes had gone badly astray. And, in connection with our present topic, they persuaded him that there is no room whatsoever for mental activity to influence motion of matter.

In effect, the conservation of linear momentum and of kinetic energy together squeeze the mind out of the class of events that cause changes in motion. Leibniz's two conservation laws, plus the standard seventeenth-century assumption of no physical action at a distance, are themselves sufficient to fix the evolution of all physical processes. The conservation of momentum requires the preservation of the same total amount of quantity of motion in *any given direction*, thus precluding any possibility of mental nudges altering the direction of moving physical particles. Moreover, the conservation of energy, when added to the conservation of momentum, fully fixes the speed and direction of impacting physical particles after the collide.[9] So there is no room for anything else, and in particular for anything mental, to make any difference to the motions of physical particles, if Leibniz's two conservation laws are to be respected.

We can simplify the essential point at issue here by noting that Leibniz's conservation laws, unlike Descartes's, ensure physical determinism. They imply that the physical states of any system of bodies at one time fix their state at any later time. Physical determinism in this sense is certainly sufficient for the completeness of physics, even if the possibility of quantum-mechanical indeterminism means it is not necessary (cf. Note 2). So Leibniz's dynamics, unlike Descartes's, make it impossible for anything except the physical to make a difference to anything physical.

Leibniz was fully aware of the implications of his dynamical theories for mind-body interaction (cf. Woolhouse, op. cit.). However he did not infer mind-brain identity from his commitment to the completeness of physics. Instead he adopted the doctrine of preestablished harmony, according to which the mental and physical realms are each causally closed, but prearranged by the divine will to march in step in such a way as to display the standard mind-brain correlations. In terms of the canonical causal argument laid out in the section on the causal argument for physicalism, Leibniz is denying premise 2 here, about the causal influence of mind on matter. He avoids identifying mental causes with physical causes, in the face of the completeness of physics, by denying that mental causes ever have physical effects.

Newtonian Physics

Some readers might wonder why this isn't the end of the issue. Given that Leibniz established, against Descartes, that both momentum and energy are conserved in systems of moving particles, then why wasn't the history of the mind-brain argument already over? Of course, nowadays we might not want to follow Leibniz in opting for preestablished harmony, as opposed to simply embracing mind-brain identity. But this is simply because we favor a different response to the causal argument laid out in the section on the causal argument for physicalism, not because we have any substantial premises Leibniz lacked. In particular, the crucial first premise of the causal argument, the completeness of physics, would seem already to have been available to Leibniz. So doesn't this mean that everything needed to appreciate the causal argument was already on hand in the second half of the seventeenth century, long before the rise of twentieth-century physicalism?

Well, it was – but only on the assumption Leibniz gives us the correct dynamics. However, Leibniz's physical theories were quickly eclipsed by those of Newton, and this then reopened the whole issue of the completeness of physics.

The central point here is that Newton allowed forces other than impact. Leibniz, along with Descartes and all other pre-Newtonian proponents of the 'mechanical philosophy,' took it as given that all physical action is by contact. They assumed that the only possible cause of a change in a physical body's motion is the impact of another physical body. (Or more precisely, as we are telling the story, Descartes supposed that the only possible *nonmental* cause of physical change is impact, and

Leibniz then argued that *mental* causes other than impact are not possible either, if the conservation of momentum and energy are to be respected.)

Newtonian mechanics changed the whole picture. This is because Newton did not take impact as his basic model of dynamic action. Rather his basic notion is that of an *impressed force*. Rather than thinking of 'force' as something inside a body that might be transferred to other bodies in impact, as did all his contemporaries (and indeed as did most of his successors for at least a century[10]), Newton thought of forces as disembodied entities, acting on the affected body from outside. An impressed force "consists in the action only, and remains no longer in the body when the action is over." Moreover, "impressed forces are of different origins, as from percussion, from pressure, from centripetal force" (Newton [1960] [1686], Definition IV). Gravity was the paradigm. True, the force of gravity always arose from the presence of massive bodies, but it pervaded space, waiting to act on anything that might be there, so to speak, with a strength as specified by the inverse square law.

Once disembodied gravity was allowed as a force distinct from the action of impact, then there was no principled barrier to other similarly disembodied special forces, such as chemical forces, or magnetic forces, or forces of cohesion (cf. Newton [1952] [1704], Queries 29–31) – or indeed vital and mental forces.

Nothing in classical Newtonian thinking rules out special mental forces. While Newton has a general law about the effects of his forces (they cause proportional changes in the velocities of the bodies they act on), there is no corresponding general principle about the causes of such forces. True, gravity in particular is governed by the inverse square law, which fixes gravitational forces as a function of the location of bodies with mass. But there is no overarching principle dictating how forces in general arise. This opens up the possibility that there may be *sui generis* mental forces, which would mean that Newtonian physics, unlike Leibnizian physics, is not physically complete. Some physical processes could have nonphysical mental forces among their causal antecedents.[11]

The switch from a pure impact-based mechanical philosophy to the more liberal world of Newtonian forces thus undermined Leibniz's argument for the completeness of physics. Leibniz could hold that the principles governing the physical world leave no room for mental acts to make a difference because he had a simple mechanical picture of the physical world. Bodies preserve their motion in any given direction until they collide, and then they obey the laws of perfect elastic impact. The Newtonian picture is far less pristine, and gives no immediate reason to view physics as complete.

You might think that the conservation laws of Newtonian physics would themselves place constraints on the generation of forces, in such a way as to restore the completeness of physics. But this would be a somewhat anachronistic thought. Conservation laws did not play a central role in Newtonian thinking, at least not in that of Newton himself and his immediate followers. True, Newton's mechanics does imply the conservation of *momentum*. This falls straight out of his Third Law, which requires that 'action and reaction' are always equal. But it is a striking feature of Newtonian dynamics that there is no corresponding law for energy.[12]

Of course, as we shall see in the next section, the principle of the conservation of kinetic *and* potential energy in all physical processes did *eventually* become part of the Newtonian tradition, and this does impose a general restriction on possible forces, a restriction expressed by the requirement that all forces should be 'conservative.' But this came much later, in the middle of the nineteenth century, and so had no influence on the range of possible forces admitted by seventeenth- or eighteenth-century Newtonians. (Moreover, it is a nice question, to which we shall return at length in the following text, how far the principle of the conservation of kinetic plus potential energy, with its attendant requirement that all forces be conservative, does indeed constitute evidence against *sui generis* mental forces.)

In any case, whatever the significance of later Newtonian derivations of the conservation of energy, early Newtonians certainly saw no barrier to the postulation of *sui generis* mental forces. It will be helpful to distinguish in the abstract two ways in which such a Newtonian violation of the completeness of physics could occur.

First, and most obviously, it could follow from the postulation of *indeterministic* mental forces. If the determinations of the self (or of the 'soul,' as they would have said in the seventeenth and eighteenth centuries) could influence the movements of matter in spontaneous ways, then the world of physical causes and effects would obviously not be causally closed, because these spontaneous mental causes would make a difference to the unfolding of certain physical processes.

But, second, it is not even necessary for the violation of completeness that such *sui generis* special forces operate indeterministically. Suppose that the operation of mental forces were governed by fully *deterministic* force laws (suppose, for example, that mental forces obeyed some inverse square law involving the presence of certain particles in the brain). Then mental forces would be part of Newtonian dynamics in just the same sense as gravitational or electrical forces: we could imagine a system of particles evolving deterministically under the influence of all these forces, including mental forces, with the forces exerted at any place and time being deterministically fixed by the relevant force laws. Even so, this deterministic model would still constitute a violation of the completeness of physics, for the physical positions of the particles would depend inter alia on prior mental causes, and not exclusively on prior physical causes.

Did I not say at the end of the last section that determinism is sufficient for the completeness of physics (even if not necessary, because of quantum mechanics)? No. What I said was that *physical* determinism (the doctrine that prior *physical* conditions alone are enough to determine later physical conditions) is sufficient for the completeness of physics. However, we can accept determinism as such without accepting physical determinism, and so without accepting the completeness of physics. In particular, we can have a deterministic model in which mental forces play an essential role, and in which the physical subpart is therefore not causally closed.

You might feel (indeed might have been feeling for some time) that a realm of deterministic mental forces would scarcely be worth distinguishing from the general run of physical forces, given that they would lack the spontaneity and creativity that is normally held to distinguish the mental from the physical. And you might think that it is therefore somewhat odd to view them as violating the completeness of physics. I happily concede that there is something to this thought. But I would still like to stick to my terminology, as stipulated at the end of the section on the causal argument for physicalism, which assumed an initial sense for *mental* (as sentient, intentional, or intelligent), and then defined the *physical* as whatever can be identified without alluding to such mental properties – which then makes even deterministically governed *sui generis* mental forces come out 'nonphysical,' because they can't be so nonmentally identified. This is the terminology that best fits with our original interest in the causal argument for physicalism. We don't want deterministic mental forces to be counted as consistent with the completeness of 'physics,' precisely because we wouldn't be able to use *this* kind of completeness of 'physics' to infer that these mental forces are always identical with some *other* (nonmental) causes of their effects.

So far I have merely presented the possibility of special Newtonian forces as an abstract possibility. However, the postulation of such forces was commonplace among eighteenth-century thinkers, particularly among those working in anatomy and physiology. Many of the theoretical debates in these areas were concerned with the existence of vital and mental forces, and with the relation between them. Among those who debated these issues, we can find both the indeterministic and deterministic models of mental forces.[13]

Thus consider the debate among eighteenth-century physiologists about the relative roles of the forces of *sensibility* and *irritability*. This terminology was introduced by the leading German physiologist Albrecht von Haller, Professor of Anatomy at Göttingen from 1736. Haller thought of 'sensibility' as a distinctively mental force. 'Irritability' was a nonmental but still peculiarly biological power. ("What should hinder us from granting irritability to be a property of the animal *gluten*, the same as we acknowledge gravity and attraction to be properties of matter in general...," Haller [1936] [1751].) Haller took the force of sensibility to be under the control of the soul and to operate solely through the nerves. Irritability, by contrast, he took to be located solely in the muscle fibers.

In distinguishing the mentally directed force of sensibility from the more automatic force of irritability, Haller can here be seen as conforming to my model of *indeterministic* mental forces. Where the force of irritability is determined by prior stimuli and is independent of mental agency, the force of sensibility responds to the spontaneous commands of the soul.

Haller's model was opposed by Robert Whytt (1714–66) in Edinburgh. In effect Whytt can be seen as merging Haller's distinct mental and vital forces, irritability and sensibility. On the one hand, Whytt gave greater power to the soul: he took it that a soul, or 'sentient principle,' is distributed throughout the body, not just in the nerves, and is responsible for all bodily activities, from the flow of blood and motion of muscles, to imagination and reasoning in the brain. But at the same time as giving greater power to this sentient principle, he also rendered its operations *deterministic*. He explicitly likened the sentient principle to the Newtonian force of gravity, and viewed it as a necessary principle that acts according to strict laws. Whytt can thus be seen as exemplifying my model of deterministic mental forces: the sentient principle is simply another deterministic Newtonian force, just like gravity and the others, in that its operations are fixed by a definite force law (Whytt [1755]).

The Conservation of Energy

In this section I want to consider how the principle of the conservation of energy eventually emerged within the tradition of Newtonian mechanics, and how this bears on the completeness of physics. It will be useful to separate some different aspects of this emergence.

Rational Mechanics

Through the eighteenth and early nineteenth centuries a number of mathematician-physicists, among the most important of whom were Jean d'Alembert (1717–83), Joseph Louis Lagrange (1736–1813), the Marquis de Laplace (1749–1827), and William Hamilton (1805–65), developed a series of mathematical frameworks designed to simplify the analysis of the motion of interacting particles. These frameworks allowed physicists to abstract away from detailed forces of constraint, such as the forces holding rigid bodies together, or the forces constraining particles to move on surfaces, and concentrate on the effects produced by other forces. (See Elkana [1974], ch. II, for the history, and Goldstein [1964], for the mathematics.)

These mathematical developments also implied that, under certain conditions, the sum of kinetic energy and potential energy remains constant. Roughly, when all forces involved are independent of the velocities of the interacting particles and of the time (let us call forces of these kinds *conservative*), then the sum of actual kinetic energy (measured by $\frac{1}{2}mv^2$) plus the potential to generate more such energy (often called the 'tensions' of the system) is conserved: when the particles slow down, this builds up 'tensions,' and, if those 'tensions' are expended, the particles will speed up again.

We now think of this as the most basic of all natural laws. But this attitude was not part of the original tradition in rational mechanics. There were two reasons for this. First, the Newtonian scientists in this tradition were not looking for conserved quantities anyway. As I explained earlier, conservation principles played little role in classical Newtonian thinking. True, Leibniz had urged the conservation of kinetic energy (under the guise of 'vis viva'), but by the eighteenth century Leibniz's influence had been largely eclipsed by Newton's. Second, the conservation of potential and kinetic energy in any case only holds under the assumption that all forces are conservative. Nowadays we take this requirement to be satisfied for all fundamental forces. But this again was no part of eighteenth-century thinking. Some familiar forces happen to be conservative, but plenty of other forces are not. Gravitation, say, is conservative, because it depends only on the positions of the particles, and not on their velocities, nor on the elapsed time. But, by contrast, frictional forces are not conservative, because they depend on the velocity of the decelerated body relative to the medium. And correspondingly frictional forces do not in any sense seem to conserve energy: when they decelerate a body, no 'tension' is apparently built up waiting to accelerate the body again.

For both these reasons, the tradition in rational mechanics did not initially view the conservation of kinetic and potential energy in certain systems as of any great significance. On the contrary, it was simply a handy mathematical consequence that falls out of the equations when the operative forces all happen to fall within a subset of possible forces (cf. Elkana [1974], ch. 2).

Equivalence of Heat and Mechanical Energy

In the first half of the nineteenth century a number of scientists, most prominently James Joule (1819–89), established the equivalence of heat and mechanical energy, in the sense of showing that a specific amount of heat will always be produced by the expenditure of a given amount of mechanical energy (as when a gas is compressed), and vice versa (as when a hot gas drives a piston).

These experiments suggested directly that some single quantity is preserved through a number of different natural interactions. They also had a less direct bearing on the eventual formulation of the conservation of energy. They indicated that apparently nonconservative forces such as friction and other dissipative forces need not be nonconservative after all, because the kinetic energy apparently lost when they acted could in fact be preserved by the heat energy gained by the resisting medium.[14]

The stage was now set for the formulation of a universal principle of the conservation of energy. We can distinguish three elements that together contributed to the formulation of this principle. First, the tradition of rational mechanics provided the mathematical scaffolding. Second, the experiments of Joule and others suggested that different natural processes all involve a single underlying quantity that could manifest itself in different forms. Third, these experiments also suggested that apparently nonconservative forces such as friction were merely macroscopic manifestations of more fundamental conservative forces.

Of course, it is only with the wisdom of hindsight that we can see these different strands as waiting to be pulled together. At the time, they were hidden in abstract realms of disparate branches of science. It took the genius of the young Hermann von Helmholtz (1821–94) to see the connections. In 1847, at the age of twenty six, he published his monograph *Uber die Erhaltung der Kraft* (*On the Conservation of Force*). The first three sections of this treatise are devoted to the tradition of rational mechanics, and in particular to explaining how the total mechanical energy (kinetic plus potential energy) in a system of interacting particles is constant in those cases where all forces are familiar 'central forces' independent of time and velocity. The fourth section describes the equivalence between mechanical 'force' and heat, referring to Joule's results, while the last two sections extend the discussion to electric and magnetic 'forces,' showing again that there are fixed equivalences between these 'forces,' heat, and mechanical energy.[15]

Physiology

At the end of his treatise Helmholtz touches on the conservation of energy in living systems. Helmholtz was in fact a medical doctor by training, and had been a student in the Berlin physiological laboratory of Johannes Müller in the early 1840s, along with Emil Du Bois-Reymond (1818–96) and Ernst Brücke (1819–92). Together these students were committed to a reductionist program in physiology, aiming to show that phenomena such as respiration, animal heat, and locomotion could all be understood to be governed by the same laws as operate in the inorganic realm.

This physiological context undoubtedly played a fundamental role in Helmholtz's articulation of a universal principle of the conservation of energy. Because of his physiological interests, Helmholtz was interested in a principle that would cover *all* natural phenomena, including those in living systems, and not just such manifestly physical phenomena as mechanical motion, heat, and electromagnetism. Thus he took the crucial step of asserting that *all* forces conserve the sum of kinetic and potential energy. Superficially nonconservative forces such as friction are simply macroscopic manifestations of more fundamental forces that preserve energy at the microlevel. This then enabled Helmholtz to view the equivalences established by experimentalists such as Joule, not just as striking local regularities, but as necessary consequences of a fundamental principle of mechanics. All natural processes must respect the conservation of energy, including processes in living systems.

It is noteworthy that neither the experimentalists such as Joule, nor the mathematician-physicists in the rational mechanics tradition, made this crucial step to a universal principle. None of the scientists working experimentally on numerical equivalences between different processes, such as Joule, generalized their discoveries into the claim that there is one quantity, energy, preserved in all natural interactions whatsoever. While it is true that a number of different scientists at the time were investigating such numerical equivalences (thus the historical thesis of the 'simultaneous discovery' of the conservation of energy), there is no reason to suppose that these scientists were generally inspired by any vision of the underlying unity of different natural processes. Similarly, there was nothing to attract mathematical physicists in the tradition of rational mechanics to the conclusion that all forces are conservative, for the reasons given previously. They simply thought of such forces as the mathematically tractable special case where changes in kinetic and potential energy always happen to balance out.

Without the desire to bring living systems under a unified science, none of these scientists had any motive for synthesizing the different strands pulled together by Helmholtz. It was Helmholtz's combination of physiological interests and sophisticated physical understanding that precipitated the crucial step. He saw that, if we assume that all fundamental forces are conservative, then this guarantees that a certain quantity, the total energy, will be preserved in all natural processes whatsoever, including the organic processes that formed the focus of his interest.

Vital Forces

Helmholtz was part of a tradition in experimental physiology that set itself in opposition to the previous generation of German *Naturphilosophen*. These nature-philosophers had developed the eighteenth-century notions of 'irritability' and 'sensibility' into a philosophy of *Lebenskraft*. By the first half of the nineteenth century, this notion of vital force had broken loose from its original Newtonian moorings and had become part of a florid metaphysics imbued with romanticism and idealism. According to the *Naturphilosophen*, organic matter was imbued with a special power, the *Lebenskraft*, which organized and directed it. They viewed this power as having a quasi-mental aspect, which enabled it to mediate between the 'archetypical ideas' or 'essences' of different species and the development of individual organisms toward that ideal form (see Coleman [1971], ch. 3; Steigerwald [1998]).

The experimental tradition that included Helmholtz can be seen as a reaction to these extreme doctrines. However, it is striking that many of those associated with this tradition, though not Helmholtz himself, continued to admit the possible existence of vital forces, both before and after the emergence of the conservation of energy. This is less puzzling than it may at first seem. These physiological thinkers did not think of vital forces as the mystical intermediaries of the *Naturphilosophen*, imbued with all the powers of creative mentality. Rather these thinkers were reverting to the tradition of eighteenth-century physiology. They simply viewed vital forces as special Newtonian forces, additional to gravitational forces, chemical forces, and so on, and which happen to arise specifically in organic contexts. Justus von Leibig (1803–73), the leading physiological chemist of the time, and Müller, Helmholtz's own mentor, are clear examples of experimental physiologists who were prepared to countenance vital forces in this sense (cf. Coleman [1971], ch. VI; Elkana [1974], ch. IV).

Does the Conservation of Energy Rule out Vital (and Mental) Forces?

The interesting question, from the point of view of this chapter, is how far this continuing commitment to vital forces is consistent with the doctrine of the conservation of energy. There is certainly some tension between the two doctrines. It is noteworthy that Helmholtz, and his young colleagues from Müller's laboratory, were committed to the view that no forces operated inside living bodies that were not also found in simpler physical and chemical contexts (Coleman [1971], pp. 150–4). Even so, there is no outright inconsistency between the conservation of energy and vital forces; and many late nineteenth-century figures were quite explicit, not to say enthusiastic, about accepting both.

In order to get clearer about the room left for vital (or mental) forces by the conservation of energy, recall how earlier I distinguished two ways in which early Newtonian theory left room for such special forces to violate the completeness of physics. First, such forces might operate spontaneously and indeterministically: nothing in early Newtonian theory would seem to rule out spontaneous forces ungoverned by any deterministic force law. Second, even if the relevant forces are governed by a deterministic force law, they may still be *sui generis*, in the sense that they may be distinct from gravitational forces, chemical forces, and so on, and may arise specifically in living systems or their brains.

The conservation of energy bears differentially on these two kinds of special forces. It does seem inconsistent with the first kind of special force, a spontaneous special force. But it does not directly rule out the second, deterministic kind.

Why should the conservation of energy rule out even a spontaneous special force? (Think of a spontaneous mental force that accelerates molecules in the pineal gland.) Why shouldn't such a force simply respect the conservation of energy, by not causing accelerations that will violate it? But this doesn't really make sense. The content of the principle of the conservation of energy is that losses of kinetic energy are compensated by build-ups of potential energy, and vice versa. But we couldn't really speak of a 'build-up' or 'loss' in the potential energy associated with a force, if there were no force law governing the deployment of that force. So the very idea of potential energy commits us to a law that governs how the relevant force will cause accelerations in the future.

However, nothing in this argument rules out the possibility of vital, mental, or other special forces that *are* governed by deterministic force laws. After all, the conservation of energy in itself does not tell which basic forces operate in the physical universe. Are gravity and impact the only basic forces? What about electromagnetism? Nuclear forces? And so on. Clearly the conservation of energy as such leaves it open as to exactly which basic forces exist. It only requires that, whatever they are, they operate conservatively.

The Death of Emergentism

So a commitment to the conservation of energy by no means settled the question of whether *sui generis* mental or vital forces should be rejected and physics declared complete. True, some few thinkers, such as Helmholtz himself, conjoined the conservation of energy with a denial of such special forces. But this was by no means mandated by the conservation of energy itself, for the reasons I have just explained. Accordingly, many other thinkers in the late nineteenth and early twentieth centuries took the opportunity to posit special forces of the kind allowed by the conservation of energy. So I still owe an explanation of what finally created a scientifically informed consensus against such special forces.

The issue is not straightforward, and there is no question of dealing with it fully here. But in this final section I would like to offer some outline conjectures. I shall proceed as follows. First, I shall take it as given that the conservation of energy at least was a settled doctrine. Of course there is a story to be told about this as well. But, for whatever reasons, the doctrine of the conservation of energy did win widespread acceptance within a decade or two of its initial formulation, and certainly none of the developments I am about to consider questioned its validity. Second, I shall lump mental and vital forces together. There are, of course, considerations that bear differentially on the existence of such forces, but I shall be proceeding at a level where these are not significant.

Two Arguments

My central suggestion will be that two rather different lines of evidence contributed to the demise of special forces. The first was an abstract argument based on theoretical physics, while the second was a more direct empirical argument based on physiological research. The abstract argument involves considerations to do with the conservation of energy, and was available from the time of Helmholtz onward (even though it was not incontrovertible, and many were not persuaded). By contrast, the direct argument has little to do with the conservation of energy, and indeed did not really gain force until the twentieth century.

At the end I shall argue that both arguments can be seen as contributing to the general modern acceptance of the completeness of physics. But the precise timing of this acceptance, and in particular the arrival of a general consensus in the second half of the twentieth century, seems to call for explanation in terms of the build-up of direct evidence for the second argument, rather than in terms of the more abstract argument that had been available since the middle of the nineteenth century.

Let me begin by presenting the two arguments in outline.

(1) *The Argument from Fundamental Forces.* The first argument is that all apparently special forces characteristically *reduce* to a small stock of basic physical forces that conserve energy. Causes of macroscopic accelerations standardly turn out to be composed out of a few fundamental physical forces that operate throughout nature. So, while we ordinarily attribute certain physical effects to 'muscular forces,' say, or indeed to 'mental causes,' we should recognize that these causes, just as all causes of physical effects, are ultimately composed of the few basic physical forces.

(2) *The Argument from Physiology.* The second argument is simply that there is no direct evidence for vital or mental forces. Physiological research reveals no phenomena in living bodies that manifest such forces. All organic processes in living bodies seem to be fully accounted for by normal physical forces.

I take both of these to be empirically based arguments, and both to have the same conclusion: namely, that there are no special mental or vital forces. But note that the evidential basis for the two arguments is quite different. The second argument appeals directly to the evidence uncovered by physiological research. It notes that observations made inside living bodies never reveal any accelerations that cannot be attributed to normal physical forces. The first argument, by contrast, appeals to the investigation of forces in general. It rests on evidence that many apparently different kinds of forces turn out to be composed of a few fundamental forces, and then applies this lesson to vital and mental forces in particular. So it need not appeal directly to any evidence about what goes on in living bodies. Instead it can infer the general conclusion inductively from the study of other forces, and then project it to the special case of mental and vital forces.

The Argument from Fundamental Forces

Let me now explain the first argument more fully. I shall return to the second argument in the following text. I take the materials for the first argument to have been available from the middle of the nineteenth century, and to relate to the reasoning that led up to the acceptance of the conservation of energy. It is true, as I have stressed, that the doctrine of the conservation of energy is itself consistent with the existence of special forces, as long as those forces are conservative. At the same time, it seems to me that the thinking that supported the conservation of energy also weighed against special mental or vital forces.

At its simplest, my thought here is that the arguments behind the conservation of energy give inductive reason to suppose that all forces reduce to a small number of fundamental forces. We have already seen how Helmholtz's formulation of the conservation of energy hinged on the assumption that friction and other dissipative forces are nonfundamental forces, macroscopic manifestations of processes involving more fundamental conservative forces. For it is only if we see macroscopic forces such as friction as reducing to fundamental conservative forces that we can uphold the universal conservation of energy. Now, this point can be viewed as providing inductive support for the general thesis that *all* apparently special forces reduce to a small stock of fundamental forces. The special forces that have been quantitatively analyzed, such as friction, turn out to reduce to more fundamental conservative forces. So this provides inductive reason to conclude that any other apparently special forces, such as muscular forces, vital forces, or mental forces, will similarly reduce.

This is of course not a knock-down argument. Vital or mental forces could figure among the fundamental forces of nature, even if they are only generated in the special circumstances associated with life or sentience. But this position does not sit happily with a continued commitment to the universal conservation of energy. An insistence on the independent existence of *sui generis* special forces inside bodies threatens to remove the reasons for believing in the conservation of energy in the first place. For there are no obvious grounds for expecting such *sui generis* special forces to be conservative.

After all, what argument was there, in 1850, say, for believing that forces operating inside bodies do not violate the conservation of energy? I am suggesting that the most persuasive argument hinged on the assumption that all forces operating in special circumstances reduce to a small stock of fundamental conservative forces. However, suppose now that it is explicitly specified that vital and mental forces do *not* reduce to other forces. Now we need independent evidence for supposing they are conservative, and it is not clear where it is to come from. In effect, then, positing *sui generis* vital or mental forces threatens to undermine the inductive grounds for upholding the conservation of energy in the first place. For it makes the assumption of their conservativeness an independent assumption, an assumption for which we lack any independent evidence.

I suspect that something like this line of thought lay behind Helmholtz's and his younger contemporaries' conviction that there were no special vital forces. Consider how Helmholtz argues in *Uber die Erhaltung der Kraft*. He takes pains to stress it is specifically *central* forces independent of time and velocity that ensure the conservation of energy. This emphasis on central forces (by which Helmholtz meant forces that act along the line between the interacting particles) now seems dated. Nowadays, conservativeness is normally defined circularly, as a property of those forces that do no work round a closed orbit, and that are therefore the gradient of a scalar that depends only on position. This definition does not require a restriction to central forces. However, Helmholtz was in no position to adopt our circular definition of conservativeness. He was aiming to *persuade* his readers of the general conservation of energy, and so needed an argument. It wouldn't have served simply to observe that energy is conserved by those forces that conserve energy. Helmholtz's actual claim was that energy is conserved by a wide range of known forces, namely, central forces. Still, this by itself doesn't show energy is conserved by all forces, *unless* all forces are central. Why should this be? Well, as previously mentioned, the most plausible thought is surely that there is a small stock of basic central forces, and that all causes apparently peculiar to special circumstances are composed out of these.

Even this is scarcely conclusive. Those thinkers who remained convinced, for whatever reasons, that there must be irreducible special forces inside living bodies, could still respect the universal conservation of energy, by maintaining that these extra forces must themselves operate conservatively. In support of this they could have offered the alternative inductive argument that, because all the *other* fundamental forces examined so far have turned out to be conservative, we should infer that any extra vital or mental fundamental forces will be conservative too.

I am not sure to what degree these alternative lines of inductive reasoning can be found explicitly laid out in the nineteenth-century debates. But they offer one possible explanation for the two different views on *sui generis* special forces that coexisted after the emergence of the conservation of energy. The thought that all apparently special forces reduce to a small stock of fundamental forces can account for the rejection of irreducible vital or mental forces by thinkers such as Helmholtz and his young colleagues. Yet there were at least as many who wanted to maintain that vital and mental forces are *sui generis*, and they had the option of arguing that, even if these forces are fundamental and irreducible, the nature of other fundamental forces provides inductive reason to suppose these *sui generis* forces will be conservative in their own right.

In connection with this latter school of thought, I have already mentioned Leibig and Müller, two eminent physiologists of the older generation, who continued to accept vital forces, even after the conservation of energy had won general acceptance. Also, Brian McLaughlin, in his excellent article on "British Emergentism" (1992), explains how the philosophers J.S. Mill and Alexander Bain went so far as to argue that the conservation of energy, and in particular the notion of potential energy, lends definite support to the possibility of nonphysical forces. (The 'British Emergentists' discussed by McLaughlin were a philosophical movement committed precisely to nonphysical causes of motion in my sense, causes that were not the vectorial "resultants" of basic physical forces such as gravity and impact, but which "emerged" when matter arranged itself in special ways. The particular idea that attracted Mill and Bain was that these "emergent forces" might be stored as unrealized potentials, ready to manifest themselves as a cause of motion only when the relevant special circumstances arose.[16,17])

The Argument from Physiology

McLaughlin explains how 'British Emergentism' continued to flourish into the twentieth century.[18] This highlights the question with which I began this chapter. Given that thinkers continued to posit special mental and vital forces until well after the Great War, why has the idea of such forces now finally fallen into general disfavor?

Here I think we need to refer to the second line of argument against such forces, the argument from direct physiological evidence. We can view this second argument as operating against the background provided by the earlier argument from fundamental forces. The earlier argument suggested that at least most natural phenomena, if not all, can be explained by a few fundamental physical forces. This focused the issue of what kind of evidence would demonstrate the existence of extra mental or vital forces. For once we know that other forces exist, then we will know which anomalous accelerations would indicate the presence of special mental or vital forces. Against this background, the argument from physiology is then simply that detailed modern research has failed to uncover any such anomalous physical processes.

The relevant research dates mostly from the twentieth century. While important physiological research was carried out in the second half of the nineteenth century (see Coleman [1971]), it did not penetrate to the level of forces operating inside bodies. At most it identified the chemical inputs and outputs to various parts of the body and showed that animals are subject to general conservation principles. (See in particular Coleman, pp. 140–3, for Max Rubner's elaborate 1889 respiration calorimeter experiments, showing that the energy emitted by a small dog exactly corresponds to that of the food it consumes.) Experiments of this kind, however, failed to provide compelling evidence against vital or mental forces. That normal chemicals are moved around, and that energy is conserved throughout, does not in the end rule out the possibility that some accelerations within bodies are due to special vital or mental forces. It may still be that such forces are activated inside cells, but operate in such a way as to "pay back" all the energy they "borrow," and vice versa.[19]

In the first half of the twentieth century the situation changed, and by the 1950s it had become difficult, even for those who were not moved by the abstract argument from general reducibility, to continue to uphold special vital or mental forces. A great deal became known about biochemical and neurophysiological processes, especially at the level of the cell, and none of it gave any evidence for the existence of special forces not found elsewhere in nature.

During the first half of the century the catalytic role and protein constitution of enzymes were recognized, basic biochemical cycles were identified, and the structure of proteins analyzed, culminating in the discovery of DNA. In the same period, neurophysiological research mapped the body's neuronal network and analyzed the electrical mechanisms responsible for neuronal activity. Together, these developments made it difficult to go on maintaining that special forces operate inside living bodies. If there were such forces, they could be expected to display some manifestation of their presence. But detailed physiological investigation failed to uncover evidence of anything except familiar physical forces.

In this way, the argument from physiology can be viewed as clinching the case for completeness of physics, against the background provided by the argument from fundamental forces. One virtue of this explanation in terms of two interrelated arguments is that it yields a natural explanation for the slow advance of the completeness of physics through the century from the 1850s to the 1950s. Suppose that we rank different thinkers through this period in terms of how much specifically physiological evidence was needed to persuade them of completeness, in addition to the abstract argument from fundamental forces. Helmholtz and his colleagues would be at one extreme, in deciding for complete-ness on the basis of the abstract argument alone, without any physio-logical evidence. In the middle would be those thinkers who waited for a while, but converted once initial physiological research in the first decades of this century gave no indication of any forces beyond funda-mental forces found throughout nature. At the other end would be those who needed a great deal of negative physiological evidence before giving up on special forces. The existence of this spectrum would thus explain why there was a gradual build-up of support for the completeness of physics as the physiological evidence accumulated, culminating, I would contend, in a general scientific consensus by the 1950s.[20]

Conclusion

The problem I set myself at the beginning of this chapter was to explain the rise of physicalist doctrines in the second half of this century. My argument has been that this is due to contemporary agreement on the completeness of physics. In the main body of this chapter I have sought to show that this consensus is not just a fad, but a reflection of develop-ments in empirical theory. Though it has not always been so, there is now good reason to believe the empirical thesis that all physical effects are due to physical causes. In particular, by the 1950s, there was enough phys-iological evidence to persuade even those scientists who were unmoved by the abstract argument from fundamental forces.

The rise of physicalism among philosophers can be seen as a reflec-tion of this development within science. Without the completeness of physics, there is no compelling reason to identify the mind with the brain. But once the completeness of physics became part of established science, scientifically informed philosophers realized that this crucial premise could be slotted into the various alternative versions of the causal argument for physicalism. There seems no reason to look any further to explain the widespread philosophical acceptance of physicalism since the 1950s.

Of course, as with all empirical matters, there is nothing certain here. There is no knock-down argument for the completeness of physics. You could in principle accept the rest of modern physical theory, and yet continue to insist on special mental forces, which operate in as yet undetected ways in the interstices of intelligent brains. And indeed there do exist bitter-enders of just this kind, who continue to hold out for special mental causes, even after another half-century of ever more detailed molecular biology has been added to the inductive evidence that initially created a scientific consensus on completeness in the 1950s. Perhaps it is this possibility that Stephen Clark has in mind when he doubts whether any empirical considerations can "disprove" mind-body dualism. If so, there is no more I can do to persuade him of the completeness of physics. However, I see no virtue in philosophers refusing to accept a premise that, by any normal inductive standards, has been fully established by over a century of empirical research.[21]

NOTES

1. Although see pages 11–12 in the following text for some necessary qualifications.
2. Or, even more precisely, to accommodate quantum mechanical indeterminism: the *chances* of all physical occurrences are fully determined by prior physical occurrences. I shall ignore this qualification in nearly all that follows, because it would only complicate the issues unnecessarily.
3. Note, however, that while this is just a doctrine about physics, it does implicitly distinguish physics from other realms, because most other realms manifestly aren't complete in this sense. The mental isn't complete, for example, because there is no mental cause for the pain I feel when I sit on a drawing pin. Nor is the economic, because there is no economic cause for the economic costs occasioned by a hurricane. (This is why we don't find arguments aiming to show that everything is mental, or economic, parallel to the completeness-based argument that everything is physical.)
4. In other writings, the relevance of the completeness of physics does not need to be excavated, because it lies on the surface. Thus see Feigl (1958); Oppenheim and Putnam (1958).
5. Equally: all chemical/biological/social occurrences have physical effects. The causal argument provides a schema that delivers physicalism for other special subjects as readily as for the mental. In the historical discussion in the following text, various special categories will be at issue at different points. But it will often be expositorily convenient to let the mental stand for the other cases, especially when addressing issues of argumentative structure rather than historical substance. The context should make it clear when the category of the mental is so being used.
6. However Sturgeon (1998) argues that an equivocation between a quantum-theoretical sense of *physical* (in premise 1) and an everyday sense (in premise 2) invalidates the argument. This raises a number of interesting issues that I shall not be able to discuss here. But see Noordhof (1999) and Witmer (forthcoming).
7. Of course, many philosophers are moved to pay this price because they cannot believe that *conscious* occurrences in particular can be identical with physical occurrences. I do not think that this is a good motivation. However, I do accept that physicalists owe some explanation of why conscious occurrences *seem* so very different from physical ones, if they aren't. See Papineau (1993, ch. 4); (1998).

8. Conversely, those philosophers who do think that mathematical or moral facts have physical effects (in our brains, say) will come under pressure from the causal argument to identify them with physical facts.
9. Leibniz took it that all basic material particles are perfectly elastic, and that no kinetic energy is lost when they collide. He explained the apparent loss of kinetic energy when inelastic *macroscopic* bodies collide by positing increased motion in the microscopic parts of those bodies. (Thus he explains, in the fifth paper of the Leibniz-Clarke Correspondence, H. Alexander, ed. [1956]: "The author objects, that two soft or un-elastic bodies meeting together, lose some of their force. I answer, no. 'Tis true, their wholes lose it with respect to their total motion; but their parts receive it, being shaken (internally) by the force of their concourse.")
10. Cf. Papineau (1977).
11. Throughout the rest of this chapter I shall talk in terms of 'forces.' However, the issues will arise in just the same way if you regard forces as otiose, and instead think of the circumstances that "cause forces" as themselves directly causing the resulting accelerations. In that case, you will replace the question of whether there are 'mental forces' with the question of whether specifically mental initial conditions (conditions of sentience, intentionality, or intelligence, depending on how you wish initially to pick out the mental) make a difference to accelerations, in the sense of entering as antecedents into special laws about accelerations that do not follow from other laws about accelerations. More simply, are there special accelerations in brains that aren't predicted by other laws about accelerations? (Cf. McLaughlin [1992], pp. 64–5.)
12. One barrier to the formulation of an energy conservation principle by early Newtonians was their lack of a notion of potential energy, the energy "stored up" after a spring has been extended or compressed, or as two gravitating bodies move apart. Given this, there was no obvious sense in that they could view two gravitating bodies, for example, as conserving energy while they moved apart: after all, the sum of their kinetic energies would not be constant, but unequivocally decreasing. And even in the case of impact, where the notion of potential energy is not immediately needed, early Newtonians displayed no commitment to the conservation of (kinetic) energy. Most obviously, Newton and his followers were perfectly happy, unlike Leibniz, to allow unreduced inelastic collisions, in which both bodies lose kinetic energy without transmitting it to their internal parts. It is also worth remarking that there is nothing in Newton's Laws of Motion to rule out even 'superelastic' impacts, in which total kinetic energy increases. If two bodies with equal masses and equal but opposite speeds both rebounded after collision with double their speeds, for example, Newton's three Laws of Motion and the conservation of momentum would be respected. True, any such phenomenon would provide an obvious recipe for perpetual motion, but the point remains that Newton's Laws do not rule it out. (It is also worth noting that perpetual motion was by no means universally rejected by seventeenth- and eighteenth-century physicists. Cf. Elkana [1974], pp. 28–30.)
13. Here I am closely following Steigerwald (1998, ch. 2).
14. One model for this preservation was the kinetic theory of heat. This account took the macroscopic kinetic energy that was apparently lost to be converted into internal kinetic energy at the microscopic level (cf. Leibniz's explana-

tion for the apparent loss of kinetic energy in inelastic impact mentioned in note 9). But the abstract point at issue did not demand acceptance of the kinetic theory, because the lost kinetic energy could alternatively be viewed as being stored in the 'tensions' of whatever force might be associated with heat.

15. Helmholtz used the word *Kraft*. This is now standardly translated as 'force' rather than 'energy,' but these two concepts were not clearly distinguished at the time, in either English or German. The general expectation at the time was that any conservation law would involve 'force' ('Kraft,' '*vis*'), where this was thought of as a directed quantity ('force of motion'), rather than as a scalarlike energy. (Here again we see the dominance of the Newtonian tradition, whose only conserved quantity was the vectorial momentum.) One of Helmholtz's most important contributions was to make it clear that even within the Newtonian tradition of rational mechanics it is the scalar energy that is conserved, rather than any vectorial 'force.' Even so, the confusions persisted for some time, as shown, for example, by Faraday's 1857 paper "On the Conservation of Force" (cf. Elkana [1974], pp. 130–8).

16. Indeed this line of thought seems to have become extremely popular in the late nineteenth century. The idea that the brain is a repository of 'nervous energy,' which gets channeled in various ways and is then released in action, is common among Victorian thinkers from Darwin to Freud.

17. My treatment of the conservation of energy raises some interesting questions in connection with quantum mechanics. (I am grateful to Barry Loewer for pressing these points on me.)

(1) An initial query relates to my continued presentation of the issues in terms of forces. How does this fit in with modern quantum mechanics, which is normally formulated in terms of Hamiltonians rather than forces, that is, directly in energetic terms? But there is no substantial issue here, because the Hamiltonians can be seen as depending on the relevant forces (cf. McLaughlin [1992], p. 54).

(2) On some interpretations, quantum systems do not always respect the conservation of energy. While energy is conserved in the 'Schrödinger evolution' of quantum systems, it is apparently violated by 'wave collapses.' Some, including myself, take this to argue against wave collapses. But, even if you don't go this way, it doesn't matter for this chapter, because (a) the argument from fundamental forces to completeness will still have weight even if conservation is restricted to Schrödinger evolutions, and (b) completeness is consistent with the indeterminacy of collapse outcomes, because the chances of those outcomes are still fixed by prior physical forces alone (cf. Note 2).

(3) On some, but not all, collapse interpretations, however, *sui generis* factors do seem to fix whether a collapse occurs or not (even though the subsequent chances of the various possible outcomes then still depends entirely on the prior physical forces). I am thinking here of interpretations that say that collapses occur when physical systems interact with consciousness (or indeed that say that collapses occur when there are 'measurements,' or 'macroscopic interactions,' and then refuse to offer any physical reductions of these terms). On these interpretations, the completeness of physics is indeed violated, because collapses don't follow from more basic physical laws, but depend on 'emergent' causes. It would seem an odd victory for

nonphysicalists, however, if the sole locus of *sui generis* mental action were quantum-wave collapses.

18. However, not all emergentists were as sophisticated as Mill and Bain. In *Mind and its Place in Nature* (1923), C.D. Broad addresses the issue of whether independent mental causation would violate the conservation of energy (pp. 103–9). But instead of simply claiming that any mental force would operate conservatively, he insists that the principle of the conservation of energy does not explain all motions, even in physical systems, and so leaves room for other causes. He draws an analogy with a pendulum on a string, where he says that the "pull of the string" is a cause that operates independently of any flows of energy, and suggests that the mind might operate as a similar cause. While it is not entirely clear how Broad intends this analogy to be read, it is difficult to avoid the impression that he has mastered the letter of the principle of the conservation of energy, without grasping the wider physical theory in which it is embedded.

19. Indeed, and somewhat paradoxically, this species of 'bookkeeping' experiment may even have weighed in *favor* of postulating *sui generis* vital forces. This is because these experiments offer a counter to the argument from fundamental forces. That argument, remember, hinged on the claim that there is no direct inductive reason to suppose that any *sui generis* vital forces are conservative, if it is denied that they reduce to more fundamental forces. But experiments such as Rubner's do offer just such direct inductive reason, in that they show that any special forces operating inside bodies must always "pay back" just as much energy as they "borrow," even if they *don't* reduce to more fundamental forces. (I owe this point to Keith Hossack.)

20. McLaughlin ([1992], p. 89) attributes the end of British Emergentism, and therewith the rise of contemporary physicalism, to the 1920s quantum mechanical reduction of chemical forces to general physical forces between subatomic components. But it seems unlikely that this could have been decisive. After all, why should anybody be persuaded against special mental causes just because of the reduction of *chemistry* to physics? (Why should it matter to the existence of *sui generis* mental forces exactly how many independent forces there are at the level of atoms?) At most the reduction of chemistry to physics would have added weight to the argument from fundamental forces, by showing that yet another special force reduces to more basic forces. But it was irrelevant to the argument that I claim swayed thinkers in the twentieth century, the argument from physiology.

21. I would greatly like to thank Barry Loewer, Keith Hossack, and David Spurrett for comments on drafts of this chapter.

2

From Physics to Physicalism

BARRY LOEWER

Introduction

Hilary Putnam explains that:

> The appeal of materialism lies precisely in this, in its claim to be *natural* metaphysics within the bounds of science. That a doctrine which promises to gratify our ambition (to know the noumenal) and our caution (not to be unscientific) should have great appeal is hardly something to be wondered at. (Putnam [1983], p. 210)

Materialism says that all facts, in particular all mental facts, obtain *in virtue of* the spatiotemporal distribution, and properties, of matter. It was, as Putnam says, "metaphysics within the bounds of science," but only so long as science was thought to say that the world is made out of matter.[1] In this century physicists have learned that there is more in the world than matter and, in any case, matter isn't quite what it seemed to be. For this reason many philosophers who think that metaphysics should be informed by science advocate *physicalism* in place of materialism. Physicalism claims that all facts obtain *in virtue of* the distribution of the fundamental entities and properties – whatever they turn out to be – of completed *fundamental physics*.

The enterprise of fundamental physics can be characterized (perhaps a little tendentiously) in terms of its ambition and the kinds of concepts it employs in attempting to satisfy that ambition. The goal of physics is, first, to discover the laws that govern or describe the motions of macroscopic material objects; and second, to discover laws that are complete in that they *completely* account for every event mentioned by those laws.[2] The attempt to formulate a set of laws that is complete resulted in the domain of physics expanding to include not only macroscopic bodies, but all material substances (solids, liquids, gases), their microscopic parts, and also entities and properties that are not in the usual sense material at all: force fields, energy, photons, curved space, strings, spins, wave functions, and so forth. While in one way the domain of physics expanded, in another it shrank. Typically, "newer" entities and properties were understood as constituents of "older" entities and properties. For example, gases and their temperatures are constituted by molecules and their motions, molecules and their dispositions for chemical combination are constituted by elementary particles and their quantum states, and so on. Whether or not the ambitions of physics can be realized is an empirical question. So far the success of this program has been much better than could have been expected in 1650. The astonishing accomplishments of fundamental physics raise the possibility that our world contains relatively few kinds of fundamental *microscopic* entities and quantities that, together with its space-time structure and a few fundamental laws, are sufficient to account for the motions of all material bodies and every other event that physics expanded to include. Steven Weinberg (1992) calls the theory that specifies the complete (in this sense) set of laws "the final theory" and suggests that physicists may not be too far from finding it. Whether or not it will ever be discovered, fundamental physics proceeds under the assumption that there is a final theory and with the ambition of discovering it. I will call the extralogical atomic concepts that appear in their formulations "fundamental physical concepts." The fundamental concepts that have so far been proposed have the following two features; they are *microscopic* and *ubiquitous*. By *microscopic* I mean that they apply to very small regions of space-time; for example, "electromagnetic field values."[3] By "ubiquitous" I mean that they (or concepts from the same family) apply at all places and times (except perhaps at the very origin of the universe). In this they differ from, for example, biological or mental concepts that apply only to certain physically complex systems.

I call the claim that the universe allows the ambition of physics (to discover the final theory) to be realized without going beyond spatio-temporal and microscopic concepts (in addition to mathematics) "PC." PC is not yet physicalism. There is no contradiction in the thought that there is a small complete set of microphysical laws that govern the motions of all material bodies, and everything else mentioned by those laws, and yet there are facts that do not obtain in virtue of facts describable by fundamental physics. In particular, PC doesn't logically exclude mental facts that do not obtain *in virtue of* physical facts. However, there is a line of thought that goes from PC to physicalism. Later in the chapter I will discuss it and also say a few words about the credibility of PC. But the first order of business is to state physicalism more precisely.

Formulating Physicalism

Physicalism is sometimes formulated (e.g., Crane [1991]) as the thesis that all God had to do to create our world was to create its physical facts and laws; the rest followed from these. Fortunately for physicalism's proponents, there are nontheological formulations. The following is due to Frank Jackson (1998):

> (P) Physicalism is true IFF every world that is a minimal physical duplicate of the actual world is a duplicate *simpliciter*.[4]

In (P) a physical duplicate duplicates the laws of physics as well as the physical facts. A minimal physical duplicate duplicates just this and nothing more than is absolutely (i.e., metaphysically) necessary. The idea behind (P) is that once one has fixed the physical facts of our world one has thereby, metaphysically speaking, fixed all the facts. Notice that (P) is itself not metaphysically necessary. There are possible worlds that contain nonphysical entities or properties. Minimal physical duplicates of such worlds are not duplicates *simpliciter*.[5]

As Jackson notes, the truth of (P) is necessary to capture the idea that all facts hold in virtue of physical facts. If (P) is false, then there is a world that completely matches the actual world physically, but leaves something out. If there is something over and above the physical that would thus be left out, obviously there are some facts that do not hold in virtue of physical facts. On the other hand, it is not clear that (P) is sufficient for physicalism. The worry is that (P) fails to capture the idea that the fundamental properties and facts are physical and everything else obtains *in virtue of* them. One problem is that (P) does not exclude there being some kind of fact other than physical facts such that minimally duplicating this kind duplicates the world. It helps to add to (P) the claim that there is no other kind of fact and I will henceforth understand (P) with this addition. But this still may not be enough. The worry is that (P) may not exclude the possibility that mental and physical properties are distinct but necessarily connected in a way in that neither is more basic than the other. In this case, it doesn't seem correct to say that one kind of property obtains in virtue of the other's obtaining.[6] Now I am not sure that this is a real possibility, because it may be that if two *fundamental* properties are really distinct then they cannot be connected by metaphysical necessity.[7] But if considerations about the nature of necessity do not rule this possibility out then we must admit that (P) is not quite sufficient for physicalism. However, it seems to me that if we had good reason to believe (P), then, unless we also had some reason to believe that despite (P) mental facts (or some other kind of facts) do not hold in virtue of physical facts, we have good reason to accept physicalism. In any case, even if (P) is not quite physicalism it is close enough to be an interesting claim. So for the rest of this chapter I will focus on the credibility of (P).

Some philosophers dismiss physicalism as a serious view because they are skeptical that the notion of a *physical* statement can be adequately characterized. The alleged problem (Crane and Mellor [1990]) is that every way of explicating "physical" will make (P) either obviously false or trivially true (or not consonant with the idea behind physicalism). If "physical" is characterized in terms of the language of current physics then it is likely that (P) is false because it is likely that the vocabulary of current physics is incomplete.[8] Certainly a complete description of the world in terms of the vocabulary of classical physics is incomplete and there are reasons to suspect that additions (if not revisions as radical as the replacement of classical physics by quantum physics) that will be needed by a more complete future physics. On the other hand, if "physical" in (P) means facts expressible in the language of the complete physical theory of the world (if there is one), then that threatens to make (P) trivial unless some conditions are placed on what makes a theory "physical." If it were to turn out that to account for certain clearly physical events physicists needed to posit fundamental intentional, or phenomenal, properties, then the resulting theory would not be physical.

The most straightforward response to this objection (Papineau [1993a]) is to require that fundamental physical predicates (the atomic predicates of the language in which the complete physical description of the world is expressed) are not mental (i.e., intentional and phenomenal). Given this, (P) implies that mental truths supervene on nonmental truths. This is nontrivial and not obviously false. Other and stronger versions of physicalism can be formulated by adding further conditions on fundamental physical predicates, for example, no biological predicates, no macroscopic predicates, etc. Another route is to add to (P) the claim that our world has a PC theory and then specify that the physical vocabulary include only the vocabulary of the PC theory (plus logic and mathematics). So (P) can be taken as formulating a number of physicalist doctrines with the strongest identifying the physical vocabulary as constructed from the predicates of the true PC theory. In what follows I will generally have this strongest version in mind.[9]

(P) has an important consequence that Jackson calls "the entry by entailment thesis" (ENT). A first, but not quite correct, formulation is:

(ENT) If B is true and $ is the full physical description (including the laws) of the world, then N(If $, then B).

(ENT) isn't quite correct, because even if (P) is true there will be some true statements, for example, "That there are no spirits", that are not entailed by $. The problem is that there are worlds at which $ is true but that contain so called "extras," for example, spirits. Jackson recognizes this problem and seeks to handle it by requiring that $ include not just the full physical description of the world but also some statement that says, as he puts it, "that's all." But it is not clear how to formulate "that's all" without going beyond purely physical and mathematical vocabulary.[10] A better approach is to restrict the statements B that appear in (ENT) to those that are in an intuitive sense "nonglobal" (Witmer [1997]). Global statements are those whose truth values depend on these being all the facts. We can make this precise by defining a proposition as global just in case it is true at some world w and for any world w at which it is true, if world w* contains w, then it is also true at w*. "There are no spirits" and "There are exactly 10 conscious beings" are examples of global propositions, while "There are at least 10 conscious beings in region R" and "John is in pain" are examples of nonglobal statements.[11] Many of the basic predicates of the special sciences are nonglobal in that statements affirming their instantiations are nonglobal. However, a true special science generalization may well be global. If so, then although it supervenes (and if it expresses a law, the law supervenes) on the physical facts, it will not be entailed (and its being a law will not be entailed) by the full physical description.[12]

Jackson thinks that if physicalism is true, then true instances of (ENT) are analytic and a priori. His argument for this surprising claim involves a generalization of Kripke's ideas for showing how necessities can be a posteriori. In fact, at one time, Jackson thought that statements concerning phenomenal consciousness do not follow a priori from the full physical description and that this showed that physicalism is false.[13] But Jackson's argument involves semantical assumptions that are no part of physicalism and, in any case, it can be demonstrated that his claim has exceptions.[14]

Fear of Physicalism

It has been claimed that physicalism has certain unpalatable consequences. Among these are:

1. Physics takes precedence over all the other sciences and other ways of obtaining knowledge.
2. All sciences (and all other truths) are reducible to physics.
3. The only genuine properties, events, and individuals are those of fundamental physics.
4. The only genuine laws are laws of physics. There are no special science laws.

5. The only genuine causation is causation by physical events; in particular, there is no mental or other higher-level causation.
6. Eliminativism: Intentionality, consciousness, rationality, and meaning do not exist.

Sometimes these alleged consequences are taken to be reasons to disbelieve physicalism and sometimes as bitter pills that physicalists must swallow. But, although each of these claims are indeed unpalatable, none is a consequence of (P). Decisively establishing this claim is beyond the scope of this chapter, but a brief discussion may lend it some credibility.

(1) It is important to keep in mind that (P) is not an epistemological or methodological doctrine. (P) doesn't imply that physics is epistemologically or methodologically more basic than other sciences. If the claims of current physics should conflict with the claims of one of the special sciences it may very well be that the latter is better confirmed than the former. Nor does the truth of (P) favor allocating federal funds to the proposed super collider over biological research, or to support the arts. (P) doesn't imply that the reductionist methodology of analyzing complex systems into simpler parts that is so successful in physics, is the appropriate method for the enormously more complex systems treated in biology. Nor does (P) imply that scientific methodology is the only, or best, way to acquire knowledge about every topic. It is compatible with (P) that hermeneutics, or verstehen, are better methods than experimental psychology when it comes to knowing the minds of our fellow human beings. (P) does require that if that is so, then this fact, just as all others, is implied by the totality of physical facts.

(2) A reduction of a special science (say biology), or a particular special science theory, to fundamental physics involves systematically locating physical truths that entail the truths (including the laws) of the special science. (P), of course, does not imply that any special science can be reduced to current physics. More interestingly, it doesn't imply that any of the special sciences can be reduced to completed physics. Because laws are expressed by global statements, (P) doesn't imply that physical truths imply special science laws. And although (P) does imply that non-global truths of the special sciences are metaphysically entailed by the truths of fundamental physics, it does not imply that these entailments are systematic or that we can ever locate and know them. Similarly, (P) does not imply that truths that do not belong to any science can be reduced to physics, even though they are implied by statements of physics. It may be, as some have suggested, that limitations in the kinds of concepts that we are capable of entertaining; the nature of the

concepts of the special sciences; or the complexity of the entailments, precludes us from ever knowing the implications that (P) requires.[15]

(3) (P) does imply that the only *fundamental* properties, events, and individuals are those of fundamental physics. But (P) doesn't exclude nonfundamental entities belonging to these various categories. Exactly what nonfundamental properties, etcetera. (P) allows for depends on the nature of properties, etcetera. Let me begin with what is sometimes called an "abundant" conception of properties. According to the abundant conception, every predicate (or concept) that can be used to make a statement (or is a constituent of a thought) with truth conditions expresses a property, although there may also be properties that are not expressed by the predicates of any language.[16] Further, two predicates express the same property only if it is metaphysically necessary that they are coextensive. Although the abundant conception is profligate with respect to the existence of properties, it is compatible with properties being nonlinguistic and (largely) mind independent, and with distinct predicates expressing the same property.[17] It is clear that on the abundant conception, (P) is compatible with the existence not only of the properties of fundamental physics, but also with many other kinds of properties. On the abundant conception, "is a storm," "is green," "is 5 miles from the Eiffel tower," "is grue," "feels painful," and "is thinking about Vienna," all express properties. It may be that given (P) some of these properties are not instantiable, but that would have to be shown for the specific property.

Contrasting with the abundant conception are so-called "sparse" conceptions of properties according to which only certain predicates express genuine properties. Lewis calls these "perfectly natural properties" (Lewis [1983], Armstrong [1978]).[18] Perfectly natural properties satisfy certain conditions, for example, they involve real similarities; figure in laws and scientific taxonomies; and are causally relevant. Such added conditions presumably disqualify "grueness" (and perhaps some of the other examples previously mentioned) from being a perfectly natural property. So whether or not the instantiation of perfectly natural properties that are not expressible in the language of physics (in particular psychological properties) is compatible with (P) depends on whether the existence of special sciences (in particular psychology) and higher level causation is compatible with (P); issues to which I will discuss in the following text.

Suppose for now that (P) doesn't exclude the existence and instantiation of perfectly natural properties other than those of fundamental physics. How might they and their instantiations relate to physical properties? If (P) is true, then these instantiations (for the nonglobal properties) are necessitated by physical facts and laws. But in some cases more can be said. It is widely and plausibly held that some nonfundamental properties are *realized* by fundamental physical properties. There are various views concerning exactly what is involved in one property instantiation realizing another, but they have in common that if an instance of P realizes an instance of F, then the P instantiation metaphysically necessitates the F instantiation; in other words, any possible world that contains the first also contains the second.[19] For example, the property of being a storm may be realized by various dynamical configurations of physical properties, but is not identical to any specific one or even to their disjunction. For it seems plausible to suppose that storms occur in possible worlds that contain none of our fundamental physical properties (these storms will be realized by alien fundamental properties).

Suppose that events are, or are correlated with, the instantiations (by individuals and times) of certain event-constituting properties (Kim and Brandt [1967]). I see no reason why nonfundamental properties cannot be event constituting. For example, the event of a storm striking the coast is composed of various physical events, though it is somewhat vague around the boundaries, but is not identical to any of them. This is clear because the storm's modal properties differ from the modal properties of the events that compose it. That is, it may be that the storm might have struck a bit to the north, but not the case that any of its constituent events might have occurred a bit to the north. Of course, these counterfactual truths must, if (P) is true, supervene on the totality of truths of fundamental physics.[20]

Similar remarks apply to particulars, for example, particular rocks, trees, or people. If (P) is true then these "higher level" particulars are constituted by the instantiations of physical properties, elementary particles possessing certain states, but are not identical to them. Of course exactly what fundamental physical entities constitutes a given particular, for example, my cat, is a vague matter. The important point is that (P) is compatible with the existence of my cat even though the cat is not identical to any fundamental physical particles (or mereological sum of them). The reason that my cat is not identical to any sum of fundamental physical entities is that there are counterfactuals true of my cat that are not true of the mereological sum (or any precisifications of the vague sum) that constitute it. Of course, as in the case of events, any such counterfactuals must supervene on the totality of physical facts.

(4) Of course, (P) is not compatible with the existence of *fundamental* laws that are not laws of physics. Whether or not (P) is compatible with there being nonfundamental laws depends on exactly what the laws

are, and that is controversial.[21] Jaegwon Kim (1993b) has argued that physicalism excludes there being special science laws. More precisely, he argues that if F and G are nonphysical predicates each of which is multiply realized, then the generalization "Fs are followed by (or cause) Gs" cannot express a law. His argument is predicated on the idea that law statements must involve predicates that are projectible, and if physicalism is true then only predicates of physics are projectible. A predicate G is projectible with respect to F (the generalization "Fs are followed by Gs" is projectible) if Fs that are Gs confirm that Fs are followed by Gs.[22] Because he holds that a generalization expresses a law only if its predicates are projectible, he concludes (P) is incompatible with the existence of laws expressed by generalizations composed of nonphysical predicates. Kim's main argument involves an example. He asks us to consider the property of being Jade that is realized by or equivalent to the disjunction Jadeite or Nephrite. Kim observes that if our evidence consists just of samples of Jadeite and we are interested in a generalization such as "Jade melts at such and such a temperature" then it would be foolish to generalize just from this sample. Of course this is correct, because we know that different molecular structures typically give rise to different melting temperatures. But this example doesn't generalize to other predicates. In the first place, whether or not a generalization is lawlike depends on the predicates in both antecedent and consequent. There are some generalizations with "Jade" in the antecedent that are confirmable by their instances; for example, "Jade is called 'Jade' by English speakers." In fact, one can see that (P) is compatible with one's assigning a probability function over certain generalizations expressed in nonphysical vocabulary, say the vocabulary of psychology or biology, which allows for their confirmation. That is, predicates of the higher level sciences may be projectible even though they express multirealizable properties. Indeed, a prohibition against such probability functions would be pig-headed, because we have reason to believe that generalizations that we can express in nonphysics vocabulary are sometimes true, or approximately true. We can see that something must be wrong with Kim's argument from the fact that there are well-confirmed generalizations of the special sciences that involve properties that are multirealized by fundamental physical properties.[23] Perhaps the best and most obvious examples are provided by statistical mechanics; for example, the probability of the entropy of an isolated body decreasing is negligible.

As far as I can see, (P) does not preclude there being true generalizations couched in nonphysical vocabulary (whose predicates do not refer to properties of fundamental physics) that are confirmable by their instances, support counterfactuals, and are entailed by highly informative and simple theories, in other words, have all the usual marks of laws. If this makes them laws (although nonfundamental laws), then (P) does not exclude special science laws.

(5) The issue of whether (P) allows for causation by nonphysical events and nonphysical properties, in particular by mental events and properties, is a vexed matter. Part of the difficulty is that there are no fully acceptable accounts of causation by either events or properties, even for fundamental events and properties. But it seems to me that any adequate account of causation must allow for causation by nonfundamental entities. For example, the storm's striking the coast caused flooding. The storm is a cause and the property of being a storm is causally connected to the flooding. Of course, if (P) is true, such causation is not fundamental, but will supervene on physical facts and laws. As far as I can see, any account that allows nonfundamental physical events and properties to be causes will do the same for at least some kinds of mental events and properties. I won't argue for that here, but I do want to sketch an account of causation that, though not fully adequate, has this consequence. The account is this: Ms causes Ps* if Ms does not metaphysically entail Ps* and at a time t immediately prior to Ms the following pair of counterfactuals are true:

(a) Ms > t Ps*;
(b) −Ms > t − Ps*.

As far as I can see, (P) is compatible with the pair of counterfactuals that, on this account, ground claims such as the storm's striking the coast caused the flooding. And, additionally, (P) is also compatible with the pair of counterfactuals that ground, for example, Fred's wanting a beer causing Fred's body to be in the kitchen. On this account, there may be many events or property instantiations, even ones that occur simultaneously, at different levels that are causally connected to a given event. For example, a neurological event that instantiates Fred's urge may also be causally connected to his body's location.

It has been objected (Kim [1998]) that counterfactual accounts of causation are inadequate, especially in the context of mental causation, because the truth of counterfactuals (such as the above pair) is compatible with epiphenomenalism. That is, it is compatible with there being mental properties that are distinct from physical properties to which they are connected by so-called "bridge" laws. If there are no causal relations between these mental properties (or events) and physical properties then the mental properties are epiphenomenal. This view is nonphysicalist, because a minimal physical duplicate of a world at which it obtains does not duplicate the mental property instantiations or the bridge laws. Kim's claim is that in the epiphenomenalist world, mental to physical counterfactuals may still obtain. But, as we will see in the next section, there is reason to doubt this. In any case, even if it is true it doesn't show that the counterfactuals are not sufficient for causation in a physicalist world. Indeed, if they or some similar account were not correct, then there could be two PC worlds exactly alike in their physical laws and instantiations of physical and mental properties, but only in one are there *genuine (sic) -causal* connections between mental properties and physical properties. These causal connections would, of course, be themselves nonphysical, because they don't supervene on the instantiations of physical properties and laws. (If they did, then physicalism could allow *genuine* causal connections). But what are these causal connections doing? They are truly "epiphenomenal"; unneeded and unknowable. The conclusion is that the counterfactual surrogate for causation (or some similar account) is really all we need to account for mental causation, as we know it.

Now, of course, Kim would reject this reasoning, because what he really wants is for mental properties to make a causal difference over and above causation by physical properties. But it is obvious from the start that this is something that a physicalist cannot allow. For the physicalist it is enough for our bodily movements to be counterfactually sensitive to our mental states. That the counterfactuals are true in virtue of more fundamental physical facts takes nothing away from that. And one can take comfort in the fact that mental properties are in the same boat as other nonfundamental properties.

The claim that mental causation is compatible with (P) is highly abstract and, of course, doesn't imply that mental causation is implemented by physical processes. Advocates of (P) would like to be in a position to show that certain physical mechanisms do implement mental causation; for example, to explain the causal processes involved when a driver notices a deer running across the road and then applies the brakes. Current psychological research is some distance from coming out with an account, but optimistic cognitive scientists think that the so-called "computational-representational theory of mind" is on the right track. If intentional causation can be shown to be implemented by computational processes, then we are on the way toward showing that it is physically implemented because we know that computational processes can be physically implemented; for example, by computers.[24]

(6) If (P) really did exclude the instantiation of mental properties (consciousness, intentionality, rationality) then it would have to be rejected because mental phenomena certainly exist. It is difficult to see

how elements of physical reality can add up to intentionality and consciousness. There have been various attempts to show that they do. These
"naturalization" projects have not met with much success.[25] But as I mentioned previously, (P) doesn't require that we can ever see how physical
statements metaphysically entail mental statements, just that the entailments hold. On the other hand, attempts to show that (P) excludes
mental facts are, if anything, even less convincing. Here I only want to
briefly mention two such attempts. One involves so-called "conceivability arguments" that claim that it is *conceivable* that the physical facts be
what they are and there be no consciousness, or intentionality, at all.[26]
These arguments assume (and sometimes argue for) the claim that,
at least in the relevant situations, conceivability implies possibility.
However, it can be shown that, at most, conceivability is defeasible evidence for possibility (Balog [2000]). The second line of argument identifies some feature of mental properties, for example, alleged normativity,
and then claims that it is not the case that physical facts that fail to exhibit
this feature can metaphysically entail facts that do. The claim is that two
kinds of facts are just too different from one another.[27] While it is not
difficult to find philosophers expressing sympathy for this line of thought
it is well nigh impossible to find an argument for the conclusion that is
sufficiently well articulated to evaluate. In any case, as we will see, given
CP if any of these arguments were sound we would be saddled with the
conclusion that mental events (or properties) are epiphenomenal, or
overdeterminants of physical effects. These consequences seem to me to
be so implausible as to cast doubt on the soundness of any argument that
claims to show that (P) excludes mentality.[28]

The upshot of the preceding discussion is that reasonable antireduc-
tionists, humanists, opponents of scientism, and so on, have nothing to
fear from (P).

PC (p. 38)?

From CP to P

What would the world be like if (P) were false? First, there would be
certain nonglobal contingent facts not metaphysically necessitated by the
full physical state description. But how would these nonphysical facts,
and more specifically the properties and entities that constitute them, be
related to physical properties and entities? One possibility is that both
physical and nonphysical properties are instantiated, but there are no
laws or metaphysical connections linking them.[29] This view makes it quite
mysterious why it is that mental properties are found associated with
only certain physical properties; why, for example, rocks or gases don't
have thoughts. Because there are no laws or metaphysical links that

connect these properties, such correlations are merely coincidental. Most opponents of physicalism reject this picture and hold instead that mental (and perhaps certain other properties) are emergent in a certain robust sense that involves the existence of *emergent* laws linking them to physical properties.[30] These laws are thought of as vertical because they link the physical state at t with the mental state at t. Emergentist views sometimes also posit horizontal laws linking instantiations of physical and mental properties with each other at different times. Such laws might ground causal relations between mental and physical events (where events are property instantiations at times). If physics is incomplete, then such mental-physical laws might also be required to give full accounts of physical events (or their chances). The important point about these Emergentist laws is that they are not among the fundamental laws of physics or entailed by them and the physical facts. If our world contains them, then God when he made the world had to make them in addition to the physical facts and laws.

Now I don't think there is much reason to believe that there are Emergentist laws, either vertical or horizontal. But not having a reason to disbelieve is not a reason for belief, so I now want to examine an argument for (P). I know of two ways of arguing for (P). One is by finding reductions of particular higher level facts (properties, events, etc.) to lower level, and ultimately physical, ones. While there are some notable reductions (or partial reductions), for example, of thermodynamics to statistical mechanics, claims of reduction are usually accompanied by a great deal of hand waving. And while each successful reduction provides some reason in favor of (P), each failed reduction provides some reason against it. So this piecemeal approach is far from conclusive. A very different line of argument seeks to establish (P) all at once based on very general considerations about laws and causation. The line of argument I have in mind has been formulated in a number of different ways (for example, McGinn [1982], Peacocke [1979], Papineau [1990], [1993a], and [1995], and Loewer [1995]). The version I will discuss proceeds in two steps. The first step argues that any property (or event) whose instantiation at t (or in time interval d) is causally relevant to a physical event at least nomologically supervenes on the physical state of the world at t. The second step argues that the laws in characterizing nomological supervenience are no more than the fundamental laws of physics. If we further assume that every property instantiation has a physical effect, and that all nonglobal facts are determined by some collection of property instantiations, then we get (P).

I will assume that the fundamental laws of physics are deterministic. It is not difficult, though a bit messier, to run the argument if the fundamental laws are indeterministic. The main premise of the argument is the deterministic completeness of physics (PCD):

(PCD) For any distinct times t and t', the physical state S(t) and the fundamental physical laws entail the physical state S(t').

I will say that a property instantiation M(t) is physically detectable by P*(t') iff at times immediately prior to t the counterfactuals M(t) > P*(t') and −M(t) > −P*(t') are true. If M(t) is physically detectable by P*(t') and M(t) occurs, then M(t) causes or is actually relevant to P*(t') in accord with the account given earlier. Now, suppose that (PCD) is true so that at times s prior to t the physical state P(s) and the laws entail that P*(t') (or −P*(t')). Then, whether or not M(t) occurs P*(t') (or −P*(t')) will occur. So if M(t) is not connected by law to P(t) it will be physically undetectable. So every property instantiation that is physically detectable at the very least nomologically supervenes on the complete physical state. This is not yet (P). There are two problems: (1) there may be some property instantiations that are not physically detectable, and (2) even for physically detectable properties the most we have shown is that they *nomologically* supervene on the physical state.[31] But among the laws may be laws that are not entailed by the full physical description of the world including physical laws.

As for the first problem, it seems to me plausible that all property instances are either physically detectable or supervene on properties that are physically detectable. But even supposing this is not so, the following principle still strikes me as quite reasonable:

(U) If some instances of M nomologically supervene on the physical state (or some instances of M supervene on property instantiations that are each physically detectable) then, unless there is some positive reason to think that other instances don't supervene on the physical state, we should suppose that all instances of M do so supervene.

I know of no reason to think of any instances of a nonglobal property that fails to have instances that are physically detectable (or fails to supervene on property instances that are physically detectable). It follows that it is reasonable to suppose that all property instances nomologically supervene on the full physical state.

Nomological supervenience is compatible both with (P) and with the Emergentist account sketched earlier on which M properties are linked by special "vertical" laws with physical properties (and perhaps also by horizontal laws with physical and mental properties). To establish (P) then I need to show that the Emergentist account is false. I know of no way of conclusively demonstrating this. However, there are some considerations that make the Emergentist picture quite unattractive when combined with (PCD). To begin with, notice that it would be bizarre to suppose that a property such as being a rock, or a cloud, etcetera is linked by special vertical law (over and above the laws of physics) to the physical state. If that were so there would be a possible world physically identical to the actual world, but where in the actual world there is a rock at a certain location in the other world there is a cloud. It is only for mental properties that the proposal of special vertical laws has any credibility. But even here the result is peculiar. It would entail not merely that zombies (physical, but not mental duplicates of people) are possible, but that either mental properties are completely epiphenomenal or if linked by causal law to physical (or other mental) properties that the instantiations of these properties are pervasively causally overdetermined. The world may be like that, but I think that simplicity considerations suggest that we don't believe it is pending persuasive arguments against (P).

Furthermore, it is arguable that if (PCD) is true then on the Emergentist account, even with horizontal mental-physical laws, physical events do not counterfactually depend on mental events. So, for example, it will not be the case that the location of my body near the refrigerator will depend on my having desired a beer. Here is why. Suppose that I form the desire to have a beer at t, call this "M(t)," and that there is a physical state P(t) that is linked by Emergentist law to M(t); in other words, "P– > M." Suppose now that P(t) leads by the complete deterministic physical laws to P*(t'). Then, I claim that –M(t) > –P*(t') is false. The argument assumes Lewis's (1983) account of counterfactuals and specifically Lewis's account of world similarity. (It doesn't presuppose Lewis's account of possible worlds as concrete entities). To evaluate the counterfactual we ask what world (or kind of world) is most similar to the actual world (where the laws of physics are deterministic and there are Emergentist vertical laws connecting physical with mental properties). For Lewis's world similarity is evaluated in terms of two factors: (1) the size of the region in which laws of the actual world are violated; and (2) the size of the departure of perfect match in matters of particular fact. There are two kinds of worlds to consider (where "L" is the conjunction of the complete deterministic laws of physics and "V" is the Emergentist law linking P with M):

W1: –M(t) & P(t) & L & –V
W2: –M(t) & –P(t) & –L & V

If W1 is more similar than W2 to the actual world, then the counterfactual will come out false because in it P*(t') will be true. But if W2 is

more similar than W1, then the counterfactual might be true depending
on what physical state occurs at t. At first, it may appear that there is a
tie in similarity because both worlds involve the violation of a law; W1
an Emergentist law and W2 a dynamical law of physics. But on Lewis's
account of evaluating similarity that is not so. The reason is that W2 will
differ enormously in matters of particular fact from the actual world,
whereas W1 will differ only to the extent required to make −M(t) true.
This being so on the Emergentist account, and assuming that the fundamental laws of physics are deterministic, it follows that physical events
don't counterfactually depend on emergent events. Whether or not I
want the beer would make no difference to the location of my body. But,
of course, it does. And (P) is no impediment to that being so. Under (P),
worlds of type W1 are metaphysically impossible because the physical
state P and the physical laws are metaphysically sufficient for M(t). This
being so, the counterfactual assumption −M(t) requires some violation
of the physical laws. If the most similar world in which −M(t) is one
at which −Q(t), such that Q(t) leads by law to P*(t), then indeed the
counterfactual will come out true. And that scenario is completely compatible with (P) depending on the exact details of the physical realizations of M. So I conclude that (perhaps somewhat surprisingly) if we
want the physical to depend on the mental, and if we think that the fundamental laws of physics are complete and deterministic, then we should
also accept (P).

The Credibility of PC

I will conclude with a very brief discussion of the credibility of PC. I think
it is fair to say that no one thinks that current physics is complete and
there is not a consensus among physicists or philosophers on whether
PC is true. Some physicists, for example Steven Weinberg (1992), think
that we are fairly close to a unified physics that would validate PC. But
there is a rather contrary view according to which our world is a much
sloppier place than the world of Weinberg's dreams. Nancy Cartwright
(1999) is a vigorous advocate of this viewpoint. She has been arguing that
the fundamental laws of physics work, to the extent they do, only under
very special contrived conditions found in laboratories. If I understand
her, the view is that the fundamental laws of physics are woefully incomplete and what laws there are are best understood as containing *ceteris
paribus* qualifications. More fundamental than laws are capacities; for
example, the capacity of a charged particle to produce an electromagnetic field. There are many capacities associated with entities and
properties at different levels that together determine the tendencies for

various courses of events to occur. She suggests that lawful regularities are more or less artifacts of laboratory situations in which interactions are shielded from the various capacities that normally affect them. And she also thinks that emergent *ceteris paribus* laws may appear at higher levels of description than fundamental physics. This is an interesting view and it would definitely be instructive to think through what a world similar to that would be like in contrast with a world at which physics is complete. Cartwright's main argument for her view is in the form of a challenge to proponents of PC. Her example is dropping a dollar bill from St. Marks Tower. Proponents of PC think that the fundamental laws of physics, and to a good approximation Newton's and Maxwell's laws, govern the trajectory of the dollar bill as it floats to the ground, though the use of those laws to predict the trajectory is not possible due to the complexity of the interactions between the dollar bill and air molecules. But Cartwright thinks this is mere dogma. She seems to suggest that although "F = ma" may hold in specialized laboratory conditions it may be false in this case (presumably that some of the changes in motion of the dollar are not due to forces).

Cartwright's arguments against PC strike me as very weak. They are merely *skeptical* arguments. She doesn't produce a single case in which "F = ma" (and other examples of fundamental laws) fails, but rather claims that extrapolating it beyond controlled laboratory conditions is unwarranted. One would expect that if a putative fundamental law fails outside the laboratory it would be possible to find evidence of it. A Nobel Prize would be in the offing for the discoverer. Even though the fundamental laws (or the equations believed to approximate them) cannot be used to give detailed explanations in complex situations, they can be used to give approximate predictions, or be used in connection with statistical models to make statistical predictions, and these are born out. Second, unless we have some specific reason to think that moving outside of the laboratory, or increasing complexity, leads to the failure of these laws then ordinary principles of scientific inference counsel that we should, pending counter evidence, suppose that they hold generally. So I think that while the completeness of physics is a contingent claim, there is now reason to believe that it may well be true and scant reason to think it false.

Conclusion

The journey from physics to physicalism is not an entirely smooth one. As we have seen, the starting place, PC, is plausible, but not obviously true. Given PC, the argument for (P) is fairly straightforward although it requires that one resist epiphenomenalism and nomological overdetermination. Once we have arrived at (P) we still have not quite reached physicalism, because we saw that there may be ways in which (P) could be true, but still not all facts obtain *in virtue of* physical facts. However, on the whole Physicalism is more plausible than any of the alternatives and well deserving the name of "scientific metaphysics."

NOTES

1. Putnam himself is no advocate of materialism or physicalism but thinks that metaphysical claims such as these involve presuppositions that he rejects. While I like the quote I disagree with his view.
2. Aristotle says that physics is "about bodies and magnitudes and their affections and changes, and also about the sources of such entities" (*De Caelo*, p. 368).
3. It is sometimes said that quantum mechanical states are not microscopic in this way, because the quantum state of a many particle system is not fully determined by the density matrices associated with each particle. While this last point is correct it shows only that quantum states are not microscopic in ordinary space-time. But that doesn't mean that they are not microscopic by my definition, because the space of any theory that interprets the quantum state realistically is configuration space in which the quantum state is a field. See Albert (1996).
4. David Lewis (1983) formulates physicalism as the doctrine that "among worlds where no natural properties alien to our world are instantiated, no two differ without differing physically." A property is alien to a world if it is not instantiated there and not constructed out of properties instantiated there. On the assumption that fundamental properties of physics are natural properties, Lewis's formulation entails Jackson's, but the converse entailment doesn't hold, at least not without further metaphysical assumptions about natural properties and laws. While both formulations employ possible worlds neither is committed to Lewis's account of possible worlds.
5. (P) is contingent but, in a certain sense, nonaccidental. If (P) is true and if Q is any proposition (true or false) that is compatible with the laws of physics, then the counterfactual "if Q were true then (P) would be true" is also true. See Witmer (Chapter 3, this volume) for a discussion of this point.
6. How might this happen? One way would be if properties are individuated by their nomological connections to other properties (Shoemaker 1998) so that, for example, F cannot be instantiated without G's being instantiated. Another way (Russell 1927) would be if fundamental properties possess both categorical and nomological/causal aspects that are metaphysically inseparable and if physical concepts refer to the nomological/causal aspect but not the categorical aspects. Some philosophers inclined to this view think of the categorical aspect as proto-mental and others as merely nonphysical and unknowable. In either case, if the properties referred to in physics possess this kind of categorical aspect it seems wrong to say that all facts hold in virtue of physical facts even though (P) is satisfied.

7. According to Lewis's "recombination principle" (1983), if P and Q are distinct fundamental properties then there are possible worlds in which one is instantiated but the other is not.
8. The trouble isn't that current physics may be false (i.e., physicists are mistaken about the laws) but that it may be incomplete. If its vocabulary were sufficiently complete to specify all the fundamental physical facts and laws then (P) would not be obviously inadequate.
9. This strong version has the apparent disadvantage of defining physicalism so that it entails PC, but because I think that PC is plausibly true and that it provides the premise for the best argument for physicalism this doesn't strike me as a real disadvantage.
10. Adding that "$" is the complete description of the world involves semantic notions.
11. Some global statements, for example, "There are no ghosts," have negations that are nonglobal while others, for example, "the average age of a ghost is a million years," have negations that are also global.
12. If the reduction of a special science to physics involves the laws of physics and statements of physics implying the laws of the special science then (P) doesn't imply that the special science laws are reducible to physics.
13. Jackson (1990). Chalmers (1996) develops this argument in great detail.
14. For general objections to Jackson's claim see Yablo (2000). For an argument that shows that the claim must have at least some exceptions see Balog (2000). Balog shows that statements about phenomenal consciousness must be exceptions to the claim.
15. McGinn (1996) claims that limitations in our concepts may prevent us from ever solving certain philosophical problems, for example, how phenomenal consciousness arises out of physical phenomena; Loar (1997) and Balog (2000) suggest that the nature of the phenomenal concepts prevent our finding any identification or realization of phenomenal consciousness by physical properties satisfying.
16. For Lewis (1983) an abundant monadic property is any set of possible entities.
17. It is important to distinguish between concepts and properties. Concepts are the meanings of predicates while properties are references of predicates. Distinct predicates can express distinct concepts, that, unknown to a thinker who understands both, express the same property, for example, is water and is H_2O.
18. Universals can be construed as special abundant properties, or as another kind of fundamental entity, that is correlated with an abundant property. Lewis (1983) points out that the work that is done by universals can also be done by tropes.
19. Shoemaker (Chapter 4, this volume) suggests that a property P realizes F when the set of F's causal powers is a subset of the set of P's causal powers.
20. The same holds for other accounts of events, including Davidson's. An interesting point about Davidson's account is that his event monism, all events are physical events, is neither necessary nor sufficient for (P).
21. It is plausible that special science laws or law statements include a *ceteris paribus* qualification. There is no fully satisfactory account of exactly what this qualification comes to, but that shouldn't prevent us from recognizing

that there are plenty of examples of special science statements that are thought to express laws.

22. Following Goodman (1979) a hypothesis "Fs are followed by Gs" is projectible (G is projectible with respect to F) IFF positive instances of the hypothesis confirm it (raise its credence and the credence of unobserved positive instances).

23. More extensive responses to Kim's argument are in Block (1997), Fodor (1997), and Antony and Levine (1997).

24. See Rey (1997) and (Chapter 5, this volume).

25. For a survey of some recent attempts to naturalize intentionality see Loewer (1997).

26. Conceivability arguments directed at showing that phenomenal consciousness fails to supervene on physical facts go back to Descartes and have recently been revived by Kripke (1980), Jackson (1998), Chalmers (1996), and McGinn (1991c). They have, in my view, been decisively refuted by Balog (1998) and (2000), Loar (1997), and Hill and McLaughlin (1999).

27. Davidson's (1969) argument against the existence of strict psychophysical laws and more generally of there being any "close connection" between physical and intentional concepts seems to be of this sort but it is very difficult to know because it is very difficult to say exactly what the argument is.

28. The arguments that are intended to show that (P) excludes mental facts might actually better be understood as showing, if anything at all, that we cannot see how physical statements metaphysically entail mental statements.

29. This view is sometimes attributed to Davidson (1969) who on the one hand holds that there are no psychophysical laws, but on the other hand accepts that the mental weakly – not strongly, as required by (P) – supervenes on the physical.

30. The Emergentist laws may be "deterministic" in that the physical state completely determines the cotemporal mental state or "indeterministic" in that the physical state only partially determines the mental state or determines the chances of various mental states.

31. Witmer (1997) commenting on earlier versions of this argument made this point about Papineau (1993a) and Loewer (1995).

3

Sufficiency Claims and Physicalism: A Formulation

D. GENE WITMER

According to Jeffrey Poland, the "basic conviction" of the physicalist is that:

> ... phenomena occur in nature in virtue of what goes on in the physical domain.... My approach will be to frame theses that express the following idea: given that all individual phenomena, all regularities, and all instances of and exceptions to regularities which occur in nature occur in virtue of physical phenomena, there are physically-based explanations of all such phenomena. (Poland [1994], pp. 207–8)

I agree with Poland that this sort of explanatory claim is central to the physicalist idea. In this chapter I explore how we may fill out and clarify that explanatory claim in terms of its modal implications. In particular, I focus on two sufficiency claims to which physicalism is committed. Ultimately, there is no way to *replace* the explanatory claim with sufficiency claims; nonetheless, there are good reasons to focus on them. They help cash out the demands of physicalism, giving us a better grasp on its content. In so doing, they also put us in a better position to evaluate apparent counterexamples to physicalism, think further about the implications of physicalism for science, and, perhaps most urgently, get clear on what sense there is to be made of so-called naturalization projects. Further, they provide a dialectically useful route to justifying physicalism itself. As I shall argue at the end of this chapter, if they are true, it is overwhelmingly likely that the overarching explanatory claim is true.

Physicalistic Explanation and Sufficiency

In what sense is the physical realm supposed to explain everything else? The explanation wanted is plainly not a causal one: the dualist can say that the state of the nonphysical realm may be such that only physical events provide information about its causal history. Such a position is, of course, familiar under the heading of dualist epiphenomenalism. The

kind of explanation wanted is rather that which is exemplified by the
following:

Amy is dead in virtue of having neither heartbeat nor brain function.

Basil's decision to rob the bank counts as his relapse into criminal
activity.

Clara is inclined to consider the interests of others as equal with her
own and is thereby moral.

In each case, the explanation indicates a close metaphysical relationship that fits the physicalist ambition to say something about the
very nature of the nonphysical entities. Such explanations may seem
a bit mysterious, but it is undeniable that they are offered and sought
after by philosophers all the time. When we ask what it is in virtue of
which a belief is justified, or what it is in virtue of which a sentence is
true, and so on, we are seeking just such explanations. The explanatory notion in question is serviceable, even though we do not have an
explicit theoretical grasp on it. I here offer no analysis of that sort
of explanation in general, only some relevant implications of one
particular use of it.

If the nonphysical realm is nothing over and above the physical realm,
then the physical state of the world suffices for its nonphysical state. In
general, if the fact that P is nothing over and above the fact that Q, then
Q suffices for P, where this sufficiency is of the broadly logical or metaphysical sort. The argument for this general principle is short and sweet.
Suppose Q didn't suffice for P. That is, suppose it is possible for it to be
true that Q while not true that P. Then something in addition to the fact
that Q is needed to make it true that P, in which case, surely, the fact that
P *is* something over and above the fact that Q.

Not every explanation of this type implies such sufficiency; sometimes we want to say that something is true in virtue of something
else being true where the explanation is only partial. For instance, we
want to say that the sentence "The cat is on the mat" is true in virtue
of the meanings of "cat" and "mat," where we do not mean that the sentence's being true is nothing over and above those words' having the
meanings they do. But the physicalist's claim, at least, is meant to be
complete: the explanation of the nonphysical by the physical is all the
explanation needed.

The idea that the physical realm suffices to fix the state of the nonphysical realm is, of course, familiar under the rubric of supervenience.

Supervenience and Three Parameters

Why has supervenience seemed of any use for physicalists? Perhaps the best known reason to focus on it is its apparent charm when contrasted with "reductionism." The notion has, after all, become prominent in the wake of Davidson's appeal to it as an alternative to the reductionism he opposed in his classic "Mental Events" paper (1970). I wish to make it clear that my motivations for looking at supervenience have nothing to do with avoiding reductionism, whatever that is. The conviction that something called "reduction" must be avoided at all costs is far too muddled at this point to bank on it. A better reason to focus on supervenience is that it provides a handy, minimal way of talking about sufficiency. To say that A-properties supervene on B-properties is equivalent to saying that there is a total state of each individual with regards to its B-properties that suffices for its total state with regards to its A-properties.[1]

Any supervenience claim needs to specify three parameters. First, which family of properties is supposed to supervene on which other family? Second, what objects are compared for discernibility with respect to those properties? Third, what is the modal status of the claim?

The first parameter seems simple enough: the nonphysical properties supervene on the physical properties.[2] Some may worry about just how the physical properties are to be classified, but I take it that we can roughly characterize them as those explicitly at issue in an idealized physical theory. Another question about the first parameter concerns the range of the nonphysical properties. Most contemporary physicalists seem content to leave the realm of abstract objects out of the domain of target explananda. I will take it that the family of nonphysical properties includes only those that are (possibly) possessed by concrete objects.[3]

The second parameter has occasioned some controversy. When we say there are no differences of one sort without differences of another, which objects are we comparing for differences? There are two salient choices at hand, namely, individuals and entire worlds. The latter kind of relation, known as global supervenience, is the sort implied by the physicalist's explanatory claim. That claim in no way requires that the properties of an individual be explained exclusively by intrinsic properties of that individual.[4]

Consider the following example. A politician's reputation is damaged by some incriminating photos. He has the property of having a damaged reputation, and his having such a property is nothing over and above the fact that the photos were published, that they depicted the politician taking a bribe, and so on. While these facts provide the explanation, they are plainly not a matter of intrinsic properties of the politician. The sufficiency claim is supposed to mirror the explanatory claim, and the sort of explanatory claim at issue in no way motivates a restriction to intrinsic properties of individuals. Rather, when we say that a certain property instance is nothing over and above certain other property instances, we allow ourselves access to any kind of property instances in the actual world.

The Modal Status of the Supervenience Claim

Having settled on a global supervenience thesis, we need to consider the issue of its modal status. Let us start by considering the following very strong thesis:

(S1) There are no two physically indiscernible worlds that are discernible in some nonphysical respect.

How well does S1 fare? Its quantification is unrestricted, so that it seems to speak of all logically possible worlds. There are, however, various ways in which one might understand "logically possible." On one reading, any sentence that fails to contradict itself given the rules of meaning governing its terms describes a logically possible situation. In this sense, there is no logically possible world in which bachelors are married, but there is a logically possible world in which Tully is not Cicero. A supervenience thesis of such strength would be far stronger than is necessary to express physicalism. Physicalism has long been understood to be a conceptually contingent claim; few physicalists want to deny the mere intelligibility of its denial.[5]

There is another way of understanding the totality of possible worlds, however, that is of more relevance for physicalism. I have in mind that modality that is sometimes called "metaphysical possibility" or "broadly logical possibility." The metaphysically possible worlds may be positively characterized as those which conform to facts about the natures or essences of entities in those worlds. That is, the metaphysically possible is what you get when you restrict the merely coherent by principles regarding *what it is to be* thus and such a thing. So, for instance, if it belongs to the very nature of belief to be part of a rational believer, then there is no metaphysically possible world in which there is an irrational believer. There is nothing mysterious about this beyond what is mysterious about essences or natures – which is, it must be confessed, admitting a fair chunk of mystery. Claims about the "nature" of things seem part and parcel of the physicalist position, however, because it is, after all, a claim about the nature of the world.

The fact that metaphysical possibility often goes by the name of "broadly logical" possibility reflects the fact that philosophers are loathe to admit that it ultimately makes sense to speak of possible situations in which metaphysical laws are violated. Following this lead, I shall presume that there are no metaphysically impossible worlds. Hence, S1 is equivalent to the claim that there are no two metaphysically possible worlds that are physically indiscernible yet discernible somehow.

Even including nonlogical constraints of metaphysics, S1 is too strong. The following example makes clear how. Let some actually instantiated property F be functional, so that F is instantiated by virtue of there being some property that plays a causal role R. Perhaps a physical property P plays role R and F is thereby instantiated in this world. Now consider another world that is metaphysically possible and that is just like this one physically. Will the physical property P realize F? Because the metaphysical truths are fixed, the truth concerning the metaphysics of the functional property F are preserved; hence if P plays role R, it will realize F. But in this other world, P might fail to play role R. For all we've said so far, this other world might be one in which the laws governing P are very different and P does not, as a result, play role R. Such a world would be a counterexample to S1 but not, it seems, to physicalism.

Because S1 is too strong and its failure seemed to turn on a neglect of the laws of nature, a plausible next step is to weaken the modality to that holding across all possible worlds with the same laws of nature as ours. Let's say that a world is *nomologically possible* just in case all and only the laws of nature at the actual world are laws therein. We can then try S2:

(S2) There are no two nomologically possible worlds that are physically indiscernible but discernible somehow.

Thesis S2 is too weak to be an adequate expression of physicalism. Its weakness may be dramatized by its compatibility with dualism. S2 allows that the natural laws may dictate that mental substances appear and behave entirely according to the evolution of physical conditions, in which case two worlds that were indiscernible with respect to those physical conditions and obeyed all the natural laws would have to be indiscernible with respect to their distribution of mental properties as well. The physical would then in one perfectly good sense determine the mental, but this determination would be quite acceptable to a dualist: This determination is a function not of the nature of the mind but of natural law. The same point can be made for properties: The laws governing interaction could dictate the appearance and disappearance of mental properties in such a way as to provide an association of each mental property with some physical property, or perhaps some complex construction of such.[6]

The essential problem with S2 is just that the factors that determine the nonphysical state of the world are allowed to include laws that do not belong to physics alone.[7] Natural laws seem capable of linking items of any kind together; the contingency of natural law is what makes the link described by S2 far too weak to be an expression of physicalism. The fact that two properties are linked by natural law in no way implies that one is instantiated in virtue of the other. Hence, a determination of the nonphysical by the physical via natural law is insufficient for the sort of explanation demanded by physicalism.

The point is easy to overlook because of the influence of the Nagelian model of reduction that has helped shape so much of the contemporary discussion of physicalism. On that model, one theory reduces another just in case the reduced theory can be derived from the reducing theory with the aid of bridge laws, understood to be empirical truths akin to the laws of nature (Nagel [1961], pp. 336–66). As a result, the following "nomological reduction" thesis has often been taken to be a physicalist thesis:

(S3) Every nonphysical property is coextensive, as a matter of natural law, with some physical property.

But, plainly, S3 is compatible with dualism. One way to demonstrate the insufficiency of S2 as a formulation of physicalism is to point out that S3 is sufficient for S2. If S3 is sufficient for S2 yet not sufficient for physicalism, then S2 is not sufficient for physicalism either.

If neither S1 nor S2 will do, what is left? The counterexamples point the way to a solution. We want to ensure that certain laws hold in all the relevant worlds, but we don't want to include laws that effect the determination of the nonphysical by the physical. The solution is to specify the class of worlds as all those in which our laws of physics hold, whether or not other laws of nature hold in those worlds.

Let the *physically possible* worlds be those in which all and only the laws of physics of the actual world are laws of physics therein. Sometimes "physically possible" is used to mean "possible according to the laws of nature," period (i.e., what we're calling "nomologically possible"). It is important to keep the distinction between these two quite clear. By definition, every nomologically possible world is a physically possible world, but it is an open question whether every physically possible world is a nomologically possible world. It may be that there are laws not necessitated by the laws of physics, in which case there are physically possible worlds that are not nomologically possible. The existence of sciences other than physics indicates that there are laws of nature distinct from the laws of physics, and in the absence of special argument we must allow that some worlds are such that the laws of physics are laws therein while some other laws – say, laws of economics – aren't.

The supervenience thesis we want, then, seems to be:

(S4) There are no two physically possible worlds that are physically indiscernible yet discernible somehow.

Thesis S4 gets the basic choice of modality right. On this thesis the facts are determined solely by reference to metaphysical facts concerning the nature of the nonphysical items and physical factors including particular physical facts and the physical laws.

Before proceeding further, we should pause to face an increasingly common objection to supervenience formulations. The contemporary popularity of supervenience seems bizarre once one recalls the use made of it by Moore (Moore [1903]; Schiffer [1987], pp. 153–4; Horgan [1993]). On Moore's view, ethical properties are not subject to naturalistic explanation even though they supervene on natural properties. How, then, can supervenience be used to express such an explanatory relationship? I agree, as I said at the outset, that the explanatory relationship cannot be replaced with a supervenience formulation. But the present objection fails to establish that thesis. (I shall later give a different reason for that irreplaceability thesis.) The simple response to it is to point out that it is not, after all, clear that Moore's position is coherent. Nothing in his position provides an account of how simple, nonnatural properties could be constrained in such a way as to conform to supervenience. He could say that this constraint is a matter of laws of nature, if he likes; but that explanation would not account for a supervenience relation of the strength of S4. In short, the example of Moore does nothing to establish the insufficiency of supervenience of the strength of S4, because Moore's position is itself mysterious.[8]

There is much more to be said by way of improving sufficiency formulations before admitting their ultimate inability to capture the full content of physicalism. The next step in that improvement is to face a problem about contingency.

Contingency and the Problem of "Extras"

As we noted, physicalists typically think the doctrine is conceptually contingent. Indeed, many now think it is metaphysically contingent; there

is nothing about the nature of the mental that precludes the existence of
Cartesian spirits, for instance. As a result, S4 is too strong. Because the
physicalist wants to allow that such things as Cartesian spirits are possible, if not actual, he will recognize a pair of physically possible worlds
that are physically indiscernible, yet mentally discernible, because each
contains a scattering of Cartesian spirits, where those spirits are all
morose in one world and all happy in the other.

One reaction to this problem is to emphasize that physicalism is
supposed to be about the *actual* world. Instead of comparing pairs of
merely possible worlds, we should, it may be thought, consider other
possible worlds that are just like the actual one physically. There are no
Cartesian spirits in the actual world; that much the physicalist clearly
wants to say.

We can then try S5:

> (S5) Any physically possible world that is physically indiscernible from
> the actual world is indiscernible from it in all respects.

The problem is not solved yet, however, given the possibility of what we
might call "extras." The "problem of extras," as I call it, has been discussed by Lewis (1983), pp. 361–4; Jackson (1993), pp. 28–9 and (1998),
pp. 11–13; and Chalmers (1996), pp. 38–41.[9] In a nutshell, S5 rules out
certain possible worlds, worlds containing physicalistically unacceptable
"extras," as impossible, whereas physicalists need not rule out such
worlds without fearing for their physicalist credentials.

The problem may be illustrated by considering extra property
instances. Suppose the actual world is such that every mental property
instance is sufficed for and explained by physical factors just as the materialist holds. Nonetheless, there is a world w such that w is just like the
actual world physically yet contains an extra property instance. In the
actual world, my computer has no feelings of regret, but in w it does. In
w that property is simply attached to the computer in a brute fashion,
with no deeper explanation possible. In other words, the property is
instantiated by the computer much as the dualist imagines our actual
mental properties to be connected to our physical selves.

The existence of such a world is not contrary to physicalism. Even
though S5 fails because of that world, it does not falsify the materialist's claim that every nonphysical property instance in our world is
necessitated by purely physical factors. The physical factors common to
the actual world and this other world w are the same, and they necessitate
the same nonphysical properties. The failure of indiscernibility is not due
to any failure of those physical factors to bear that determinative, explanatory relationship to the nonphysical properties in the actual world.

The most helpful reaction to this problem is to weaken S5 in the way suggested by Jackson, using his notion of a "minimal physical duplicate," explained thus:

> A minimal physical duplicate of our world is what you would get if you – or God, as it is sometimes put – used the physical nature of our world (including of course its physical laws) as a recipe in this sense for making a world. (Jackson [1993], p. 28)

The physicalist's idea that the physical will suffice for those cases of nonphysical properties we care about is captured here. Every actual property is such that it would reappear, just as it actually is, in a world constructed without any extras, with only the physical conditions listed as the "recipe." Jackson explicitly includes the physical laws in this recipe, but I wish to exclude them, because I want to keep it clear that the worlds over which we are generalizing are physically possible worlds. This would be implied by the meaning of a minimal physical duplicate if we kept the laws in the recipe, but it would not be as salient.

The supervenience thesis we seem to want, then, is:

> (S6) Any physically possible world that is a minimal physical duplicate of the actual world is indiscernible from it in all respects.

While we have weakened the supervenience thesis so as to allow extras, we have not weakened it so far as to be a claim only about all nomologically possible worlds that are minimal physical duplicates. The fact that the physically possible minimal physical duplicates are just like the actual world in all respects is still to be explained by purely physical factors, without recourse to any fundamental bridge laws.

The Problem of Lucky Materialism

We are not out of the woods yet. S6 is not as weak as the nomological supervenience thesis S2, but it is too weak in a different sense. Because S6 restricts itself to minimal physical duplicates of the actual world, it says nothing about worlds that differ from the actual world physically. We may dramatize its weakness by pointing out that it is compatible with the truth of the following counterfactuals:

> (CF1) If Desmond had remembered to shave yesterday, a ghost would have appeared in the mirror to congratulate him.
>
> (CF2) If the Industrial Revolution had never occurred, humans would have developed, in addition to their present physically based minds, Cartesian spirits as additional psychic mechanisms.

Suppose that those are true, as well as S6. In that case, saying that physicalism is true would be just as misleading as it would be to say that physicalism is true in a world in which no Cartesian spirits exist simply because the requisite organisms haven't been born yet. On the face of it, physicalism is not that sort of contingent doctrine; metaphysically contingent it is, but it is not a mere matter of luck. This is what I call the problem of lucky materialism.

The problem is not just that S6 allows true counterfactuals that mention conditions that are, as I shall say, physicalistically unacceptable. Surely the physicalist will want to accept the truth of certain counterfactuals concerning those worlds in which physicalism is false; that commitment comes with accepting that the doctrine is contingent. The following counterfactual, for instance, seems true.

(CF3) If a ghost had appeared in Desmond's mirror to check up on his shaving habits, he would have been alarmed.

In this counterfactual, the offensive conditions are introduced into the world by brute force. The problem with CF1 and CF2, in contrast to CF3, is that the truth of the former implies that physicalistically acceptable conditions would lead of their own accord to physicalistically unacceptable conditions.

The problem is not just that physicalistically unacceptable conditions appear in "nearby" worlds – those that don't require a considerable departure from the actual. It can't be solved simply by incorporating into our formulation of physicalism the claim that, whereas physicalistically unacceptable conditions are possible, they only appear in very far away possible worlds. Consider the following counterfactual:

(CF4) If Quine had been convinced of the soundness and certainty of the ontological proof of the existence of God, a ghost would have appeared in his study to congratulate him.

If this is true, it's made true by events in some very far off world. Nonetheless, the truth of the above counterfactual would be repugnant to a physicalist. By contrast, the counterfactual CF3 is not. Acknowledging the truth of CF3 admits the possibility of physicalistically unacceptable phenomena, which is something we've admitted by supposing the doctrine contingent. Admitting the truth of CF4, however, would be admitting something much more radical, that the sort of phenomena we now see as physicalistically acceptable could bring about *on their own* the existence of ghosts.

The troublesome counterfactuals include every counterfactual such that: (1) the consequent implies some physicalistically unacceptable condition; (2) the antecedent does not imply any physicalistically unacceptable condition; and (3) it is not a counterlegal. If all such counterfactuals are false, then none of the physicalistically acceptable conditions that could obtain would lead to physicalistically unacceptable conditions. Physicalism should imply that once we're in a physicalist world, there is no legal counterfactual route out of it, except through brute force – introducing the offensive condition via the antecedent itself.[10]

How, then, could we ensure that all such counterfactuals are false? The key is to focus on the factors that determine the truth-value of counterfactuals. I take it those are limited to two: the particular facts and the laws of nature. The supervenience thesis S6 concerns only the particular facts. Let me first show explicitly how S6 fails to rule out troublesome counterfactuals and then show how an additional thesis about laws succeeds in ruling them out.

Consider again the troublesome counterfactual CF1. There is some world or other that is the one that determines the truth-value of CF1, that is "nearest." Let that world be w_S. CF1 is true only if w_S contains a ghost. Now, let $w_S{}^*$ be a minimal physical duplicate of w_S.[11] Given how we've specified the notion of a minimal physical duplicate, any world that is a minimal physical duplicate (of any world) is going to be one such that everything nonphysical in it is necessitated by purely physical factors. Hence, all minimal physical duplicates, including $w_S{}^*$, are ghost free. If w_S and $w_S{}^*$ are indiscernible, then CF1 is false, as both would be ghost free. Hence, if CF1 is true, they differ. But the difference must be due solely to the fact that w_S has some phenomena in it not necessitated by the physical factors in common to w_S and $w_S{}^*$. If CF1 is to be true, w_S, unlike $w_S{}^*$, introduces physicalistically unacceptable phenomena.

In evaluating CF1 we must make no gratuitous departures from the actual world. Given S6, there is nothing in the actual world not necessitated by physical factors. Because the actual world doesn't contain any ghosts, it would be prima facie gratuitous to suppose them existent in w_S unless the antecedent of CF1 directs us explicitly to a world containing them. The antecedent of CF1 doesn't so direct us, of course. Because the ghost-free $w_S{}^*$ is available as a possible world, it seems we should let $w_S{}^*$ determine the truth-value of CF1, not w_S.

But – of course – we've neglected the role of laws. The truth of S6 isn't enough to rule out troublesome counterfactuals because S6 is compatible with there being some actual law L that links shaving and ghosts such that L is preserved in w_S while broken in $w_S{}^*$. In this case, w_S would be closer than $w_S{}^*$ and CF1 could be true. So we need a thesis about laws – but what thesis? A natural candidate is a sufficiency thesis once again, parallel to S6. If the explanation of the particular nonphysical facts implies a sufficiency claim, the explanation of the nonphysical laws implies a similar sufficiency claim about laws – namely, that the laws of nature are entailed by the laws of physics.

Let's first consider a simple law entailment thesis, namely:

> (LE1) If L is a law of nature in the actual world, then L is a law in every physically possible world.

Return to CF1 and our w_S and w_S*. If LE1 is true, then the situation we considered earlier is not possible. It cannot be the case that there is an actual law linking shaving and ghosts that obtains in w_S but not w_S*, as LE1 implies that any law in the actual world is a law in any physically possible world – including w_S*. Hence, LE1 in conjunction with S6 implies that CF1 is false.

Unfortunately, many will find LE1 too strong. Some laws are *conditioned* in the sense that, even though they are laws, they are relativized to certain background conditions. I have in mind laws that may be called "hedged" or "*ceteris paribus*" laws, laws such that some particular condition C is invoked as part of what the law depends on. Without that C, the law might fail to obtain. Hence, we should qualify the law entailment thesis by saying that, for the conditioned laws, the physical laws plus particular actual physical conditions entail the law. We may divide and conquer, then, and propose the following thesis:

> (LE2) If L is an unconditioned law of nature in the actual world, then L is a law in every physically possible world. If L is a conditioned law of nature in the actual world, then there is a physical condition C on which L depends such that L is a law in every physically possible world in which C obtains.

Now I want to show that the weaker thesis LE2 *also* suffices to get around the problem of lucky materialism. Turning again to CF1, let w_S and w_S* be as before, but this time suppose that the law L, which links shaving and ghosts, is conditioned and depends on condition C.

Is it now possible for w_S to be closer than w_S*? The key question is whether L could be a law in w_S but not in w_S*, thereby forcing us to consider w_S to be closer than w_S*. Because L is dependent on C, we should ask if C obtains in w_S. If C does obtain in w_S, we can easily show that CF1 is false. Because w_S and w_S* are physically indiscernible, and because C is a physical condition, C obtains in w_S* as well. Because by LE2 the laws of physics and the obtaining of C suffice for L's being a law, L is a law in w_S*. Hence, we cannot appeal to a difference between w_S and w_S* as to whether L is a law to get w_S to be closer to the actual world.

Suppose, however, that C doesn't obtain in w_S. In that case, it doesn't obtain in w_S* either, because they are physically indiscernible worlds. The failure of C to obtain in either world doesn't, however, imply that L isn't a law in the two worlds. The fact that L depends, in the actual world, on the particular condition C, does not imply that L generally can't be a law unless C obtains. It only implies that the actual-world incarnation of L depends on C. So, perhaps L is a law in w_S but not in w_S*, and in w_S L is a law without depending on C.

Does that mean that CF1 could turn out to be true compatibly with LE2 after all? No. The law L in w_S is entirely gratuitous. In the actual world, L is a law because of the combination of physical laws and the obtaining of C. In w_S it's a law for some other, entirely new reason, perhaps as a basic law added onto the world, or as a law that emerges from the physical laws combining with some nonphysical condition, or whatnot. In either case, treating a world with such a law in it as nearest, when a world without that law is available, is to insist on the relevance of entities that are plainly unmotivated by anything about the actual world or the directions given in the counterfactual.

Whether L is conditioned or unconditioned, then, the conjunction of the law entailment thesis LE2 and the supervenience thesis S6 ensure that CF1 is false. Because the argument depends only on those features of CF1 that make it troublesome, it generalizes to all troublesome counterfactuals, and the problem of lucky materialism is solved. In this way we can retain the idea that physicalism is contingent without having to make it a matter of luck.

The Limits and Uses of Sufficiency

We've arrived at two very demanding sufficiency claims, the supervenience claim S6 and the law entailment claim LE2. These two neatly mirror the two sorts of phenomena that the physicalist thinks can be explained by the physical: both the particular distribution of and the laws governing the nonphysical properties. The relevant explanatory claim may now be given the following formulation, which I call "Demanding Physicalism" because of its strict, rigorous character.

> (DP) Every law of nature and every particular fact is either physical or to be explained by the physical in such a way as to imply that the nonphysical facts are nothing over and above the physical facts, where the physical facts include the actual distribution of physical properties and the laws of physics.

Given the necessitation implied by a "nothing over and above" explanation, DP implies both S6 and LE2. However, DP cannot be analyzed as the conjunction of S6 and LE2, because they do not imply DP. Nonetheless, if they are true, then DP is very likely true as well. I elaborate on the latter two points in the rest of this chapter.

I confine myself to the case of particular facts, showing how S6 could fail to imply that every particular nonphysical fact is to be explained by the physical. (Analogous remarks may be made about the law facts.) Suppose there is a kind of property (utterly unknown to us) I shall call "quizzical" such that (1) the physical realm is as it is solely in virtue of the way the quizzical realm is, and (2) the realm of the neither physical nor quizzical is as it is solely in virtue of the way the quizzical realm is. In other words, imagine the quizzical as a sort of common cause that explains both the physical and the rest of reality, while any correlation between the physical and the neither physical nor quizzical is not indicative of an explanatory relationship, but is only a side effect. More precisely, suppose there is a one-one function between the quizzical and the physical so that each physical property P is necessitated by, and necessitates, some quizzical property Q, and vice versa. Fixing the physical thereby fixes the quizzical, which fixes the remaining properties. Hence, fixing the physical indirectly fixes the remaining properties. In that case, S6 would be true even while physicalism is false. (A version of this objection has been given by Jack [1994, p. 437].)

The implication runs from physicalism to sufficiency but not vice versa. But the failure of implication relies on an extremely odd situation. If we have excellent evidence for S6 and LE2, then, barring evidence of something such as quizzical properties, we have every reason to suppose that DP is true. More precisely, the truth of S6 and LE2 would seem to require an explanation. DP provides a simple explanation, while any hypothesis introducing something such as quizzical properties would provide an explanation that begs for Occam's razor. In other words, the sufficiency theses provide a key step in an argument to the best explanation.[12]

It is important to see here that it is implausible in the extreme to take S6 and LE2 as brute, metaphysically necessary truths. They are hardly in the form of identity or essence-stating claims. That is why they need an explanation that yields DP. Of course, DP doesn't look like a brute metaphysical truth. It doesn't look like an essence-stating claim either. My claim is not that DP will be at the bottom level of explanation; rather, what will be at the bottom level are facts about what it is to be thus and such physical and nonphysical phenomena, and those together imply that nonphysical phenomena are instantiated in virtue of physical facts. My claim regarding DP is that the only plausible explanation of S6 and LE2 will include enough to make DP true. If the nature of each nonphysical item is such that it explains S6 and LE2 in a plausible way, that explanation will imply that they are instantiated in virtue of physical facts in the way required by DP. In sum, any plausible story about the sufficiency claims will be one that secures the explanatory component of physicalism by saying enough about the metaphysics of the nonphysical items involved to imply that the nonphysical realm is as it is in virtue of the physical realm being as it is.

The formulation of physicalism I have offered renders it both contentious and reasonably clear, so that it is of use in evaluating the consequences and plausibility of physicalism. Nonetheless, it is not a formulation that straitjackets the physicalist into a particular view of just how the explanation of the nonphysical is to go. Instead of relying on the more specific notions of realization, property identity, or whatnot, the appeal to some explanation or other that renders nonphysical phenomena nothing over and above the physical phenomena is attractively flexible. We ought not to underestimate the varieties of possible physicalistic explanation. This flexibility is not matched, however, by a comparable obscurity in the claim. And if one is unclear on the relevant notion of metaphysical explanation, the two salient consequences – the two sufficiency claims – should pinpoint well enough the sort of explanation that is at issue. Those who think that physicalism has no adequate expression may be referred to this flexible yet demanding formulation.

NOTES

1. For seminal discussions of supervenience see Kim (1984) and McLaughlin (1995).
2. There may be some question about what we are to admit as genuine properties in the first place. Some may wish, for instance, to rule out such "gruesome" properties as that of *being hungry if human or green if reptilian*. I can see no motivation for such a view. The physicalist will want to explain why the world is the way it is with regards to the applicability of such predicates as "hungry if human or green if reptilian." If we want to cash out (partly) the explanatory demand of physicalism by appeal to supervenience, we need to take account of the applicability of such predicates by including such properties in the supervening class.
3. This neglect of abstract objects doesn't amount to the advantages of theft over honest toil. Such nonphysical properties as that of knowing that $2 + 2 = 4$ are not borne by abstract objects but by concrete sentient beings, and those will be caught within the physicalist's net. Accommodating those properties within a physicalist picture is no easy task.

   In any case, assuming that the properties of abstract objects are to be included makes no real difference to the plausibility of the supervenience thesis. See Note 12 for discussion.

4. Kim has objected that global supervenience is too weak a relation to be suited for physicalism ([1990], p. 155). His objection fails, however. For thorough and conclusive responses in print see Paull and Sider (1992) and Post (1995).
5. In their (1994) attack on the idea that an interesting physicalist thesis can be formulated, Stich and Laurence note the failure of a global supervenience of the strength of S1 and proceed straightaway to the following pessimistic conclusion:

> At this point, we fear, a resolute opponent might begin fiddling with the notion of *possibility* that is embedded in the definition of global super-venience. . . . The path on which our imagined opponent has embarked is not one we're tempted to follow, for we suspect that it leads directly to a metaphysical swamp. (Stich and Laurence [1994], p. 178)

The reader may judge for him or herself whether the remainder of my discussion is thus swampy.
6. This, in fact, is the view of Chalmers (1996) concerning phenomenal properties; in accordance with the claim I'm making in the text, he does not consider himself a physicalist.
7. This point has been well emphasized by Horgan (1993).
8. This mystery has been used against Moore in the context of metaethical discussion. See both Strawson (1949) and Mackie (1977a), where he finds moral properties intolerably bizarre because of their dependence on nonmoral properties.

> The wrongness must somehow be 'consequential' or 'supervenient'; it is wrong because it is a piece of deliberate cruelty. But just what *in the world* is signified by this 'because'? (Mackie [1977a], p. 113)

9. I provide a full-dress presentation of the problem and its solution in Witmer (1999).
10. Why can't we just build into the formulation of physicalism the claim that no counterfactuals of the troublesome sort are true, where the troublesome kind are as we just defined them? Answer: We specified the "troublesome" counterfactuals in terms of "physicalistically unacceptable" conditions, hence relying on a prior notion of physicalism.
11. Some such world is bound to exist, because any world will have some minimal physical duplicate. Just as there needs to be some result or other of a recipe, a world will have some minimal physical duplicate or other.
12. There are limits to this strategy. There are three ways in which S6 and LE2 might be rendered *trivial*, so that their truth can be explained in a way that bypasses physicalism:

(1) *Abstract Objects*. Suppose that the physicalist wants, after all, to include in the target explananda the features of abstract objects. If those objects exist and have their features necessarily, then a trivial version of S6 is true of them. More precisely, if we let the A-properties be those that are exclusively borne by abstract objects, it is necessarily true that every pair of worlds is indiscernible with respect to its A-properties, and, hence, any minimal physical duplicate of the actual world is indiscernible from the actual world with respect to those properties.

(2) *Worldbound Properties*. Suppose there is a property P such that P is instantiated in only one possible world, namely, the actual world. If P is

included in the base of physical properties, then S6 is trivially true. It's quite doubtful that there are any such physical properties, of course, but the case of worldbound properties is worth noting for another reason. Suppose our worldbound P is one of the nonphysical properties in the supervening class. In that case (assuming there are no worldbound physical properties) S6 is trivially *false*. Its falsity, in that case, certainly couldn't be used to argue against physicalism. So, to make dialectical use of S6 in either way requires that we rule out of consideration all such worldbound properties. (See Jackson [1998], pp. 17–18, for some discussion of singular thought properties that might cause this sort of trivialization. His response, however, is not the same as mine; he curtails the worlds at issue while I curtail the properties.)

(3) *Necessitarianism about laws.* If we agree with the necessitarians that the laws of nature are absolutely necessary, so that every possible world is nomologically possible (see Shoemaker [1980]; Swoyer [1982]), then LE2 becomes trivial: anything entails an absolutely necessary proposition. Of course, a physicalist who buys S6 and necessitarianism may have an interesting argument for part of DP but not for the claim about the explanation of laws.

4

Realization and Mental Causation

SYDNEY SHOEMAKER

The problem of mental causation is at the heart of the mind-body problem. And for physicalist or materialist views of mind, the key to solving the problem of mental causation is getting a satisfactory understanding of how the mental is realized in the physical. Recent discussions of physicalism have focused on the notion of supervenience; but I think that the focus should instead be on the notion of realization. Supervenience comes in a variety of forms – and the form we need to understand, in order to understand mental causation, is that in which the properties in the supervenience base can be said to realize the properties that supervene on them. Any physicalist theory, whether or not it is a functionalist theory, needs to maintain that the mental is realized in the physical, and so needs an account of realization. But my main focus will be on the realization of functional properties.

I

I take as my point of departure a recent paper by George Bealer that attempts to show that functionalist accounts of mind cannot give a satisfactory account of self-consciousness.[1] Although Bealer's primary target is functionalism, he takes his arguments to establish a version of property dualism. They are supposed to show that mental properties are "first-order properties," not the higher-order properties functionalists take them to be. And because Bealer thinks that there are decisive reasons for rejecting type physicalism, he thinks that the only way for mental properties to be first order is for them to be nonphysical. His central claim is that functionalist views are incoherent, because they imply that when a person self-ascribes a property such as pain, the property self-ascribed is a first-order property, a physical "realizer" of the second-order functional property the mental property pain is supposed to be, rather than that second-order property. The only way pain can be what is self-ascribed in such self-ascriptions is if pain is a first-order property, contrary to what Bealer takes functionalism to hold. And given the falsity of type physicalism, the only way for pain to be a first-order property is for it to be a nonphysical property. Property dualism follows.

Rather than expound Bealer's rather complex argument, I will present a simpler and cruder argument (not to be ascribed to him) that I hope conveys its flavor. This argument shares with Bealer's argument an assumption that I shall later question.

Bealer's central argument is directed against what he calls "Ramsified Functionalism," which defines mental states in terms of the Ramsey sentence of a folk-psychological theory in the way proposed by David Lewis.[2] On Bealer's interpretation (a standard one) the quantifiers prefacing the Ramsey sentence of the psychological theory range over first-order properties. So what the definition of a particular mental property or relation says is that an individual instantiates that property or relation just in case the individual instantiates some first-order property or relation that occupies a certain position in a complex network of causally interrelated first-order properties or relations. For short, it says that an individual instantiates the mental property just in case it instantiates some first-order property that plays a certain causal role, where playing the causal role is a matter of belonging to a family of properties that are such that their instantiations stand in certain causal relations to one another and to sensory inputs and behavioral outputs.

It is part of the causal role of pain that under certain conditions its instantiation results in an awareness on the subject's part that it has this property. As we might put it – and here begins my cruder version of the argument – it is part of its causal role that its instantiation results in its being self-ascribed. But if the instantiation of this property is a matter of some first-order realizer of it being instantiated, and if a realizer of it is a property that plays this causal role, then the instantiation of it should result in some first-order realizer property of it being self-ascribed – or, more precisely, in some first-order realizer property of it standing to the subject in a first-order relation that realizes the self-ascription relation. And this is the wrong result. Assuming that the property of being in pain is not identical with any first-order property, the self-ascription of pain cannot consist in, and should not involve, the self-ascription of any first-order property.

There is an interesting parallel between this argument and the argument that functionalism makes mental properties epiphenomenal. Again, functionalism is taken to hold that mental properties are higher-order properties. Being in pain, for example, is the higher-order property something has just in case it has some first-order property or other that plays a certain causal or functional role. But then whatever causal work we might be inclined to attribute to the mental property will be done by one or another of its first-order realizer properties. The first-order properties will "preempt" whatever causal role the mental property might be supposed to have. So where Bealer's argument faults functionalism for coming to the wrong conclusion about what properties we introspectively self-ascribe, this argument faults functionalism for coming to the wrong conclusion about what causes the things mental events and properties are supposed to cause.

Perhaps the second argument needn't be taken as showing that functionalism is incoherent or false – perhaps it only shows that functionalism has the surprising consequence that mental properties are epiphenomenal. But there does seem to be a threat of incoherence here. For what is the causal role that the realizers of a mental property are supposed to play? It is (at least on some versions of functionalism) precisely the role that the mental property is taken to play in "folk psychology." And it is precisely that role that is supposed to define the mental property. It hardly seems coherent to say that a mental property is defined as the property that plays a certain causal role, and then say that what plays this causal role is not the mental property itself but rather one or another of the physical properties that realize it.

What we need if we want to avoid the conclusion of the second argument is a notion of realization on which realizer properties do not preempt the causal roles of the properties they realize. And I think that a notion that satisfies this need will also enable us to avoid the conclusion of Bealer's argument. Bealer considers the suggestion that we drop from the Ramsey definitions the requirement that the properties be first order, so as to allow the mental properties themselves to be the properties that play the defining functional roles. He argues that this will have the consequence that the mental properties will themselves be first-order properties. And, as already mentioned, he thinks that because there are compelling reasons to reject type physicalism (the view that mental properties are identical with physical properties), the view that mental properties are first-order properties leads to property dualism. I shall argue that this whole line of thought rests on a mistaken conception of realization, and a distorted conception of the distinction between "first-order" and "higher-order" properties.

II

It seems tautological to say that if mental properties have defining causal roles, then it is the mental properties that play these roles. Of course, someone might think that it is only a first approximation to the truth that it is the mental property that plays the defining causal role. The truth behind the intuition that this is so is that there is a causal role "associated with" each mental property and in some sense defining it – but, the suggestion would be, it turns out on investigation that this causal role is played not by the mental property itself but by a physical property that realizes it. If what it means to say that a physical property realizes a given mental property is that it plays the causal role associated with that property, and if we cannot suppose without introducing an absurd sort of overdetermination that in each case of (supposed) mental causation the causal role is played twice, once by the mental property and once by whatever physical property realizes it on that occasion, such a view would seem to be forced on us. But such an error theory about our mental concepts is to be avoided if at all possible.

What we need is a different account of realization. The account I am about to suggest is partly due to Michael Watkins, and draws on a view about properties that I advanced some years ago.[3] While parts of the latter view are controversial, the part on which I will draw seems to me not to be so.[4]

Any property whose instantiation can be a cause or partial cause of something will be such that its instantiation bestows on its subject a set of what I call "conditional powers." A thing's having a power *simpliciter* is a matter of its being such that its being in certain circumstances, for example, its being related in certain ways to other things of certain sorts, causes (or contributes to causing) certain effects. A thing has a *conditional* power if it is such that if it had certain properties it would have a certain power simpliciter, where those properties are not themselves sufficient to bestow that power simpliciter. So, for example, the property of being knife-shaped bestows on its possessor the conditional power of being able to cut wood if it is made of steel, and the conditional power of being able to cut butter if it is made of wood. Some properties confer powers simpliciter all by themselves; and we can think of powers simpliciter as a special case of conditional powers. But the more usual case is for the powers simpliciter of a thing to be determined jointly by a number of different properties of it – as the knife's cutting powers are determined jointly by its composition, shape, and size. Saying what conditional powers a property confers specifies what contribution its instantiation can make to the powers simpliciter of the object in which it is instantiated.

The controversial part of my account of properties consists in the claim that it is essential to a property that it confers the particular set of conditional powers it does in the actual world, so that these are conferred by it in any possible world in which it can be instantiated, and that properties that confer exactly the same sets of conditional powers, and also are alike with respect to the possible causes of their instantiation, are identical. But here I shall not assume this part of the account. I assume only that in the actual world the same property always confers the same conditional powers, and that no two properties confer exactly the same conditional powers.

Now sometimes the conditional powers bestowed by one property will be a proper subset of those bestowed by another. This will be true where the one property is a determinable of which the other is a determinate. The set of conditional powers bestowed by redness will be a proper subset of the conditional powers bestowed by scarlet, for example. The different determinates of redness will each confer its distinctive set of conditional powers – but these will have in common the set of conditional powers conferred by redness. Stephen Yablo has given us the example of the pigeon Sophie, who has been conditioned to peck at red things.[5] Being red, together with being of an appropriate size, confers the power of evoking a pecking response from a pigeon such as Sophie under certain conditions. And so does the property of being scarlet. The latter, of course, confers powers not conferred by redness. For example, it confers the power of evoking a pecking response in the likes of Sophie's sister Alice, who was conditioned to peck at scarlet things but not at things of other shades of red. In such a case we could say that the determinate property realizes the determinable in virtue of the fact that the conditional powers bestowed by the latter are a proper subset of those bestowed by the former.

It is likewise true that the conditional powers conferred by a functional property will be a proper subset of the conditional powers bestowed by whatever physical property realizes it on a particular occasion. Suppose, then, that pain is a functional property, and that someone is in pain in virtue of instantiating a particular physical realization of pain, physical property P1. What makes P1 a realization of pain is that the conditional powers conferred by the instantiation of P1 include the conditional powers conferred by the instantiation of the property of being in pain. Of course, the instantiation of P1 bestows a number of conditional powers that are not among those associated with the property of being in pain – powers that are specific to it, and are not conferred by other properties that are realizers of pain. For example, it might bestow the power of producing a "P1" reading on a cerebroscope attached to the subject's head.

In general, then, property X realizes property Y just in case the conditional powers bestowed by Y are a subset of the conditional powers bestowed by X (and X is not a conjunctive property having Y as a conjunct).[6] Where the realized property is multiply realizable, the conditional powers bestowed by it will be a proper subset of the sets bestowed by each of the realizer properties. The different realizer properties will differ from one another in the total sets of conditional powers they confer but will be alike in conferring the conditional powers conferred by the realized property.[7] Being such as to confer a certain conditional power can be said to be a "forward-looking causal feature" of a property. So we can also say that property X realizes property Y just in case the forward-looking causal features of Y are a subset (a proper subset in cases of multiple realization) of those of property X.[8]

III

Before developing this account further, let us see how it deals with the problem of mental causation, and with the threat that the causal role we attribute to mental properties is preempted by their physical realizers. Suppose physical property P1 is one of the realizers of the property of being in pain, and that in a particular case the causing of a piece of "pain behavior," say taking an aspirin, involved the exercise of some of the conditional powers conferred by P1. But suppose further that these conditional powers were all ones belonging to the subset that the property of being in pain and the property P1 both confer. Which of these property instantiations, that of being in pain or that of P1, should we say was a cause or partial cause of the piece of behavior? It seems natural to say that it is the instantiation of the property of being in pain. Of course, the person was in pain *by* having P1. But if we say that it was (in part) in virtue of the instantiation of P1 that the causing occurred, we should add that it was in its capacity of being a realization of pain, that is, by conferring the conditional powers constitutively bestowed by the property of being in pain, that the instantiation of P1 made its causal contribution. It is qua realization of pain that P1 made its contribution to causing the behavior; for the conditional powers it conferred that are independent of those conferred by the property of being in pain were irrelevant to its making this contribution.

Some writers have suggested that when a determinable property is instantiated in virtue of a certain one of its determinates being instantiated, the instance (instancing, instantiation) of the determinable and that of its determinate are identical.[9] So, in a particular case, the instance of redness and that of scarlet are one and the same. Similarly, it is suggested that when a mental property is instantiated in virtue of the instantiation of a physical property that is a realization of it, the instance of the mental property and the instance of its realization are the same. This, of course, has the consequence that the mental property instance causes whatever

effects the physical realizer instance causes. It might seem that this provides a neat solution to the problem of how the mental can be causally
efficacious in a physicalist world.

Even supposing the claim about the identity of instances to be correct,
it is not clear that this would solve the problem of mental causation. As
a solution to that problem it might be held to have the same drawback
that a number of writers have charged against Davidson's anomalous
monism, as a solution to the problem of mental causation. Anomalous
monism claims that token mental events are identical with token physical events, and so cause whatever those physical events cause. But it does
not follow from this that these events cause what they do in virtue of
being mental events of the kinds they are; on the contrary, it rather seems
that they don't, because (Davidson holds) they cause what they do in
virtue of being subsumed under physical laws, and they are subsumed
under physical laws in virtue of their physical properties, not their mental
properties. A similar worry might be raised here. If what is in fact an
instance of a mental property causes something (or contributes to
causing something), but does so in virtue of being an instance of a physical property rather than in virtue of being an instance of that mental
property, then the causal efficacy of the mental does not seem to have
been adequately vindicated.

But in any case, it seems doubtful that we should identify the mental
property instance with the instance of the physical property that realizes
it – or that we should identify the instance of red and the instance of
scarlet. If we think of the instantiation of a property as the conferring on
something of the conditional powers associated with that property, then
when properties confer different sets of conditional powers, the instantiation of one of them is not identical with the instantiation of the other.[10]
But it does seem right to say that properties are causally efficacious in
virtue of their instances being efficacious. And there is an intimate relation between an instance of a determinable and the instance of the determinate that realizes it on a particular occasion. Likewise, there is an
intimate relation between an instance of a functional property and the
instance of the property that realizes it on a particular occasion. While
it seems wrong to say that a determinable property is part of each of its
determinates, or that a functional property is part of each of its realizer
properties, it does not seem inappropriate to use the part-whole relation
to characterize the relationship between the instances of these pairs of
properties.[11] The instantiation of the determinate entails the instantiation of the determinable, and can quite naturally be said to *include* it. It
seems natural to me to say that being scarlet is in part being red. Likewise, the instantiation of a realizer property entails, and might naturally

be said to include as a part, the instantiation of the functional property realized.[12] The conditional powers conferred by the instance of the determinable or functional property are a proper subset, and in that sense a part, of the conditional powers conferred by the instance of the more determinate property that realizes it on a particular occasion.

Suppose then that we say that the instance of scarlet involved in Yablo's Sophie example has the instance of red as a part. Because the part-whole relation is not identity, we cannot argue that the instance of red caused whatever the instance of scarlet caused. But given that Sophie's pecking was a consequence of the instance of scarlet, we can ask whether what caused it was this instance as a whole or some proper part of it. (Compare: Someone's dying might be said to be a consequence of the fusillade of shots from the firing squad, but because many of those shots may have missed it may be that what caused his death was not the fusillade as a whole but some part of it.) And here it seems appropriate to say that it was a part of it, namely the instance of red, that did the causing, because it was the conditional powers conferred by that part that were relevant to the effect (they are the ones that were conferred in other cases, when Sophie pecked at things of other shades of red). Similar circumstances exist in the case where the instances are instances of a functional property and of one of its physical realizations.

Stephen Yablo has suggested that where one event is a determinate of another, in the way Socrates' guzzling hemlock is a determinate of Socrates' drinking hemlock, the events do not compete for causal relevance to a particular effect or for causal sufficiency for that effect, but do compete for the status of being a cause of that effect.[13] And he suggests the one that is the (or a) cause is the one that is, in a sense he spells out, "proportional" to the effect.[14] I think that Yablo's notion of proportionality can be applied here. Where the only causal features of property P1 that play a role in producing an effect are ones that belong to property P2, of which P1 is a determinate or realizer property, there seems a good sense in which considerations of proportionality favor the instantiation of P2 over the instantiation of P1 as a cause of the effect.

IV

I will now explain more fully how this view of realization works. It is a commonplace that the behavior we attribute to mental states is typically the manifestation of a combination of mental states rather than any single state taken by itself.[15] Assuming that the manifestations of mental states are caused by them, we can illustrate this by saying that a given belief causes a piece of behavior in conjunction with certain of the subject's desires and certain of the subject's other beliefs. So the conditional powers conferred by the property *believes that it is raining* include, among countless others, one that can be roughly characterized as *being such that if one wants to keep dry and believes that umbrellas keep off rain, this will result in one's taking an umbrella if one goes out*. Suppose that on a particular occasion the belief that it is raining, call it Br, is realized in physical property P1. I say that the conditional power just characterized is among those conferred by P1. P1 is such that in combination with certain other mental states, certain desires and other beliefs, it causes certain behaviors.

But of course, those other mental states will themselves be physically realized. Suppose that in the case just envisioned the relevant desires and other beliefs are realized in physical properties P2, P3, and P4. P1 will "combine" with the mental properties in question to produce the behavior by combining with the realizations of those properties, in other words, P2, P3, and P4. So in the first instance the conditional power bestowed by P1 is *being such that if one has P2, P3, and P4, this results in one's taking an umbrella if one goes out*. But given that P2, P3, and P4 are realizations of the mental states in question, being such as to confer this conditional power will amount to being such as to confer the conditional power that belongs to the belief-property that P1 realizes. Being such as to confer a certain conditional power is a forward-looking causal feature of a property. Let's say that such a causal feature is a *mental causal feature* if the properties referred to in specifying the conditional power are mental properties, and that it is a *physical causal feature* if the properties referred to in specifying the conditional power are physical properties. We can now say that when mental property Br is realized by physical property P1, the mental causal features of Br are realized in physical causal features of P1. But I should emphasize that these mental causal features of Br are shared by P1; they are realized in P1 by its physical causal features.

Assuming that Br is multiply realizable, it will have possible realizations other than P1. Each of these will share the mental causal features of P1 and Br. But they will not necessarily share the physical causal features in which these are realized. A creature in which Br cannot be realized by P1, because P1 is not in its repertoire of possible properties, will most likely be such that P2–P4 are also not in its repertoire of possible properties. Its having the causal feature that interests us, that is, being such as to confer a certain mental conditional power, will not consist in its being such that in combination with P2–P4 it causes certain results. For it will not be capable of combining with those properties. Its mental causal features will be realized in some quite different physical features, including its being such that in combination with some quite different physical properties – call them Px, Py, and Pz – it causes certain behavior.

It should be clear that when mental properties M1 . . . Mn combine to produce certain effects, and these properties are physically realizable, it will not be the case that just any set of physical properties P1 . . . Pn that are, respectively, realizations of M1 . . . Mn will combine to produce those effects. This will be so only if P1 . . . Pn are jointly instantiable. The different physical properties that are realizers of mental properties will fall into a number of different "families" of properties, the members of each family being jointly instantiable. The forward-looking causal features of a realizer property will have to do with how instantiations of it can combine with other members of the same family to produce various effects. Presumably the physical realizations of mental states in earthlings and the physical realizations of the same mental states in the martians and supercomputers of philosophical fiction will typically not be jointly instantiable, and will not belong to a single family.[16]

V

Now let us return to Bealer's argument that functionalism leads to the wrong result about what a person is self-ascribing when self-ascribing pain. It will be recalled that his argument assumes that the properties quantified over in Ramsey-Lewis–style functional definitions are first-order properties, presumably physical ones, and that according to functionalism mental properties are second-order properties. The undesired result is that what a person self-ascribes is not pain but one of the first-order properties that realizes it.

Bealer takes it to be a primary tenet of what he calls ontological functionalism that mental properties are "definable wholly in terms of the general pattern of interaction of ontologically prior 'realizations'" (p. 105). He clearly takes ontological functionalism to be committed to the notion of realization I have rejected, that which seems to make mental properties epiphenomenal.

On the alternative view of realization I have suggested, realized properties can be causally efficacious, and it can sometimes be the case that it is the instantiation of a realized property rather than an instantiation of a realizer of it that should be regarded as causing a certain effect. So on this view, there is every reason not to require that the properties quantified over in a Ramsey-Lewis–style functional definition be restricted to the first-order realizer properties. The properties quantified over turn out to include the mental properties. And then there is no route to Bealer's conclusion that Ramsified Functionalism leads to the absurd result that what should be self-ascriptions of pain are really self-ascriptions of physical realizers of pain.

Does that mean that we should reject Bealer's characterization according to which the properties quantified over are first-order properties? That depends on whether functional properties can count as first order. Bealer tells us that first-order properties of individuals are "either primitive properties or properties of individuals definable in terms of primitive properties of individuals plus quantification over individuals" (pp. 70–1), but he does not tell us what it is for a property to be primitive, or how "definable in terms of" is to be understood. If the fact that functional properties are realized in properties other than themselves makes them nonprimitive and "definable in terms of" the realizer properties, then functionalism denies that mental properties are first order. But if it is sufficient for a property's being first order that its instantiation can be causally efficacious, then functional properties can count as first order.[17]

I think that functionalists (including myself) who have championed the sort of Ramsified functional definitions Bealer discusses have gotten into trouble by trying to combine two tasks. They have tried to define (or to provide a recipe for defining) mental states in terms of their causal or functional roles. And they have tried to give an account of how mental properties are physically realized. These are combined by saying that to have a certain mental state, or instantiate a certain mental property, is to instantiate some realizer property or other that plays a certain causal role. If Bealer is right, this leads to the wrong result about what we self-ascribe in what should be self-ascriptions of mental properties such as being in pain. And it also leads to epiphenomenalist worries, because it lends support for the view that physical properties preempt the causal roles we want to ascribe to mental properties.[18]

So I suggest that functionalists should separate these two tasks. Their definitions of mental states should be of the sort Bealer envisages "ideological" functionalists as giving – mental properties should be characterized in terms of *their* causal relations to one another and to inputs and outputs. And then they should give a separate account of what it is for these properties to be realized. The latter account will be along the lines I have been suggesting. The realizer properties will be physical ones whose forward-looking causal features include those of the mental property as a proper subset.

Does this mean that, in Bealer's terms, I advocate abandoning "ontological functionalism" in favor of "ideological functionalism"? In advocating separating the two tasks just distinguished, I do favor a formulation of functionalism that does not incorporate one ontological claim that virtually all functionalists accept, namely the claim that mental properties are realized in properties with which they are not identical. But I do not see why the claim that mental properties are themselves defined by certain causal roles, and have certain causal features essentially, should not itself count as an ontological thesis, and should be said to have "only 'ideological' significance" (p. 90).[19]

VI

On the account I am suggesting, traditional examples of the determinable-determinate relation are instances of the relation between a property and a realizer of it; for example, being red can be said to be realized by being scarlet. And while this may depart from the traditional notion of the determinable-determinate relation, I shall sometimes speak of realizers as determinates of the properties they realize, and so shall construe the relation of mental properties to their physical realizers as an instance of the relation of determinables to their determinates.[20] In any case, it seems clear that properties fall into hierarchies, where the properties higher in a hierarchy are those whose forward-looking causal features are included in the causal features of properties lower in the hierarchy.

One thing that could be meant by "first-order property" is a property that is, as I shall say, *self-realized* – in other words, is such that its instantiation does not consist in the instantiation of some other property of which its causal features are a proper subset. To understand *first-order property* in this way would be to restrict its application to properties that are ultimate determinates. There is, I think, no plausibility in the view that only such properties can be causally efficacious.

A self-realized property will be at the bottom of one of the hierarchies mentioned previously. It will realize properties above it in the hierarchy, which in turn will realize properties still higher in the hierarchy.

It might be supposed that if we start with the set of causal features of a self-realized property, there will be a property associated with every subset of this set, and each of these will have the self-realized property as a realizer. If this were so, then what is grounded in the self-realized property would not be a single hierarchy but a very complex treelike structure.

But it clearly will not do to say that given a property and its set of causal features, there is a property corresponding to every subset of that set. It also will not do to say that in every case in which the causal features of one property are a subset of the causal features of another, the second is a realizer of the first and is determinate relative to it.

Let me start with the last point. Assuming that there are conjunctive properties, it is clear that the causal features of such a property will have as subsets the sets of the causal features of its conjuncts. But plainly we do not want to say that each of the conjuncts of a conjunctive property is a determinable relative to it, and is realized by it. Assuming there is a conjunctive property corresponding to every pair of properties that can be instantiated together, and that every property belongs to such a pair, this would have the consequence that every property is a determinable relative to other properties. Clearly, if we are to define realization in terms of the subset relation, we need to impose some restriction that rules out conjunctive properties as realizers of their conjuncts.

Let's turn to the suggestion that there is a property corresponding to every subset of the causal features of a property. I have said that the causal features of the property of being red are a subset of the causal features of being scarlet. But consider those causal features of being scarlet that are *not* included in the set associated with being red. If there is a property corresponding to the subset consisting of these, then the property of being scarlet is the conjunction of the property of being red and some other property. Intuitively this is not so. And it is commonly said about the determinate-determinable relationship that a determinate cannot be regarded as the conjunction of the determinable and some other property.

What we saw previously is that what is commonly said about the determinate-determinable relationship should also be said about the relation between realizers and the properties they realize – realizers cannot be just conjunctive properties having the realized property as a conjunct. A realizer of the property of being in pain cannot be being in pain *and* being F, for some F. And that goes with the fact that not every subset of a property's causal features defines a property having just that set of causal features. To put it in another way, not every subset of the conditional powers conferred by a property is such that there is a property that confers just that subset.

What we need here is an account of the conditions under which a set of conditional powers is such that there is a property that confers just that set of conditional powers. Given such an account, we can say that property P realizes property Q just in case the conditional powers conferred by Q are a subset of the conditional powers conferred by P *and* there is no property R such that R confers just the conditional powers that are conferred by P and not by Q. This, of course, rules out conjunctive properties as realizers of their conjuncts.

In an earlier paper I addressed this issue, for a different reason, and suggested the following as a "unity relation" for properties: conditional powers X and Y are conferred by the same property if and only if it is a consequence of causal laws that either (1) whatever has either of them has the other, or (2) there is some third conditional power such that whatever has it has both X and Y.[21] In line with this, we could suggest there is a property that confers all and only the members of a set just in case every pair of members of the set satisfies this condition. This has the disadvantage that it rules out conjunctive properties. Obviously, if for any coinstantiable properties P and Q there is a property something has just in case it has both P and Q, then where P and Q are nomically independent (neither is such that its instantiation requires that the other be coinstantiated with it) there will be conditional powers C1 and C2, conferred by P and Q respectively and conferred by the conjunction of the two, that will not satisfy this condition. We might, however, give this as an account of what it is for there to be a basic, nonconjunctive, property that confers all and only the conditional powers in a set, and then allow for conjunctive properties by saying that there is a property that confers all and only members of a set just in case either (1) the set satisfies the condition just stated, or (2) the set can be partitioned into two or more sets, each of which satisfies that condition.

While I am inclined to think that satisfaction of the condition I have just formulated is a necessary condition for a set of conditional powers being such that there is a property corresponding to it, I am not sure that this is so. In any case, it is not sufficient. A further requirement is that the set be closed under nomic and metaphysical entailment – that for every conditional power contained in the set, the set contains every conditional power nomically or metaphysically entailed by that conditional power.[22] In what follows, I will assume only this necessary condition for a set of conditional powers having a property corresponding to it.

Let us return to the example of red and scarlet, and let us consider the set of conditional powers that are conferred by scarlet and not by red. These will include the power to elicit pecking in the likes of Alice (the pigeon conditioned to peck at scarlet things, but not at things of other shades of red), the power to produce an experience having a certain phenomenal character in human observers, and so forth. Although these are not conditional powers conferred by the property of being red, it would appear that they cannot be instantiated in something unless it is red and so has the conditional powers conferred by the property of being red. So the set in question fails to contain conditional powers that are nomically entailed by conditional powers in it; it is not closed under nomic and metaphysical entailment. That being so, there cannot be a property corresponding to that set of conditional powers.

I think the same will be so if we consider a physical realizer of a functional property and consider the conditional powers bestowed by it that are not bestowed by that functional property. The property of being a braking system is a multiply realizable functional property. Consider then a complex physical property the instantiation of which would give us a mechanical braking system of a certain design. This property confers whatever conditional powers are conferred by the functional property of being a braking system, but confers a number of others that are not conferred by other physical realizers of that functional property, for example, those that give us hydraulic braking systems, or electronic ones. So consider the conditional powers it confers that are not conferred by the functional property. I think it is clear that there is no property that confers these and only these conditional powers. If there were, the realizer property would be a conjunctive property having two nomically independent conjuncts, one of which is the functional property. And that is certainly not the case.

VII

On the account I am defending, functional properties are genuine properties whose instantiations confer conditional powers and play a role in the production of various effects. But a number of recent writers have questioned the genuineness of functional properties. Sometimes the challenge is based on the worry that the causal efficacy of functional properties is preempted by their realizations.[23] I have tried to show that that worry is baseless. A related worry, recently voiced by Jaegwon Kim, is that functional properties fail to be inductively projectible, and are for that reason unsuited for entering into causal laws.[24]

Kim compares pain, as construed by functionalists, with the property of being jade. Jade is a "disjunctive kind" rather than a natural kind. The two kinds of jade, jadeite and nephrite, are entirely different minerals that are alike only in their superficial properties (and in properties common to all minerals). And according to Kim, the property of being jade is not inductively projectible. This is supposedly shown by the fact that if our inductive sample consisted solely of pieces of jadeite, or solely of pieces of nephrite, the fact that all members of the sample are F would not give inductive support to the generalization that all pieces of jade are F. Kim suggests that if being in pain is a functional property, realizable in a variety of different physical properties, it fails to be projectible in the same way. For Kim this makes it questionable whether, assuming functionalism, there really is a genuine property shared by the things the predicate "is in pain" is true of.

But compare the property of being jade with the property of being an acid, which I assume Kim would count as a genuine property, well suited to figuring in causal laws. Being an acid is a multiply realizable property. There are many different ways of being an acid – being sulfuric acid, being hydrochloric acid, being citric acid, and so forth. And just as we will go wrong in our inductions about jade if we rely on a sample consisting of only jadeite, so we will go wrong in our inductions about acids if we rely on a sample consisting of only sulfuric acid. For example, we may conclude, falsely, that all acids contain sulfur.[25]

There is a difference having to do with projectibility between the property of being jade and the property of being an acid, but it is not happily put by saying that the latter is projectible and the former is not. What is true is that if we do induction on a sample containing various kinds of acid, we stand a good chance of turning up generalizations true of acids generally. While if we do induction on a sample containing the various (two) kinds of jade, we are unlikely to turn up generalizations true of jade generally, except where these are generalizations true of minerals generally and so not specific to jade. If indeed we do find that the members of our sample share some property beyond those used to pick them out as jade, and not shared by minerals generally, we can take this as supporting the claim that that property is shared by pieces of jade generally. So the hypothesis that it is so shared is inductively projectible. But believing what we do about jade, we do not expect that to happen. (If it did happen, we might revise our beliefs about jade, and decide that it is a "natural kind" after all.)

But what underlies the difference between these two properties? Both properties confer sets of conditional powers, and both are multiply realizable. Why should they differ with respect to inductive projectibility?

The kind of induction we are here concerned with aims at discovering the causal features of a property, that is, discovering what conditional powers it confers. Obviously, if a property is picked out as the property having all and only a certain set of causal features, there is no room for this sort of induction concerning it – in picking it out we already know what this sort of induction seeks to discover. Assuming that properties are picked out by their causal features, it would seem that induction is possible only when a property is picked out by some proper subset of its causal features. We "fix the reference" of a property term by a description specifying such a subset, and then proceed to investigate empirically what further causal features the property referred to possesses. But as we have noted, the same set of causal features can belong to a number of different properties; so a description of the form "The property having thus and such causal features" will not in general be uniquely referring. And as we have also noted, a description of the form "The property having all and only thus and such causal features" will not pick out a property we can proceed to do induction on.

What will give us what we want is a description of the form "The most determinate property having thus and such causal features that is instantiated around here – or is instantiated in thus and such objects." This can pick out a unique property, and one that we can learn about by induction. If we think of the reference of terms such as *acid* as fixed by descriptions of this sort, we can understand how induction with respect to them is possible. Let's use the term *acidish* as a name for the property having all and only the causal features by reference to which the property of being an acid was initially picked out, and let's call those features acidish causal features. These features will include such powers as corrosiveness, and the disposition to turn blue litmus paper red. It may be that something could be acidish without being an acid. We cannot exclude a priori, or by simple induction, the possibility that being acidish relates to being an acid as being jade relates to being jadeite. And with respect to projectibility, the property of being acidish would be on a par with the property of being jade. But we can suppose that the reference of the term *acid* is fixed by the description "The most determinate property shared by thus and such things that has the acidish causal features." We can then set about to discover what other causal features the property so designated has – and can eventually discover the subatomic basis of acidity, namely that acids are proton donors. A functional definition of a property can be thought of as specifying a set of conditional powers and saying that anything having those conditional powers has that property; or as specifying a set of causal features and saying that anything having a property having those causal features has that property. It might be thought that this amounts to defining the property as the property having all and only certain causal features. But this isn't quite right. While a functional definition leaves open the possibility that the property defined is multiply realizable, it does not, taken by itself, exclude the possibility that there is just one nomologically possible way of realizing it, or the possibility that while there are a number of different ways of realizing it, all of the nomologically possible realizer properties share causal features in addition to those that define it. Should either of these possibilities be realized, it would seem that the functional property would have causal features over and above those that define it – it would have those that belong to its sole nomologically possible realizer, or those shared by all of its nomologically possible realizers.[26]

So there is room for an empirical discovery of a "hidden nature" of a functional property. But such a discovery is unlikely to be made by enumerative induction. It could not be an extrapolation from the fact that in examined cases the realizers of a functional property share some causal feature not included in the set of features that define the property – for such a fact would give scant support to the claim that it is nomically impossible for a property lacking that feature to realize the property. (At one time all computers contained tubes, but the inference from this to conclusion that it is nomically necessary for computers to contain tubes would surely have been unwarranted.) What might ground such a discovery are theoretical considerations showing that, given the fundamental laws governing the physical entities out of which possessors of the functional property are built, only microphysical properties of a certain sort could realize the functional property.

But let us return to properties, such as being an acid, that are prime examples of projectible properties. I have suggested that it is characteristic of these that reference to them is fixed by reference to paradigm exemplars of them in a way that leaves open what many of their causal features are. Such a property might be picked out as the most determinate property having certain causal features that are commonly found in a certain class of things, a class whose specification might be in part indexical, and we might well find that such a property has additional causal features. But there is more to it than this. When a property is picked out in this way, we expect not only that the property will have causal features beyond those by which it is picked out, these being shared by its different realizer properties, but also that there is something in common to the various realizer properties that *explains* their shared causal features. The property of being an acid has many different realizations, differing from one another in many of their causal features. But in addition to sharing the "acidish" causal features, they share microphysical features, including those that make their possessors proton donors, that explain their acidish causal features. The causal features of the microstructural chemical property that realizes the property of being an acid on a particular occasion will include as a subset the causal features of that property. But that won't be the explanatory relationship. The explanatory relationship will be between, on the one hand, certain properties of, and certain relations between, protons and other subatomic particles and, on the other, the macroproperties of assemblages of these that have the conditional powers that go with acidity. The former will be the properties and relations that make something a proton donor and account for the fact that proton donors do the things acids do. Precisely what properties and relations of these sorts are involved will vary from acid to acid – but there will be a good deal in common to the explanatory stories in the case of different sorts of acid, and different realizers of the property of being an acid.

We can, of course, be wrong in expecting there to be this sort of commonality between different ways of realizing a property – but if we do turn out to be wrong, we will cease to regard the property as well suited for doing induction on.

In the case of functional properties we do not expect there to be this sort of commonality. As already indicated, the ways these are picked out make them unsuited for induction. And while it is possible that we might find theoretical reasons for supposing there is some commonality in the explanatory basis of different realizations of them, nothing in the way they are picked out gives us reason to expect this.

Where the defining functional role of a functional property is fairly thin, its explanatory potential will be limited. Being a functional property, it will (most likely) have no hidden nature that suits it for being invoked in explanations beyond the obvious ones, those that invoke the defining functional role. And when the defining role is thin, the obvious ones are likely to seem superficial – as in the explanation of someone's going to sleep in terms of the dormativity of the pill he took. This does not at all call into question the causal efficacy of such properties. Saying that taking the pill caused sleep because it was dormative can be true even though it fails as an explanation because it fails to give us causal information we did not already possess, or causal information of the sort we were after.

In any case, what is distinctive about mental properties, on a functionalist understanding of them, is that their defining functional roles (unlike that of dormativity) are extremely rich, and make possible illuminating explanations that are far from obvious. Arguably, there are no properties whose causal and explanatory roles are richer. They differ, in the ways I have indicated, from such properties as being an acid. The differences are what we should expect, given the differences in the ways the properties are picked out. But these differences provide no reason for denying that these properties have either explanatory or causal efficacy.

If mental properties are not functional properties, but are nevertheless multiply realizable, the way they are picked out must be more similar to the way the property of being an acid is picked out than was supposed previously. It will still be the case that each mental property will confer a set of conditional powers, which will amount to its playing a distinctive causal or functional role. And on a causal theory of properties this will be essential to it. But the way mental properties are picked out may carry the presupposition that there is the sort of commonality between the different realizers of a mental property that we expect there to be between the different realizers of a property such as being an acid, and do not expect there to be between the different realizers of a functional property. This is what I have called a "parochial" view of mental properties, and it allows for the possibility of "ersatz" mental states – states functionally similar to the mental states of various kinds that do not count as mental states of those (or any) kinds. To my way of thinking, the reality of the properties with which such a view would identify mental properties is no more robust than that of the functional properties with which functionalism identifies them. Both sorts of properties are "there," instantiated in creatures that are said to have mental states. It is a semantic question, which I do not here address, which sort our mental terms refer to, or our mental concepts pick out.

VIII

I have suggested that one property's realizing another is a matter of the forward-looking causal features of the first containing the forward-looking causal features of the second as a subset, with the proviso (discussed in Section VI) that the realizing property not be a conjunctive property of which the realized property is a conjunct. Such a view makes it unmysterious that the causal efficacy of a multiply realized property is not preempted by that of its realizer properties, especially if combined with Stephen Yablo's point that causes should be proportionate to their effects. It has the added benefit that it disarms George Bealer's argument that functionalism leads to the wrong conclusion about what property a person is self-ascribing when, so we would think, she is self-ascribing pain.[27]

NOTES

1. Bealer (1997).
2. See Lewis (1972).
3. See my (1980) and (1998). I am indebted to Michael Watkins for pointing out to me that one can think of what I call the forward-looking causal features of a functional property as a proper subset of the causal features of the physical properties that realize it. Watkins develops his version of the view in his *Discovering Colors* (forthcoming). The same view is suggested, independently, by Lenny Clapp in his paper "Disjunctive Properties: Multiple Realization" (2001).
4. I think, however, that we get a more satisfactory account of realization if we adopt all of my theory of properties rather than just this part. See Notes 12 and 26.
5. Yablo (1992).

6. The need for the condition added in parentheses will be discussed in Section VI.
7. Here I oversimplify. When a concept is a cluster concept, the corresponding property (if we allow there is one) will be disjunctive, and instead of there being a single set of conditional powers corresponding to it there will be a number of overlapping sets.
8. Because the only causal features of properties I shall be concerned with here are forward-looking ones, I shall sometimes omit the qualifier "forward-looking." But properties also have "backward-looking" causal features, which consist in their being such that their instantiation can be caused in certain ways. These have as much claim to be essential to the properties that have them as do the forward-looking causal features. But it cannot be said that the backward-looking causal features of a property are a subset of the backward causal features of the properties that realize it. On the contrary, the backward-looking causal features of the realizer property seem to be a subset of those of the realized property. The possible causes of instantiations of scarlet are a subset of the possible causes of instantiations of red, and the possible causes of instantiations of P1 (a realizer of pain) are a subset of the possible causes of instantiations of pain. But I see no need to bring the backward-looking causal features into the account of realization.
9. See MacDonald and Macdonald (1995). See also Robb (1997), although what his account identifies are mental and physical "tropes," rather than instances of mental and physical properties.
10. Another reason for not identifying instantiations of determinates and instantiations of determinables with them is given in Yablo (1992), p. 259, fn. 32.
11. At one time I thought that one could simply *identify* a property with a "cluster" of conditional powers having a certain kind of unity. If one could do that then, because the conditional powers associated with the property of being in pain is a proper subset of each of the sets of conditional powers associated with the properties that realize pain, one could say that the property of being in pain is literally a *part* of each of the realizer properties. In that case there is certainly no question of the realizer properties "preempting" the realized property with respect to causal efficacy – not if the realized property is a part of the realizing property, and is the part that includes the conditional powers involved in the episode of causation. For reasons I cannot go into here, I no longer want to identify a property with a cluster of conditional powers (see my [1998]). While rejecting that identification bars me from construing realized properties as parts of their realizer properties, it does not bar me from construing instances of realized properties as parts of instances of realizer properties.
12. Here it matters whether the causal features of a property belong to it essentially (as on the causal theory of properties I favor), or belong to it only contingently. If they belong to it essentially it will be straightforwardly true that the instantiation of the realizer property entails the instantiation of the realized property. If they belong to it contingently then what entails the instantiation of the realized property is not the instantiation of the realizer property by itself, but its instantiation *having the causal features it in fact has*, or, what comes to the same thing, *being governed by the causal laws that in fact hold*. If *realize* means something similar to *make real*, perhaps we should

say that the realization includes the possession of those causal features, or the holding of those causal laws – so that where the causal essentialist view says that the realizer property is physical property P, the contingency view says that it is *P and such that L*, where "L" stands for the causal laws that actually obtain. Then it will be true on both views that the instantiation of the realizer property entails the instantiation of the realized property.

This seems required if we are to say that realizations of functional properties are determinates of them; for I think that it is part of the usual conception of the determinable-determinate relationship that the instantiation of a determinable is entailed by the instantiation of any of its determinates.

13. Yablo (1992).
14. Proportionality requires that effects be *contingent* on their causes, and that causes be *adequate* for their effects, *required* by them, and *enough* for them. See Yablo (1992) for details.
15. This point, commonly attributed to Roderick Chisholm and Peter Geach, is the core of an important criticism of philosophical behaviorism.
16. There is one challenge to this view of realization that requires a more extended treatment than it is possible to give here. Some mental states have "wide content," which makes the associated mental properties partly historical and relational. For example, the property of believing that there is water in the glass is a property one has partly in virtue of having a certain sort of history of interaction with a certain sort of environment (Earthlike rather than Twin Earthlike) – having this history is partly constitutive of having the property. Any realization of this property will itself have to be a property that is partly historical and relational. But in that case, how can the relation between realizer property and property realized be simply a matter of the conditional powers bestowed by the former being a superset of those bestowed by the latter? It is natural to suppose that the causally efficacious part of the instantiation of such a realizer property, what bestows the conditional powers, will be the contemporary intrinsic state of the subject's brain, and that the historical/relational part will be without causal efficacy. Yet given that the realized state essentially has wide content, and so is partly historical and relational, this causally efficacious part of the realizer property will not be sufficient for the instantiation of the realized property.

The first step toward answering this objection is to notice that it is possible for the possession of a power to require, constitutively, the having of properties that are partly historical and relational. For example, only someone with a certain sort of history, the details of which are spelled out in the U.S. Constitution, has the power to veto acts of Congress. Other examples involve the power of ministers to make couples husband and wife, the power of professors to pass and fail students, and the power many of us have to make purchases with credit cards. I think that if we get a satisfactory understanding of the sort of causation involved in these cases, we will be in a position to see how the powers bestowed by mental properties can be such that they can only be bestowed by properties that are partly historical and relational. Here I think Fred Dretske's distinction between "triggering causes" and "structuring causes" can be put to use (see Dretske [1993]). But that is a topic for another paper.

17. There is a sense in which any determinable property, and any multiply realizable property, is second order. Each such property is associated with a class
of properties, of which it is not a member, such that it is necessary and sufficient for something's having that property that it have some property or
other in that class. (Of course, unless we put some restriction on what count
as properties, any property whatever will be second order in this sense. For
let P be any property, and Q any other property. P is not a member of the
class [P&Q, P&-Q], yet it is necessary and sufficient for something's having
P that it have some member or other of this class. So we will want to stipulate that the members of the class are not logical compounds involving our
property.)

18. One way to avoid these difficulties is to follow David Lewis in denying that
terms such as *pain* are rigid designators, and holding that they always refer
to one or another of the realizers of a functional property rather than to the
functional property. See Lewis (1980). I dissent from Lewis's view in my
(1981), although I do not there consider this reason for holding it.

19. There is one strand in Bealer's paper I have not discussed. He gives a "diag-
onal argument" to show that there is "a system of nonstandard properties
that behave with respect to each other and the external environment in
exactly the same way that the standard mental properties behave with
respect to each other and the external environment" (p. 107). And he takes
this to show that even ideological functionalism fails, unless it allows that the
standard mental properties, which he thinks he has already shown to be first
order and nonphysical, are "natural" universals as well.

Now I have already argued that Bealer's argument fails to show that
the mental properties are first order in a way that precludes their having
physical realizations, and so fails to show that they are nonphysical.
And I take it that their "naturalness" is a consequence of the fact that
their instantiation plays a role in the causing of what goes on in the world.
I have no idea whether Bealer's argument succeeds in establishing that
mental properties are necessarily coextensive with "deviant" properties
such as his "thunking," the deviant relation that supposedly mimics the
functional behavior of thinking, for I confess to being unable to take the
argument in. But supposing there are such deviant properties, he could not
hold that these are causally efficacious in the way mental properties are
without holding that the behavioral effects of mental property instantiations
are massively overdetermined. And because in any case he holds that thunking and its ilk are not natural, presumably he does not want to hold this. So
functional definitions as I would want to formulate them, ones that require
that the properties being defined have genuine causal efficacy, could not be
satisfied by Bealer's deviant properties. Bealer points out (personal communication) that logically equivalent sentences are substitutable *salva veri-
tate* within the scope of causal-necessity operators. So, if thinking and
thunking are necessarily coextensive, and if the causal role of properties is
specified only by the use of such operators, thunking will have a causal role
that parallels that of thunking. This can be avoided either by using causal
idioms of a different sort (e.g., "x's being F causes . . .") in one's functional
definitions, or by stipulating that the properties quantified over in the
definitions are natural ones.

20. Here I follow Yablo, in his (1992).

21. See Shoemaker (1980).
22. One conditional power nomically entails another just in case it is a consequence of causal laws that whatever has the first has the second; and one metaphysically entails another just in case it is a metaphysically necessary truth that whatever has the one has the other. On the causal theory of properties I favor, nomic entailment is a special case of metaphysical entailment – but I do not assume this here.
23. See Block (1990), and various papers by Jaegwon Kim in his (1993b), including his (1993a).
24. See Kim (1993a).
25. A similar point is made by Louise Antony and Joe Levine in their (1997).
26. Here is a place where it may matter whether one accepts my view that it is true generally of properties, and not just of (what are generally regarded as) functional properties, that their causal features are essential to them, and that nomological necessity is a special case of metaphysical necessity. On this view, if it is nomologically necessary that a certain functional property be realized by a property having certain causal features, then this is metaphysically necessary. Given this, the case would seem very strong for saying that those causal features belong to the functional property. On the other hand, if one thinks that causal laws are contingent, and that while the causal features of functional properties are essential to them the causal features of other properties are not, then it may seem possible to hold that the causal features that belong to all of the nomologically possible realizers of a functional property do not belong to the functional property itself, on the grounds that in other possible worlds the functional property can be instantiated without being realized by a property with those features. Of course, if a proponent of this view holds that what are essential to functional properties are only their defining causal features, and does not insist that these are their only causal features, he can hold that functional properties possess, although only contingently, those causal features that belong to all of their nomologically possible realizer properties.

It occurs to me that one reason why some philosophers find functional properties suspect is that they assume that it is true of paradigmatic "natural" properties that they have their causal features contingently. From this vantage point, properties defined as having certain causal features essentially may seem to be a kind of artifact. On the view I recommend, that all properties have their causal features essentially, there will not be this difference in status between functional properties and other properties.

A related reason why functional properties may be found suspect is that on the usual view that "ordinary" properties, including all first-order properties, have their causal features contingently, it will be possible for things in different possible worlds to be exactly alike in their intrinsic first-order properties, and so (it would seem) to be duplicates, and yet differ in their functional properties. And then it may seem that functional properties fail to be intrinsic, despite the monadic character of the predicates that express them. On the view that properties have their causal features essentially there of course will not be this reason for regarding functional properties as nonintrinsic. (Of course, externalism about content provides a reason for regarding some mental properties as not intrinsic; but this is a consideration independent of functionalism.)

27. A shorter version of this chapter was delivered in August 1998 at the 20th World Congress of Philosophy, and was published in volume 9 of the proceedings of that congress. I am grateful to George Bealer, Barry Loewer, Zoltan Szabo, Michael Watkins, and Steve Yablo for comments on an earlier version of the chapter.

5

Physicalism and Psychology: A Plea for a Substantive Philosophy of Mind

GEORGES REY

1 Introduction

There has been considerable worry for the last thirty years about the causal efficacy of the mental: How, given the closure of physics and the apparent "irreducibility" of the mental to the physical, can mental phenomena play any causal/explanatory role in the world? Aren't they mere "epiphenomena"? In reaction to these worries, Tyler Burge (1993) has reasonably argued that:

> [T]hey are symptomatic of a mistaken set of philosophical priorities. Materialist metaphysics has been given more weight than it deserves. Reflection on explanatory practice has been given too little. The metaphysical grounds that support the worries are vastly less strong than the more ordinary grounds we already have for rejecting them. (p. 97)

And Lynn Rudder Baker (1993) has rightly suggested that we:

> take as our philosophical starting point, not a metaphysical doctrine about the nature of causation or of reality, but a range of explanations that have been found worthy of acceptance. (p. 92)

Baker and Burge are applying the sensible point, suggested years ago by Moore and emphasized by Quine (1953a), that there seems to be no specially privileged position outside of common sense and science from which philosophers can effectively dismiss them. It would take a pretty powerful metaphysical argument indeed to give us reason to give up our belief in familiar forms of mental causation.[1]

For all the wisdom of this position, however, I fear that Burge overstates the case in a crucial way. The problem of "epiphenomenalism" that many of these "metaphysical" discussions have been addressing arises in part from the difficulty of specifying a mechanism linking the mental and the physical. About this, Burge writes a few pages later:

> I have no satisfying response to the problem of explaining a mechanism. But I am sure that there is less reason to think it a decisive consideration

in favor of materialism than is often thought. What is unclear is whether the question is an appropriate one in the first place. Demanding that there be an account of mechanism in mind-body causation is tantamount to demanding a physical model for understanding such causation. It is far from obvious that such a model is appropriate. It is not even obvious why any such model is needed. The argument I have just cited presents no clearly formulated problem about mental causation that need force us to embrace materialism, including the computer model's version of materialism, as a solution. (Burge [1993], pp. 113–14)

Indeed:

> The flood of projects over the last two decades that attempt to fit mental causation or mental ontology into a 'naturalistic picture of the world' strike me as having more in common with political or religious ideology than with a philosophy that maintains perspective on the difference between what is known and what is speculated. Materialism is not established, or even deeply supported, by science. (p. 117)

This seems to me too sweeping a dismissal of a quite large and diverse set of projects, only some of which are susceptible to the earlier criticism of being insufficiently rooted in explanatory practice. There are, to be sure, purely philosophical motivations to physicalism, some of which may well be as "religious" as many of the dualisms they oppose. But there are scientific motivations as well.

In the first place, the attempt to fit spatio-temporal phenomena in general into mechanistic and ultimately physical accounts of the world lies at the heart of the most successful explanatory practices we know:[2] for example, the cellular theory of anatomy, the microbe theories of disease, the DNA account of genetic inheritance and fetal development, the atomic theory of chemical combination, and the thermonuclear theory of stellar radiation. The different physical theories of these phenomena may yet await complete unification, and there may well be specific phenomena that have yet to be fully explained, but these and similar scientific successes provide overwhelming support not only for mechanism and materialism about a wide diversity of phenomena, but for pursuing them as rewarding research strategies in any spatio-temporal domain.

Indeed, it certainly appears as though every regularity in the spatio-temporal world is, in one way or another, susceptible to an ultimately physical (and/or mathematical) explanation. The route may be circuitous: fetal development may first need to be explained at an anatomic level, significant portions of which are then explained at the level of evolutionary biology and genetics, each of which in turn is explained historically and biochemically, and, only then, in terms of atomic and then subatomic physics. These different explanatory levels may be in important ways relatively "autonomous," bearing diverse and complex relations to one another, and it may well be essential to a proper understanding of an arbitrary macrophenomenon that one pass through many such levels. But I think there can be no doubt that paths through such levels, each one providing, inter alia, more fine-grained mechanisms than the last, appear to exist at least for every *non*mental regularity. One reason for applying the strategy to the mind is the reasonable expectation that mental regularities, particularly those involving patently spatiotemporal phenomena, will not prove to be some odd exception.

Moreover, on pain of circularity, if mental phenomena are ultimately to be explained, they must be explained in terms of *nonmental* phenomena, and it's a significant fact that *the only nonmental phenomena we know of are physical.* Despite erstwhile doubts, even the biological turns out to be physical.[3] Of course, it's conceivable that the mental should turn out to be "brute" (cf. Chomsky [1996], p. 44). But what is it for a phenomenon to be *ultimately* brute – not only unexplain*ed* but unexplain*able*? Physicists seem to regard even most of their basic postulations as only provisionally brute, and search for grand, unified "Theories of Everything" (see Hawking [1980], Weinberg [1992]). Establishing that the mental is ultimately brute would require a very unusual argument indeed.

Quite aside from these general arguments for physicalist projects, there is a special urgency for it in the case of the mind. Despite what a surprising number of prominent philosophers sometimes seem to suggest (see section 2, "Supposed Insularity of Folk Psychology"), we don't really have anything remotely like a serious understanding of the mind. We have no adequate explanations of such basic activities as perception, thinking, reasoning, language, decision making, and motor control, much less of the more special phenomena of consciousness, creativity, scientific insight, or morally responsible action. It's not that we know nothing. We have lots of folk insights into this and that overt behavior, some reasonable ideas about general architecture (perceptual versus cognitive versus decision-making systems), and, here and there, some understanding of some internal workings (e.g., vision, the neurochemistry of moods) (see section 3, "Different Stages of Physicalism"). However, most of us are in not much better a position than that of children, who know how to play fancy games on their computers, but haven't the slightest idea of how they work, in particular, of the ways in which transducers, transistors, operating systems, "virtual machines," and specific programs are responsible for the images produced on their monitors. Imagine a child wondering why pushing a certain button causes spectacular displays, and another child citing Burge, in an analogous dismissal of "projects to fit computer causation" into a naturalistic account: Why should this be any less absurd in the case of the mind – particularly in view of the fact that the main explanatory model in present psychology is in fact the computer (see section 3.2, "Substantive Physicalism")?

A particular danger of Burge's dismissal is that it could be construed as supporting a general resistance to scientific psychology that in one form or another has been highly influential for the last fifty years. Whether or not Burge intends to share in this resistance,[4] the thought that materialism is irrelevant to existing explanatory practice is frequently expressed by many of those who insist that existing folk psychological practice is essentially complete and in important ways insulated from scientific advance. I want to examine some of these insularity claims (see section 2.1, "Its Sanctity") and what strike me as the rash conclusions drawn from them. Too much of the discussion is limited to a small diet of examples of rationality, particularly of the practical sort (see section 2.2, "Rationality"), and many of the grand theses about, for example, the "normativity" "(ir)reducibility" or causal (in)efficacy of the mental seem to me undernourished in this way (see section 2.3, "Rash Pronouncements"). Deciding these issues requires considering a much wider range of examples, and knowing a good deal more relevant empirical theory than anyone yet knows (see section 3, "Different Stages of Physicalism").

Indeed, it seems to me that much contemporary philosophy of mind is much too philosophical. Although there are plenty of philosophical issues *within* psychology that need addressing, many of the discussions, particularly of "physicalism," seem to me to lie beyond it, and are, therefore, seriously premature. We are simply not remotely in the position that Burge and Baker recommend, of basing our metaphysics on adequate explanatory practice. Again, it's not that we know nothing. But our grasp of physicalism comes in grades. We have abundant reason to believe what I call *"simple bodily physicalism,"* roughly, what Burge ([1993], p. 98) acknowledges, that there are no exceptions to present physics peculiar to our bodies (see section 3.1, "Simple Bodily Physicalism"). But we don't know nearly enough about a *substantive, explanatory* physicalism (see section 3.2, "Substantive Physicalism") – much less about metaphysics generally – to know how to settle the difficult issues of *philosophical physicalism* (see section 3.3, "Philosophical Physicalism"), in which very specific claims (e.g., "identity theories") are proposed about mind-body relations in general. At best, we have a sketch of a promising naturalistic research program: the very "computer model's version of materialism" (see section 3.2, "Substantive Physicalism") that Burge and others dismiss. This program is nowhere near a finished theory, and there are serious conceptual problems that are (in Carnap's phrase) "internal" to it, and that are rightly the object of substantive philosophical concern. But, I submit, it's the best approach we have, and until we develop it further, or replace it with something better, Burge's dismissal of it seems to me as misguided as the "external" epiphenomenalism that he and many others reasonably oppose.

2 The Supposed Insularity of Folk Psychology

2.1 Its Sanctity

Many contemporary discussions in the philosophy of mind begin in the shadow of the later work of Wittgenstein and Ryle, who often expressed opposition to most any mentalistic explanation that departed far from ordinary thought. Wittgenstein (1981) is sometimes surprisingly explicit about this:[5]

> How does it come about that I see the tree standing up straight even if I incline my head to one side [so that] the retinal image is that of an obliquely standing tree?" "Well, I am conscious of the inclination of my head, and so I supply the requisite correction in the way I take my visual impression." ... We do not in truth supply any correction here – that explanation is gratuitous. ... *How does it come about* that we act, react, in this way? But must there be a physiological explanation here? Why don't we just leave explaining alone? (§614)

As is Ryle (1963):

> [W]hen we are in a less impressionable frame of mind, we find something implausible in the promise of hidden discoveries yet to be made of the hidden causes of our actions and reactions. (p. 325)

Wittgenstein's student, Norman Malcolm ([1959], p. 81), went on to claim that it's impossible to use R.E.M. data to establish the existence of forgotten *dreams* – without the memories, he argued, the data would perforce be about a different phenomenon. And he later (Malcolm [1977]) rejected "the myth of cognitive processes and structures," writing, for example, with regard to a cognitive explanation of such a phenomenon as a man or child recognizing a dog:

> we could, just as rationally, have said that the man or child *just knows* without using any model, pattern or idea at all, that the thing he sees is a dog. We could have said that it is just a normal human capacity. (p. 168)

Well, I suppose one could have said that it is just a normal human capacity for people to die of cancer, but I would hope that this observation wouldn't discourage a search for something more substantive to say.

One might have thought that this sort of opposition to the scientific development of mentalistic explanation had long subsided with the decline of these various (broadly speaking) behavioristic tendencies both in psychology and philosophy of mind. It is, therefore, with some alarm that one finds Thomas Nagel (1985) writing:

> The reductionist program that dominates current work in the philosophy of mind is *completely misguided*, because it is based on the groundless assumption that a particular conception of objective reality is exhaustive of what there is. Eventually, I believe, current attempts to understand the mind by analogy with man-made computers that can perform superbly some of the same external tasks as conscious beings will be recognized as *a gigantic waste of time*. The true principles underlying the mind will be discovered, if at all, only by a more direct approach. (p. 16, emphasis added)

Most recently, Jennifer Hornsby (1997) goes so far as to claim:

> If 'folk psychology' is construed by analogy with 'folk physics' or 'folk linguistics', then it carries the implication that folk psychology is the perhaps defective version of a subject matter that others (physicists, linguisticians [sic]) study with more appropriate methods than the folk. The implication is to be shunned: *we ought not to assume at the outset that the basis of our everyday understanding of one another is susceptible of correction and refinement by experts in some specialist field where empirical considerations of some non-commonsensical kind can be brought to bear.* (pp. 3–4, emphasis added)

It's hard to believe these passages are intended seriously. Is Nagel really prepared to defend the claim that *all* of the fairly detailed research of the last forty years into computational models of, for example, human vision, language, memory, reasoning, decision making, and motor control, is a "gigantic waste of time"? Does it not tell us *something* about, for example, the phenomenology of color and visual illusions, the details of sentence parsing, the patterns of fallacies to which we're prone, the risks we're willing to undertake? Is Hornsby really not prepared to turn to specialists to learn more about the bases of our everyday understanding of these phenomena? Surely, it is obvious "at the outset" with regard to any explanatorily interesting project that people who have studied the phenomena more systematically than is ordinarily possible will be in a position to correct and refine the basis of our ordinary thought. I fear Nagel and Hornsby are augmenting standard Cartesian first-person privileges with Wittgensteinian "folk" ones.

What room Hornsby does make for psychological theory, she tries to confine entirely to the "sub-personal" level ([1997], ch. 9), along lines recently urged also by John McDowell (1985):

> Proper attention to this contrast [between personal and sub-personal phenomena] subverts the idea that sub-personal cognitive psychology might supersede 'folk psychology' and the idea that it reveals hidden depths of something whose surface 'folk psychology' describes in a rough and ready way. (p. 397, fn. 29)

However, I must confess to not grasping exactly how this distinction is to be drawn, much less why all scientific inquiry should be confined to one side of it. True, it's *persons*, not mere brains, that ordinarily *act* for *reasons*. But it's also mostly *persons* who see visual illusions, grasp (however unconsciously) the principles of grammar, have all manner of repressed motives, and are able to anticipate the trajectories of baseballs (which is not to say that there aren't obvious differences in their relations to unconscious versus conscious material). Insisting otherwise strikes me as a little like insisting that biology doesn't account for the evolution of *animals* but only for some "sub-animal" counterparts, nor Newton for the motion of *planets*, but only "sub-planets."[6] Such pronouncements do sound more like the "religious ideology" that worries Burge than serious assessments of the prospects of scientific research. That research may not solve *all* the problems in the theory of mind – perhaps it will never provide a full account of free will or consciousness or the beauty of a summer day. But does it really tell us *nothing*?!

One reason that is often adduced for insulating folk psychology in this way is a widespread view that, unlike other ordinary "kind" concepts, say, of chemical elements or diseases, whose definitions are often filled out by deeper scientific research, our mental concepts are entirely defined by ordinary use. In a useful and influential proposal about the logical "Ramsified" form of "functionalist" definitions,[7] David Lewis (1972) went on to burden them with platitudinous content:

> Think of commonsense psychology as a term-introducing scientific theory, though one invented long before there was any institution as professional science. Collect all the platitudes you can think of regarding the causal relations of mental states, sensory stimuli, and motor responses. . . . Include only platitudes which are common knowledge among us – everyone knows them, everyone knows that everyone else knows them, and so on. For the meanings of our words are common knowledge, and I am going to claim that the names of mental states derive their meaning from these platitudes. (p. 212)

Incorporating these platitudes into Ramsified definitions has the star-tling consequence that, should any *one* of them turn out to be substan-tially mistaken, *no one would have any mental life at all!*[8] But perhaps we are not to be worried by this prospect. Colin McGinn (1991c) claims that "our mental concepts are happily superficial," and, like Hornsby,

> doubt[s] that our naive psychological classifications could be overturned ... under pressure from *any* sort of scientific theory of the mental. (pp. 132–3, emphasis added)

But, again: Why on earth should we think that folk ideas are any better off here than in any other explanations? It's legend that widespread plat-itudes about the mind involve extravagant beliefs about dualism, free will, and immortal souls; about racial and characterological dispositions, sexuality and gender roles; and about how we "learn" language and other capacities that may turn out to be largely innate. Whatever their merits, most of these claims surely aren't *analytic!*[9] To be sure, these philoso-phers might claim that only *some* platitudes must be right. It's unlikely we're wrong about *everything* about the mind (or anything else, for that matter). But which ones? Why? Serious candidates, for example, the "practical syllogism," principles of simple inference, when articulated within the resources of common sense, seem either hopelessly vague or obviously false (notoriously people don't do what they think they ought, and one person's *modus ponens* is likely as not to be another's *modus tollens*). We don't even know really the terms in which to begin to for-mulate such principles: should we speak of what people *believe* and *desire*, or, more carefully, about what they *notice*, or *judge*, or "make up their mind" to avow?

In trying to decide on the right platitudes or other claims for Ramsification, I can't see why we shouldn't be as prepared at the outset to be as informed by empirical theory as we are in developing, say, a theory of disease, where there is also every reason to expect that some of that improvement will afford insight into the concepts, proper-ties, and even natures of the states picked out by ordinary talk.[10] Many mental classifications (regarding, e.g., intelligence, sexuality, character, or neuroses) are reasonably being revised all the time in the light of a variety of psychophysiological investigations. Consider just the compli-cations visited on the ordinary notions of belief and desire by psychia-try, or, more recently, by the data about introspection reviewed by Nisbett and Wilson (1977).[11] The folk *know* this: They know they are often as mistaken about their understanding of their minds as they are about their bodies, and so, *pace* Hornsby and McGinn, regularly consult specialists.

2.2   *Rationality*

One motivation for this insularity claim, which figures prominently in recent discussions, is a concern with *reason*, particularly with practical rationality. The concern is hardly surprising: practical reason tends to be what first comes to mind in thinking about intentional explanation, from Aristotle to Max Weber, and is obviously central to our conceptions of people as moral agents, as in Kant. This is no doubt what leads Kim (1985) to claim that:

> our commitment to the intentional framework is a reflection of our nature as rational agents, and our need for it arises out of the demands of practical reason. . . . (p. 386)

McDowell (1985) similarly writes:

> The concepts of the propositional attitudes have their proper home in explanations of a special sort: explanations in which things are made intelligible by being revealed to be, or to approximate to being, as they rationally ought to be. This is to be contrasted with a style of explanation in which one makes things intelligible by representing their coming into being as a particular instance of how things generally tend to happen. (p. 389)

Because determining "how things rationally ought to be" is presumably a project of a priori philosophy and logic, intentional psychology is not properly regarded as an empirical inquiry.

Quite apart from what one might think about the actual status of normative projects of that sort, all of this fixation on practical rationality seems to me to do a great injustice to merely folk intentional ascription. As Wittgenstein and Austin emphasized, philosophy often suffers from too restricted a diet of examples. It's true, of course, that much human thought and action falls into rational patterns. But, even in the case of action, there is far more to the mind than reason alone. Intending to wriggle a finger brings about its wriggling whether or not one has a good reason to do so. Some actions, what Kent Bach ([1978], p. 363) has called "minimal actions," such as scratching an itch, doodling, or automatically tying a shoelace, don't require intentions, although (as he argues) they may still involve rich representations. Moreover, many fully intentional actions are performed without reasons. Rosalind Hursthouse (1991) discusses a significant range of fully intentional actions – she calls them "arational actions" – such as kicking a car in anger, jumping up and down in glee, and screaming in agony, that are not done in order to achieve some *end*: although they may in fact express one's feelings, they are not typically performed *in order* to do so (indeed, their being so performed can undermine their authenticity). She draws attention also to *symbolic* actions – such as washing one's hands for absolution, or, rather more dramatically: "taking a cigarette and burning out the eyes of a photo of one's rival in love" – which, again, seem not to involve any serious rational plan (or, if they did, would involve pretty irrational use/mention confusions!). And, of course, there are all sorts of effects of intentional states that are not *actions* at all: startle at the unexpected, laughter at jokes, tears at bad news, ulcers due to anxiety, and trembling at the thought of speaking in court.

Bearing all these sorts of cases in mind, it should be plain that intentional states are not invoked merely to rationalize actions, but to explain an extremely wide range of actions and events, any one of which could be taken to be evidence for any one of those states. Someone's belief that a friend has died not only explains her making reasonable funeral arrangements, but also her tears, grief, exclamations, beating her breast, inattention, sleeping late, and placing the friend's photo in a special box, etcetera, from each of which we might infer that belief.[12] In this way, we would certainly appear to be, as it were, *triangulating* onto such internal states as the common causes of these events, much as a doctor triangulates upon some malady from a set of symptoms. It is this triangulation onto a common cause that makes plausible the idea spurned by Hornsby "of items inside people that we latch on to when we give action explanations" ([1993], pp. 167–8), as much in the case of the mind, as in the case of physiology.[13] *Pace* Kim and McDowell, fitting into patterns of practical and other forms of reason is only one of a multitude of demands on intentional explanation, only one of the many "proper homes" of our concepts of the propositional attitudes. (Perhaps tears, laughter, and cries of despair should temporarily replace practical reason as paradigms of the mind.)

True, some of these philosophers might claim there's a limit to the way the physical can mix with the mental. Nagel, for example, writes:

> My reason for doing [some action] is the *whole* reason why it happened, and no further explanation is necessary or possible. . . . Intentional explanations must simply come to an end when all available reasons have been given, and nothing else can take over where they leave off. . . . It does not explain why this rather than another equally possible and comparably intelligible action was done. That seems to be something for which there is no explanation, *either intentional or causal*. (Nagel [1985], pp. 115–16, emphasis added)

An idea that is seconded by Hornsby:

> There is the thought, that Thomas Nagel has made especially vivid, that it is essential to our conceiving of ourselves as agents that we take ourselves

to be *completely* accounted for in terms that we use as agents; the possibility of treating actions from the impersonal point of view would then seem to subvert our ordinary conception of ourselves. (Hornsby [1993], pp. 161–2, emphasis added)

But surely this overstates the autonomy and adequacy of "personal" explanation. While it's true that one doesn't ordinarily worry about the further details that influence a person who, wanting a beer, buys one, it's plainly false there aren't further investigations that might be made. Advertisers are engaged in them all the time, finding all sorts of ways in which our voluntary choices can be influenced by patently ridiculous associations with power and love. Or, in a more reputable vein, consider the various effects of subliminal cues on choice and problem solving in the array of experiments reviewed by Nisbett and Wilson (1977); or the nonrational explanations of the speech errors we make, not only for the salacious reasons suggested by Freud, but for the structural reasons explored, for example, by psycholinguists like Gary Dell (1995); or merely the familiar effects of mood-altering drugs on our thoughts, decisions, and actions. I don't know exactly at what point Nagel and Hornsby think intentional explanations are in fact genuinely complete, and that nothing further "either intentional or causal" could be said; but I see no reason to think that anyone has reached that point yet, nor why people should find their ordinary conception of themselves seriously "subverted" by their learning it is further along than they ordinarily suppose.

This is not to say there aren't serious problems understanding deliberate action and the full richness of our personal lives. Philosophers have been rightly puzzled by the difficulties of integrating "free" morally responsible choice into any objective account of the world, and of justifying our related "reactive" attitudes, such as gratitude and resentment. And there are the familiar problems of qualia and consciousness.[14] Moreover, what we are conscious of, and especially what a person, herself, *identifies with* as "her" reason for action, may play a very special role in our ordinary lives, public and private. Perhaps some of these important phenomena will never be *completely* integrated into a scientific psychology. But a lack of *complete* integration doesn't, of course, imply a total lack of integration at all. Perhaps no objective account can be "exhaustive of what there is," whatever that might mean. But just how far an objective account can go would seem to be a terrifically interesting, but entirely open empirical question, not to be settled simply by a priori fears about threats to our freedom, autonomy, or rich personal conceptions of one another.

Nor do I mean to suggest that, even were we to attain a fully "objective" account of human psychology, further demands might not be plausibly made on human *understanding*. Much evidence suggests that people are often able to engage in various kinds of empathic "simulation" of the psychological states of others: They are able to acquire insight into others by "putting themselves in their shoes." If someone is unable to do this, then arguably they lack a certain sort of genuinely interesting understanding. However, I see no reason to suppose this sort of (in Max Weber's phrase) "*verstehen*" understanding involves any substantive claims whose truth is accessible only from such a perspective, or which are somehow insulated from standard, "*erklären*" inquiry. Empathy is just that: a *perspective* on a fact (or proposition), not an access to some special fact, rather as 'I am ill' is a perspective on the fact that G.R. is ill, not a further fact over and above, much less somehow insulated from the fact of G.R. being ill.[15]

There's often a simpler issue at stake in these discussions: whereas folk explanation is largely concerned to explain *individual* behavior, psychological explanation – much as scientific explanation anywhere – is concerned to explain *regularities*, and it seems very unlikely that the interesting regularities are available at the gross level of ordinary behavior. Ordinary human behavior is arguably the result of interaction among a multitude of probably quasi-independent subsystems of the mind (for example, perception, memory, reasoning, attention, motivation, language processing, motor control, interpersonal understanding, spatial orientation, mathematical ability, and so forth), and where there is such complex interaction, one seldom expects there to be any clear, scientifically respectable *laws*, at least not at the level of the interaction.[16] The laws concern regularities about the *subsystems*, for example, how visual representations are constructed, how a heard sentence is parsed, why certain patterns of reasoning are hard, and why certain preferences are systematically discounted. For all its moral and practical importance, practical reason may in fact be the last place to look for the right claims to Ramsify or otherwise ground intentional concepts.

2.3   Rash Pronouncements

A disturbing consequence of this presumed insularity of folk psychology is the proliferation of various pronouncements about the "autonomy," "irreducibility," "indeterminacy," and "normativity" of the mental. The merits of these pronouncements vary in proportion as they are informed by serious psychological theory. But some of them are advanced quite independently of it – indeed, are intended to call any such theory into question. In an influential article that enlarged on the "principle of charity" discussed by Quine (1960), Donald Davidson (1970) claimed that, in ascribing propositional attitudes to other people:

> We must work out a theory of what he means, thus simultaneously giving content to his attitudes and to his words. In our need to make him make sense, we will try for a theory that finds him consistent, a believer of truths, and a lover of the good. (p. 253)

In so doing, however, we are committing ourselves to norms that are not dictated by the physical description of the world:

> It is a feature of physical reality that physical change can be explained by laws that connect it with other changes and conditions physically described. It is a feature of the mental that the attribution of mental phenomena must be responsible to the background of reasons, beliefs, and intentions of the individual. There cannot be tight connections between the two realms if each is to retain allegiance to its proper source of evidence ... (pp. 253–4).

Jaegwon Kim ([1993e], p. 194) endorses a component of this view of Davidson, the "anomalousness of the mental," writing of its significance:

> Science is supposed to be nomothetic ... so that where there can be no laws there can be no science and ... we have no business pretending to be doing science. ... In advocating the lawlessness of the mental [Davidson] joins a small but influential group of philosophers who have taken a dim view of the scientific prospects of psychology. ... [His] argument has far-reaching implications regarding some basic issues about the nature of mind, ... and points to a conception of the mental that I find both intriguing and appealing. (pp. 194–6)

And Dennett writes in a similar vein:

> Deciding on the basis of available evidence that something is (or may be treated as) an intentional system permits predictions having a normative or logical basis rather than an empirical one. ... *Intentional theory is vacuous as psychology because it presupposes and does not explain rationality or intelligence.* (Dennett [1978], pp. 13, 15; emphasis added)

But, so far as I have read, few real candidates for mental laws are discussed (say, from psychophysics, vision theory, linguistics, attribution theory, decision making, to name just a few fields in which research has been fairly detailed).[17] Indeed, in reply to familiar empirical problems with his own Davidsonian-like claims ("a system's beliefs [and] ... desires are those it *ought to have* given its biological needs" ([1987], pp. 48–9)), Dennett simply writes:[18]

> I would insist, however, that all this empirically obtained lore is laid over
> a fundamental generative and normative framework that has the features
> I have described. ([1987], p. 54)

After all:

> No other view of folk psychology . . . can explain the fact that we do so
> well explaining each other's behavior. ([1987], p. 51)

Well, perhaps; but – given that what's at stake is the *vacuity* of intentional theory! – it would be nice to have seen some empirically informed discussion of exactly how the explanation goes, and the defects of some plausible alternatives. The actual processes underlying the successful deployment of folk psychology are in fact as difficult to understand as most any other feature of our minds.[19]

There is not space here to examine all the various reasons Davidson, Dennett, and others have adduced for this conception of psychology.[20] Suffice it to say that they are based either upon a demonstrably inadequate behaviorism, or upon a priori arguments whose appropriateness at this stage of our theorizing is uncertain at best. Indeed, the complaint I want to press here is not with specific arguments, but with the incredible *presumption* of so many of them. One sometimes gets the impression that many of these philosophers think they are in the position of Einstein in 1905 declaring absolute velocity to be indeterminate. But once the comparison is really made explicit, surely we ought to be embarrassed. What in our understanding of the mind is remotely comparable to Newton's or Maxwell's equations, or to the closure principles that physicists at that time were increasingly in a position to propose seriously? Imagine making analogous grand generalizations about insularities, indeterminacies, and "disparate commitments" of biology or chemistry on the basis merely of our *folk* knowledge of those domains!

Of course, it will be claimed that we do know enough, for example, to know that intentional ascription is "normative," and that we couldn't really make sense of someone who didn't believe by and large what they ought to believe. After all, isn't the *point* of belief truth and rationality? Perhaps it is; perhaps believers, *ceteris paribus*, ought to be controlled by these "norms" if they are to qualify as genuine believers. But none of this implies much about actual practice. Actual believers may deviate from these norms just as actual gases may deviate from the Ideal Gas Laws: with believers, as with most gases, *cetera* are seldom *paria*. Beliefs are notoriously subject to all manner of nonrational influence, playing, as we noted in the previous section, a variety of roles in relation to the sub-

systems of which we are composed. Idealized norms of truth and rationality (whatever these ultimately are determined to be) are at best only
some among many determinants of those roles, alongside limitations on
perception, memory, attention, the influence of habits and desires, the
sway of charismatic authorities, and the sudden impulses of a moment.[21]
Indeed, it is not at all clear at what level of abstraction to even begin to
apply any such rational norms, just which things are to be treated as
cetera and which as part of the idealized system: Should our short-term
memory and processing limitations be regarded as intrinsic to our
reason, or should we be regarded as rational gods, closed under deduc-
tion? But then who needs any mental *processes*?

It seems to me that once one puts certain philosophical preconcep-
tions aside and focuses on these uncertain complexities, it is hard to
see why psychological ascription really need involve any sort of charity
or special normativity.[22] It's not as though, even *ceteris paribus*, people
satisfy Davidson's or Dennett's norms. Indeed, it would be astonishing,
calling for quite special explanation, were someone actually to turn out
to be entirely consistent, a believer of only truths, an unqualified lover
of the good, etcetera (imagine someone utterly impervious to any standard temptations or illusions, or a novice refusing to accept naive set
theory because it was – "obviously"? – inconsistent!). Human beings
often fail to see the most immediate consequences of their thought, are
notoriously inconsistent, say the most bizarre things about religion,
history, psychology, biology, physics, want things they don't need, and
have positively alarming views about the good.

Of course, these appearances are supposed to be explained away by
the fact that "disagreement and agreement alike are intelligible only
against a background of massive agreement" (Davidson [1984], p. 137),
and that consequently the stated norms do hold on the whole. But think
of the complexity of the networks of states that, as we noted in section
2.2, "The Supposed Insularity of Folk Psychology", are "triangulated"
from now this, now a bit of rational, arational, symbolic, or nonrational
behavior. And think of how even more complicated this triangulation
becomes when we allow for the various subsystems of perception,
memory, attention, and the like that together are responsible for all that
behavior. Why shouldn't there be systematic interferences from these
subsystems that largely subvert the efforts at truth and rationality that
an agent might otherwise display? In any case, who yet has a sufficient
grip on the *whole of these triangulations, networks, and subsystems* to say?
Who is in a position to make any sweeping claims about the character
and commitments of intentional ascription? I have no such grip, and am

daunted by the serious difficulty of achieving one. Moreover, we have every reason to think that further empirical research will improve our grip (see Note 40).

Notice, in any case, that the contrast we saw McDowell ([1985], p. 389) wanting to draw between intentional and ordinary explanation requires showing that rational norms, *qua norms*, are somehow crucial to intentional ascription. To show this, it's not enough merely to point out that we make someone's actions "intelligible" by citing their "reasons." Intelligible reasons are not always normative reasons: bad news may be the "reason" for someone's depression, but not because depression is really a *rational* response to bad news (depressive convictions notwithstanding, it's not *irrational* to fail to be depressed!). And people laugh at silly jokes, weep at sentimental movies, and deliberately tousle their loved one's hair, often for no *good* reason at all. Sometimes, that is, *intentional states can and regularly do have their causes and effects quite independently of norms of rationality*. Pace McDowell, the 'intelligibility' of such cases consists in seeing them merely as "instance[s] of how things generally tend to happen":[23] at least in these cases, *verstehen* seems simply a specific form of *erklären*.

Nor is it enough to point out that people usually are pretty rational, often because they think they ought to be, and that it would often be hard to understand them if they weren't. Rationality in this respect can be considered to be just another regularity, perhaps one more central than some, but not different in kind from regularities that might figure centrally in other domains. After all, one would have trouble understanding something as a gas if it didn't, *ceteris paribus*, obey the gas laws (note that "If it's gas, it ought to behave thus" is not an appeal to any serious normativity). What a defender of a genuinely contrastive form of intentional normativity needs to show is that somehow the theorist's acceptance of certain norms, *qua norms*, is *essential* to certain intentional ascriptions. Especially in view of the kinds of nonrational cases I've mentioned, this would seem to me very hard to do. In any case, I certainly doubt it could be done until we have a far firmer grip on the whole of our psychology than is presently available. Until then, I don't see why we shouldn't suppose that psychological ascription is informed by precisely the same kind of explanatory interests that inform the ascription of states to other parts of nature.

If we are in such a terrible epistemic position, then perhaps, precisely as Burge insists, "materialism is not established, or even deeply supported by science." In the next, concluding section I'd like to lay out roughly what I take our present scientific position as regards the materiality of the mind to be.

3 Different Stages of Physicalism

'Physicalism,' of course, covers a wide variety of hypotheses about the world, and our epistemic position varies with respect to different ones of them. I want to distinguish three different kinds of claims that seem to me often run together in this regard: Simple Bodily Physicalism, Substantive Physicalism, and Philosophical Physicalism.

3.1 Simple Bodily Physicalism

I think we certainly know enough to know the following:

> *Simple Bodily Physicalism* (SBP): The overwhelming majority of individual nonmental phenomena produced by human mental activities do not per se provide explanatory counterexamples to present physics.

In other words, physics is not presented with any special problems in explaining any physical results of mentation simply by virtue of their being results of mentation: The movement of a finger can be explained by reference, for example, to electrical impulses down efferent nerves whether or not it is also true that it was produced by an intention. This, of course, doesn't entail that there aren't counterexamples to physics; finger movements may be among them. Nor does it rule out macrolevels of description that are in some important sense causally explanatory but not "reducible" to physics.[24] Perhaps "mental state" and "action" descriptions are at such a nonreducible macrolevel. Fine. All that SBP claims is that, if these states and actions somewhere down the line cause any purely physical events at all, such as the *motion* of a finger, these latter events are not thereby counterexamples to present physics (although they could, of course, be counterexamples for some other reason).

There are some who do contest SBP. Perhaps in the passage we cited previously ([1985], pp. 115–16), Nagel could be taken to be doing so. John Foster (1991) explicitly thinks that our ordinary knowledge of mental causation and the failure of various reductionist programs makes it reasonable to suppose "that the brain is subject to certain non-physical influences which do not affect the other physical systems which science investigates" (p. 200). But there certainly has been sufficient investigation of the brain to refute this.[25] At a certain point, the absence of evidence of any physical violations becomes evidence of absence. In any case it would certainly come as a surprise to most researchers were the success of mentalism to depend upon the failure of SBP in the way that Foster is prepared to discover (p. 201).

I've phrased SBP in such a way as to be neutral about a number of issues:

(i) Paranormal phenomena: whether *some* events are produced by, for example, "psychokinesis" or the like. Although the evidence for such phenomena is notoriously slim (see Stairs [1998]), there seems to me no reason for philosophers to take a stand about it. Philosophy of mind has headache enough with the explanation of perfectly *normal* cases of "mind over matter," such as wriggling a finger as the result of an intention to do so.

(ii) The general adequacy and "closure" of present physics: whether physics forms a completely adequate, "closed" explanatory system. These are obviously much stronger claims than SBP, involving issues far beyond the concerns of psychology, about which a mere philosopher of mind ought make no commitments.

(iii) The ultimate characterizations of the notions of *mind* or *body* or *physical*. Chomsky ([1993], pp. 38–9; [1994], p. 157; [1996], p. 6) sometimes claims that mind-body problems can't be coherently posed in post-Newtonian science, what with its postulation of "action at a distance" and its abandonment of "Cartesian mechanism." Even if this were true (and I'm not at all convinced by Chomsky's discussion – last I heard, "locality" is quite a live issue in physics), still SBP would be true and interesting.[26]

3.2   Substantive Physicalism

Can we say anything more at this time? Of course, SBP does invite questions about how, specifically, the mental and the physical are related, and there has been a great deal of virtually a priori speculation about the topic: type and token identity theories, and a wide variety of forms of "functionalism." But most of them are so extremely abstract and programmatic that one can feel that little has really been understood.[27] A *substantive physicalism* is one that provides some *genuinely explanatory framework* in which psychological states can actually be understood as some kind of physical state.[28] Such substantive proposals are not easy to come by. The only serious one I know of is what has come to be called the "computational/representational theory of thought" (CRTT). This is the general framework that has been emerging mostly in work in the "cognitive sciences," and has been taken seriously only by those philosophers interested in making sense of that work. I offer here only the briefest summary.

CRTT can be regarded as the hypothesis that mental processes should be treated as computations defined over representations that are encoded in our nervous systems on the model of processes in a computer. It might really be regarded as simply a species of a *causal*/representational theory of thought, because what the idea of computation does – or, anyway, what essentially Turing did with the notion of computation – is to suggest ways in which rational processes could be caused purely physically.[29] In this way CRTT promises to provide the "mechanism" many have sought to link mental and physical phenomena, as well as a way of thinking about what I described earlier as the "triangulated" states we infer from both rational and nonrational behavior. It provides a framework for understanding how a physical event (e.g., a retinal stimulation) could cause a thought (that there's an abyss ahead) that could in turn cause another thought that it rationalizes (that there's danger ahead), which in turn could cause both a rational act (stepping aside) and a purely physical event (a rush of adrenalin). Physical events cause tokenings of representations that, sometimes in rational, computational patterns, cause other tokenings that sometimes cause rational acts and also other purely physical events.

I emphasize that CRTT "promises" such an account. As things stand, CRTT is not so much a theory as a research program. Dan Osherson once compared it to Boyle's postulation of "atoms" as constituents of chemical phenomena, without any clear idea of what the precise character of those atoms might be. It leads us to ask interesting and often empirically testable questions about, for example, the precise character of the medium of representation – its expressive power, the kind of information it needs to represent, whether it consists of sentencelike structures or of "mental images" and "models" – as well as about the character of the computations defined over or between those representations – whether they are serial, parallel, sometimes "connectionist" or "dynamic," or to what extent they are modularized or "encapsulated" from one another. Discovering the subtle principles and algorithms by which we understand the world and adjust our behavior to it is, of course, not something to be expected in our grandchildren's lifetimes, if ever.[30] But CRTT does seem to be the only serious framework in which these questions can be posed.

In any case, CRTT has been fruitfully enlisted in a variety of psychological domains such as vision, memory, learning, reasoning, decision making, and the comprehension and production of natural language. For example, many perceptual illusions can be accounted for by presuming people compute specific algorithms that capture inferences about the relations of surfaces in a three-dimensional space. In theories of decision making, contradictory attitudes toward the same decision problem can be explained by different evaluative attitudes toward represented gains versus losses. And standard accounts of natural language parsing and production seem to involve computing quite elaborate structural descriptions of acoustic input.[31]

Most such models, however, focus largely on the computational aspects of the processes. There has been some, but by no means equal progress in understanding the notion of representation. Even though computations can be *specified* and studied without appeal to content, content is arguably *presupposed* by any computational theory: in vision, representations of, for example, edges and surfaces; in decision making, of options, losses, and gains; and in parsing, of nouns and verbs. Discussion of just what sorts of representations are needed, whether they can make do with some sort of "nonconceptual" content, however, has not been wanting.[32]

3.3   Philosophical Physicalism

As programmatic as CRTT is, it is philosophically interesting in a number of ways.

(i) For starters, it allows us to begin talking about propositional attitude states in a way that is potentially independent of our merely folk mentalistic ways. Recall that Hornsby (1993) rejected all such talk of "discrete things combining . . . in the production of action" (p. 167). And one reason Burge adduces for resisting at least Davidson's (1970) "token" materialism is that

> The system of intentional content attribution is the fundamental means of identifying intentional mental states and events in psychological explanation. . . . In fact we have no other systematic way of identifying such states and events (p. 110).

If CRTT is correct, however, then we have at least the promise of such a way: we could at least identify the *representations* and *the causal/computational relations* defined over them, independently of a quite possibly "external" semantic component, in rather the way a physicist abstracts mass from weight.[33] We could then treat a propositional attitude state as having two components, one involving a causal/computational relation to a representation and the other a perhaps externally determined content of that representation. This helps the materialist program by then allowing us to treat the relation between the first component and a physical state as a species of the "realization" relations that obtain between the computational states of a computer and the physical processes that are responsible for executing the computation.

(ii) In a quite substantial way, CRTT supports the suspicion of multiple realizability that was otherwise a mere "intuition" about the mental, that creatures with different physiologies could enjoy much of our psychology. This suspicion is vividly borne out by the possibility of running the same algorithm on any of an indefinite variety of physical machines. It also supports the idea that certain parts of psychology may well be as "autonomous" from physiology as the understanding of an algorithm may be from an understanding of its electronic implementation.

However, it's important not to exaggerate this multiple realizability.[34] Given the diversity of subsystems of which the mind is likely composed, it would be surprising if the mind were perfectly unified by a theory at simply one level of abstraction. *Functionalism* is too often defined as "characteriz[ing] mental states in terms of . . . their causal relations to sensory stimulations, behavioral outputs, and other mental states" (Block [1980b], p. 172). Not only does this inappropriately invite a monolithic definition of *all* mental terms at once (see Note 9), it ignores the possibility that there may be *other* nonmental terms appealed to in a definition (for starters, consider the probably crucial role of *relative times* that processes take). Recalling the Lewis "Ramsification" technique for defining functional notions (see Note 8), *it's a nonobvious theoretical question what "old" terms are to be included in the Ramsey sentences.* They could include physical descriptions of both human biology and maybe even aspects of the surrounding environment. Until we have really serious computational theories about the various subsystems of the mind, and can ascertain their appropriate level of abstraction, there is simply no way of assessing how much multiple realizability actually obtains. Perhaps sensation and color vision are tied rather closely to our peculiar biology. Perhaps linguistic semantics depends heavily on its embedding in a social world, but logical reasoning is entirely abstract.[35]

(iii) Multiple realizability, of course, is one main source of the worries about epiphenomenalism of the past thirty years, because it seems to imply that mental properties are distinct from causally adequate physical ones (Kim [1993e], [1998]). Here, then, emerge the issues of *philosophical physicalism*, or the ultimate statement of the exact relations between mental and physical phenomena. I have said (with deliberate caution) that CRTT "treats" attitudes as computational states: Is this "treatment" to be spelled out finally as an *identity* or as an *analysis*? Are even purely computational phenomena *identical to, constituted by*, or *composed of* physical phenomenon? These seem to me to be extremely difficult issues, whose resolution depends upon a far more satisfactory account of metaphysics generally than is available anywhere. It's a philosophical commonplace that there is no settled account of properties, tropes, events, states, facts, individuals, the bewildering mereology of all these things, or the nature of intertheoretic "reduction." Put aside beliefs and desires: Are, for example, *storms* or *wars* really "identical to," "composed of," or "reducible to" microphysical events? Do they include, for example, the movement of the termites on the uprooted trees, the sunlight that breaks through the clouds, and the cries of the dislocated people? Is the property (or a trope) of being a storm composed of the corresponding properties or tropes of these subevents? If not, then are we really no longer in a position to say that storms and wars "cause" the massive destruction that is "also caused" by the movements of elementary particles? I hope not, and not merely because I believe in the occasional causal efficacy of the mental. Here, again, the observation of Baker and Burge: philosophy ought to play second fiddle to successful explanatory practice. In any case, surely it's hard to see why we should lose much sleep if epiphenomenalism about the mind is no different from epiphenomenalism about storms, wars, digestion, and metabolism.

The point is that there is simply no need for CRTT to be clearer on these issues than anyone else. It would be a major advance if CRTT could merely show how psychology is no worse off in this regard than meteorology, biology, computer science, or any other discipline that adverts to large-scale, often "functionally" defined states. Philosophers interested in the causal metaphysics of mind would do well to *first* work out the complicated causal metaphysics of not only storms and wars, but of hearts and kidneys, and then of transistors, "or-gates," "machine states," "information," "instructions," "computations," "virtual machines," and the like. Only after we have solved the problems of "computer/body interaction" on systems whose operation on many levels is relatively well understood should we turn to the vastly more difficult problems of the mind and brain, whose operations on most levels are largely opaque. Hard cases make bad law.[36] Kim (1998) thinks that this reliance on other sciences should provide little solace:

> This is a little like being told that we shouldn't worry about, say, being depressed because everyone else has the same problem. (p. 78)

A better analogy might be: if you're a homeless alcoholic schizophrenic, don't fret about common melancholia! Philosophy of mind has sufficient problems of its own to warrant what I have elsewhere ([1997], p. 27) called a "Principle of Fairness": *don't burden the philosophy of mind with everyone else's problems*. Enough that we might replace the neurotic misery of psychology with the common unhappiness of the other sciences.

It is interesting to note that Kim is

> inclined to think that ontological schemes are optional.... Concerning such questions as whether there "really are" events ... along with similar

questions about facts, properties, continuants, time-slices, and so forth, it just seems wrong-headed to think there are "true" answers. ([1993e], p. ix)

He suggests that the purely philosophical questions he's posing are like Carnap's "external" questions that do not seriously impinge on the "internal" issues of a science ([1993e], p. x). Insofar as Kim holds by his recent claim ([1998], p. 61) that he is concerned not with *whether* but *how* mental causation is possible, this is plausible.[37] But then it would certainly seem wildly premature to be addressing external questions before the internal theory has been seriously spelt out (imagine trying to settle the "external," ontological questions about biology without any understanding of natural selection or genetics).

(iv) On the other hand, CRTT does present a valuable, empirically informed framework in which to consider a number of *substantive* philosophical problems that are serious *internal* issues for a scientific psychology: for example, the specific kinds of intentionality required for different portions of psychology (how much can be handled by "nonconceptual content," how much by differences in internal representations? Is there an explanatorily distinct subsystem for processing of "semantic" information?);[38] the nature of observation and qualitative states (Are there perceptual modules? Are inverted qualia not only *imaginable* but *actually possible*? Would a purely CRTT account of qualia suffice, or must there be a further physiological component?);[39] even the nature of conscious and unconscious processes (What are the processes underlying introspection? "Blindsight"? "Repression"? Linguistic competence?).[40] It is these sorts of detailed internal issues, as opposed to the purely metaphysical issues that have occasioned so much worry, that seem to me to deserve our immediate philosophical attention.

In this regard, given the pessimism of philosophers such as Nagel, McDowell, Hornsby, and McGinn about our ability to provide a scientific account of people's mental lives, it is disappointing that they discuss few serious empirical efforts to do so. They seem to treat all psychological research as somehow on a par, too often on the model of mere psychophysical *correlations*, which, of course, do leave one "amazed that this vivid experience of red could result from chemical perturbations in that little bit of wet cortex" (McGinn [1991c], p. 86).[41] But this amazement may be due merely to being mesmerized by certain superficial appearances, in the way that (to return to my opening comparison) children might be amazed when told a television image could result from electrical perturbations in their computers. The only way to get over this amazement is to stop staring at the screen and study some substantive theory.[42] In the case of the mind, this would appear, *pace* Burge, to involve CRTT and the materialist program of which it is a part: for starters in the case of experiences of red, computational theories of visual illusions, Fechner-Stephens accounts of phenomenal intensities, and opponent-processing accounts of vibratory colors. The mind – like God, the devil, and the activity of any computer – is in the details.[43]

NOTES

1. It is worth noting that one of the chief targets of Burge's and Baker's remarks, Jaegwon Kim, has recently moved significantly in their direction, conceding in reaction to just these passages that the problem that concerns him is "*how* mental causation is possible, not *whether* it is possible" (Kim [1998], p. 61). This does seem some distance from his ([1993e], pp. 92–5) defense of "epiphenomenal causation," in which he likens the (apparent?) "efficacy" of mental phenomena to successive mirror images of some genuine causal process.

2. Some terminology: by *mechanical* I presume Burge means the postulation of increasingly "local" causes of phenomena, and by *physical*, the ultimate phenomena of *physics* (including mathematics). By *mental* I want to include not only phenomena that immediately involve intentionality and/or consciousness, but also phenomena, such as nations and economies, that presuppose intentional agents. "Explanatory practices" I take to include more than merely specific causal claims, but also the search for them within fruitful explanatory strategies, as in the case of, for example, medicine.

3. Which is not to say that it can be "reduced" to physics, in all the enticing senses of that overused and misleading phrase (as though the "reduced" phenomena were somehow "less" than what they had previously been taken to be). Note that theology is mental in the sense of the previous note, and that the concern here is with only spatiotemporal phenomena.

4. In correspondence, Burge has claimed to be opposed only to "philosophical" and not to "scientific" interpretations of physicalism and the "computer model." Especially with regard to the latter, it's unclear to me what distinction he has in mind. If it's the distinction between "philosophical" and "substantive" physicalism that I will draw in the end (see the section, "Different Stages of Physicalism"), perhaps our views are not as far apart as I fear.

5. By *physiological* I take him here to mean any explanation that adverts to unintrospectible brain processes, whether described physically or psychologically. Wittgenstein's opposition to nonordinary mentalistic explanations surfaces at quite a number of places. There is the famous dictum at the very beginning of the *Investigations*, "Explanation comes to an end somewhere," said in reply to the question: "And how does the shopkeeper know where and how to look up 'red' and what he is to do with the word 'five'?" And there are the attacks on "inner processing" models at ([1953], §308, 571), as well as the rejections of specific postulations involving, for example, color perception ([1977], pp. 37–40), reading ([1953], §160), understanding of other people ([1981], §220), aesthetic reactions ([1978], pp. 17–20), and animal thought ([1953], §25; [1981], §117; [1980], §192). My favorite example is his pontification: "The question 'Do fishes think?' does not exist among our applications of language, *it is not raised*" ([1981], §117). In my (1995b) I try to salvage something nevertheless quite valuable in Wittgenstein's view.

6. But perhaps Hornsby would not be fazed. She also writes, "The scope for casting light at all directly on ordinary things by thinking about their invisible parts' interaction is rather limited" (p. 193). One wonders what she makes of the scientific successes I enumerated in the preceding paragraphs.

7. *Very* briefly, and because it matters later: Lewis proposes defining any specific mental term t_i by the sentence:

$$t_i = \text{the } x_i \text{ such that } (E!x_1) \ldots (E!x_{i-1})(E!x_{i+1})(E!x_n) \, (C_M \, (x_1 \ldots x_i \ldots x_n, o_1 \ldots o_m))$$

where '$C_M \, (x_1 \ldots x_i \ldots x_n, o_1 \ldots o_m)$' is some long conjunction containing variables, $x_1 \ldots x_n$ in place of the n mental terms being defined in this way, and m number of "old" (e.g., physical) terms, $o_1 \ldots o_m$, included in specifying the relations among $x_1 \ldots x_n$. Thus, to take Lewis's own specific proposal, C_M might be a conjunction of platitudes that contain commonsense mental terms, as well as lots of physical terms about people's bodies and their environments.

8. This is because the Ramsified definitions essentially define any mental terms explicitly in terms of *all* the platitudes. Ned Block has suggested to me that Lewis has in mind logically complex Ramsifications, involving "clusters" (e.g., disjunctions of conjunctions) of platitudes that might protect the definitions "nearly enough" from any specific failure. Well, it would be interesting to see this worked out, especially in light of the very substantial errors common platitudes probably involve. But why should one think this reliance on even clusters of platitudes is any more plausible as an approach to mental, than to biological or chemical concepts or kinds? Perhaps even false platitudes are useful for fixing the reference of our concepts (cf. Kripke [1972]); but why restrict our analyses of them in this way? I suspect an uncritical empiricist semantics, whereby meanings must be "derived from experience," in particular from the observation of ordinary behavior (see Rey [1994] for discussion). It is interesting to note that Lewis ([1994], p. 416) has recently backed away from this direct reliance on platitudes, proposing, instead, "principles of folk psychology that govern our judgments, analogous to the tacit principles of grammar." If current linguistics is any indication, they may of course be a far cry from the platitudinous judgments.

   Although this "commonsense" functionalism is quite widespread – for variants of it see McGinn (1991c), and Jackson and Pettit (1993) – there are plenty of other ways of deploying Ramsification. In my ([1997], chs. 6–7), I resist both Lewis's excessive holism and the reliance on platitudes, defending instead a "molecular, anchored psychofunctionalism," whereby Ramsifications are confined to subsystems of the mind, appropriately embedded in an environment. See Lycan (1987) for a similar proposal.

9. Perhaps in the present, intellectually turbulent times, what with eliminativisms on the one hand and "new age" mysticisms on the other, it may be hard to determine exactly what would count as platitudinous any more. So go back a hundred years or so, when many mental words surely meant what they do today, but the platitudes were probably more plentiful – and less true.

10. Which is not to say there mightn't be an a priori component to such investigations. But I suspect it is less substantial and much harder to isolate than philosophers have tended to suppose (see Rey [1998a] for discussion).

11. These data lead Stich ([1983], p. 231) to doubt that the ordinary concept of belief is even coherent. In Rey ([1988], pp. 273–7), I argue this is rash; but the methodological point remains.

12. Think of how much is presently being learnt about the intentional states of prelinguistic infants from mere observation of their involuntary startle responses (cf. Spelke [1991]).

13. This triangulation from nonrational effects of intentional states also gives the lie to claims such as those of Rosenberg (1985): "Intentional psychology does not have even the strength of phlogiston theory, for its causal variables are not subject to any actual or practically possible independent measurement" (p. 404).

14. See, for example, P. Strawson (1974) and G. Strawson (1987) regarding the intractability of free will, and Levine (1983), Chalmers (1996), and Rey (1997) regarding qualia and consciousness.

15. Cf. the various "ability" and "perspectival" responses to Nagel's (1974) worries about "knowing what it's like to be a bat," or Jackson's (1986) worries about what his newly color-sighted Mary comes to know. See for example, Lewis (1990), Loar (1997), and Nemerov (1990). In Rey ([1992], [1997], pp. 290–301) I develop at length the analogy between sensory and first-person reflexive states.

16. This may explain some of what is right in the preceding remarks of Nagel about how intentional explanation often doesn't determine a unique act, or, as others have put it, that mental states "incline" without "compelling" (Chomsky [1980a], p. 7; [1986], pp. 222–3). This is precisely what to expect in the case of subsystems governed by *ceteris paribus* laws: They have their standard effects only when lots of other conditions are *just right*. Whatever else it may also be, voluntary action is surely a complex interaction effect, such as the precise path of a leaf in a lake, blown now by the wind, engulfed in a moment by a wave, about which general, systematic theorizing or prediction may be quite idle.

17. To the contrary, Davidson oddly confesses about his work in the 1950s on actual choice behavior: "I found it impossible to construct a formal theory that could explain [it], and gave up my career as a cognitive psychologist" (Davidson [1980], p. 236). See Tversky (1975) for criticism of Davidson's specific work on intransitive preferences.

18. He's replying to the trenchant objections of Stich (1984), who is commenting on Dennett ([1978], pp. 18–19, 21–2, 106, 281–2).

19. See, for example, Fodor (1981), Gordon (1986), and Rey ([1995a], [1997], pp. 277–87) for further discussion of both Dennett's proposal and some alternatives.

20. I address some of them in Rey (1995a) and ([1997], §10.3). One reason often cited is Quine's ([1960], ch. 2) argument for the indeterminacy of translation. It would take us too far afield to assess Quine's claims, but note that (1) unlike the claims I'm considering, they are at least based upon what he *takes* to be the best science of psychology available, viz. Skinnerian behaviorism; (2) that basis, however, has been fairly conclusively shown to be scientifically bankrupt, and, although the argument has been admirably run on nonbehavioristic assumptions by Bealer (1984) and Gates (1996), we are still not in the position that "one has only to reflect on the nature of possible data and

methods to appreciate the indeterminacy" (Quine [1960], p. 72) (indeed, one wonders what a confirmation holist such as Quine (1953a) is doing speculating about "the nature of possible data" in the first place!; cf. the next note); and (3) the argument for indeterminacy doesn't entail the positive "charity" principles that these writers offer as an account of our interpretative practice.

A related reason arises from the argument Kripke (1982) gleans from Wittgenstein's worries about rule following. In our (1995), Paul Pietroski and I argue that it suffers from far too simplistic a conception of *ceteris paribus* clauses, and so fails to consider how a reasonable psychology could settle the worries. Another recent discussion, Zangwill ([1998], pp. 184–6), seems to me to suffer from a similar defect.

21. Perhaps the worry is this: without actual patterns of practical rationality, we couldn't ordinarily *identify* intentional states. However, the sorry history of verificationism has surely taught us that such observations, even if true, entail little about the *nature* of those states, any more than the way we ordinarily identify salt tells us much about its nature. Moreover, as the same history shows, there is a tendency to overlook atypical and indirect evidence: imagine someone suffering from severe abulia, unable to engage in any voluntary action, but still capable of reacting emotionally to the contents of stories and jokes. Merely an inference to the best explanation might suffice for the ascription of quite detailed intentional states, quite independently of practical rationality.

22. This is not to say that intentional idioms are not committed to normative vocabulary ("right," "wrong"); just that it has yet to be established that this sort of normativity isn't integratable into standard explanatory projects, particularly ones that avail themselves of more appropriate *ceteris paribus* laws than are cited in any of the standard discussions (cf. Note 21). See Horwich ([1998], ch. 8) for a good discussion of many other confusions regarding "normativity" in this regard.

23. Perhaps *these* are the sorts of cases about which the earlier quote from Malcolm ([1977], p. 168) is partly apt. Unlike the cognitively complex case of recognizing a dog, depression, rage, laughter, and tears may be nothing more than "normal human capacities," for which at least any *rationalizing* explanation would be otiose.

24. Of course, it may do so given further claims of a *philosophical physicalism*, to be discussed in the next section. The blocking of the inference from "ideological" irreducibility to "ontological" dualism was a welcome contribution of the Davidson (1970) article that I have been maligning, although the nice logical point (and the terminology for it) was implicit in Quine (1953b) and provides a useful way of distinguishing, respectively, *physicalism* from *materialism* (Rey [1997], pp. 179–80). See also van Gulick (1993) for an especially good discussion of this whole issue. Note, as I mentioned earlier, despite his dismissal of physicalistic projects, Burge ([1993], p. 98) essentially defends SBP.

25. It's actually hard to find a neuroscientist who bothers to point this out. The closest I have been able to find is Churchland and Sejnowski ([1992], pp. 1–2).

26. I discuss Chomsky's somewhat undulating views of mentalism in my (forthcoming-a).

27. It's important to note that one could deploy Lewis's technique of Ramsification (Note 8) and so be a "functionalist" about almost any domain (see Rey [1997], pp. 175–6).

28. Barry Loewer (1997) calls it a "perspicuous physicalism."

29. It is astonishing how this point is *still* missed. Thus, McDowell (1985) writes:

> It is important not to be misled by the role of rationality in, e.g., computational accounts of sub-personal processes. The illumination that such accounts can undoubtedly yield is not a product of a deeper understanding of the mind. It is rather a matter of understanding the workings of the brain – in a way whose possibility is wholly unmysterious – by modelling them on certain mental processes. (p. 397, fn. 29)

But the whole point of a computational account is to show how any "mental processes" appealed to in it are ultimately *inessential* in that they are so stupid they can be obviously replaced by a machine (cf. Dennett [1978], pp. 80–1). The idea is that what's rational is computational and what's computational is mechanical and so does *not* rely on mentalistic modeling. Perhaps what McDowell means is merely that the *intentional* interpretation of a computation is not explained in this way. Fine. But then he needs to show that it isn't provided by the usual embedding of these computations in an explanatorily adequate descriptive psychology.

30. See Fodor (1983) and (forthcoming) for expressions of pessimism in this regard.

31. Excellent surveys of recent CRTT-driven research can be found in the four volumes of Osherson (1995–8), especially the many articles on language acquisition and processing by Nakayama, He, and Shimojo in vol. 1; by Biederman on vision research in vol. 2; by Shafir and Tversky on decision making in vol. 3; and by Gallistel on animal navigation, along with Sternberg and Dosher on object and face recognition in vol. 4.

32. See much of the work of Dretske, Stalnaker, Devitt, Burge, and Fodor, a survey of which I provide in Rey ([1997], ch. 9). Crane (1992) is a useful anthology on nonconceptual content. For some skeptical discussion, see the aforementioned reworking of Quine's indeterminacy arguments for nonbehavioristic psychologies in Bealer (1984) and Gates (1996). I worry about the role of intentionality and CRTT in current linguistic theory in Rey (forthcoming-a).

33. Burge ([1991], p. 208, 213, fn. 13) seems to begin to allow as much.

34. Certainly, it should not be interpreted as liberally as Searle (1992) allows, whereby "for any object there is some description of that object such that under that description the object is a digital computer . . . thus, for example, the wall behind my back is right now implementing the Wordstar program, because there is some pattern of molecule movements that is isomorphic with the formal structure of Wordstar" (pp. 208–9). CRTT is intended as a genuine explanatory hypothesis, and so is justified as a literal description of the world only insofar as there is nontendentious evidence for it that could not be otherwise explained (moreover, surely a mere isomorphism is not enough for science: one reasonably wants, for example, systematic decomposition, counterfactual support and integration into other theories). This is abundantly available in the case of people, many animals, and some machines – but presumably not in the case of the wall. It is this disregard of these

further explanatory demands that leads Searle to his views about the "observer relativity" of any computational theory such as CRTT. See Rey (forthcoming-b) for discussion.

35. In this regard, Burge's own work on externalist semantics, and the debates between him, Segal (1989), and Davies (1991), have been a significant contribution. Burge's apparently sympathetic discussion of Marr's (1982) explicitly *computational* theory of early visual processing does make one wonder about his dismissal of "computer models" that I cited at the beginning of this chapter.

36. This is not to deny that significant insights into the metaphysics of the mind might not emerge, as indeed they have, by direct philosophical inquiry (I really don't mean to be telling people how to spend their time!). I'm concerned largely with avoiding the kinds of a priori obstacles to psychology (cf. Kim's endorsement of Davidson) that seem to me to be based on a metaphysic that has not dealt satisfactorily even with comparatively easy cases.

37. I'm not endorsing Carnap's distinction in any but a provisional way. In this connection, it is indeed worth noting that nothing in Kim's argument turns on any finding about the mind or brain, or on much of any science. It's a quite general argument that could be applied to any *atomistic* world (although it's an irony about the discussion that in the case of our present atomistic theory, it is often argued that the basic laws are not causal at all!).

38. In this connection, it is worth distinguishing at least two orthogonal challenges raised by Quine's famous attacks on the notion of "meaning": a "*vertical*" challenge to "naturalize" intentionality that is largely "external" to psychology, and a "*horizontal*" challenge to specify *within psychology* a principled distinction between matters of meaning and matters of factual belief. Although I think the former involves issues of the kind of purely philosophical physicalism that I believe is premature, the latter arguably turns on complex details of empirical linguistics and psychology (see, for example, Jackendoff [1990], Schein [1993], Larson and Segal [1995], Fodor [1998], Rey [1998a], Pietroski [forthcoming]).

39. See, for example, Fodor (1983), Pylyshyn (1999), Block (1995), Palmer (1999), Rey ([1997], [1998b]). Another nice example of how CRTT might settle an issue in this domain that has been deemed prematurely "indeterminate" is afforded by the familiar wonder about whether, in coming to like beer since childhood, it's one's experiences or preferences that have changed. Dennett ([1991], pp. 392–6) argues that, because the matter couldn't be settled by recourse to introspection or ordinary behavior, there is "no fact of the matter" about it. CRTT could supply a potentially perfectly good way to settle the question by determining whether there is a subsystem for gustatory perception distinct from one for preferences. If children have more taste buds than adults, then despite having the same preferences for bitter titillation as adults, their gustation system might reach a painful threshold sooner with the same quantity of bitter substance. The important point here is that the issue might only be settled by the kind of detailed internal investigation of the mind that CRTT invites (see Rey [1995a] for further discussion).

40. See Ericsson and Simon (1984/1993) regarding introspection, Weiskrantz (1986) on blindsight, Dwyer and Pietroski (1996) on linguistic competence. It is interesting to contrast in this regard the "external" question of

epiphenomenalism raised by philosophers such as Kim with the quite "internal" one raised by Libet (1985), who produces interesting (although not overwhelming) evidence that people's awareness of their intentions occurs significantly later than the neural events responsible for the intended act, which would appear to render that awareness "epiphenomenal" at least with regard to that act.

41. More recently, McGinn (1999) writes: "Neurophysiologists find correlations between brain states and conscious states, but nothing in neurophysiology even begins to explain such correlations" (p. 45).

42. Cf. Wittgenstein (1953): "it shows a fundamental misunderstanding, if I am inclined to study the headache I have now in order to get clear about the philosophical problem of sensation" (§314).

43. I am grateful to Barry Loewer for the invitation to write this paper, and to him and to my colleagues Michael Devitt, Jerry Levinson, Michael Slote, Allen Stairs, and especially Paul Pietroski for much useful discussion. Some of its animus arose from lively discussions over the years with Naomi Scheman, whose views for some reason nevertheless continue to differ. Drafts were presented at Cornell; at the ESAP conference in Maribor, Slovenia; at the Universities of Edinburgh, London, Oxford, Sheffield, Stirling, and St. Andrews; at CREA in Paris; and at the Eastern APA in 1999. In reaction to various of these, Tyler Burge provided some clarification of some of his views, and Jonathan Adler, Rogers Albritton, Kent Bach, Martin Davies, Brian Loar, Nenad Miscevic, Jesse Prinz, Gabe Segal, and Tim Williamson made valuable suggestions. I am particularly indebted to Mark Greenberg for quite detailed comments, and to both him and Barry Smith for admirably charitable readings of many of those whose views I oppose. I found that I wanted to reiterate points I made elsewhere, especially in my (1993), (1997), and (forthcoming-a), and so have occasionally used some of the same material to do so.

6

Davidson and Nonreductive Materialism: A Tale of Two Cultures

HOWARD ROBINSON

I

I shall argue in this chapter that the discussion of *nonreductive materialism* has been conducted under the shadow of an ambiguity in the sense of *reductive*. One sense is specific to the philosophy of mind, and here the reductive tradition is marked by the attempt to give an account of the mind in behavioral or functional terms, without remainder. The other sense derives from the philosophy of science, and it concerns the possibility of giving some kind of systematic account of "higher" sciences in terms of "lower" ones, and, ultimately, in terms of physics. I shall argue that failure to distinguish these senses in Davidson's "Mental Events" has led to serious confusions in the discussion of "nonreductive materialism" and in the attendant notion of 'supervenience.' Davidson has clarified the confusion in "Mental Causes", but in a way that makes his original contribution much less interesting than it had seemed to be. In the course of the discussion, I hope to clarify the various senses in which theories, properties, and predicates can be 'reduced' or 'emergent.'

II

Story 1. In order to vindicate a materialist theory of the mind it is necessary to show how something that is a purely physical object can satisfy psychological predicates. Those features of the mind which seem to be, prima facie, incompatible with this physicalism – such as consciousness and the intentionality of thought – must, therefore, be explained in a way that purges them of their apparently Cartesian elements, which would be incompatible with materialism. Overt behavior is expressive of mentality and is a purely physical phenomenon, so it is necessary to provide some kind of analysis, or looser gloss, of psychological predicates that shows how they need be no more than dispositions to behave – or, more probably, functional states defined by their ultimate contribution to behavior: in this way, it can be shown that there is no principled objection to physicalism.

Story 2. In order to vindicate a physicalist theory of the mind it is necessary to integrate psychology into a unified science resting on physics. Such a *scientific reduction* requires that there be bridging laws relating the properties or concepts of any science higher than physics to those of the science below it, until nomological correlation with physics is achieved. In the case of psychology, this means that, at the first stage, there be laws connecting psychological states with neurological states.

Story 3. Reductionism never looked plausible. Fortunately, a materialist theory of the mind requires only that each mental event be also a physical event. This will be so if a given mental event and a given physical event have all and only the same causal relations. Nothing is required in the way of reduction of psychological predicates or properties to physical ones.

Question. Is the reduction that is not required for materialism according to Story 3 the analytic reduction advocated in Story 1 or the scientific reduction of Story 2, or both, and does it make a difference whether it is understood primarily in relation to one of them or to the other?

III

The analytical reductionism of Story 1 is the approach to the mind-body problem associated with analytical behaviorists such as Ryle, Australian central state materialism, analytical functionalism, and the computational theory of the mind. It is analytical because there is an explication of the possession of particular mental states in terms of the kinds of behavior paradigmatically associated with them, and it is reductive because it purports to show how, through the behavioral connection, mental states need be no more than – "nothing but" – physical states, contrary to one's Cartesian intuitions: the mind is ultimately its contribution to behavior, and nothing more.

The scientific reductionism of Story 2 is part of the logical positivist program to produce a unified science: one rationale for it is the belief that such nomological reduction is necessary if the different sciences are to be thought of as being genuinely true, but different, ways of talking about the same subject matter, namely the one physical world.[1]

What I have called Story 3 represents, of course, Donald Davidson's (1970) nonreductive physicalism. Many of Davidson's readers including, I would hazard, most, if not all, of his British ones, understood his theory to be nonreductive in the sense of avoiding analytical reductionism, as well as scientific reductionism (if they gave that issue any thought). It was, for them, an alternative to the counterintuitive theories of Ryle, Smart, and Armstrong. Thus, very recently David Charles has written:

> In his writings [Davidson] sought to support the conviction that the mental is dependent on the physical, while at the same time holding that the mental need not, and indeed should not, be reductively defined in terms of the physical or functional. (Charles [1992], pp. 265–6)

Nor does Charles make this attribution carelessly. He quotes Davidson on the kind of supervenience his theory involves. Davidson says:

> Supervenience of this kind does not entail reducibility through law *or definition*. (Davidson [1970], p. 88, emphasis added)

Nothing would seem to be plainer than that Davidson is disowning reductionism as it appears in both Story 1 and Story 2. The argument of this chapter is that, despite this apparent avowal, Davidson is actually concerned only with forms of nomological reduction, and that his theory positively requires analytical reduction; and that this fact is brought out by the way he defends his doctrine in "Thinking Causes." If one is interested in developing a 'soft materialism,' free from the counterintuitive rigors of functionalism and similar theories, Davidson is no ally.

If this is true, how can he say what Charles quotes him as saying? Shortly after the passage quoted, Davidson considers, as an example of the *reduction by definition* that he eschews what he calls 'definitional behaviorism.' He asks "[w]hy are we willing . . . to abandon the attempt to give explicit definitions of mental concepts in terms of behavioural ones?" He illustrates what such a program would be committed to by citing an attempt to analyze having a certain belief in terms of having the disposition to utter certain sounds. The goal is the explicit definition of the mental in terms that contain no mentalese: it is the matching of a mentally characterized type of behavior with behaviors that are types in purely physical terms. Reduction by explicit definition is not, therefore, something different from nomological reduction, but is a strengthened version of it – it replaces mere nomological correlation with definitional correlation, which entails nomological correlation. Twenty-three years later, in "Thinking Causes," he still has the same notion of reduction.

> Supervenience . . . obviously applies in an uninteresting sense to cases where [some higher level vocabulary] *p* is . . . *explicitly* definable by means of the predicates in [some more basic vocabulary] *S*, and to cases where there is a law to the effect that the extension of *p* is identical with the extension of a predicate definable in terms of the predicates in *S*. The interesting cases are those where *p* resists any of these forms of reduction. (Davidson [1993], pp. 4–5, emphasis added)

The definitional reduction of mental predicates to explicitly physical ones, so that the mental predicate can be identified in meaning with some kind of physical process, characterized in wholly nonmental terms, is associated with Carnap, but not with an analytical behaviorist such as Ryle, nor with the topic neutral analyses, nor with any functionalist, nor computational approach. Ryle's emphasis on the "multitrack" nature of psychological dispositions ([1963], p. 42ff) rests on his belief that the manifestations of those dispositions need possess no unity as physical kinds, thereby ruling out nomological reduction, and, hence, explicit definition in terms of bodily movement. Putnam (1975) introduced the term *functionalism* as explicitly nonreductive in Davidson's sense. One of the toughest analytical functionalists, Sydney Shoemaker ([1994], p. 56), has described his position as "radically 'nonreductive,'" meaning that the functions can be multiply realized, and, hence, is neither nomologically nor definitionally reducible. These latter theories might be called *token behaviorism* and *token functionalism*, in contrast with *type behaviorism* and *type functionalism*, because they identify each individual expression of a mental state with physical behavior, or some other purely physical change, but do not identify types of mental states with types of physical process. The *topic neutral* analysis of the mental, such as are provided by Smart and Armstrong, is devised precisely to avoid defining the mental in explicitly physical terms, substituting instead terms that leave room for the possibility of wholly physical realization. But can it be denied that these topic neutral analyses are reductive analyses? As far as I can tell, Davidson shows no awareness of the existence – or, at least, the special relevance to his project – of such theories, yet they constitute paradigms of reductionism in the philosophy of mind.

IV

There are two lines of objection that might be taken against my claim that Davidson's targets are straw men and that the form reductionism has taken in the philosophy of mind is different from the form it takes in the philosophy of science. First, it could be argued that those forms of physicalism that uphold a type-type identity between mental and physical states – such as Armstrong's central state materialism – *are* reductive in the sense of Story 2. They do not adopt an explicit analysis of mental predicates in physical terms, but type-type identity seems necessarily to involve nomological reduction. Second, it might be argued that, because of the absence of definitional type reduction, token behaviorism and token functionalism, as represented by Ryle, Putnam, and Shoemaker, are neither analytic nor reductive, and so need not be among the theories Davidson is concerned to deny; they are genuinely forms of nonreductive, 'soft' materialism.

(1) *Are type identity theories reductive in Story 2?* It might seem that just because they are type identity theories they, *ex hypothesi*, meet the criteria for scientific reductionism. This is not so, however. Suppose Theory 1 says that *A*s cause *B*s, and that it is claimed that *A*s are type identical with *F*s in lower level Theory 2. This is not enough for a reduction of the law in Theory 1 to a law in Theory 2. This would require that there be some *G*s in Theory 2 to which *B*s are reducible. This latter condition is not met by type identity theories in the philosophy of mind. Pain, for example, might be thought type identical with some physical state-type – traditionally the firing of C-fibers. But the pain-behavior that the pains cause is not identical with some standard neurological state (obviously) or behavioral movements (physically described), for they are physically varied. If it be asked how this is possible, given the sameness of the physical cause, appeal can be made to the vast complexity of the other factors that condition our reactions: the results do not correspond to the types of any lower-order science. So the mere type identity of the mental state with a neural state is not enough to reduce psychological explanation to some more physicalistic kind of explanation; it would require that the behavior they produce also be type identical with some physicalistically characterized kind. So it seems to me to be true that reductionism of Story 2 figures nowhere in modern philosophy of mind, not even in type identity theories, which makes it odd that Davidson should be at such pains to circumvent it.

(2) *That token functionalism, et al. are not analytic or reductive.* The main support for this claim comes from the fact that most functionalists deny that they are reductionists, in both the nomological and explicit definitional senses. There are four reasons why these disavowals do not possess the significance that they seem to possess. First, as the quotation from Charles shows, as a matter of fact, standard forms of functionalism are taken to be among the theories that Davidson is circumventing, and it is from this fact that much of the interest in his theories derives. Second, Davidson famously claims of his theory that

> in any case it is not apt to inspire the nothing-but reflex ("Conceiving the *Art of Fugue* was nothing but a complex neural event" and so forth) (Davidson [1970], p. 88).

It is plain that behaviorism and functionalism of any kind are apt to produce this result, for each act of thought or artistic creativity is nothing but some physical event, even if types of thought do not form physical types. 'Nothing but' reduction is ontological rather than analytic, and, as Davidson realizes, it is at the heart of the issue.

Third, a quick inspection of the writings of Ryle, Armstrong, or Shoemaker easily reveals that a great deal of philosophical analysis is required to make any kind of behavioral or functional theory square with the apparent phenomena: such analysis is what they are largely engaged in in their writings. What has to be explained is how various types of mentality can be no more than the production of something physical and observable.

The most that can be said for discounting the relevance of token behaviorism and token functionalism to Davidson's project is that, though these theories are analytic and reductionist, they are not *analytically reductionist*. The materialist reduction is factual; the analysis clarifies the concepts to show how this factual reduction is possible. This, indeed, is how Smart (1959) and Armstrong (1968) characterize their topic neutral analyses of mental ascriptions. It is not explicit definitional physicalism, it is philosophical analysis, clearing the way for a science-based physicalism. But such theories are plainly ones that a 'soft' or 'nonreductive' materialism is meant to avoid, so the fact that they are not analytically reductionist in a particularly strong sense does not mean that they are compatible with such a 'soft' materialism.

My fourth response is that even this concession to those who would deny that functionalism can appropriately be called 'analytic reductionism' is perhaps too generous when one recalls that, according to token functionalism, the physical base (construed broadly enough to include context) is a priori sufficient for the mental. Although Story 1 analytic reductionism does not require any nomological or extensional equivalence, the lower or reducing level stands in a very strong relation to the higher or reduced level, for it is conceptually sufficient for it. So, according to analytic reductionism, if a world were just like this one physically, it follows a priori that it would be just like it mentally. There is logical sufficiency of the base for the superstructure, though there could, in principle, be different bases. This rules out a priori the possibility of what some philosophers have called 'zombies' – that is, creatures with exactly similar physical states to humans (in roughly similar contexts, it is assumed) without their possessing any conscious states. This makes it natural to think of psychological predicates as topic neutral, for they refer to *whatever it is* that is organized in the right functional or behavior-producing way. The relations here are sufficiently strong to be naturally described as 'reductionist.' Indeed, the a priori exclusion of zombies, is, I think, something taken as paradigmatic of what it is to be reductionist in the philosophy of mind, for it makes passing the Turing Test sufficient for mentality, and this a benchmark for reductionism in the philosophy of mind.[2]

This is reductionism by analysis. The fact that the base is conceptually sufficient, but not necessary, distinguishes it from the positivist theories, but hardly disqualifies it from being an analytical reduction. Indeed it is essential to the topic neutral analysis of the mental as *whatever it is* that produces behavior of such and such a kind. When Putnam or Shoemaker call their theories *nonreductive*, it may surprise some philosophers, but it only shows that they are taking their sense of *reduction* from Story 2, not Story 1, and the matter is merely terminological. Because they are explicit about the nature of their functionalism, no one need be confused. But confusion is at the center of Davidson's project, or, at least, at the center of the interpretation he is given by most of his readers, for, as we shall see, the relation in which he stands to the normal forms of functionalism has been almost wholly obscured.[3]

V

Davidson's Theory, Naively and Sophisticatedly Understood

As naively, naturally, and usually understood, Davidson's theory involves a kind of property dualism that is sufficiently dualistic to render any kind of functionalist understanding of mentalistic concepts unnecessary. The theory seems to be presented as if no kind of analytic preparation of our psychological concepts is required as a preliminary for the type of token identity theory that Davidson is giving. This is because the identity in question is not between mental and physical states or properties, but between mental and physical events, where the identity of events seems to place no constraints on the nature of any monadic qualities or properties involved in the event, because it is entirely a function of causal relations.

This theory of event identity might be pictured as the 'flagpole' theory of events. The same event can be thought of as possessing or instantiating quite different properties, just as two or more quite dissimilar flags could be flying from the same flagpole at the same time. The same event could instantiate some neurological property, and also be the having of a deep-red quale, with the latter conceived in as 'qualia-freakish' way as one prefers, or be the having of some fully self-conscious thought-content. The only requirement is that the causes that bring about the having of the quale, or the conscious thought, and the occurrence of the neural event are the same, and so are their consequences.[4] The identity of the event is no more dependent on, nor does it impose constraints upon, the nature of the noncausal properties involved, than the identity of a flagpole depends on or constrains the color or shape of the flags it flies. In property and state terms, this theory permits full-blooded dual-aspect theory.

It is this theory, when combined with his doctrines of the nomological nature of causation and the anomolousness of the mental, that has left Davidson's theory open to the accusation that it entails epiphenomenalism. This accusation is put in two ways. First it is claimed that the irrelevance of mental states or properties to causal explanation is constitutive of epiphenomenalism, for interaction involves causal explanatory relevance. The second ground for the accusation is that, given the strict causal monopoly he allows to the physical, the world would have followed just the same path if the mental had been absent. There is a possible world physically and nomically just like this without the mental. It follows that the presence of the mental makes no difference and so it is epiphenomenal.

The first ground for the charge of epiphenomenalism is rendered inconclusive in two ways. First, there is a clash of intuitions concerning what interaction requires. It is possible to insist that it is mere causal relatedness that is relevant, not explanatory relevance.[5] But, second, and more importantly for our purposes, in "Thinking Causes" (Davidson [1993], p. 9ff) Davidson explains what he means by 'strict causal explanation' in a way that radically alters the situation. Most readers seem, rightly or wrongly, to have read "Mental Events" as saying that there was nothing worth calling proper causal explanation, such as applies in the physical world, operating in the mental realm. The thesis, however, turns out to be rather more specialized than this. It is that strict causal explanation operates only at the level of physics, not 'only at the physical level;' it is the science of physics that supports the rest.

> I made clear that what I was calling a law in this context was something that one could at best hope to find in a developed physics: a generalisation that was not only 'law-like' and true, but was as deterministic as nature can be found to be, was free from caveats and *ceteris paribus* clauses; that could, therefore, be viewed as treating the universe as a closed system. I stressed that it was only laws of this kind (which I called 'strict laws') that I was arguing could not cover events when those events were described in the mental vocabulary. I allowed that there are not, and perhaps could not be expected to be, laws of this sort in the special sciences. Most, if not all, of the practical knowledge that we (or engineers, chemists, geneticists, geologists) have that allows us to explain and predict ordinary happenings does not involve strict laws. The best descriptions that we are able to give of most events are not descriptions that fall under, or will ever fall under, strict laws. (Davidson [1993], pp. 8–9)

What we have here is a residue of the positivist doctrine of the unity of science. Davidson does not believe that science need be unified in the strong sense, with all sciences nomologically reducible to physics, but he does believe that only physics (and, perhaps, consequently, those sciences that are strongly unified with physics – that is, reducible as in Story 2) are the strict bearers of causal explanations. There are looser forms of causal explanation at higher levels, including the psychological, and so it becomes just as proper to explain causally human action by reference to human thought as it is, for example, to explain the destruction of a village by reference to the force of a hurricane, given that meteorology is not nomically reducible to physics. In neither the psychological nor meteorological cases are there strict causal explanations – nothing wholly deterministic or as probabilistic as nature allows – but there is what we intuitively recognize as causal explanation. If Davidson's theory allows our mental states to be causally on a par with hurricanes, it would not seem just to accuse him of epiphenomenalism. We shall see in the following text why nobody originally read him in this way.[6]

The second ground for the accusation of epiphenomenalism is also affected by the new interpretation of his theory, if not quite so obviously. The suggestion that the world would have followed just the same path if the mental had been absent only gets a hold if there is a possible world physically and nomically just like this without the mental. Denying the argument naturally involves, therefore, denying that there could be a world physically but not mentally similar to this. Davidson says that the mental supervenes on the physical, in the sense that a mental difference presupposes a physical one, but seems to apply this only to the actual world. If there is a genuine absence of property reduction, it is difficult to see how it could apply to all worlds. Though it might be a brute fact that the mental supervenes in a given world, it could hardly be a brute fact that it supervened in all – a rationale would be required. Token functionalism would provide such a rationale, but that is a form of reductionism in the sense of Story 1. In fact Davidson requires the truth of some such theory as functionalism if the relation between psychology and physics is to be similar to that between physics and other sciences that are not reducible to it. Let us suppose that meteorology is such a science. There is no logically possible world that, at the level of physics, is just like one in which a hurricane is destroying a village, but in which there is not a hurricane destroying a village: the physics base is a priori sufficient. There is no need to invoke some elusive conception of supervenience here. In the broadest sense of "logically possible," there is no possible world with the same physical base as the given one and no hurricane; the relation is one of entailment in the strongest sense. Also, the hurricane is strictly constituted by the things physics describes, and that is why there is no problem about attributing causal power to hurricanes. A hurricane is *nothing but* the action of physical particles, though talk about hurricanes is not nomically reducible to physics. It is because Davidson's readers took him to be claiming that mental properties are irreducible in a stronger sense than this that they feared he was in danger of epiphenomenalism.

The sophisticated reading of anomalous monism, which only becomes clear on reading "Thinking Causes," is, therefore, as follows:

> Strict causal laws only apply in physics and in those sciences – if any – nomically reducible to physics. All other special sciences – and that includes psychology – employ only loose causal explanations that depend on the potential availability of the tight account provided by physics. Psychology is irreducible just in the way that geology or meteorology is irreducible, and its properties are causally explanatory to a similar extent.

But this parallel with the other special sciences requires some such theory as token functionalism to preserve the conceptual sufficiency of the physical base that characterizes the relation in those other cases. If this feature of the parallel with the other special sciences is lost, the monism is lost. Mental properties lose the appropriate involvement in the causal explanatory network, for it becomes at least logically possible, in a broad sense, that the base be present without the higher properties. Hence the threat that a fully fledged property dualism leads to epiphenomenalism. There was no need for the long and ultimately fruitless literature on supervenience, or the attempt to dragoon Kripkean *de re* necessities into the mind-brain relation, both of which were meant to facilitate the combination of fully fledged property dualism with a dependence strong enough to frustrate the charge of epiphenomenalism; for such an impossible relation was never required by Davidson's program.[7] It does not face the danger of epiphenomenalism for mental properties are not, in the image used, independent flags at the same mast as physical properties; they are just high level descriptions of the array of physically present signals. Davidson's supervenience is constituted by the anomalous logical sufficiency of physics. In his own limited postpositivist project, Davidson is quite successful. He shows how there can be different descriptions of the same subject matter that are not nomically related to each other, without this rendering any of them wholly otiose in causal explanations and without impugning the unity of the subject matter. This was not, however, perhaps generally controversial.[8]

Davidson does nothing to show that this general model can plausibly be applied to the mental, for he does not discuss whether mental ascriptions can adequately be treated in the same way as meteorology – that is, whether admitting the logical sufficiency of the physical base entails too reductive an account of mentality.

Davidson concludes, in "Thinking Causes":

[s]o if (non-reductive) supervenience is consistent . . . so is A[nomolous] M[onism]. (Davidson [1993], p. 5)

As the comparison with hurricanes shows, this is correct only if one restricts the sense of *nonreductive* to that of Story 2, and positively embraces reductionism in the sense of Story 1.

VI

It might be thought surprising that I have said nothing about the famous 'normativeness' of mentalistic language, which is supposed, in Davidson's view, to be what marks it off from the physical.[9] This notion was relevant and important while it seemed that it was what explained the anomolousness of the mental and thereby explained the divide between the mental and the physical. Once we realize, however, that all or most of the physical special sciences are also anomalous, then 'normativeness,' however interesting a feature of the mental it is in its own right, is supererogatory as an explanation of the mental's anomolousness. It merely gives an extra reason for the presence of a feature that would anyway be expected in a special science such as psychology.

Near the beginning of "Thinking Causes" Davidson says that his argument "will involve some clarification, and *perhaps modification*, of the original thesis" (p. 3, emphasis added). Davidson (1987) shows these modifications being brought about. At the beginning of "Problems in the Explanation of Action" (1987) he says:

I hold that there is an irreducible difference between psychological explanations that involve the propositional attitudes and explanations in sciences like physics and physiology. (p. 35)

It is natural to jump to the conclusion, on reading such a passage against the background of his earlier work, that this particular irreducible difference between psychology and *all* the physical sciences is what makes anomalous monism possible. That would lead one to assume that anomalous monism tracked the mental-physical divide, and so was itself special to the mental. It would not lead one to think that anomalous monism was relevant to the special sciences as a whole.

Further on in the same article, Davidson reinforces the impression that the crucial theoretical divide is that between the physical sciences as a whole and psychology.

> The laws of many physical sciences are also not like the laws of physics, but I do not know of important theoretical (as opposed to practical) reasons why they cannot be reduced to the laws of physics. But there *is* a reason why psychological concepts like belief, desire, and intentional action, and the laws containing them, cannot be reduced to physical concepts and laws. (Davidson [1987], p. 45)

The in-principle reducibility of the physical sciences seems here to be important, and to be inconsistent with what he says about the irreducibility of the special sciences in the passage from "Thinking Causes" quoted in the previous section. But even on the same page of "Problems in the Explanation of Action" he appears to have undergone a change of mind.

> Explanations in terms of the ultimate physics, though it answers to various interests, is not interests relative: it treats everything without exception as a cause of an event if it lies within physical reach . . . Special sciences, or explanatory schemes, take note of more or less precise correlations between effects of certain kinds and far more limited causes of certain kinds. These correlations, of the sort we find in economics, geology, biology, aerodynamics and the explanation of action, depend on assumptions of other things being more or less equal – assumptions that cannot be made precise. (Davidson [1987], p. 45)

He then admits:

> In these remarks, I have made no distinction between a science like geology and the explanatory scheme of 'folk psychology'; the big distinction came between physics and the rest. If there is a distinction between reason-explanation and the rest, it must depend on some further feature of reason-explanations. (And of course there may be a significant sense in which geology, for instance, cannot be reduced to physics.). (Davidson [1987], p. 46)

There are two fundamental divisions: that between physics and the rest of the special sciences, especially the physical ones; and that between all the physical sciences and psychology. Davidson seems to move from believing that the divide between physics and the other physical sciences can be crossed by the relation of in-principle reducibility, to believing that it cannot. He always affirms that psychology is irreducible to any physical science. If reduction were correct within the physical sciences, the only fundamental divide would be between psychology and the rest. But if the special sciences are not reducible to physics, there remain two fundamental divides, that between physics and the rest and that between psychology and the physical sciences. The crucial question is which of these divides is doing the work in Davidson's nonreductive physicalism. What feature of psychology is it that reconciles it with physicalism; is it a feature it shares with the other special sciences, or is it something special to the mental? Davidson does not seem sure on the matter, but if what reconciles it are the logical features of anomalous monism, and if those features are present in all or most physical special sciences, then any further properties of the mental will be irrelevant to defending physicalism – psychology must bear the same relation in the relevant respects to the physical base as that in which the other special sciences stand.

The normativeness of the mental might be sufficient to show that it is irreducible and that it is anomalous, but it does not of itself show how the mental is reconcilable to monism.[10] That task can be performed either by means of the account of event identity that, on its own, left the theory open to the charge of epiphenomenalism or by closely following the model of anomalous monism that applies to the other special sciences, which, we have seen, is reductive. Davidson's clarification-cum-modification of his theory consists in acknowledging more plainly that, if epiphenomenalism is to be avoided, monism must be achieved by the latter route.

Davidson admits that his view on reduction and the special sciences in general is no different from Fodor's. It transpires that his difference from Fodor on psychology in particular consists in the fact that he is less of a realist about folk psychology than is Fodor.

> Let me make clear that in my view the mental is not an ontological but a conceptual category. . . . To say of an event . . . that it is mental, is simply to say that we can describe it in a certain vocabulary – and the mark of that vocabulary is semantic intentionality. (Davidson [1987], p. 46)[11]

It cannot be much comfort to those who wish to see Davidson as propounding a 'soft' form of materialism, to learn that his nonreductiveness rests on a kind of nonrealism about the mental that places him somewhere between Fodor and Dennett.

VII

A more systematic taxonomy of kinds of reduction and emergence will help to sort out the confusion I claim to find in Davidsonianism, and, I will argue, in much of the rest of what passes for nonreductive or 'soft' materialism, and in the debate on 'supervenience.' In decreasing strength, the positions on reduction are as follows:

(1) (a) *Conceptual reduction through the specification of necessary and sufficient conditions.* This involves the provision of definitionally necessary and sufficient conditions for being F in terms belonging to

some lower-level discourse. For these purposes, let us assume that it is ultimately physics. This is the kind of theory Davidson rejects as definitional reduction.

(b) *Scientific reduction through the specification of nomologically necessary and sufficient conditions.* The provision of nondefinitional nomological necessary and sufficient conditions for being F in terms of some lower-level discourse, ultimately physics. This is the relation between sciences required for the positivists' 'unified science.'

These together constitute the positivist program in Story 2.

(2) *Reduction of the superstructure to the base, in the sense that the base is conceptually sufficient, but not necessary, for the higher level states.* This is, I have argued, the situation between physics and all the 'irreducible' special physical sciences. Any attempt to treat the relation of the mental to the physical such as that between the special sciences and physics must, therefore, fall under suspicion of being reductionist in this sense. But it is also reductionist in a further, analytic sense. There is no controversy about the purely physical nature of the objects of the special physical sciences, for there is no intuitive problem about how a hurricane could be just a mass of particles in motion. One might say that *hurricane* is already understood functionally, as the concept of an object that behaves in a certain kind of way. No doubt, within meteorology a fairly strict definition of this sort is available. But it is far from obvious to many people that mental states can be treated in this way. This is why serious philosophical analysis is required in the attempt to render plausible the claim that psychology can be completely understood in this fashion. To render it so understandable is the objective for all those physicalist theories, reductive in the sense of Story 1, which attempt to rule out the logical possibility of zombies.[12]

(3) *(Mere) explanatory irreducibility.* This is the situation for all discourse with causal explanatory force, which is not nomically reducible to the base, but for which the base is conceptually – a priori – sufficient. This is the situation for all the physical special sciences. This kind of irreducibility is not weaker than (2), but its natural concomitant. It occupies the space vacated in the retreat from (1) to (2).

From this point it is convenient to talk not in terms of degrees of reductionism, but of degrees of emergence.

(4) *Weak property emergence.* This is the position of a property in a special science with explanatory value, but for which conceptually sufficient conditions exist in the physical base. A nominalist approach to such properties is prima facie plausible, because it is plausible to see them as just different, higher order *ways of describing* the base subject matter.

(5) *Real property emergence.* This is the status of a property with no conceptually sufficient conditions in the base for its exemplification. This is the status allowed to emergent properties by those who believed in emergent evolution. It is also the status allowed to psychological properties by anyone who allows the conceptual possibility of zombies. It involves the rejection of reduction as in (2). In the philosophy of mind, it is a realist version of a dual-aspect theory of mind. I think most of Davidson's readers thought his theory allowed for it, while also providing an original proof, via his treatment of event identity, that such real property emergence was consistent with materialist monism.

How do these theories relate to interaction between levels? Numbers (2), (3), and (4) are concomitants. The base is conceptually sufficient, but explanations are irreducible, and higher level properties are weakly emergent. There is no problem for interaction, prima facie. Hurricanes causally explain the weather and also causally explain why certain elementary particles ended up where they did, though without the same kind of strictness, perhaps, as an account in physics would supply.[13] The problem only arises with (5). It seems to me that the difference between (4) and (5) is not noticed much because the difference between (1) and (2) – or, perhaps one should say, the very existence of (2) – is generally ignored in this debate. It is as if, between the Scylla of the too strong (1) and the too weak and too dualist Charybdis of mere causal dependence between levels, there are only the murky waters of 'supervenience.' In fact there is a perfectly clear position that seems exactly to meet all Davidson's formal requirements. Unfortunately, it is what would otherwise be regarded as the standard form of reductionism in postwar philosophy of mind: namely, that given by (2), (3), and (4).

In fact, most of the debate about supervenience and 'soft' materialism has concerned an attempt to create a weak version of (5):

(5w) *Real but supervenient property emergence.* This is the status of a property with no conceptually sufficient conditions in the base for its occurrence, but with some stronger dependence on that base than the merely causal and contingent. The dependence has to be strong enough to spoil the counterfactual argument for the accusation of epiphenomenalism, by rendering the supposition that the physical might occur without the mental somehow improper.

As I shall illustrate later, the attempt to give any good sense to (5w) has run into the sand, yet this was the sense of 'nonreductionism' that most interested those philosophers of mind who wished to be nonreductive physicalists.

VIII

Why does Davidson seem not to notice the difference between the two kinds of reductionism? There are other ways of putting this question. One could ask why he fails to notice that there could be more to irreducibility in the case of the mental than the absence of nomological reduction or explicit translation. Perhaps the most revealing way of posing the question would be to ask why he does not register the difference between irreduciblity of different levels of description and the real irreducible existence of different properties. When put this way, an answer to the question suggests itself. Once again, Davidson's positivist heritage, in the shape this time of nominalism, might be the key to understanding him and why he is usually misunderstood. On the nominalist understanding, there is no other sense to the irreducibility of a property than the ineliminability by law or translation of a predicate, for there is no other sense to the existence of properties than the applicability of predicates. So the idea that mental states and properties might be irreducible in some stronger sense than that the descriptions cannot be eliminated means nothing.

It is not clear, however, that Davidson is so completely nominalist. In the passage quoted toward the end of VII, Davidson seems to demote the mental by saying that the mental is a conceptual, not an ontological category, and that seems to suggest that some predicates (presumably some or all physical ones) are to be taken realistically and some (including the mental) are to be taken nominalistically. Nevertheless, the quotation does make it clear that he is a nominalist about the mental, which is enough to rule out its real emergence. Moreover, he sometimes seems more thoroughgoingly nominalist, for example, in his defense of the extensionality of causal relations. Some of those who accuse Davidson of epiphenomenalism argue that he makes all causal relations hold *by virtue of* the physical properties involved in an event and never *by virtue of* the mental ones. Davidson rejects this way of talking.

> Given [my] extensionalist view of causal relations, it makes no literal sense
> . . . to speak of an event as causing something as mental, or by virtue of its
> mental properties, or as described in one way or another. (Davidson [1993],
> p. 13)

This version of extensionalism seems to me to work only with a thoroughgoing nominalism. If the different properties of events are essentially different ways of describing them, then they could not be expected to be efficacious in moving the world. If the only thing "out there" is the bare event, then only the bare event enters into the causal relations.[14]

But, in so far as properties are out there in the world answering to the descriptions, then it would seem natural that they had their individual impact on events. *How an event is described* would not be expected to influence what it does, but *how it is constituted* might be expected to influence its effects, with the different constituents making different contributions. Only if the distinction between constitution and description is abolished in favor of the latter can Davidson's reply to the criticism be maintained.

His nominalism about the mental, however, does not wholly explain the failure to notice the distinction between full-blown property dualism and that permitted to the functionalist, because that distinction can be brought out by asking whether the physical is logically – or a priori – sufficient for the mental. This Davidson never seems to consider. His nominalism does, however, help to make his criterion of event identity less counterintuitive. If one is a full-blown property dualist, with no logically sufficient physical conditions for the satisfaction of mental predicates, then it is counterintuitive to treat the event of, for example, the occurrence of a bright red quale or an interesting thought as the same event as the firing of some neurones: the properties just seem too separate. But if the mental ascription is similar to a large-scale description of the physical proceedings, it does not seem counterintuitive to treat them as the same event, differently described. In general, the causal criterion for event identity can be thought of as a criterion for determining whether two event descriptions from different sciences, or, in a looser sense, from different levels, with the same ultimate subject matter, are descriptions of the same event. Because of his form of monism, Davidson thinks this covers all event identities, but it need not be treated as a wholly general theory, and need not come into conflict with a suitably constrained property-based account.[15]

IX

It is not Davidson alone who is misled by the failure to notice the importance of reduction, understood as the a priori sufficiency of the base. Almost all the discussion of 'nonreductive materialism' is bedeviled by it. In this section I shall very briefly sketch four recent examples.

(1) Adrian Cussins (1992) argues that the different levels of description to which the world is subject must be "coherent" if they are to be compatible with naturalism. They fail to cohere if it is a "miraculous coincidence" that the two levels of explanation march in step, both predicting that a given body ends up at the one place, but with no rationale for how they achieve coordination. This means that some kind of rationale

is needed for why and how they fit together. Cussins leaves this as an intuitive matter, but I think that it is fairly clear that the a priori sufficiency of the base is both necessary and sufficient for this, given that no level is supposed to be without causal explanatory power. Obviously, if the base is sufficient to determine the higher levels, then it is sufficient to explain coherence between the levels, because it is sufficient to explain why the higher level should be as it is. If the base were not logically sufficient, then the causal explanatory content of the higher could, in principle, diverge from that of the base, and there would not be nonaccidental coherence between the two. So coherence is equivalent to the a priori sufficiency of the base. Cussins nowhere recognizes it as the same principle as drives the various token functionalist theories of the mind.

(2) Kim (1992) argues that, for nonreductive physicalism to be genuinely physicalist, it must treat the causal powers of a particular mental state as a subset of the causal powers of the physical system in which it is realized, thus excluding the mental from having a causal contribution in its own right. He concludes:

> ... it seems highly plausible that the only solution to the exclusion problem and the problem of the physical causal closure lies in some form of reductionism that will permit us to discard, or at least moderate, the claim that mental properties are distinct from their underlying physical properties. (p. 210)

The identification of the token mental powers with the token physical powers is exactly what token functionalism achieves. It also achieves a reductive – because purely functional – gloss on what mental properties are. But Kim, too, talks as if no one has yet come up with a theory of the kind he says is required.

(3) A similar obliviousness to the rationale of the options already available is to be found in Tyler Burge (1992), but in a more complacent direction. Burge rejects token identity and reduction, but thinks that this should not worry a materialist because of the "general supervenience" of the mental on the physical. Unlike Cussins or Kim, he shows no sign of thinking that supervenience need be given a constraining rationale. He happily adopts what I previously called (5w). This is indicative of the belief – away from which Cussins and Kim are struggling – that, once one has abandoned the reductionism of Story 2, there is no constraint on the relations of different explanatory levels. No one could simply assume this if they were aware of the rationale of the neo-behaviorist traditions in the philosophy of mind after Ryle.

(4) In a way, the most striking example of the syndrome is Searle, though because his case has been so effectively discussed I shall say even

less about it.[16] Searle compares the irreducibility of mental states with the irreducibility of liquidity to any properties of individual atoms. In his original expression of his own nonreductive materialism, he showed no sign of noticing the difference that his own use of the "Chinese Room" argument should have shown him between the cases. Namely that, in the one case, the base of atoms taken collectively was logically sufficient, and, in the other, it was not: It is a priori impossible that the atoms should be moving in the way they do when a liquid flows and the macroscopic mass that they constitute does not behave as a liquid. Again, he is victim of too generic a sense of 'nonreductive,' with its roots in the philosophy of science, not the philosophy of mind.

X

The argument of this chapter has been that there are two senses to the expression 'nonreductive physicalism.' According to one, what the antireductionist is trying to preserve is the phenomenology of the mental, in either or both its sensory and intellectual aspects, and he is trying to preserve this against attempts to cash it entirely in terms of its role in modifying behavior. According to the other, the nonreductionist is concerned with the conceptual autonomy of psychology. Much of the discussion of the latter would be as relevant for almost any of the special sciences as it is for psychology. Indeed, it seems that carrying out the discussion in terms of psychology creates confusion, by making it seem that issues that are general to the special sciences are relevant to our particular worries about physicalism and the phenomenology of the mental.

This has been a tale of misunderstanding between two cultures. On the one hand, there are most of Davidson's readers – including, I would guess, all of his British ones – who take as their paradigm of reductionism in the philosophy of mind a tradition running from Ryle, through Armstrong, to functionalists such as Putnam and Shoemaker and the computational theory of the mind. It is all more or less behavioristic, but has nothing particularly to do with the program of a unified science, nor with the elimination by translation of mental language, though it does involve an explanatory gloss, of a roughly behavioral kind, on how psychological predicates work. For them, positivism means the verification principle, and has been an historical curiosity since about 1950. On the other hand, there is Davidson and certain other American philosophers brought up in the shadow of positivist philosophy of science, for whom 'reduction' is intimately concerned with the unity of science and nominalism. The former group – call them Davidson's British readers – thought that anomalous monism was addressed to their condition.

Under interrogation Davidson reveals that his theory is really only addressed to his fellow Americans, and then only to a relatively small group of them.[17]

NOTES

1. This rationale might seem rather too ontologically based to be the positivists' reason. Carnap's reason, at the end of his (1955), is that we could not apply a variety of sciences to one problem – as we often need to do – if there were not a strict unity of the laws of the various sciences. This, I think, is only a *de dicto* way of making the same point.
2. Some functionalists claim that passing the Turing Test alone is not sufficient for the possession of a mind: one must also possess the right kind of internal causal structure. There could, according to this theory, be 'Turing zombies,' which behaved similar to humans but lacked the right kind of internal causal structure. Kirk (1994), for example, argues that such creatures would not be conscious. What view one takes on this matter is not important for my point here.
3. There is another reason for resisting the denial that Story 1 is really reductionism, and that is that *even within some of the accounts of reduction provided in philosophy of science* it is reductive. I have talked as if the type-type reductions of Carnap (1955) and Nagel (1961) were definitive of reduction in the philosophy of science. These, too, are the standards that Fodor (1974) applies for reduction, in his attack on it, as well as Davidson. But the definitions provided by Kemeny and Oppenheim (1956) and Oppenheim and Putnam (1958) are wholly consistent with token reduction. The requirements for reduction there provided are:

   > given two theories T1 and T2, T2 is said to be *reduced* to T1 if and only if:
   > (1) The vocabulary of T2 contains terms not in the vocabulary of T1.
   > (2) Any observational data explained by T2 are explained by T1.
   > (3) T1 is at least as well systematized as T2.

   These criteria are satisfied without type reduction, as are their criteria for microreduction. They are satisfied by any case in which the base is a priori sufficient, as it is in any behaviorist or functionalist account of mind. What is true is that, at this stage of the debate, not enough attention was given to what might turn on the distinction between type and token reductionism. When Oppenheim and Putnam proceed to discuss the actual reductive achievements of science, the cases are type-type. Nevertheless, it is fair to say that Davidson has chosen the easiest target, but pretends to have shot the bull. (That those who attack reductionism usually choose the easiest formulation of that idea to attack, and thereby miss important distinctions, is pointed out by Peter Smith [1992]).
4. It might be objected that it is wrong to bring qualia and similar creatures of consciousness into this debate, for Davidson is only concerned with propositional attitudes. There are two reasons for rejecting this objection. First, if Davidson's strategy does not apply to such conscious states, it hardly represents a general physicalist approach to mind. (Perhaps Davidson, like other

postpositivist Americans, is an eliminativist about qualia, and this is essential to his overall strategy. If so, it is something we should know.) Second, as Strawson (1994) has reminded those mesmerized by our neo-behaviorist tradition, thoughts can be just as much conscious states with introspectable contents as can qualia. Whatever might be the contribution of causal relations to giving thoughts their content, that content, however derived, is a monadic property of the mental event.

5. There is another argument employed by Macdonald and Macdonald (1986). They argue that the mental property cannot be idle if the physical property is active, for given the token identity of the mental event with the physical event, the instance of the mental property is identical with the instance of the physical property; so anything one does is done by the other, for they are the same instance. This argument seems to me to confuse two senses of *instance*. The fact that the same particular – be it event or object – instantiates two properties does not entail that the two property instances are identical. If, for example, a ball is red and round, it does not follow that the instance of redness is the same thing as the instance of roundness. The property instances that are realized in an object are not simply all identical with the object itself. It is, therefore, perfectly possible for the instance of one property in a particular to be causally relevant and the instance of another to be causally idle. What is true of objects as particulars is also true of events.

6. Davidson's indignation in his (1994) at having been misunderstood is exceeded only by his critics' incredulity at his protestations of injury. It seems to me that, apart from his blatantly misleading denial of 'nothing but' materialism, his (1970) is entirely consistent with his later interpretation; but his critics' misreading is entirely due to their having believed that he was saying something of relevance to avoiding reductionism as then found in the philosophy of mind. If I am correct, they flattered him in their error.

7. The fruitlessness of the literature on supervenience is, perhaps, crucially admitted by Kim (1993). An instance of the attempt to employ Kripke is Peacocke (1979). For an attempt to show that this will not work, see Robinson (1982, p. 22–4).

8. The drift of this chapter might seem to suggest that I do not believe that the issue of scientific reduction, as found in Story 2, is of serious interest, at least to the philosophy of mind. This is not my view. The argument of this chapter is that reductionism in the philosophy of mind is different from scientific reductionism, and that failure to notice this has caused much confusion. The problem of scientific reduction as discussed nowadays seems to me to have two moments. In the first, the existence of the knowing subject is implicitly taken for granted, and the question concerns the kinds of constraints that are imposed on various descriptions if they are to be taken, by the subject, to be descriptions, at different levels, of the same subject matter. I think that the a priori sufficiency of the base rationalizes such relations adequately. Extra problems arise, however, when one tries to incorporate the subject into this picture, for one then has to construe the *knowing* into the world. This carries, first, the problem of giving something such as a token functionalist account of our cognitive states, as required by Story 1, but that is only the beginning. The fact that the special sciences can be reconciled with the base via token identities when the knowing subject is given as outside the system rests on the fact that that subject can be thought of as having different

perspectives on the world and a variety of interests. It is in the light of these that he can cut the world up in ways that do not reduce in the sense of Story 2. But once these activities of the subject are integrated into the world, as relatively high-level activities, they can no longer be held responsible for the different ways of seeing the world. They themselves must be thought of as emerging from the basic reality. From this perspective, basic properties of human thought must be conceivable as natural from the perspective of the base: such properties as intentionality must emerge as a natural kind. I believe that George Bealer (1993) has shown that this is not plausible. I think it is to the credit of the positivists that they never passed through the first of these two moments. It was always their ambition to construe the natural sciences with the mind as a part, whereas, in practice, most of the discussion in the 'nonreductionist' tradition takes for granted the role of interests and explanatory strategies as making possible the different irreducible explanations. The nonpositivist view of the sciences is, therefore, essentially incomplete from a physicalist perspective. Furthermore, there is the problem that Dennett addresses in "True Believers," of why any but the most basic level should be considered real. Dennett argues that higher order patterns are objective, and that the human level is essential if we are to see ourselves and others as persons, but has no account of why this particular level of description should be *unavoidable* and not merely available (see Robinson [1994], pp. 134–5).

9. I am grateful to Dan Hutto for drawing my attention to Davidson (1987) and for persuading me that it was necessary to discuss the normativeness of mental language.

10. Ralph Walker (1993), for example, uses the ineliminability of the normative functions of reason as a ground for rejecting physicalism.

11. See the following text for further discussion of Davidson's nominalism.

12. The kind of physicalism resulting from reduction in this sense is essentially similar to that defended under the label 'strict implication' by Kirk in his (1994) and other places.

13. The problem with Kim's (1993b) attack on nonreductive materialism, in which he tries to show that the materialist must accept either reduction or elimination, is that it works as well for meteorology as it does for psychology. If he is right, there are no nonreducible physical sciences. This cannot be correct. He argues that either there is local supervenience, which should be convertible into nomological reduction, or there is only global supervenience, which would allow a difference anywhere in the base world to license any difference, however great, in the supervening world. He misses a middle position. What is required is that the difference in the higher level is somehow explained by the difference in the lower. Does this portend reduction? Houses supervene on bricks, and *house* is not definable in *brick* terms. But a minor alteration in the configuration of bricks at the other side of the universe does not license a radically different description of the housing situation in Budapest. Case-by-case explanation does not entail reduction. Not every rationale of supervenience is nomological.

14. This theory is reminiscent of Strawson's in his attack on Austin's theory of truth. When discussing the sentence 'The cat has mange,' Strawson insists that, though the cat is in the world, its having mange is 'on the side of language.' The position appears to be that, though the cat is in the world, all its

properties are language dependent. This seems to me to make no sense, and the same goes for Davidson's theory of causal relations.

15. Such a modified property-based account is sketched in Robinson (1982, pp. 13–19).
16. One comprehensive source for Searle's theory is Searle (1992). A powerful account of why any such nonreductive theory cannot work is to be found in A.D. Smith (1993).
17. Versions of this chapter have been read at the Technical University of Budapest; Eotvos Lorand University, Budapest; the University of Hertford-shire, the University of Liverpool; Trinity College Dublin; and to a discussion group in Oxford. I am grateful for the comments of many people, but especially Bill Brewer, Amita Chatterjee, Barry Dainton, Katalin Farkas, Gabor Forrai, Dan Hutto, and Adrian Moore.

7

Substance Physicalism

NOA LATHAM

How should we define *physicalism* or *minimal physicalism*? In my view, this question calls for stipulation because these are theoretical terms without a uniform use. Different views of psychophysical relations are physicalistic in different ways and to different degrees, and there is an obvious interest in clarifying and distinguishing these views and determining which are true. My aim in this chapter will be to do some of the clarifying and distinguishing. Stipulation of a unique thesis as physicalism or minimal physicalism must come with a rationale, and as I have none to offer I shall not pursue this.

Some regard physicalism as the thesis that all first-order properties instantiated in the spatiotemporal world are physical properties. I shall refer to this as *type physicalism* or *property physicalism*. It can be presented in the form of a supervenience thesis – another popular way of defining physicalism – on the assumption that a property is physical if and only if it logically supervenes on microphysical properties. This is one way, or a first approximation of a way, of characterizing a physical property in terms of microphysical properties. But as I think that the following discussion will apply on any reasonable view of physical property, I will mostly continue to talk of physical properties without getting more specific. I shall assume that it will be clear enough to think of a microphysical property as an assignment of fundamental microphysical parameters in some type of spatial or spatiotemporal region, where the fundamental microphysical parameters are those featuring in an ultimate microphysical theory.

A few decades ago, physicalism would more often have been characterized as the supposedly weaker thesis of *token physicalism* or *ontological physicalism* – the view that every token or particular in the spatiotemporal world is a physical particular. Many people who are discontented with physicalism would not be content with a mere denial of property physicalism, but are opposed to ontological physicalism. I do not share this opposition, but I think it is an interesting question that has not been satisfactorily answered, whether a coherent thesis of ontological physicalism can be articulated that is genuinely weaker than property physicalism. And of all views about mind-body relations, I think it is ontological physicalism whose truth or falsity has major practical consequences for how people lead their lives.

There are many kinds of particular to consider in inquiring what it is for a particular to be physical, the most important of which are events, objects, substances, and states. I take events of a certain class and state to be property exemplifications. For such particulars, ontological physicalism reduces to property physicalism. But I do not think all particulars are property exemplifications. Many have held that there is an important notion of particular, sometimes referred to as a concrete particular, for which ontological physicalism amounts to a weaker claim than property physicalism, and it is ontological physicalism for such particulars that is the topic of investigation here. I focus, for the most part, on providing a characterization of ontological physicalism for substances (including objects), which I shall call *substance physicalism*. Then I suggest that an analogous argument would yield an equivalent characterization for concrete event physicalism. Many have thought substance dualism a mysterious, perhaps incoherent, doctrine and token physicalism for events to be clear by contrast. Here I want to argue that substance physicalism and concrete event physicalism are equivalent versions of ontological physicalism and are best understood as the view that the world is governed by laws of succession with purely physical antecedents.

To this end I'm going to focus on mental substances, which I shall often refer to simply as minds, as the obvious candidates for nonphysical substances, and seek a characterization of a substance dualistic world, in other words, a world in which there are nonphysical minds and non-mental physical substances. The account could also be adapted to provide a characterization of a world containing vital substances or any other putative nonphysical substance.

The term *substance* may seem antiquated and unsuitable for modern philosophical inquiry, so let me clarify my usage here. It is often said that a substance is capable of independent existence, and I shall take this to be an essential feature of substances insofar as it rules out properties, because they need something to inhere in, as well as nonbasic, in other words supervenient, entities such as property exemplifications. A further feature of substances I shall take to be essential is that they are continuants, in other words particulars that occupy spatial regions and endure through time, rather than events. However, the discussion can be adapted to apply also on a four-dimensional view of substances, by reinterpreting talk of three-dimensional substances, where necessary, as talk of time slices of four-dimensional substances. On the account I'm offer-ing, substances include physical objects, as well as identifiable bits of liquid and gas that wouldn't readily be described as objects. Human bodies, brains, and nervous systems are thus examples of substances that are relevant to this inquiry, along with minds. But as minds are some-times thought not to be occupants of spatial regions, I'm not going to take spatial location or extendedness to be a further essential feature of substances.

When Descartes refers to *res extensa* and *res cogitans*, he seems to have in mind a spatially extended physical substance, the totality of matter, and a nonspatially extended mental substance, the totality of minds. But he sometimes refers to individual minds as substances in discussing their relations to individual bodies. So Cartesian substance dualism can be formulated as the thesis that there are physical bodies and nonphysical minds, or as the thesis that there is a physical *res extensa* and a nonphysical *res cogitans*. These appear to be equivalent, for if *res cogitans* is nonphysical, then the individual minds it comprises must be nonphysical,[1] and if every mind is nonphysical, then the totality of those minds, *res cogitans*, must be nonphysical. So for the sake of convenience I shall ignore these big Cartesian substances, unless otherwise specified, and focus instead on individual minds and bodies.

What is a substance dualistic world? Let us consider first a popular way of characterizing physical particulars and thereby ontological phys-icalism proposed by Geoffrey Hellman and Frank Thompson.[2] It is that every physical particular is one that satisfies a basic positive physical predicate at a place, or is a part or sum of such particulars. Those predicates are given by a list that, according to Hellman and Thompson, might include "is a neutrino," and "is a four-dimensional manifold."

One problem with this is that it is hard to make sense of a sum of particulars of different spatiotemporal kinds. Hellman and Thompson include fields along with substancelike entities such as electrons. And one might also expect a fundamental theory to contain predicates such as "is an alpha decay" and "is a measurement" satisfied by eventlike entities. For this approach to have the best chance of succeeding it seems that a restriction must be made to particulars of some spatiotemporal kind, such as events or substances, in forming sums. But in both cases it would be necessary to show how a sum is formed when there are overlaps and gaps between particulars satisfying the designated predicates. And this would clearly be revisionary in the sense that not any sum of substances or events would commonly be regarded as a substance or event.

Furthermore, it may not be clear into what spatiotemporal category to classify the particulars satisfying the various predicates proposed even by current theories of fundamental physics. Does a neutrino, photon, or quark essentially occupy a spatiotemporal region, or is it essentially capable of enduring through time? It seems better to represent fundamental physics exclusively in terms of fields rather than as dealing with microscopic events and substances.

However, the main problem with this approach is that it fails to provide an analogous positive account of what it could mean for nonphysical substances to exist in a world alongside physical substances. Some might be inclined to say that a nonphysical substance is one made from some nonphysical stuff such as ectoplasm. But it seems to me that we have no idea how to characterize nonphysical stuff, and hence no idea how any nonphysical substance could be shown to be built up from such nonphysical stuff.

What positive characterization can be offered of a nonphysical substance? If a mind is not spatially located, then it is nonphysical. But I shall argue that we can make sense of a nonphysical mind being spatially located and extended, and hence should not define a nonphysical substance as lacking spatial location or extension.

In seeking an alternative approach, let us begin with the assumption that a substance is a bearer of properties that satisfy certain conditions. A physical substance bears certain intrinsic physical properties and is spatially located and extended within a spatial region. This spatial region must satisfy certain conditions that may not be precisely specifiable, such as having a recognizable boundary given purely conventionally or in terms of different types of material. Likewise, a mental substance bears certain intrinsic basic mental properties, such as having a certain (narrow content) belief or sensation, which satisfy certain holistic coherence conditions. In each case the conditions are hard if not impossible to specify, but I do not think such specification is necessary for the purpose at hand.

Now let us consider the options for conditions under which a mental substance would also be a nonphysical substance. It might be suggested that a substance is nonphysical if and only if *none* of its intrinsic properties are physical. But such a condition does not appear to be necessary, for it would seem that a substance could be nonphysical in virtue of any intrinsic nonphysical properties it might have.[3]

Suppose, instead, we say that a substance is nonphysical if and only if *at least one* of its intrinsic properties is nonphysical. This strikes me as necessary for a substance to be nonphysical, and I do not think it would be altogether implausible to say that it is sufficient as well. On this view, if there are mental substances and any of their intrinsic properties are nonphysical, then there will be nonphysical substances. So property dualism would entail substance dualism provided that some nonphysical properties are properties of minds. This would accommodate the traditional view that one species of substance dualism is a kind of epiphenomenalism. However, it has also been thought that substance dualism is a significantly stronger thesis than property dualism, and an interestingly different one – a difference that cannot be accounted for by the minimal further condition that some nonphysical properties are properties of minds.

The only way to capture this strong view of substance dualism, as far as I can see, is to deny that having a nonphysical intrinsic property is sufficient for a substance to be nonphysical, and to add as a further condition for a substance to be nonphysical that it *play a causal role* (in virtue of the causal relevance of some of its nonphysical properties). I do not think we would be prepared to say that there are, or could be, any *physical* substances in our world that do not have any effects. In general, a substance must play a causal role. Thus I shall seek a characterization of substance dualism that requires that in order for there to be nonphysical minds in a world in addition to physical substances, those nonphysical minds must also play a causal role in virtue of the causal relevance of some of their nonphysical properties. I shall be aiming at a fully general characterization, in other words one that covers worlds that quite obviously don't match ours.

Substance dualist theories are typically divided into interactionist, epiphenomenalist, and parallelist theories, though I shall be pointing out later that there is at least one further kind that fits into none of these categories. Interactive substance dualism is the most natural and popular version of substance dualism. It is the view that there is interaction between substances in *both* directions. Minds and bodies certainly appear to interact. There would be physical-to-mental interaction when events such as skin piercings cause sensations such as pains. And there would be mental-to-physical interaction when mental events of deciding to do something cause voluntary movements of one's body (in action), or when thoughts or perceptions give rise to involuntary bodily movements and secretions such as trembling and sweating (in expression of emotion).[4]

Epiphenomenalism is the view that there is physical-to-mental interaction, but that minds have *no causal powers*. As should now be clear, I think that it is better classified as a species of substance physicalism. The parallelist view is that minds and bodies do not interact in either direction, but unfold fully according to laws or principles of their own special sort. I shall give an argument later that this view is probably incoherent – an argument that tells equally against the view that the world contains substances that aren't involved in any causal relations at all.

However, I do want to argue that interactive substance dualism is coherent, and to this end I want to respond to the well-known objection raised in the seventeenth-century literature, most famously by Princess Elisabeth in her correspondence with Descartes, that interaction between different substances, and in particular mental-to-physical interaction, is inconceivable.[5] It is an objection that to this day finds adherents.

Now the question how substance-to-substance causation is conceivable can be raised about all four types of it: physical-to-physical, mental-to-mental, physical-to-mental, and mental-to-physical. A good answer for Descartes to have given Elisabeth would be to say that no further explanation of the intelligibility of substance-to-substance causation is needed than that there are fundamental laws or principles of succession in accordance with which such causation occurs. How is it conceivable that the earth keeps the moon in orbit? Answer: it accords with a fundamental physical law, in this case gravity. How is it conceivable that deliberation can lead to one's choosing a course of action? In response, the substance dualist may invoke mental-to-mental laws, or state that deliberation brings before the agent's mind some available options from which a selection is made by a libertarian free choice. It is only this libertarian case that I need to describe as governed by a mental-to-mental *principle* (for lack of a better term) to distinguish it from those governed by laws. (This explains my frequent reference to laws *and principles*.) How is it conceivable that bodies cause sensations? To answer this Descartes need do no more than point to the physical-to-mental laws that he invokes in his sixth *Meditation*, where he says that "whenever [the brain] is disposed in a given way it gives the same indication to the mind."[6] And finally to the case of special interest to Elisabeth – how is it conceivable that minds cause body movements? The substance dualist should offer a similar account of the intelligibility of action and expression of emotion, this time invoking mental-to-physical laws. Indeed Descartes suggests that such an account can be offered in the case of emotion.[7] In sum, laws and principles of succession of these sorts would suffice to account for the intelligibility of any case of substance-to-substance causation, unless there were some further reason for thinking that they conflicted with other laws or logical truths, or were incoherent.[8]

Let us look in more detail at these four kinds of laws and principles. The physical-to-physical laws would state that when the fundamental physical parameters are distributed a certain way in someone's body, or more generally in a spatial region, then they will be distributed a certain other way after a specified time interval in that region. They are not fundamental physical laws, such as the inverse square law of gravitational attraction (or some more accurate law of gravitation). Rather, they are derived from such laws by taking as antecedent a physical description of a body or region of space and allowing the consequent to give a physical description of the body or region of space after a specified time interval in accordance with all the fundamental physical laws.[9] Such laws are derivable for any choice of specified time interval. Let us assume for the moment that they are deterministic. I will examine the consequences of relaxing this requirement later.

The physical-to-mental laws governing sensation would state that when a body or brain moves into a state of a certain kind, then after a specified time interval an associated mind experiences a sensation of a certain kind. To give these laws the best chance of matching our world, the specified time interval would presumably have to be less than one second. Again let us initially assume that such laws are deterministic. Descartes effectively offers such a law-based view of mental-to-physical interaction in the passage quoted previously from his sixth *Meditation*. He refers to such laws to explain thirst and pain and would presumably do so for all types of sensation.

In the case of mental-to-physical interaction, the governing law would state, for example, that whenever a mind wills[10] a certain kind of limb movement, then after a specified time interval an associated body moves into a state of a certain kind. To give the best chance of matching our world, the specified time interval would again have to be less than one second, and the kind of body state would not be the willed kind of limb movement, but rather an electro-chemical configuration of a certain kind in the brain that typically causes that limb movement through the workings of fundamental physical laws.[11] This is effectively just reversing Descartes's account of physical-to-mental interaction, as he suggests in the letter quoted previously for the case of emotion. Again let us assume for the time being that such laws are deterministic. Having the body respond deterministically to the mental act of willing should not be held to compromise the freedom of the will, for the locus of freedom on any account must be in the mental process up to and including the mental act of willing.

Mental-to-mental laws and principles are the hardest to characterize. They could be used to explain the conceivability of directed thought, as when one tries to solve a problem or remember something; undirected thought, as in free association and reverie; and finally decision making. But it is worth noting that these cases could be explained instead on a substance dualist view by way of an interactive law from mental to physical, a physical law governing a cerebral event, and then an interactive law from physical back to mental.[12] (I set aside the question whether it is possible to give a coherent account of a substance dualistic world that includes laws governing direct, telepathic communication between minds.)

Consider the case of decision making as a purely mental process, and let us focus on the act of the will embodying the final decision to do something now, whether or not one has made up one's mind beforehand. The act decided upon may involve a movement of one's body, such as writing something, or it may be a purely mental act such as thinking about a problem. Such an act of will might have followed a deliberation process involving many other decisions, such as what evidence to look for, when to spend time deliberating, when to cut off deliberation, and perhaps even how much weight to assign individual reasons. Each such auxiliary decision is amenable to the same analysis as I am offering here for the final decision.

A set of laws might say that whenever the agent sees more reason to K now than to refrain from K-ing now, then after a specified short time interval, she wills to K, and whenever she sees her reasons for K-ing and against K-ing as equal, then she has a 0.5 propensity to will to K. There could also be a more complex set of deterministic laws detailing when the agent acts irrationally. Or there could be a fully indeterministic set of laws allowing for the possibility of irrational action, saying, for example, that if an agent's reasons for K-ing now are stronger than her reasons against K-ing now, then she Ks with a propensity that is some function of her reason strengths.

But none of these views of decision making can accommodate libertarian free will. To see why, consider first a number of attempts to make sense of libertarianism within a substance materialistic framework as a view in which physical indeterminacies yield indeterminacies in mental states at suitable points in the deliberation process. For example, Daniel Dennett has discussed the point at which reasons relevant to the action do or don't occur to the agent. Robert Nozick mentions, but explicitly declines to pursue, the view that locates the indeterminacy in the weighting of different reasons. And Robert Kane locates it in the amount of effort one makes in struggling to do what one considers best when there are powerful countervailing inclinations.[13] But on a probabilistic view of physical law, such as is provided on some interpretations of quantum theory, events are accorded some propensity to occur given the laws and antecedent conditions. And this means that on a non-Humean view of law,[14] events would be regarded as being made to happen by a random procedure such as an idealized version of dice rolling. It is hard to see how the difference between an indeterminacy of this sort and full determinacy could be thought relevant to whether punishment or reward for the ensuing action is justified solely on the basis of backward-looking considerations, which is integral to the libertarian notion of freedom. This is particularly clear for the theistic view that largely fuels the quest for a coherent libertarianism; it seems absurd to think that this dice-rolling alternative to full determinacy could justify divine punishment or reward on Judgment Day.[15]

We can see now that it is necessary for a decision to be free in the libertarian sense that it not be determined or accorded a certain propensity to occur by *any* antecedent conditions, whether physical or mental. For events rendered certain or accorded some propensity to occur given the laws and antecedent mental conditions, on a non-Humean view of law, would also be regarded as being made to happen by some mechanical process or by a random procedure such as an idealized version of coin tossing.[16] A person programmed to act rationally 90% of the time depending on the toss of a coin would be thought just as devoid of libertarian freedom as one programmed to act on the basis of antecedent *physical* circumstances and the toss of a coin.

It seems, then, that libertarianism requires a special kind of substance dualistic world in which decision is neither determined nor accorded an objective propensity by reasons, yet is in some sense made for reasons. Many have described the libertarian process of decision making as involving causation by the agent rather than by antecedent conditions. But there are well-known problems in making sense of how there can be agent causation in addition to event causation, and how an agent can act for reasons without the agent's having those reasons serving as an event cause of the action. Furthermore, given that libertarian probability judgments, for example in such assertions as "it's unlikely that Clinton will resign," are not statements of propensities, some alternative account must be provided of them, and it's hard to see what this could be. But it is beyond the scope of this paper to pursue these objections. If a libertarian notion of freedom is coherent, then the only way of accommodating it within the framework of laws that I have been developing would seem to be to add to those laws a special kind of purely mental principle that I shall call the 'Principle of Libertarian Choice' – that what the agent wills to do from among the perceived options is a free decision made in the light of reasons, but not related via any law of succession, probabilistic or deterministic, to prior conditions.

I have not encountered any substance dualists who are not also libertarians. Nevertheless, in the interest of generality, I shall allow for both libertarian and nonlibertarian views of decision making in developing this characterization of substance dualism.

I have argued that substance-to-substance *interaction* is conceivable for the same reason as *noninteractive* substance-to-substance causation is conceivable, namely because it can be seen as according with the laws and principles governing a world. (Laws governing a world are either fundamental laws of that world or derivable from such fundamental laws together with some state description.) Given that a substance dualistic world contains physical and mental substances with causal powers, I now wish to argue that it can be conceived as one that is governed by laws or principles of these four types, or hybrids of them. We can represent such laws in the deterministic case in their fullest generality as taking the form $P_iM_j \rightarrow P_{ij}M_{ij}$, where the M_j and M_{ij} are complete mental properties capturing the mental states of a given mental substance, or mind, at two moments in time, and the P_i and P_{ij} are complete intrinsic physical properties (together with some relational physical properties) of an associated physical substance, or body, at those moments in time. Some of the laws may not have both a physical and a mental property in antecedent and consequent. The physical properties are complete in the sense that they consist of an assignment of all the fundamental microphysical parameters throughout the body (and throughout some surrounding region in the case of relational properties), and the mental properties are complete in the sense that they capture the conjunction of all the mental states of the mind. The double subscript is used simply to indicate that the mental or physical properties in the consequent may depend on both the mental and physical properties in the antecedent.

As formulated so far, these laws just express the generality of all possible ways that minds and bodies can causally influence themselves and each other. Nothing as yet guarantees that worlds governed by such laws contain nonphysical minds or nonmental bodies. To accomplish this and make being governed by such laws a sufficient condition for a world to be substance dualistic (and thereby take the first step toward a full characterization of a substance dualistic world), we need to add some conditions discussed earlier. We need to stipulate that some of the laws governing the world contain nonredundant nonphysical antecedents M_j, and that some laws contain nonredundant nonmental antecedents P_i.

The condition that some of the M_j are not also physical properties is necessary if there are to be minds that are not also bodies. And the condition that some of the physical properties P_i are not also mental properties is necessary if there are to be some bodies that are not also minds. The nonredundancy clauses are needed to guarantee that both bodies and minds have causal powers, thereby ruling out substance monism. For if the M_j were redundant, we'd have substance physicalism, and if the P_i were redundant, we'd have substance mentalism. When the M_j are nonredundant in the effecting of the P_{ij}, the properties P_{ij} must differ from what would have followed from the P_i alone given the fundamental microphysical laws. In that case, the laws $P_iM_j \rightarrow P_{ij}$

would commonly be described as characterizing instances of 'downward causation,' because the properties M_j are at a higher level than microphysical properties, and their instances cause effects at a lower, microphysical level.

Jaegwon Kim has raised a problem for the coherence of substance dualism that suggests that we cannot make sense of the association described previously between a mental and physical substance.[17] Suppose that the simultaneous firing of two guns A and B results in the simultaneous deaths of two persons Andy and Buddy. We would have a way of pairing the firing of A with Andy's death because we could trace a causal chain from one to the other, and there would be appropriate spatial relations between them involving the proximity and orientation of the gun. Thus we can make sense of the claim that one physical substance rather than another is causally relevant to the occurrence of a given physical effect. But if instead we have simultaneous acts of will of nonphysical mental substances (call them souls) A and B giving rise to two simultaneous arm movements in Andy and Buddy, there would be no such way of pairing A's act of will with Andy's movement. Thus we cannot make sense of the claim that one soul rather than another is causally relevant to the occurrence of a given physical effect, and hence we have no way of making sense of the association between a physical and a nonphysical substance.

I am inclined to respond that the psychophysical pairing could be grounded in laws of the form 'for all souls S, there is a unique body B such that if S wills that p, then B goes into brain state K' and 'for all bodies of a certain sort B, there is a unique soul S such that if S wills that p, then B goes into brain state K.' Kim is prepared to concede that there might be fundamental laws relating physical and nonphysical properties involving a necessary connection beyond mere correlation. So laws of this form would allow us to say that the willing of a certain soul is causally related to Andy's brain and thereby to his arm movement, but not to Buddy's brain. And they would allow us to assert such counterfactuals as 'if that willing had not occurred, Andy's arm wouldn't have moved, but Buddy's arm would have moved anyway because of the willing of a certain other soul.'

Now what establishes that it is soul A's willing that is causally related to Andy's arm movement, rather than soul B's willing? This depends on the reference of expressions 'A' and 'B.' If 'soul A' refers to the soul having proximate causal relations, in accordance with fundamental causal laws of this form, to a certain brain, namely Andy's, then soul A's willing is paired with an event in Andy's brain by way of these laws, and from there to a movement of Andy's arm by way of a story about the physical causal chain from brain event to arm movement. If 'soul A' refers to the unique bearer of a certain intrinsic mental feature, then the pairing is more circuitous. A will be disposed to will certain things characteristic of that mental feature, allowing A to be paired with some body and hence brain by way of certain characteristic bodily expressions of such willing. For example, if 'soul A' refers to the soul with a certain knowledge of topology, and if it is Andy's body, not Buddy's that writes down certain topological proofs when pressed, then A can be paired with Andy's brain. And from this the pairing of A's willing with Andy's brain event an arm movement follows. (If souls A and B are intrinsically indistinguishable, then the only way of uniquely identifying them would be in terms of the brains they are causally related to.)

This is somewhat analogous to the pairing in the purely physical case. If 'gun A' refers to the gun in region of space R, then gun A's firing is paired with Andy's death by way of a story about the physical causal chain from the firing of a gun in R to the death of a suitably spatially related person. If 'gun A' refers to the gun with some uniquely identifying intrinsic feature, such as being a certain shade of red, the pairing is more circuitous. Gun A will be disposed to cause certain sensations characteristic of that color, allowing it to be paired with some region of space (we see a gun with that shade of red in only one place). And once we can identify gun A's spatial location and orientation, we have the previously mentioned story to tell about the causal chain leading from its firing to Andy's death.

Thus I take it that we have not found any incoherence in the suggestion that a sufficient condition for a world to be substance dualistic is that it be governed by $P_iM_j \rightarrow P_{ij}M_{ij}$ laws with nonredundant nonphysical M_j and nonredundant nonmental P_i, in which quantification is over pairs of a mind and body whose association is grounded in the laws.

Adopting this sufficient condition for a substance dualistic world, we get at least one species of substance dualism that doesn't fit into the usual categories. A case in point is that in which the M_j are nonredundant in the effecting of M_{ij} but redundant in the effecting of P_{ij}, in other words the case in which there is mental-to-mental causation but no mental-to-physical interaction. A world (clearly not ours) in which this is the only way that mental properties in the antecedent of such laws of succession are nonredundant should be regarded as substance dualistic, I claim, because it allows for some aspects of thought to be independent of the physical world, for example free association, directed thought, and choosing what to think about. The mind's impotence with respect to affecting the physical world might suggest labeling this view epiphenomenalism. But this would be a misnomer because minds would have genuine causal powers to affect their own future mental states.

And adopting this sufficient condition, psychophysical parallelism would also count as a species of substance dualism. For it would appear that there could be parallelist worlds in which all minds conform to $P_iM_j \rightarrow P_{ij}M_{ij}$ laws with M_j nonredundant in effecting M_{ij} while having no influence upon P_{ij}, and P_i nonredundant in effecting P_{ij} while having no influence on M_{ij}. Yet, as I mentioned earlier, I am skeptical that parallelism is coherent, or rather, that it is a coherent view of a *single* world.

First, it encounters an epistemological problem. Defenders of the coherence of parallelism would say that our apparent perceptions of, and actions upon, the physical world are closely correlated with actual events in the physical world, and although the close correlation seems to be explained by causal relations between the world and our mental states, the two may not in fact be causally related at all but instead unfold in accordance with their own principles or laws. But if we take away the supposition of causal relations and focus on our access to our own minds, then we take away all reason for believing that there is any physical world at all, and a fortiori that there is a correlation between the content of one's mental states and a physical world.

And this introduces the metaphysical problem that if there is no causal interaction between a mind and some particular body, it is hard to see what can be meant by saying that the mind is even part of the same world as the body, let alone united to or associated with this body and unfolding concurrently with it. Leibniz uses the metaphor of two clocks perfectly synchronized to illustrate his parallelist preestablished harmony. But this seems to make sense to us only because we can imagine a spatiotemporal frame of reference in which the two clocks are side by side, ticking away at exactly the same times, but not exerting any causal influence on each other. In the mind-body case we must replace the two clocks by the physical world and some mind, and there is no independent frame of reference in which they can both be embedded to allow us to say that they are synchronized.

One might think that the metaphysical link could be established not in terms of causation, but in terms of the representational content of mental states. For example, one might say that a mind runs parallel to a particular body so long as the body closely resembles that mind's representation of a body it calls its own. But this will not do, for if there were different yet similar bodies matching such a representation of a mind there would be no determinate body to associate with that mind. And there might be no body sufficiently resembling such a representation.

Consider the case of deluded or impaired minds, or a world containing brains-in-vats as philosophers have conceived them.

Perhaps the metaphysical link could be established in some possible worlds where mental and physical substances are correlated by way of being effects of a common protophysical cause. But I cannot imagine any advance in our understanding of microphysics that would not be regarded as unearthing a deeper microphysical layer, as was the case in advancing from a molecular theory to an atomic theory to a subatomic theory.

The formulation I have offered so far of a sufficient condition for a world to be substance dualistic is that it be governed by laws $P_iM_j \rightarrow P_{ij}M_{ij}$ that quantify over mind-body pairs, in other words persons, and times, in which some M_j are nonredundant and nonphysical, and some P_i are nonredundant and nonmental. That formulation does not explicitly require that minds be spatially extended, but it is consistent with such a view. Descartes eventually conceded a kind of extension to mental substances, claiming that minds can be regarded as having the same extension as the bodies to which they are united.[18] Another reasonable view to take would be to hold that minds have a spatial extension defined at any moment by their proximate causal relations with the physical world. From now on I shall grant some such spatial extension for minds.

Consider now whether we get an equivalent sufficient condition for a world to be substance dualistic by requiring the $P_iM_j \rightarrow P_{ij}M_{ij}$ laws governing it to quantify instead over all regions of space, thereby removing all mention of substances. In comparing this with the substance-based condition, I do not think we need to worry about the fact that quantifying over different kinds of particular will require laws involving different kinds of property. That is because for every property P of a substance we can find an appropriate corresponding property of a spatial region occupied by the substance, namely the property of being occupied by something with P. And for every property P of a spatial region, there is a corresponding property of a substance occupying the region, namely that of occupying a region that is P.

I think it is clear that a world in which there are such laws quantifying over substances will be one in which there are such laws quantifying over spatial regions, because we are supposing that every substance occupies a spatial region. In the reverse direction, suppose we have such laws quantifying over spatial regions. The only way I can see in which we may fail to have laws quantifying over substances is if there are some regions unoccupied by a substance that have physical and mental properties that conform to the laws and thus do not correspond to any physical and mental properties inhering in substances.[19] However, it seems that we should grant that the world is substance dualistic if at least *some* of the nonredundant nonphysical properties M_j correspond to properties inhering in a mental substance, and *some* of the nonredundant nonmental properties P_i correspond to properties inhering in a physical substance. And if there can be worlds governed by such laws in which none of the relevant nonredundant properties correspond to properties inhering in substances, I think it would be a small but warranted revisionary step to assert that they too are substance dualistic. Thus, although it is a little broader than the original substance-based condition, I think we should also accept the condition that quantifies over regions of space as sufficient for a substance dualistic world.

Emergent properties are typically regarded as those entailing downward causation that supervene but do not logically supervene on microphysical properties.[20] So if there are emergent mental properties in a world, they will satisfy laws of the form $P_iM_i \rightarrow P_{ii}M_{ii}$ with nonredundant M_i, and where there are logically contingent supervenience conditionals $P_k \Rightarrow M_k$. This I classify as substance dualistic provided that the M_i are nonphysical properties. And indeed many would grant that properties failing to logically supervene on microphysical properties must be nonphysical, though as mentioned earlier there is room for dispute about how physical properties are to be characterized. Yet the classical emergentists held that it was an advantage of their view that it didn't require the postulation of nonphysical substances for the emergent properties to inhere in. I would agree that a view requiring the postulation of some nonphysical stuff should be rejected. But I have argued that we should not construe nonphysical substances in terms of nonphysical stuff as this would be of no use in understanding their relation to nonphysical properties and how they function in the world. If instead, as I have urged, we think of nonphysical substances simply as property bearers of a certain kind, then I think we'll see no obstacle to regarding emergent properties as inhering in nonphysical substances, or simply in spatial regions on the view I have just presented.[21]

The sufficient conditions discussed so far involve deterministic laws. Another sufficient condition for a world to be substance dualistic is that it is governed by certain indeterministic laws (traceable to an indeterminacy in substance-to-substance laws, such as indeterministic purely physical laws). We can formulate such laws by requiring that instead of a single $P_{ij}M_{ij}$ in the consequent there is a disjunction of such psychophysical properties, $P_{ij}M_{ij}$ or $P_{ij}'M_{ij}'$ or . . . , where each disjunct has a precise objective probability indicating its propensity to occur. And to provide a sufficient condition in which room is to be left for libertarian free decision, we would need the law to have a similar disjunctive consequent. But in this case, the consequent would have to be a bare disjunction without any statement of objective probabilities, and the law would need to be supplemented by the Principle of Libertarian Choice to account for which disjunct is selected. The suppression of objective probabilities in the disjunctive laws amounts to an extraordinarily strange adjustment to our conception of a law of nature, but I see no other way of accommodating libertarian choice.

Can we now say that being governed by laws and principles of one of these sorts – the deterministic, the disjunctive probabilistic, or the disjunctive libertarian – is necessary as well as sufficient for a world to be substance dualistic? A further obstacle to necessity needs to be addressed.

We might have a nonlibertarian substance dualistic world in which no $P_iM_j \rightarrow P_{ij}M_{ij}$ laws hold for any time interval, because even when P_i contains relational properties covering a large region of space, there are other persons sufficiently close whose mental properties have a downward causal influence on the physical properties that will influence P_{ij}. This can be accommodated, I think, by globalizing the necessary and sufficient conditions, reformulating them to take the laws to quantify over spatial regions that cover the entire universe, or over the big Cartesian substances mentioned earlier.

Thus we may conclude that a substance dualistic world either involves laws in which nonphysical properties play a nonredundant role in the antecedent, noninteractively or via downward causation, or it involves libertarian choice. And now finally we can define a substance physicalistic world as one that is governed by laws of succession whose antecedents are purely physical properties, in other words contain no nonphysical properties. This may seem quite a departure from the familiar construal of a substance dualistic world as containing some mysterious nonphysical stuff. But it is the only intelligible account I can find. And it seems to me to preserve everything the traditional substance dualist could want, except for the ectoplasm.

I have been treating substances as occupants of spatial regions, but I think that the argument can be adapted to hold also on the four-dimensional view of substances, as I suggested earlier, by regarding the laws as quantifying over time slices of four-dimensional substances rather than over three-dimensional substances. A four-dimensional substance is a concrete event that could be described as the life or complete history of a three-dimensional substance. Assuming a three-dimensional substance is physical if and only if its life is physical, the argument can effectively be construed as providing a characterization of ontological physicalism for those concrete events consisting of four-dimensional substances (or the lives of three-dimensional substances). We can also see how a similar argument could have been constructed to provide a fully general characterization of concrete event physicalism parallel to the one I have offered for substance physicalism. Construing nonphysical concrete events as causally efficacious bearers of properties associated with a spatiotemporal region would have led to the claim that worlds containing them are either governed by laws of succession with nonredundant nonphysical antecedents or contain libertarian choice.[22]

Ontological physicalism for concrete particulars is the view that both substance physicalism and concrete event physicalism hold. I have argued that this is equivalent simply to the view that the world is governed by laws with purely physical antecedents. And from this definition its close ties to the principle of physical closure can be seen. The basic idea behind physical closure is that the best explanations of physical phenomena are physical. Ontological physicalism can now be seen to entail physical closure, because a world governed by laws with purely physical antecedents will be one in which every physical phenomenon is fully explained by physical laws and prior physical conditions. But the converse is false. Physical closure does not entail ontological physicalism, because it holds in the noninteractive substance dualistic world we considered in which minds can perceive and think but cannot influence the physical world. However, physical closure does entail that the effecting of *physical* states is governed by purely physical laws, and this can indeed be taken as an equivalent formulation of the principle.

In conclusion, I have argued that ontological physicalism for concrete particulars is best regarded not as some primitive thesis but as the thesis that the world is governed by laws of succession with purely physical antecedents. In coming to understand in what ways the world is physicalistic, we are interested in whether all first-order properties instantiated in the spatiotemporal world are physical (on the various plausible interpretations of this),[23] whether there is libertarian choice, and whether there is downward causation. I have argued that these questions absorb the question whether there are nonphysical particulars.[24]

NOTES

1. *Res cogitans* could be nonphysical if some minds it comprises are nonphysical and others are physical. But there is no reason to suppose that some minds could be nonphysical while others are physical.
2. Hellman and Thompson (1977, p. 310). A more complex and formal characterization is given in Hellman and Thompson (1975, pp. 554–5). Their account is adopted by Post (1987, pp. 125–7).

3. I argue in my (forthcoming) that it is plausible to hold that physical entities are physical through and through, in other words they cannot have non-physical components, so that entities with a trace of the nonphysical are nonphysical.
4. A substance dualist needn't assume that the direct mental cause of these physiological manifestations is a feeling or emotion, but could allow the James-Lange view that the physiological manifestations cause the feeling or that the emotion and physiological manifestations have a common cause.
5. See Descartes (Adam and Tannery [1964], III 661–8, 684–6, and 690–5).
6. (Adam and Tannery [1964], VII 89). He does not call these laws.
7. In his letter to Chanut of February 1st, 1647, when discussing the emotion of love, he says "when the same conditions recur in the body they induce the soul to have the same thought; and conversely when the same thought recurs, it disposes the body to return to the same condition." (Adam and Tannery [1964], IV 604).
8. Descartes or some of his fellow seventeenth-century thinkers might have doubted that some of these cases of substance-to-substance causation were intelligible because they thought that such causation conflicted with some aspect of God's nature, or that A's cannot cause B's unless A's are similar to B's, have at least as much reality as B's, or are more perfect than B's. But I do not think any of these ideas provide *us* with compelling reasons for doubting the intelligibility of any form of substance-to-substance causation.
9. To fit our world the antecedent of such laws must also give as background conditions a complete physical description of a large region of space (perhaps a time slice of the whole universe).
10. For lack of a better term I use *willing* to denote a mental act that typically precipitates action, though its colloquial use (such as that of *trying*) is narrower. Some may doubt that a purely mental act of willing a limb movement can be distinguished from a composite mental and physical act of moving a limb. But in rare cases of paralysis, someone may do what she normally does in moving her arm but find the arm immobile. It is what she does in this case as well as the usual cases that I am calling a purely mental act of willing. It is a mental act that occurs on both materialistic and substance-dualistic views of action, and the question of what it is that is willed is relevant to both views. Thus I disagree with Williams (1978, p. 291), when he argues that the lack of a suitable content for such an act of willing provides a special problem for substance dualism. I also disagree that a self-referential account of the intentional content must be wrong. See for example, Searle (1983, ch. 2).
11. And in order to fit the way we experience action as continuous willing that occurs throughout the duration of a body movement rather than as an instantaneous mental triggering of subsequent movement, the substance dualist would need to provide an account of how intrusive electrical activity occurs throughout the duration of the willing. I do not see that this would be an impossible task, dooming the substance dualist to a ballistic account of action, as Williams argues, op. cit. p. 289. Likewise with the way perceptions may be continuous rather than instantaneous in the causing of involuntary physiological manifestations of emotions such as fear.

12. This is in fact how Descartes explains directed thought (Adam and Tannery [1964], pp. 360–1).
13. Dennett (1988), Nozick (1988), and Kane (1996).
14. On a Humean view of law, advocated in recent times by Lewis and Loewer, laws are construed as supervening on the facts and as providing the best systematization of those facts.
15. I take Kane's account of libertarian freedom in terms of the satisfaction of Production, Rationality, and Ultimacy Conditions (op. cit. p. 126) as failing to satisfy this essential aim of libertarianism and hence as insufficient for genuine libertarianism. Furthermore, I think his Ultimacy condition – that no other explanation of the agent's choosing A can be given apart from the agent's doing it for reasons of a certain sort by means of an effort of the will (as dictated by the Production and Rationality conditions) – fails to hold in the case in which quantum indeterminacies are the source of indeterminacy in willpower. That is because there will also be an underlying purely physicalistic explanation upon which the rationalistic explanation supervenes, in the sense that from a chain of physical conditions there will be supervenience conditionals linking each physical condition to a mental condition featuring in the rationalistic explanation. Kane says that such a physical explanation would not explain why the agent did A rather than something else (p. 137). But this seems, unreasonably, to allow nondeterministic explanations in the rational case but not the physical case, and, implausibly, to disallow all nondeterministic physical explanations.
16. This does satisfy Kane's Ultimacy condition, but as I've indicated, I don't think the satisfaction of his three conditions suffices for libertarianism.
17. See Kim (forthcoming-b). He accredits Foster (1968, pp. 64–70), for drawing his attention to this problem. See also Foster (1991, pp. 163–72).
18. In his letter of June 28th, 1643 (Adam and Tannery [1964], III 690), and in the Sixth Replies (Adam and Tannery [1964], VII 442).
19. We need not worry if a world governed by laws quantifying over spatial regions can be understood to be governed by laws quantifying over substances, but in which *different* substances feature in antecedent and consequent of the laws. For I think it is clear that such a world should be classified as substance dualistic.
20. One exception is Byrne (1993) who regards emergent properties as supervening with metaphysical (a posteriori) necessity.
21. On this view we also see how it is possible for some forms of psychophysical supervenience to be consistent with substance dualism, though not *logical* supervenience, which is ruled out if physical properties are construed simply as those logically supervening on microphysical properties.
22. Some might be inclined to think at this point that there could be alternative ways of characterizing concrete event physicalism that haven't been considered here. In "What is Token Physicalism?" (Latham [unpublished]) I reach the conclusion that concrete-event physicalism cannot be defined independently of substance physicalism, as no plausible characterization of a physical concrete event is available without closely aligning it with the notion of a physical substance. I argue there that concrete-event physicalism can be shown equivalent to substance physicalism on the assumption that all nonphysical concrete events contain the thought or activity of nonphysical substances.

23. Other questions that may go beyond the various interpretations of property physicalism concern the various kinds of supervenience on the physical, the status of the necessity of supervenience conditionals, and whether any of these supervenience conditionals hold as biconditionals.
24. I'd like to thank Alan Gabbey, Barry Loewer, Marleen Rozemond, and Dean Zimmerman for helpful comments on earlier drafts of this chapter.

8

Possibility: Physical and Metaphysical

STEPHEN LEEDS

It is a commonplace that much of contemporary metaphysics is deeply bound up with the metaphysical modalities: metaphysical possibility and necessity. To take one central instance, the mind-body problem, in its most familiar contemporary form, appears as a problem about property identities, and it is hard to imagine discussing any issue about property identity without calling on the idea of metaphysical possibility. If we want to ask whether the property of being conscious, or being in pain, or having *this* sort of pain S, is identical with some physical or functional property P – say, the property of having such-and-such neurons firing in such-and-such a way – we typically begin by asking whether I *could* have had these neurons firing in this particular way, without experiencing S. And the *could* here is the *could* of metaphysical possibility.

As we all know, these questions about what could be the case – metaphysically could – are far from easy to answer. There are, it seems to me, two features of the notion of metaphysical possibility that combine to make them hard to settle, either negatively or positively. What makes them hard to settle negatively is that because metaphysical possibility is supposed to be a kind of possibility distinct from physical possibility, styles of argument that work very well to show that various describable situations are not physically possible do not carry over to show that the same situations are not metaphysically possible. Most of us would agree that the standard correlations between brain and pain already give us excellent reasons for believing that it is not physically possible for there to be a perfect neurological duplicate of me who feels no pain at the dentist's. Whatever the principles are in virtue of which of these *are* excellent reasons – presumably some version of the idea that the same cause must always have the same effect – these principles plainly do not carry over, or do so very weakly, when we ask whether such a situation is metaphysically possible, and no analogous principles replace them.

What makes questions about metaphysical possibility hard to settle positively is the fact that the metaphysical possibility of a describable situation is supposed to be something distinct from the conceivability of that situation, and that this remains true however you might idealize the notion of conceivability (e.g., by requiring some high degree of vividness or coherence). This is why, supposing that we agree that I can conceive of my zombie duplicate in the dentist's chair, we cannot automatically conclude that such a thing is metaphysically possible. The claim that conceivability is conclusive evidence for possibility is not one that follows trivially from our notions of conceivability and possibility – it needs to be argued for. And the distinctness of metaphysical possibility from conceivability, similar to its distinctness from physical possibility, is part of what gives the notion its importance; if we could understand no difference between saying that my zombie duplicate is conceivable and saying that it is metaphysically possible, then showing the metaphysical possibility of my zombie duplicate would be entirely without interest. Why should anyone *care* that I can conceive a zombie duplicate, unless my ability to conceive it were in some way evidence for something else – evidence that (as we say) there actually could be one?

Why do we think, however, that there is such a thing as metaphysical possibility (or its correlative necessity) or that we have made sense of any notion that meets the conditions just mentioned? Here and there in the literature – less frequently than you might think – one can find philosophers who deny that we have made sense of it: typically, they acknowledge that there is a useful notion of *physical* possibility, but they attempt in one way or another to explain away our intuitions about metaphysical possibility as intuitions about conceivability. I do not think any of these attempts have so far succeeded. I do think, however, that the thing can be done, and in this chapter I propose to do it. Where I take my predecessors to have missed saying what needs to be said – this includes Hilary Putnam, whose general views on this issue come close to my own[1] – will emerge in the course of the chapter. By way of a rough indication of what is new here, let me say, first, that I think that no attack on metaphysical modality can be persuasive unless it pays due respect to the intuitions that make any identification between possibility and conceivability seem so problematic. By 'pays due respect,' I mean that one needs to show that, for example, our intuitions about the impossibility of certain apparently conceivable situations – our intuition, for example, that water's being H_3O, though conceivable, is not possible – are genuinely insights into *something* of importance – if not quite what a modalist takes them to be. And second, that the only way to pay respect to these intuitions is to take physical possibility much more seriously than antimodalists have been accustomed to. The central message of this chapter is that, if you take physical modality seriously enough, you will see what people are after when they speak of metaphysical modality.

A few preliminary matters. I will be arguing that the right sort of conceivability – about the right sorts of things – comes close enough to capturing what we want to say about metaphysical possibility to allow us – indeed rationally to compel us – to identify the two notions. I need a term of art for this sort of project, and the one I've chosen is *reduction*. I will say that we are reducing metaphysical possibility to conceivability. One hears the term *reduction* most often in situations in which empirical matters play a greater role than they do here. For a case such as the present one, in which all the argument is 'conceptual,' think of the reduction of *algorithm* to *recursive function* – in any case nothing much hangs on the term.

I will want now and then to refer, by way of an analogy, to another reductive project – one that has been so successful that we tend to forget there ever was a notion that needed to be reduced. We speak of propositions[2] as probable, or as probable given other propositions: we say, for example, that given what we know about the present-day world, it's probable that it has existed for many years. Now it is clear that, outside the very narrow domain where it makes sense to talk of *chances*, most of us don't think of the property of *being probable*, or the relation *p is probable on q* as an objective property of, or relation between, propositions. We don't think, for example, that in cases of disagreement over whether p is probable given q, there is inevitably or even usually an answer to the question as far as which of the parties is right. We don't take seriously the idea that, once all our standards have been met for saying that p is probable given q, it might nonetheless be the case that really, objectively, p is not probable given q. So our attitude toward probabilities is nonrealistic. What accounts for this? Surely it is our conviction that the notion of probability is in some sense reducible to a notion that is openly subjective – that of a subjective or personal probability assignment. Roughly, we think that for p to be probable on q is for everybody to set their personal conditional probability of p on q high.

Now, of course, this is only a first approximation. We have norms – few of which we have much of an idea how to make explicit – for setting our personal probabilities; a large part of our education consists in internalizing these norms. A reasonable gloss of 'p is probable on q' needs to acknowledge the importance of these norms, and there are various ways to do it. We might understand 'p is probable on q' as meaning that the norms constrain setting the conditional probability high. We might instead take it to mean that, in fact, everyone who follows the norms in other respects also sets the conditional probability high. That we have different options will be one of the points of the analogy

I will be drawing with metaphysical possibility, although a relatively minor one. More important are, first, that our subjective probability assignments are not justified 'internally' by our opinions about objective probabilities – always putting aside the special case of chances, you and I do not set one or another conditional probability high because of what we believe about the objective probabilities. And secondly, that our subjective assignments are not justified 'externally' by the objective probabilities – it is not the case that one tracks the other.

The general outline of the analogy is of course clear: probability corresponds to metaphysical possibility; subjective probability to *some* sort of conceivability. Exactly what sort will not appear until Section II; I will first need to say something about physical possibility.

I

I will begin by indicating – I do not think a definition is possible here – what I shall mean by 'physical' necessity and possibility. The simplest way to do this is to pretend that you and I understand both the metaphysical modalities and the term *law of nature* better than I think we actually do; then I can say that I count as physically necessary all the propositions that hold in all (metaphysically) possible worlds in which the laws of nature hold. So I am counting the law of conservation of momentum as physically necessary: likewise "2 + 2 = 4" and "water = H_2O." My use of the word *physically* should not be read as implying a special commitment to the traditional subject matter of physics. If there is a law of nature that certain physical states are accompanied by certain qualia, then it is physically necessary that one accompany the other – so it might be better to speak as Quine does of 'natural' necessity and possibility. I use *physically* because it is after all one standard usage – notice, however, that some people who talk about physical necessities mean only what follows by logic, or by logic and mathematics, from the laws of nature. Unless one counts "water = H_2O" as a law of nature, it will not be counted, in this usage, as physically necessary. As I use the term, all metaphysical necessities count as physically necessary.

I am eventually going to be offering a reduction of metaphysical modality in which physical necessity plays a central role; of course such a reduction won't be at all persuasive if one thinks that we come to understand the notion of physical necessity only in virtue of already understanding what metaphysical modality is. So this explication can't be read as a prescription for how to come to have the concept of physical necessity if you don't have it already. I intend it rather as a way to tell you how to locate, among the various concepts you already have, the one I am calling 'physical necessity.' Then how, according to me, can one acquire this concept without first understanding metaphysical possibility and necessity? By learning a practice in which it plays a role.

To say that at least one of the notions, metaphysical necessity, physical necessity, causation, or law of nature, needs to be explicated in terms of something closer to 'rules of use' than to a reductive definition, is hardly to say anything controversial. Although there are various projects for reducing some of these notions to some of the others, there is virtually no one these days who proposes to reduce all of them to nonmodal notions. What is more controversial is to claim that physical necessity is the best place to break into the circle of physical and metaphysical modality. Why not say instead that it is metaphysical necessity that we understand by learning 'rules of use'? Two reasons. First, because we would then still need to give an account of, for example, law of nature, and this is not an easy thing to do. Next, and more important, because whatever 'rules of use' control our decisions about what is and what is not metaphysically necessary are evidently not definite enough to allow us to reach agreement on more than a smattering of the cases that interest us. By contrast, we are much better at deciding what is and what is not physically necessary.

This is because of the close connection between the notion of physical necessity and the scientific practice of setting the actual against the background of the possible. Any science that claims to be explanatory rather than merely descriptive will aim at constructing a state-space of 'permissible' states of the universe and identifying a set of permissible trajectories through that state-space. It is this set of trajectories – what we might call the 'possible worlds' – that we appeal to when we explain the current state of the world in terms of initial conditions. What we show is that the actual world is the only permissible trajectory (or, a not saliently improbable one) that passes through the initial conditions. And likewise we appeal to this set of trajectories when we explain the whole history of the world, initial conditions included, by arguing that it is in some way a typical point in the space of permissible worlds. In either case, identifying the set of possible worlds is a crucial element in the project of giving explanations.

The separate sciences, and the separate parts of a single science, present us with rather limited state-spaces and sets of possible worlds: what is permissible in general relativity alone may not be permissible when one takes quantum field theory into account. But the idea of a unified state-space and set of worlds – one whose trajectories are not those permissible according to one or another science, but permissible tout court – is one that we already understand, well enough. We understand it because enough of the methodology for constructing it is already in place. Although in fact no one knows how to combine General Relativity with quantum field theory, or both with a science of qualia, if there is one, we know what to count as progress toward combining them. This is the sort of project the sciences have been engaged in from the beginning. And, of course, the set of worlds we are after is the set of physically possible, not metaphysically possible worlds. Whatever the interest may be in exhibiting all the ways the solar system might have behaved under various metaphysically possible force laws, the worlds that are crucial for *explaining* the behavior of the solar system – one might better say, the set of worlds such that to exhibit it (and to identify the boundary conditions) *is* to explain that behavior – are worlds in which gravity falls off as the inverse square of distance (roughly).

Our methodology for constructing sets of worlds – the immensely varied set of techniques, styles of reasoning, etcetera that collectively we call 'the scientific method' – involves recognizing as physically necessary both laws of nature and metaphysical necessities: conservation of momentum and "water = H_2O" both hold in all the possible worlds. Learning to use our methodology doesn't require us antecedently[3] to be able to recognize which is which. Whatever the distinction is (and I am not questioning that there is one) between the metaphysically contingent physical necessities – the laws of nature, in one reasonable sense of the term – and the metaphysical necessities, scientific practice places no weight on it at all. Open a book on quantum mechanics, and you may find the word *law* used to label certain truths about the subject – usually, relatively peripheral ones – but you will not find any attention paid, even implicitly, to the question as to which of the claims of quantum mechanics are laws in the sense of metaphysically contingent physical necessities and which are not. Is it a law that electrons have spin 1/2, or is it the case that an object wouldn't be an electron unless it had spin 1/2? Is it a law that physical systems evolve by a Hamiltonian, which has a certain connection with energy? Or is that a consequence of what energy *is*? Our texts don't care about such issues, and I think we know the reason: the texts concern themselves only with setting up the set of physically possible worlds – they are treatises on what worlds are physically possible, so far as we can learn from quantum mechanics – and in these worlds metaphysical necessities and laws of nature hold equally. That the metaphysical necessities hold also in a wider class of worlds is, however interesting it may be in other contexts, of no interest here.

Against this, it might be said that what appears in the textbooks is only a finished product. Although the metaphysically necessary and the (contingently) physically necessary appear on an equal footing in what a completed science identifies as the possible worlds, it might be that some of the reasoning along the way requires us antecedently[4] to distinguish metaphysical necessities from laws of nature, or indeed – what would be equally damaging for our reduction – to put the notion of metaphysical necessity to use in some other way. I think the only way to argue for either of these alternatives is to produce a persuasive example in which our reasoning about the physically necessary requires us to make use of metaphysical modality. I know of no such examples; in particular, I do not think that we can produce the required sort of example merely by discovering a case in which our grounds for believing some p to be physically necessary in fact warrant the conclusion that p is metaphysically necessary. There is indeed a great deal of scientific reasoning that is a priori, or broadly conceptual, or that depends on checking to see what we can and cannot conceive, and much of this reasoning issues in propositions that are metaphysically necessary. But it does not follow that we note this fact, or need to, in using the same reasoning to establish that some p are physically necessary. There is no reason to suppose that, in concluding that p is (presumptively) physically necessary, on the grounds that we find not-p inconceivable, we need *first* to argue that p is metaphysically necessary and *then* to conclude that it is physically necessary. We can, and in scientific contexts typically do, move directly from the inconceivability of not-p to its truth in all physically possible worlds.[5]

So the notion of physical necessity is one that we can reasonably claim to understand independently of metaphysical necessity. It is in fact the modality on which our common speech has the firmest grasp: the educated man or woman in the street says, without seeming to equivocate, that you can't build a perpetual motion machine, or trisect the angle, or make water out of helium. What he or she needs to be talked into (our students certainly require a lot of persuading) is the idea that there is a sense of *can* in which there can be a perpetual motion machine after all. Of the other physical modalities, 'law of nature' is I think best understood via physical and metaphysical necessity – in other words, as metaphysically contingent physical necessity.[6] As for causation, I take it as obvious that there is no way to explicate 'law of nature' or, for that matter, metaphysical necessity in terms of causation. I do think one can explicate causation in terms of physical necessity and metaphysical necessity, and therefore in terms of physical necessity alone, but that won't concern us here.

II

The project of reducing metaphysical possibility to some kind of conceivability is one version of a familiar idea that we might call *conceptualism*: the thesis that in talking about metaphysical modality we are really talking about, in a broad sense, our concepts. Some other versions of conceptualism include the view that the necessary is what in some sense follows from conventions, rules of use, or the structure of our innate lexicon.[7] All these accounts have lately fallen on evil days, and it will be helpful at this point to review how this has happened.

The problem for conceptualism that has seemed to so many of us to be fatal is that raised by the a posteriori necessities. Take for example necessities of origin: let us suppose, for the sake of an example, that we agree that a man, say Clinton, must have come from the egg he in fact did. Then the difficulty for the conceptualist is that, although it's necessary that Clinton came from egg E (supposing he in fact did), 'Clinton came from E' is not a priori, so 'coming from egg E' is presumably not part of the concept 'Clinton.' Now can't a conceptualist claim that it *is* a conceptual matter – a fact about the concept *man* – that a man comes from the egg he actually comes from? If we can agree to this, then perhaps we can see our intuition that Clinton must have come from egg E as really an ellipsis – what we mean to say is that a man must (conceptually must) come from the egg he comes from; also, Clinton is a man, and he came from egg E.

Well, what's wrong with this? For someone who takes de re necessities as seriously as Kripke did in *Naming and Necessity*, the suggestion is, of course, completely beside the point. For Kripke, it is simply a fact about this object, Clinton, that he necessarily came from egg E. I suppose Kripke would allow that we are free to invent a concept, say *man*, and stipulate that it is to apply to an object only if that object has the same origin in all possible worlds. But, for him, this cannot have very much to do with whether Clinton necessarily came from this egg. Rather, if we do invent such a concept, we will then need to ask whether Clinton falls under it; and the answer to this question will lead us right back to ask whether he has the same origin in all possible worlds.

Despite the intuitive pull of Kripke's position, it does not seem to me that his irreducible de re necessities have carried the day, even among philosophers who are otherwise realists about modality. Instead, committed modalists can now choose among a great variety of pictures, all of which agree on, in one way or another, attributing the necessity of Clinton's coming from this egg to something similar to the concept we apply to Clinton. We can say, with Lewis, that all counterparts of Clinton, under one particular counterpart relation, come from the same egg as the actual Clinton. And there is at least a close connection between this particular counterpart relation and the general term *man*. For example, I signal that I have this relation in mind by saying 'I don't mean the same lump of flesh or collection of atoms: I mean the same *man*.' And other accounts run variations on the same idea: one can for example say that there is an individual concept 'Clinton' that we apply to an object in another world just in case it shares origins with the actual Clinton.

So one can take modality seriously and still allow a certain kind, or degree, of conceptualism. Of course this doesn't much look like the conceptualism we began with: it's all about possible worlds. But can't we see the possible worlds as just a metaphorical way of saying what the reductive conceptualist wants to say? Namely, that just as our intuition that rabbits are necessarily animals really comes down to the fact that 'rabbits are animals' is a priori, which itself rests on the fact that our concept *rabbit*, our convention governing the use of *rabbit*, or the innate position in the lexicon into which we've inserted *rabbit*, requires us to accept the inference from 'a is a rabbit' to 'a is an animal,' so it's part of our concept of *man* that we can't call *d* a man unless *d* has the origins he actually has.

Unfortunately, putting things this way is entirely empty. One can't make a convention that no one is to count as Clinton if he doesn't share Clinton's origins. That already goes without saying, as it goes without saying that no one counts as Clinton unless he shares Clinton's path through space-time, or indeed any property whatever of Clinton's. Of course we might make a convention about a particular egg that somehow fell into our hands, that we will call a man 'Clinton' only if he issues from this egg; but such a convention, although one we could make, is plainly not one that we do. And, of course, we can make a convention about telling stories. You tell me stories about variously described people, and we'll agree that you won't call anyone 'Clinton' unless you also say that he comes from the same egg as Clinton really does. But if our intuitions about necessity of origin are to be taken seriously – if we are, as I said earlier, to pay them due respect – they cannot merely be intuitions about how we might choose to tell stories. At the very least, one has to connect our storytelling conventions with something we do in a serious context.

I've put the point in terms of conventions, but of course it goes for any form of conceptualism. If concepts are anything similar to rules for identification or rules for what to say or what to think, then there is no way to make sense of the idea that the concept 'Clinton' or 'man' has necessity of origin built into it unless we also propose to identify Clinton in other possible worlds. Allow in possible worlds, and the idea becomes a natural one: one can reasonably make a convention to the effect that a creature in another world will count as Clinton only if he shares origins with the man before us. In fact, it is arguable that Kripke's discussions persuaded many of us to adopt such a convention. And where it makes sense to have an explicit convention, it also makes sense to have an implicit rule or an innate rule. The lesson of the example is that, unlike the rule to call things rabbits only if they're animals, which I might decide to adopt or which might reasonably be part of my innate conceptual endowment, even if I was not concerned to make identifications in other worlds, the conventions governing necessity of origin are empty if confined to the actual world. They are essentially conventions concerning what to call things in worlds other than this one in terms of how they are related to things in this world.

So a conceptualist really needs possible worlds. Indeed, I suspect that part of the reason that Kripke is so much less 'conceptualistic' than, for example, Lewis is that he is also less realistic about possible worlds. Notice however that there's nothing here that requires the full galaxy of metaphysically possible worlds. All that the example shows is that one needs *some* notion of alternate worlds, so that you can have a convention or a rule that whoever is the Clinton in them must share origins with the actual Clinton. And these could just be the physically possible worlds. Certainly if you want to speak about physically possible states of affairs involving Clinton, it would be good to have a convention stipulating or at least restricting who is to count as Clinton in them.

Let me make the same point, or close to it, with another famous example. Water is H_2O, and, let us suppose, necessarily so. How close can we come to giving a conceptualist account of this necessity? Well, someone might argue that our concept of water is that of compositional stuff or, more weakly, that our concept of water is such that, given that all the lakes and streams are predominantly filled with one chemical compound, it follows that, for us, nothing will count as water unless it has that composition. Let us assume, for the sake of the example, that this is correct. Now, could it have been that all the lakes and streams had been filled with some compound other than water, which behaved indistinguishably from it? Of course, we all say. Suppose you disagree: according to you, under the conditions described, the lakes would still have been filled with water, only water with a different chemical structure. Then, we say, you've misunderstood our convention. Our convention is not to call water whatever is chemically similar to the stuff in the lakes and streams, it's to call water whatever is chemically similar to the stuff that's *actually* in the lakes and streams. Now this is a distinction without a difference, unless we're planning to deal with some nonactual lakes and streams. But, again, these don't have to be metaphysically possible lakes and streams; if I want to identify water in other physically possible worlds, and I think there are some worlds with various compositionally different liquids that have the superficial properties of our water (or even if I'm not sure in advance whether there are any such worlds or not), it would make sense to adopt a convention governing what is to count as water, and a convention about composition is plainly a reasonable one.

This is the main idea about how a conceptualist can handle a posteriori necessities. As it stands, it can't be quite right. As you read the clause in parentheses in the last sentence, you probably said to yourself, "But what if I *am* sure there are no such worlds?" This, and related difficulties, can best be handled after we restate the same idea in the context of what I think is the most plausible form of conceptualism – one that talks about conceivability rather than conventions. Our ideas about conventions and rules of use are really, I think, theories about why some things are conceivable and others not. I suspect they're incorrect theories. I think what we can conceive depends more holistically on what we already believe than these accounts allow; in any case, I don't want to be relying on them. Talking about conceivability has in addition a certain dialectical advantage; people who take metaphysical modality seriously (and those are the people to whom this chapter is primarily addressed), whatever they think about conventions and rules of use, will agree that there's something to the idea of conceivability, however vague it may be at the borders – after all, it's their main epistemological tool.

For the project of reducing metaphysical possibility to conceivability, the delicate question about conceivability is not whether there is such a thing, but whether our reduction has the right to use it. Let us consider the analogy with objective and subjective probability. If all a reductionist could say about subjective probability was that to assign a subjective probability of, for example, 2/3 to a proposition p was to be in a state in which one was willing to offer two-to-one odds on p, then I think we would not find a reduction of objective to subjective probability persuasive. For we have said nothing to rule out the possibility that to assign p subjective probability 2/3 is just to believe that it has objective probability 2/3. The reductionist project would have failed if our notion of subjective probability had turned out to depend so directly on that of objective probability. The project would also be threatened by subtler dependencies between the two notions. For example, if it were the case that, even though no particular assignment of subjective probability to a particular p requires a particular belief about objective probabilities, nonetheless the entire practice of assigning subjective probabilities is so closely tied in with beliefs in objective probabilities that if you delete objective probabilities our talk about subjective probabilities fails in some way to cohere or make sense. For an analogy, think of the way that talk about appearances fails to cohere when we delete all mention of physical objects.

In the case of conceivability, the most blatant way in which the notion of conceivability might presuppose metaphysical modality would be if it turned out that to conceive that p *is true* is to believe p metaphysically possible. This seems unlikely, given our sense that, much of the time, we come to believe that a certain p is metaphysically possible via discovering first that we find p conceivable. But there are other, less blatant ways in which one notion might presuppose the other. It might be that to conceive p is to take an epistemic attitude toward p that makes sense only *in relation to* the attitude of believing p possible. Conceiving p might be in some way taking p prima facie as possible. This is the sort of idea that is suggested by Steve Yablo's phrase, 'conceiving involves the appearance of possibility,' and indeed Yablo's analysis (Yablo [1993]) of what it is to conceive that p is explicitly an analysis in terms of possible worlds.

The situation is saved in the case of the reduction of objective to subjective probabilities by our conviction that, whether or not there exist objective probabilities, there is a story to be told about the rationality of making our way in the world by setting subjective probabilities, and then going on to update, for example by conditionalizing, as new information comes in. Notice that this sort of story is appealing even if we have little to say about the details of how we set up probability assignments. The reason is surely that we don't think that our rationale for setting up our probability assignments would be clarified if we did bring objective probabilities into the story. Always with the exception of chances, we don't use our antecedent knowledge about objective probabilities to help us set subjective probabilities. Of course one might say that, whether we know it or not, the objective probabilities guide our subjective probability assignments, but most of us are unwilling to put forward so mysterious a picture. Rather than treat our subjective assignments as dictated by a faculty of intuition into the objective probabilities, we prefer to say that the subjective assignments are constrained by rough rules, some perhaps innate, some perhaps taught – by our human or twentieth-century or personal sense of what's natural.

Can we make sense of a notion of conceivability that has an analogous independence from any ideas about metaphysical modality? I think we can, but to do so we need to use the word *conceive* a little differently from the way in which, since Kripke, many of us have been using it. We can't allow ourselves to say that, being convinced that Clinton came from egg E, I now can no longer conceive that he came from egg E', or that if I once took myself to conceive that he came from E', I was mistaken about what I conceived. Not that there is no sense of *conceive* in which we can say these things, but I would not want to try to argue that one might learn *that* sense without understanding metaphysical modality. Our judgments about what we conceive here seem on the face of it to be driven by our views about what's metaphysically possible.

The notion of conceivability that our reduction needs is that in which it is appropriate to say that even though I am convinced that Clinton came from egg E, I can conceive his having come from a different one. This is the sense of conceiving in which being able to conceive that p amounts to being able to understand what someone who asserts p is claiming; it is regarding p as something that is available as an option for me to believe. If you suggest that Clinton came from a different egg than E, I do not immediately say, "Oh, that's inconceivable; you must be thinking of someone other than Clinton"; instead, I take the claim to be an intelligible claim (as it happens, a necessarily false one) about Clinton, and one that needs to be argued against – for example, by inspecting the DNA or birth records. And I know what it would be like to be convinced, finally, that you were right.

Under this conception, it is a sufficient condition for p to be conceivable (*for me* – this sense is always relativized to a person and a time) that p has for me a subjective probability greater than zero. Are there p that I find conceivable even though the probability of p, for me, is zero? There are attractive pictures of our cognitive economy – I'm thinking in particular of the account offered by Isaac Levi[8] – in which we at all times have a large core of "accepted" beliefs to which we assign a probability of one. Levi thinks of this core as typically containing a great variety of empirical propositions, including many whose negations are conceivable in the present sense: for example, some laws of physics might be found in the core. Of course, Levi may be wrong about this, but it seems to me that, given the impreciseness of subjective probability assignments and the fact that some conceivable propositions are plainly very unlikely, one would be unwise to try to identify the conceivability/inconceivability line with the line between zero and nonzero probability. So I think it's reasonable to suppose with Levi that a proposition can be conceivable in the present sense even though its probability is zero.

Allowing that there are propositions that you might become convinced of, but that have for you probability zero, leads to a more realistic picture of our epistemology than a classical Bayesian can offer, but also leads to one in which difficult new questions arise. Because one cannot rely on conditionalization to shift beliefs in and out of the core, one needs some other account; much of Levi's work has been concerned with just this issue. Suppose you disagree with me about whether whales are mammals, but the proposition – sentence – "whales are mammals" is a core sentence for me. Then how am I to give your view a hearing, to reassess the evidence pro and con, when, for me, the conditional probability of all whales are mammals is one on any evidence whatever? In Levi's terminology, I contract my core: I retreat to a position neutral on the question at issue and then assess the evidence. How do I choose the appropriate neutral position? Speaking for myself rather than for Levi, I think that this question is quite similar to the question, how do I choose my subjective probabilities, given a particular core? There are regularities about this: some normative, some that no one has thought about enough to decide whether to impose them as norms or not, some deep, and some trivial. There is no reason to think they settle all the cases you might think up, but plenty of reason to think they settle a lot of ordinary ones, because you and I can, by and large, predict each other's subjective probabilities or neutral positions.

This gives us a clue to what the importance of conceivability might be. The p we can't conceive are the p for which the usual contraction procedures in one way or another fail. Either we can't see how to contract, or we see various ways, but they all lead to theories that are in some way inadequate as a background from which to assess p. Putnam's one-criterion words provide cases where what goes wrong is most nearly on the surface: I know how to give up my belief that all bachelors are un-married – nothing easier – but what do I do now by way of figuring out whether you're right about *this* married man's being a bachelor? I've contracted into a theory in which I have no reason to say anything about anyone's being a bachelor, one way or the other. But I think that there are many cases where we sense that something goes wrong with con-tracting, but it is much harder to say what. You suggest that I give up one case of transitivity of identity. I can perhaps think of ways to do this, but now I'm left with a position from which assessing the evidence for your view is still not something I see how to do. It would be nice to be able to say exactly what goes wrong here – that is to say, it would be nice if we understood what conceivability amounts to better than we do – but I think for present purposes the notion is clear enough.

Does a conceptualist have the right to use this notion? In other words, is it a notion that we can make sense of without appealing to metaphys-ical necessity? It is, of course, not the case that in this sense of conceiv-able, what is conceivable by me, or even a wonderfully idealized version of me, is metaphysically possible. No matter how much you idealize my conceptual abilities, I may forever be able to conceive both the truth and falsity of the Continuum Hypothesis, or Clinton's coming from a different egg. There is this much connection between what we can conceive and what is metaphysically possible: that usually we conceive that p if and only if we conceive possibly p. I would not overrate the significance of this, however. Of course we all know that if p is true, so is possibly p. It is likewise the case that once I've taken it as an intelligible hypothesis that p could happen, I often can make sense of the hypothesis that it actually is happening. But this needn't always hold. Although I can understand the claim that there is a possible situation in which right now I'm completely unconscious or no longer exist, I'm not so sure I would know what to make of the suggestion that that's actually the case – what neutral position to which I might retreat to assess the merits of that hypothesis.

So this plainly very epistemic notion of conceivability is the one I offer as, for our purposes, suitably independent of metaphysical modality. Although you need to understand the notion of metaphysical possibility to find a statement about metaphysical possibility conceivable, there is no reason I can see to suppose that our conceivability judgments about the actual or about the physically possible require us to have grasped the notion of metaphysical modality. This is a notion of conceivability that would remain important to us if we had no conception of metaphysical modality at all. Of course this doesn't rule out that "externally," so to speak, there's some connection between conceivability and metaphysical modality – that an explanation of why we draw the line between conceivable and inconceivable in just the places we do will somehow call on metaphysical modality. Notice, however, that for such an explanation to undercut our reductive project, it must show the modal facts not merely as summarizing our conceivability judgments; it must show the modal facts being the way they are as in some way accounting for our making the conceivability judgments we make. So far as I can see, this can only happen if there is a causal influence of modal truth on our conceivability judgments, in other words, a faculty of modal intuition. As at a similar point in the case of the reduction of objective to subjective probabilities, I think we should believe this only as a desperate last resort.

III

We now have the ingredients in hand for dealing with the a posteriori necessities. Putting them together is not entirely straightforward, however, and I think I can best show you why I put them together as I do by comparing what I want to say with what Putnam says in a very interesting article (Putnam [1992]) that seems not to have been widely noticed. In that article, Putnam takes positions on physical possibility and on conceivability, which are very close in spirit to what I have been saying here. His discussion of metaphysical modality comes right after a discussion of conceivability, which Putnam here, as elsewhere, treats as an epistemic notion. In his account of metaphysical modality, however, conceivability plays no role. Rather, Putnam says in effect: what we count as metaphysically possible is what we allow to be true in stories we tell about imagined situations. We have conventions about how to label things in the stories – not Clinton [my example: SL] unless the same origins as the actual Clinton; not water unless H_2O. Now part of this seems reasonable enough, especially given that Putnam looks with a friendly eye on physical possibility. We want to describe Clinton in other physically possible situations, so we have a convention about origins, etcetera. Putnam's imagined situations extend, however, beyond the physically possible. It is presumably physically necessary that H_2O is a fluid above 32°F (at standard pressure). Suppose we tell a story in which things behave a little differently – H_2O remains frozen up to 60°F. Then does water remain frozen, in this story? It is clear that Putnam thinks the answer to this sort of question is: yes, our convention extends that far, or anyway we can decide to make it extend that far. But now, what is the point of having conventions about how to describe physically impossible situations, if you really don't think there are any? Putnam has nothing to say about this, and yet surely there's a natural answer. We are interested in stories about situations that we take to be physically impossible because sometimes they are epistemically possible – in other words, conceivable – and we have a strong interest in epistemic alternatives to our own theory: what you think physically impossible today you may come to believe tomorrow.

Putnam does not give this answer. Indeed, he can't, since the stories we want to tell do not match what we find conceivable. Clinton's having an origin other than egg E is conceivable, but our stories rule it out – that's why Clinton's originating from egg E turns out metaphysically necessary. I take it that this is the reason that Putnam does not connect his discussion of imagined situations with his earlier discussion of conceivability: whatever the point may be of imagining physically impossible situations, it cannot be to test what we can and cannot conceive. The trouble is that, once you sever the connection between the stories we tell and the activity of figuring out what we can and can't conceive – in other words, regard as in principle believable – you've lost your best chance at saying *why* anyone would tell stories about imagined situations, or why it might matter to us how we ought to describe them.

Here is, I suggest, what we ought to say. The alternative theories of the world we want to consider are, similar to our own theory, theories about both the actual and the physically possible. The Kripke-Putnam intuitions are indeed, as conceptualists believe, intuitions about what we allow epistemically – what we can conceive. But what we can and can't conceive are not alternative worlds; rather they are whole theories about the actual and the possible together – the physically possible – and the relations between the two. Believing that Clinton came from egg E, we don't rule out theories in which Clinton actually came from E' as conceivable alternatives to our own. What we rule out are theories in which Clinton actually came from E but in a different physically possible world came from E': these are the theories we find inconceivable. The intuitions about a posteriori necessity are thus intuitions about both epistemic and physical possibility. They concern the epistemically possible relations between the actual and the physically possible.

What then, is metaphysical possibility? Let's begin by saying what it is for an agent S to take a proposition p to be metaphysically possible. S takes p to be metaphysically possible if she can conceive the conjunction of possibly p (physically possibly) with the "appropriate" facts. Different notions of what counts as an appropriate fact lead to different notions, or different strengths, of metaphysical possibility. The two extreme options are to count every truth as appropriate, and to count none. The first leads to a very restrictive version of metaphysical possibility. For example, my flying through the air unaided would be ruled out as metaphysically possible, in virtue of the truth that it is physically impossible for me to do so. The second isn't restrictive enough – it counts Clinton coming from E' as metaphysically possible.

The choice we make in practice lies somewhere between the two extremes. it is almost correct to say that we count as appropriate all facts about the way the world actually is – the Humean truths, in Lewis's phrase. That the lakes and streams are actually filled with H_2O counts as appropriate, as does the fact that I *don't* fly through the air; the fact that I *can't* do so does not count as appropriate, because it goes beyond a description of the actual. Working through our formula, you'll see that this allows me to take my flying through the air to be metaphysically possible, but not water as H_3O. The reason I think the characterization isn't quite right is that facts about Clinton's actual origins count as appropriate – what rules out Clinton's coming from egg E' is his actually having come from E – and facts about a man's causal origins are facts not merely about the actual, but about the physically possible too. So we need to say that, although the appropriate facts never include the whole truth about the physically possible they often include some facts about the physically possible. I think this is because we are a little Davidsonian about causation: we tend to think of at least the singular facts about what caused what as ground-level constituents of the actual world. This goes for all of us, not just those unskilled in modality. When David Lewis imagines a talking donkey in some world, he is imagining a donkey participating in some causal process – this too is going beyond the Humean description of that world. In principle I suppose we might limit ourselves to Humean descriptions of the actual, but it seems clear we don't. We allow some causal facts to count as appropriate, without perhaps deciding in a principled way just where to draw the line.

That's what it is for an agent to take p to be metaphysically possible. We speak of p being in fact metaphysically possible, as we speak of p being probable tout court – not just for you or me – by idealizing the agent. A big part of conceiving involves calculation: if you ask me to conceive some p, I need to see how to embed p in a wider theory, how to change my own theory to accommodate that wider theory – someone can in various ways not foresee how the calculation would go in detail. We idealize the notion of conceiving by imagining ourselves able to see it all – no hidden contradictions; no failures to conceive simply in virtue of a sentence being too long or complicated to process. Another direction of idealization is that what you can conceive depends somewhat on your theory of what's actual and possible. I think it is natural to count as ideally conceivable what you would conceive if you had the correct theory – again of the actual and physically possible. And, of course, we have norms for conceiving: what we can conceive has something to do with what contracted theories we find acceptable, and this is a norm-governed matter. The ideal conceiver follows the norms, whatever they are. All of this enables us to make a little sense of a contrast between thinking p is metaphysically possible and it actually being so. Not as much as we wanted, or thought we had, I believe, but let me postpone this issue until I've dealt with the prior question: why should we accept this as the right analysis of metaphysical possibility?

Here's why. First, it's extensionally correct, or largely so: clear cases of the metaphysically possible will work out metaphysically possible according to our formula and conversely. The reader will want to test this against examples (see the end of the chapter for the important case of mathematics). I predict you will find that the examples work out well, and I want to suggest a blanket reason why this is so. Suppose you think some p is metaphysically possible. Then you will find conceivable the conjunction of 'p is metaphysically possible'; with the truth about the actual – indeed, you will believe this conjunction. Will you also find conceivable the conjunction of 'p is physically possible' with the truth about the actual? Here it is important to bear in mind our admonition not to take the "physical" in "physically possible" too seriously. There is a huge difference between physical and metaphysical possibility, but the difference is entirely in what we take as a sufficient reason for a judgment of physical versus metaphysical possibility. The conceivability of p is little evidence for 'p is physically possible,' and is easily overruled by other considerations; it is much better evidence for 'p is metaphysically possible.' This is a big difference, but it's not a difference in what you might call the content of the two notions. It's hard to see what might count as being able to conceive the metaphysical possibility of some p without being able to conceive its physical possibility.

Next, given that our formula accommodates the clear cases: why think it in fact captures what we are after in talking about metaphysical modality? Because the notions of physical modality and conceivability are indispensable for us, and our suggested analysis of metaphysical possibility is a natural way to put them together. What's more, it's an important way to put them together. It's one that is of deep interest as shedding light on the conceptual structure of our theories. Why not suppose that we have already been working with this idea, under the name *metaphysical possibility*?

I've been arguing that our reduction is right; now I want to return to the question, whether it is all too right. That is, whether in allowing that metaphysical possibility has to do with ideal conceivability, we are in effect leaving everything where it is: whether every interesting question about metaphysical possibility simply reappears in the new format. My hope rather has been to walk the line that good reductions always walk – one captures the important distinctions, and in some way the essence of what drives them, but the impossible questions get trivialized. I think this is exactly what happens here. The metaphysical possibility of my having exactly my current neural configuration but being in pain isn't one whose answers depend crucially on the distinction between conceiving and idealized conceiving. It is obvious that we can conceive what the dualist asks us to conceive; there is not the slightest reason to think that thinking more about the implications of the dualist hypothesis will expose hidden difficulties in doing so. Of course, in principle, all this might shift if we changed our conceptual scheme in radical ways, but I think that in all but the most troubled sciences it is generally reasonable to suppose this won't and shouldn't happen. So 'there are physically possible zombies' is, we have a right to believe, ideally conceivable, as is the conjunction of 'there are physically possible zombies' with whatever might turn out to be the truth about the actual, however materialistic – say, that everything is made out of particles and fields. So our zombie duplicates are metaphysically possible. Of course, none of this has any interest whatsoever – as I said at the outset, my ability to conceive a zombie duplicate can only matter if it's evidence for something else – either for physical possibility or for metaphysical-possibility-other-than-conceivability. The latter doesn't exist in this framework. Of course, my ability to conceive a zombie duplicate is extremely poor evidence for the physical possibility of anything at all.

Finally, mathematics. The view about mathematics that, on this account, leads most easily to the metaphysical necessity of mathematics is a plain old-fashioned Platonism. In this view the pure sets are entities that actually exist, about which we can conceive neither the possible nonexistence of the ones that actually exist, nor the possible existence of other ones. If you try to tell me about a possible situation in which, say, you have the finite von-Neumann ordinals but not the omega that collects them, I don't understand how it is supposed to be that the omega that exists in the real world is somehow absent in the situation you describe. If you tell me about a situation in which there is some new subset of the integers, I can't see how it can be that that subset does not exist already. So the truths of mathematics are metaphysically necessary in this account, and, of course, physically necessary too. Of course, what you and I can conceive does nothing to explain the genuine necessity of mathematics – its physical necessity. I think that to be a realist about any kind of necessity – and the position taken here is meant to be realist about physical necessity – is to abjure any explanation of the necessary in terms of what you and I say or think. The present account does explain the metaphysical necessity of mathematics in terms of what we can conceive, and that's to say that our position is not a realist account of metaphysical necessity.[9]

NOTES

1. Although I had arrived at most of the views set out here before I happened across Putnam (1992), the resemblance between my ideas and his – up to a point – is hard to miss. I do not find this at all surprising: my first introduction to the topics of this chapter was as a student of Putnam's back in the 1960s, and, similar to everyone in our profession, I have kept learning from him ever since. I'm happy to be (for once!) agreeing with him in print – indeed, as I hope, taking his positions a little further in a direction he would approve.

2. I often speak of propositions, rather than sentences, for stylistic reasons: it sounds intolerably odd to me to speak of probable *sentences*. But my usage can always be replaced by talk of sentences and translation, in familiar ways.

Similarly, what I say about *concepts* can be replaced by talk in terms of translation.

3. I say "antecedently" because, after all, I do think we have a usable notion of metaphysical possibility: one that we can explicate once we have in hand the notion of physical necessity and a certain notion of conceivability. What I am denying is that, in order to learn the practice in which our understanding of physical necessity consists, you need already to be able to draw distinctions involving metaphysical necessity.

4. "Antecedently" again, for the reasons in Note 3.

5. Next, causation. Lewis thinks one needs metaphysical modality to analyze causation, that one needs to look at physically impossible nearest worlds. I disagree, but the issue doesn't run very deep: his use of metaphysically possible but physically impossible worlds will turn out consistent with my reduction. That is, the worlds in which small miracles happen are metaphysically possible on my account as well. So I can claim that we first understand physical necessity, then (via our reduction) metaphysical necessity, and then causation. I suspect there is a kind of bootstrapping involved here: the notion of causation in place, we can allow it to play a role in the reasoning by which we decide which worlds are physically possible. (I might mention that I am in fact skeptical whether an analysis of causation really needs to draw on physically impossible worlds. Lewis's reasons for thinking so are deeply bound up with his views about the direction of causation, views that I for one do not find persuasive.)

Here are some specific cases in which our reasoning about physical necessity might be held to "pass through" reasoning about metaphysical modality. To begin with, much scientific reasoning involves talk about properties. I agree with David Lewis that, in the context of metaphysical modality, one can think of a property either as an extension across possible worlds, or else as an ordered pair of extension and something along the lines of a Fregean sense. Let the available possible worlds be limited to the physically possible worlds, and exactly analogous options present themselves; both notions have some claim to be called the notion of *physical property*. To the extent our reasoning about physical possibility needs any notion of property at all, I suggest that one of these two will do.

Finally, mathematics. My view about mathematics is standardly Platonist: I think the pure mathematical sets exist in this and all physically possible worlds (the impure sets exist where their elements do). For reasons set out in the text, I do not think our reduction is threatened by the recognition that some of our reasoning about mathematics is a priori. There are however non-Platonist views of mathematics that are incompatible with our reduction, for example Geoffrey Hellman's claim in his (1989) that the axioms of set theory should be read as asserting the (metaphysically) possible existence of certain structures that don't actually exist. If true, this account would place metaphysical modality at the heart of our mathematical reasoning, and indeed in a way that the reduction I will propose cannot accommodate: Hellman's thesis and my reduction jointly entail that the Continuum Hypothesis and its negation are both metaphysically possible. I disagree with Hellman's account on independent grounds – I do not see why the claim that there could exist some vastly transfinite number of objects should be any more plausible than the claim that there actually exist that many sets – indeed, if the objects are supposed to be concrete, I'm not sure I understand how so many concreta could exist, whereas if they are supposed to be abstract, I do not understand how they could not exist already. (For my positive views on mathematics, see the very end of this chapter.)

6. What about breaking into the circle of modalities by giving an explication of *law of nature*? The best known attempt at an explication is Ramsey's idea, as taken up and improved by David Lewis, according to which a law of nature is (that which is expressed by) a sentence describing a regularity that would show up as a theorem in any deductive codification of the truth about the world that had the appropriate balance of simplicity and strength. Even if this is right, it will not lead to an explication of metaphysical necessity – not even if we allow ourselves to use the notion of physical necessity as well. The reason is that we cannot identify the metaphysical necessities as the physical necessities that are not in Lewis's sense laws of nature. We plainly cannot do so if "water = H_2O" qualifies as a law of nature, whereas if "water = H_2O" does not so qualify, then either "Burning hydrogen in oxygen produces (only) water" or "Burning hydrogen in oxygen produces (only) H_2O" must also fail to be a law of nature (else, by deductive closure "water = H_2O" would be a law after all). But then whichever of the two fails to be a law of nature will be wrongly counted as metaphysically necessary.

   In any case, I do not think that the Ramsey-Lewis idea can be right: our two sentences about burning surely should be counted as laws of nature – how then can we avoid counting "water = H_2O" as a law of nature too? My suggestion is that we should not try to avoid this. The natural notion here is precisely the one that puts "water = H_2O" in the same category as our laws about burning: not *law of nature* but *physical necessity*.

7. There is a use of *concept* in which a concept is a property-like entity that is in some way what our mental tokens are "about" – if indeed our thinking is not held to manipulate them somehow directly. That's not what's meant here: the sorts of conceptualism I have in mind are those in which the relevant sense of *concept* is something closer to a Mentalese word: what is crucial here is that the notion can be explicated without drawing on modal metaphysics.

8. See for example, Levine (1980), passim.

9. I would like to thank Brian Garrett, Jerry Katz, and Barry Loewer for helpful comments on earlier versions of this chapter.

Part II

Physicalist Discontents

9

The Roots of Reductionism

SCOTT STURGEON

Humans live in quotidian contexts. We plan trips, cook meals, and do the wash. Our time is spent within narrow boundary conditions. Our thought needn't stray from the commonplace. Our expectation needn't stray from everyday possibility. For this reason, we're disposed to mistake the contours of quotidian possibility for those of intelligibility. Yet the resulting bias is a kind of modal tunnel vision. We overlook certain conceptual possibilities. We discharge others due to their alien face alone.

In this note, I locate four features of everyday life. They generate blinkered expectation that large builds from small without remainder. I note they're contingent features of reality at best, discuss how they might fail, and use that discussion to unearth quotidian bias in two spots. First, I claim the stock argument for physicalism rests on unsound presuppositions induced by everyday life; second, I claim the stock expression of physicalism is modally misguided due to such presupposition as well.

The Roots

Everyday life renders common sense reductively oriented. There are four reasons why. Three are widely recognized. The fourth is not.

(A) In quotidian contexts: the large is the small writ big, and the small is the large writ small. Conceptually identical phenomena appear on different levels of scale. For instance: large-scale objects have shape, and so do their smaller cousins; large-scale objects have color, and so do their smaller cousins; large-scale objects move, and so do their smaller cousins. Differences across level are not differences of type. They are differences of scale alone. One range of concepts is apt for both levels. *Large and small are conceptually homogenous* (LASCH).

(B) In quotidian contexts: the properties of complex objects add up from properties of their constituents. Complex synchronic facts are nothing but complexes of lesser such facts. For instance: large-scale objects have shape, but those shapes are nothing but sums of smaller shape (and relational) facts; large-scale objects have weight, but those weights are nothing but sums of weight of smaller parts; large-scale objects have color, but those colors are nothing but aggregations of smaller colors. In each case, bottom-up reductions exist for large-scale phenomena. Quotidian properties (and relations) are *bottom-up reductive properties (and relations)* (BURPs).

(C) In quotidian contexts: macrochange is explained by microchange. Large-scale diachronic facts are produced by independent change in smaller facts. For instance: large-scale objects change shape, but those changes spring from independent change of smaller spatial facts; large-scale objects change weight, but those changes spring from independent change of smaller weights; large-scale objects change color, but those changes spring from independent change of smaller color. In each case, bottom-up explanation exists for large-scale change. Quotidian change is *bottom-up change* (BUCH).

(D) In quotidian contexts: a property is realized by other properties only if it's realized whenever it could make an appearance. A property is always realized or never realized. Realization is all or nothing. For example: large shapes are realized by lesser shapes throughout everyday possibility; large weights are realized by lesser weights throughout everyday possibility; and large colors are realized by smaller colors throughout everyday possibility. In each case, a quotidian realizee never appears unrealized, nor could it within everyday life. Such properties are realized throughout everyday possibility. They show *modally invariant realization* (MIR).

Within the sphere of quotidian possibility, then, reality is conceptually homogenous across levels of scale, filled with bottom-up reductive properties, bottom-up explicable change, and modally invariant realization. Everyday life is LASCH. Everyday properties are BURPs. Everyday change is BUCH. Everyday realization is MIR (Sturgeon [1994], [1998]).

These are the roots of reductionism. Common sense is reductively oriented because (A)–(D) characterize everyday life. They generate reasonable expectation that large builds from small without remainder. Within quotidian life, after all, that's how things work.

Pulling the Roots

(A)–(D) needn't have characterized reality. Consider how things might have been:

LASCH-free reality. It's not necessary that large and small facts are conceptually homogenous. One way to state Sellars's puzzle, in fact, is in just these terms: quotidian facts and microscientific facts are conceptually heterogeneous. The concepts involved in their canonical conception seem starkly unrelated. For this reason, one wonders how microscientific facts add up to quotidian facts. One wonders whether the two blend into one reality. The puzzle has bite precisely because conceptual homogeneity prompts reductionism. Once it's lost – as we find across the manifest and scientific divide – the viability of reductionism is unclear. Not only is it unnecessary that large and small are conceptually homogenous, then, it's not even true they're so homogenous.

BURP-free reality. It's not necessary that properties are bottom-up reductive. After all, it's one thing for a property instance to be small. It's quite another for it to be basic. The former issue concerns scale alone. The latter concerns whether the instance is something over and above other facts, whether it belongs in the minimally complete description of things. The issues pull apart. They generate four conceptual possibilities: a property might be large scale and basic; large scale and reductive; small scale and basic; or small scale and reductive. The first three are relatively uncontentious. The fourth normally goes unmentioned.

But consider the color-cube world. In it substantivalism about space is true. And colors are fundamentally instanced by one-cubic-foot regions of space. There are pink cubes and blue cubes and yellow cubes, say. And they perdure: cubes persist by having temporal parts. Further, cubes have their own mechanics. Their creation, destruction, and movement is fully described by closed theory. Smaller-scale facts don't come into it. But there are such facts in this world. Small tiles move about that are normally invisible. They have no color. When one slots into the surface space of a cube, however, its surface instantly participates in the color instance of that cube.

In such a world, large- and small-scale color facts are conceptually homogenous. But the latter reduce the former. Small-scale color facts are nothing over and above large-scale color facts in which they participate. We have top-down reduction of color. We have top-down reduction of conceptually homogenous properties. Not only is it unnecessary that properties are bottom-up reductive, then, it's unnecessary that LASCH properties are so reductive. Our quotidian world isn't like that, of course, but it might have been.

The point does not rest on the coherence of color playing its role in this story. It rests merely on the intelligibility of that role. Even if color cannot sensibly fill its role in the color-cube world, it's a sensible role to fill. It's intelligible that properties fill it. No incoherence results from the thought that large-scale property instances explain their smaller-scale cousins. Perhaps such properties make no appearance in our world. Perhaps they're alien properties. That doesn't matter. What matters is that properties can sensibly fill their role in the color-cube world. It's conceptually possible. And when they do, we have top-down reduction of conceptually homogenous properties. It's unnecessary that properties are bottom-up reductive.

BUCH-free reality. It's not necessary that change is bottom-up explicable. After all, it's one thing for change to be small. It's quite another for it to be basic. The former concerns scale alone. The latter concerns whether it belongs to the minimally complete list of explainers. The issues pull apart. They generate four conceptual possibilities: a change might be large scale and basic; large scale and derivative; small scale and basic; or small scale and derivative. Here too the first three are more widely recognized than the fourth. But we can easily see how to make sense of the latter. Just augment the color-cube story: add that cube and tile movements relate so that changes of tile color are due to cube movements. When a tile goes from pink to blue, say, that fact springs from color-cube movement. Small shifts of color are produced by large shifts in color. Small color change is derivative. It tags along with color-cube movement.

Or consider the box-and-ball world. In it there are large-scale boxes and small-scale balls. The boxes have their own mechanics. Their creation, destruction, and movement is fully described by closed theory. Small-scale facts don't come into it. Further, balls remain still unless their center occupies that of a box. When that happens, the counterpoints remain coincident. Balls move because boxes do.

In such a world, large- and small-scale movements are conceptually homogenous. But the former yield the latter. We have top-down explanation of movement. We have top-down explanation of conceptually homogenous change. Not only is it unnecessary that change is bottom-up explicable, then, it's unnecessary that LASCH change is so explicable. Our quotidian world isn't like that, of course, but it might have been.

Once again the point rests on the intelligibility of the example's form. Even if colors cannot sensibly fill their role in the dynamic color-cube story, and even if box and ball movements cannot sensibly fill their role in the box-and-ball story, the roles are nevertheless sensible. It's intelligible that properties fill them. No incoherence results from the idea that large-scale change explains small-scale change. Perhaps such change makes no appearance in our world. Perhaps it's alien change. That doesn't matter. What matters is that change can fill its role in these stories. It's conceptually possible. And when it does, we have top-down explanation of change. It's unnecessary that change is bottom-up explicable.

MIR-free reality. It's not necessary that realization is modally invariant. A property might be basic in some worlds and derivative in others. So far as intelligibility goes, in fact, a property might be basic and derivative in one world. Were that to happen, some but not all of its instances would belong to the minimally complete description of things. Take dispositions. Orthodoxy says they need categorical realizers. If correct, they show modally invariant realization. But orthodoxy doesn't seem right. For it's coherent that dispositions are realized by other dispositions. There's no conceptual need for categorical realizers. Indeed, it's even coherent that *bottom-rung* dispositions are basic, that they simply go unrealized. And if one were to appear elsewhere in a world's realization hierarchy, some but not all of its instances would be basic. Some but not all would belong to the minimally complete description of things. The disposition would be basic and derivative in one world. The idea is perfectly coherent.

For example, large-scale objects spin, and they do so derivatively. Their spin consists in cross-temporal relations between smaller-scale parts. Their spin is realized phenomena. The spin of electrons, however, isn't like that. It does not consist in cross-temporal relations between smaller-scale parts. Electrons have no smaller-scale parts; *a fortiori* they lack parts that realize spin. Spin is basic and derivative in the actual world. Some but not all of its instances belong to the minimally complete description of things.

Some will say two notions lay behind the single word *spin*: everyday spin and scientific spin. They'll say the former is conceptually tied to realization while the latter is not. They'll insist *spin* takes different truthmakers in science and everyday life. On their view, a single word stands for distinct phenomena within distinct explanatory practices. If that's right, *spin* doesn't name a property that makes basic and derivative appearances in reality.

But it doesn't seem right. After all, it's no accident the everyday word gained use in microphysics. Spinning electrons and baseballs take one quantified treatment (via the so-called rotation group). And just as electron spin helps explain electron movement in a magnetic field, baseball spin helps explain curveballs, sliders, etc. The use of *spin* in microphysics is unlike that of *color*. There's nothing colorlike about microphysical color. (Roughly: microphysical color is that upon which the strong force acts.) There's much spinlike about microphysical spin.

But even if spin cannot sensibly fill its role in the spin story, it's a sensible role to fill. It's intelligible that properties fill it. The thought that a property is basic in one world and derivative in another is coherent. So is the thought that a property is basic and derivative in one world. Perhaps such properties are alien to our world. That doesn't matter. What matters is that properties can play this role. It's conceptually possible. It's unnecessary that realization is modally invariant.

The Overdetermination Argument

Most philosophers of mind are physicalists. But they're microreductionists as well. They believe actuality is exhausted by microphysical reality. And they base their view on (a generalization of) the Overdetermination Argument (OA):

(1) Mental events have macrospatial effects (e.g., arm movements).
(2) Such effects are constituted by quantum spatial events (e.g., quantum tunneling).
(3) Every quantum spatial effect has a fully disclosive, purely quantum history.
(4) For spatial events C, E, and E*: if C causes E and E constitutes E*, then C causes E*.
(5) The spatial effects of mental events are not generally overdetermined.

Therefore:

(6) Mental events are quantum events.

OA rests on several quotidian prejudices. Some are false. Still others beg the question. And the truth value of the former undercuts the viability of the latter. To see this, consider two spots where quotidian tilt is prominent.

First, premise (4) is meant to be obvious. Yet only when large and small are conceptually homogenous is it obvious that causation rides atop spatial composition. Otherwise, it's not at all obvious (Sturgeon [1988]: 423ff). In effect (4) assumes:

(i) large and small spatial properties are LASCH,
(ii) large spatial properties are BURPs, and
(iii) large spatial change is BUCH.

But now we're in trouble. For consider:

- Quotidian and quantum spatial phenomena are conceptually distinct. There's a conceptual gap between them. In fact, superposition and projection open a conceptual Grand Canyon between the two. The large and small of OA are conceptually heterogeneous. Assumption (i) is false.
- Assumption (ii) assumes microreduction for large spatial facts; and (iii) does so for large spatial change. Yet OA is meant to establish such reductionism about reality. Assumptions (ii) and (iii) beg the question. They presume (some of) what OA sets out to prove: namely, that micromonism is true of reality.
- Because large and small are conceptually heterogeneous, it's unclear quotidian spatial properties are BURPs, and unclear quotidian spatial change is BUCH. The truth value of OA's false presupposition undercuts the viability of its question-begging presuppositions. Assumption (i)'s falsity undercuts (ii) and (iii).

The details here are subtle and unsettled. But the take-home message is neither: OA rests on unsound everyday prejudice in favor of microreduction.

Second, OA is meant to be causally univocal throughout. Premise (5) aims to preclude effects standing on the catching end of a single relation twice over. In turn this is meant to combine with (1)–(4) so as to entail (6). But the entailment requires quotidian and quantum causation are a single relation writ to different levels of scale (Crane [1995]; Sturgeon [1998]). In effect OA assumes:

(iv) large and small causal relations are LASCH,
(v) large causal relations are BURPS, and
(vi) large causal change is BUCH.

But now we're in trouble again. For consider:

- Causal notions make no explicit appearance in the postulates of quantum theory; and when they do show their face – say, in application or discussion of wavepacket collapse – the notions at work are probabilistic. Orthodox quantum-theoretic causation is probabilistic causation. Quotidian causation is not. It's conceptually deterministic. That's why the founding fathers of quantum theory took it to force *revision* of our ordinary causal notion. Quotidian and quantum causation are conceptually heterogeneous. Assumption (iv) is false.
- Assumption (v) assumes microreduction for large-scale causation, and (vi) does so for large causal change. Yet OA is meant to establish such reductionism about reality. Assumptions (v) and (vi)

beg the question. They presume (more of) what OA sets out to prove: namely, that micromonism is true of reality.

- Because the large and small of OA are conceptually heterogeneous, it's unclear quotidian causal relations are BURPS, and unclear quotidian causal change is BUCH. Once more the truth value of a false presupposition undercuts the viability of question-begging presuppositions. Assumption (iv)'s falsity undercuts (v) and (vi).

Here too the details are subtle and unsettled. But the take-home message is neither: OA rests on unsound everyday prejudice in favor of microreduction.

Modest Physicalism

Most philosophers of mind are physicalists. But they're modally modest as well. They say reality is purely physical, but admit it might have been otherwise. When pressed to say how physicalism might have failed, however, full-blown reductionism shines through. The response is inevitably this:

(*) Mental properties might have been realized by nonphysical properties. They might have been realized by "ectoplasm," for example. And if they had been, physicalism would have been false. Because mental reality isn't – but might have been – something more than physical reality, physicalism is contingently true.

Forget ectoplasm (whatever that is). But note (*)'s hardened reductionism. It allows mind to be realized by nonphysical properties. But it requires mind to be realized by something. In effect (*) presupposes:

(vii) Mental properties enjoy MIR throughout all possibility.

Once (vii) is in place, (*) is the only "modesty" left to a physicalist. Yet its reductionism about mind is decidedly immodest. Mental properties can never add to a world. They can only be realized by nonmental properties. According to (*)-based physicalism: it's contingent that mind deflates to matter, but necessary that mind deflates. Mind is perforce an ontic-free ride.

This is yet another quotidian tilt to reduction. In everyday life a property is realized somewhere only if it's realized everywhere it might show up. In general that's not so. A property can be realized in one world and basic in another. A property can be both realized and basic in one world.

Truly modest physicalism should make modal space for irreducibly mental facts. It should say something such as:

> (MP) Mental properties are realized by physical properties. But that's contingently so. They might have been realized by nonmental properties. They might have been simply basic. In the latter case, mental properties would have genuinely contributed to the world. They would have belonged to the minimally complete description of things. They don't in fact do that, but they might have.

MP says our world is purely physical. It also says the mind could have been basic. It's a truly modest physicalism. Its absence from the literature, and the ubiquity of (*), spring from yet another unsound reductive prejudice induced by everyday life.

Prospects

There's good news and bad news for physicalism. I close by speaking to each:

(1) The good news is simple. Physicalism can be weaker than previously supposed. Once MIR is unmasked as quotidian bias – and dropped as a constraint on the form physicalism might take – the view can become truly modest. It can say not only that mind contingently shrinks to matter, but that mind contingently shrinks full stop.

This lowers the physicalist's burden of proof. It generates a burden-lifting asymmetry, for instance, between zombies and ghosts. (Recall zombies are physically similar to us but lack minds; and ghosts are mentally similar to us but lack realizing bodies.) The standard view is that physicalism precludes the possibility of either. Once MP is distinguished from (*), however, incompatibilities become asymmetric. Zombies are incompatible with MP and (*). But ghosts are incompatible with (*) alone. Their possibility poses no threat to MP. To establish truly modest physicalism, then, one needn't rule out the possibility of ghosts. One need only rule out that of zombies. To establish (*) one must rule out the possibility of zombies and ghosts. It's easier to establish MP than (*). And that's good news for physicalism.

(2) The bad news is simple. OA rests on prejudice induced by everyday life. Some of its presuppositions are false. Others beg the question. And the truth value of its false presuppositions undercuts the viability of its question-begging presuppositions. Thus physicalism needs a new argument, one based on uncontentious premises, one freed of quotidian bias. It's unclear what that might be. And that's bad news for physicalism.[1]

NOTE

In Sturgeon, S. 2000. *Matters of MIND*. Routledge, Sections 6.8–6.11.
1. For helpful discussion I thank Marcus Bremer, Dave Chalmers, Tim Crane, Dorothy Edgington, Steve Laurence, Barry Loewer, Mike Martin, David Papineau, and Maja Spener.

10

The Significance of Emergence

TIM CRANE

This chapter is an attempt to understand the content of and motivation for a popular form of physicalism, which I call *nonreductive physicalism*. Nonreductive physicalism claims that although the mind is physical (in some sense), mental properties are nonetheless not identical to (or reducible to) physical properties. This suggests that mental properties are, in earlier terminology, *emergent properties* of physical entities. Yet many nonreductive physicalists have denied this. In what follows, I examine their denial, and I argue that on a plausible understanding of what *emergent* means, the denial is indefensible: nonreductive physicalism is committed to mental properties being emergent properties. It follows that the problems for emergentism – especially the problems of mental causation – are also problems for nonreductive physicalism, and they are problems for the same reason.

The structure of the chapter is as follows. In the first section, I outline what I take to be essential to nonreductive physicalism. In the second section I attempt to clarify what is meant by *emergent*, and I argue that the notion of emergence is best understood in terms of the idea of emergent properties having causal powers that are independent of the causal powers of the objects from which they emerge. This idea, 'downward causation,' is examined in the third section. In the final section I draw the lessons of this discussion for the contemporary debate on the mind-body problem.

Nonreductive Physicalism

In his discussion of the mind-body problem in *The View from Nowhere*, Thomas Nagel claims that

> what is needed is something we do not have: a theory of conscious organisms as physical systems composed of chemical elements and occupying space, which also have an individual perspective on the world, and in some cases a capacity for self-awareness as well. In some way that we do not now understand our minds as well as our bodies come into being when

these materials are suitably combined and organised. The strange truth
seems to be that certain complex, biologically generated physical systems,
of which each of us is an example, have rich nonphysical properties.[1]

It seems to me that the position Nagel describes, and the conception of
the problem this position generates, are quite widely held in current philosophy of mind.[2] According to this position, mental properties are not
physical properties, yet Cartesian dualism is false: minds are 'biologically
generated physical systems,' yet mental properties are 'nonphysical' and
'come into being' when the elements of thinking organisms are 'suitably
combined.' Furthermore, according to Nagel, the mind-body problem
consists in the fact that we do not understand how these claims can all
be true. For Nagel, and for many others, the mind-body problem is
not solved by physicalism – rather, physicalism is what gives rise to the
problem.[3]

I shall call the position described by Nagel, 'nonreductive physicalism.' Nonreductive physicalism is characterized by (at least) the following two theses:

Distinctness: Mental properties are distinct from physical properties.

Dependence: Mental properties are properties of physical objects.

Nonreductive physicalism can therefore be distinguished from the
property or "type" identity theory on the one hand, and Cartesian
dualism on the other. The identity theory asserts that mental properties
are identical with physical properties, which is the denial of *Distinctness*;
and Cartesian dualism asserts that mental properties are properties of
mental substances, which is one way of denying *Dependence*. The
commitment to Dependence is what makes nonreductive physicalism
physicalism, and the commitment to Distinctness is what makes it nonreductive. (*Nonreductive* and *physicalism* have meant many things in
recent philosophy. Here I intend these terms simply to be labels for the
characteristic positions expressed by the principles of Distinctness and
Dependence.)

In recent years, nonreductive physicalists have felt the need to distinguish their own doctrine from a doctrine that, similar to theirs, upholds
Distinctness and Dependence: this is the doctrine that the mind is emergent.[4] According to those who hold this doctrine – emergentists – mental
properties are distinct from physical properties, Cartesian dualism is
false, and mental properties "emerge" from complex arrangements of
matter in a way that is inexplicable from the perspective of the sciences
of matter. Emergentism was held to be the truth about many nonphysi-

cal (or "special") properties by a number of British philosophers of the late nineteenth and early twentieth centuries.[5] More must be said to clarify this doctrine, but the essential idea of emergentism is that special properties "emerge" from their underlying physical substrates, in a way that cannot be predicted or explained from the perspective of the sciences of these physical substrates.

So why do nonreductive physicalists distinguish themselves from emergentists? Terence Horgan claims that according to emergentism, the laws that determine the emergence of higher-level properties are "metaphysically and scientifically basic, in much the same way that fundamental laws of physics are basic; they are unexplained explainers."[6] And this, Horgan claims, is what must be denied by any form of physicalism or materialism:

> A materialist position should surely assert, contrary to emergentism, (i) that physics is causally complete (i.e., all fundamental causal forces are physical forces, and the laws of physics are never violated); and (ii) that any metaphysically basic facts or laws – any unexplained explainers, so to speak – are facts or laws within physics itself.[7]

Horgan's view is that emergentism denies that nonphysical facts and laws (e.g., psychophysical laws) must be ultimately explicable in terms of physical facts and laws. And because it is this claim that, according to Horgan, is essential to a genuine form of materialism (or physicalism),[8] it is the emergentists' denial of the claim that distinguishes their doctrine from nonreductive physicalism.

Looked at in this way, the difference between nonreductive physicalism and emergentism appears quite significant. Emergentism holds, for instance, that mental properties have causal powers that are not explicable in terms of the causal powers of their physical substrates (see section 3). But nonreductive physicalism apparently holds that the causal powers of the mental are explicable in terms of underlying physical properties and laws. For this reason, it appears important for nonreductive physicalists to deny that mental properties are emergent properties.

The aim of this chapter is to argue that this appearance is an illusion. For when the notion of an emergent property is examined, it turns out that the distinction between emergentism and nonreductive physicalism cannot adequately be drawn on metaphysical grounds. The only satisfactory way of drawing the distinction is on epistemological grounds: in terms of the limits of our a priori expectations of what must be explicable. While this distinction is important, it is not the one by means of which nonreductive physicalists hope to distinguish their view from emergentism. For this distinction was supposed to be a metaphysical one: some properties were claimed to *be* emergent by the emergentists, and this is what the nonreductive physicalist is supposed to deny. But it turns out that on the nonreductionist's view, mental properties are emergent properties too, in the only interesting and plausible sense that can be given to the term.

Once this is recognized, then nonreductive physicalists must accept that whatever problems attach to emergentism attach themselves to nonreductive physicalism too. In essence, emergentism is generally thought to encounter two problems: first, it is committed to mental properties having their own causal powers and second, it is committed to the inexplicability of the mind-body relation. But if I am right, then nonreductive physicalists must share these commitments. This is problematic for nonreductive physicalists, because their physicalism ought to commit them to the causal closure of the physical world, and to the physical explicability (in principle) of the mind-body relation.[9] These issues have been greatly discussed in recent philosophy of mind: the standard physicalist response is to develop distinctive accounts of mental causation, and to declare the inexplicability of mind (especially consciousness) to be the 'hard problem' of closing the 'explanatory gap.'[10]

Emergentists, by contrast, are quite happy to accept these consequences of their position. The British emergentists of the early twentieth century, for instance, were happy to accept that mental properties have independent causal powers, and happy to accept that the mind-body relation is (in some sense) inexplicable. What for the nonreductive physicalist is the 'hard problem' about mind, is for the emergentists a brute fact that must be swallowed with what Broad called the 'philosophic jam' of 'natural piety.'[11] This is an aspect of what we can think of as the *epistemological attitude* of emergentism, not its *metaphysical content*. If emergentism is coherent, which even its critics admit it is, then surely this epistemological attitude is coherent too.

However, my aim here is not primarily to defend the truth of British emergentism, but to examine the significance of the doctrine in helping us to understand current debates in philosophy of mind. For it seems to me that there is more to be said for the attitude of 'natural piety' than is often recognized in recent philosophy of mind. I will suggest at the end of this chapter that if we must accept mental properties as nonphysical properties, then we would do well to consider favorably the epistemological attitude of emergentism as one of the available options for 'bridging the explanatory gap.' But first I must clarify the doctrine of emergence.

Emergent Properties

Emergentism, similar to nonreductive physicalism, is committed to the truth of Distinctness and Dependence. Similar to nonreductive physicalism, it is also a 'naturalistic' view, in the (admittedly vague) sense that it regards the natural sciences as employing the correct method for investigating mental and other macroscopic and higher-level phenomena. The apparent difference between the two views is that emergentism accepts, and nonreductive physicalism officially denies, that there are *emergent properties*. But how should we understand the idea of an emergent property? The intuitive idea of an emergent property is the idea of a "novel" property of a whole or complex that "emerges" from the parts of the whole and the way the parts are put together. But how should we make this idea more precise?

There are many ways the properties of things are related to one another. Some properties of wholes are straightforward combinations of properties of their parts. Suppose an object weighing ten kilos has ten parts, each weighing one kilo. Then the property of the whole is determined by adding the properties of its parts. Weighing ten kilos is a distinct property from weighing one kilo, of course, but nonetheless it is not a different kind of property: weighing one kilo and weighing ten kilos are determinates of the determinable property *weight*. So such cases are not cases where the property of the whole is a novel property: simpler properties combine to form other properties from what Ernest Nagel calls the "additive point of view."[12]

Richard Spencer-Smith defines the novelty of a property thus:

> a property P is *novel* in x if x has P, and there are no determinates P' of the same determinable as P, such that any constituents of x have P'.[13]

This rules out weight, age, and most spatiotemporal properties of objects as candidates for being novel, which seems correct. However, the definition would fail to classify an object's color as novel, and this seems wrong. For consider a uniformly blue object O that can be divided into two parts, both of which are blue. Here O has a color, and two of its parts have a determinate property – blueness – of the determinable *color*. So color is not a novel property, according to this definition. Yet a color is something objects can have only when they reach a certain size, so surely it ought to be classified as novel. Spencer-Smith's definition would similarly misclassify the *wetness* of a liquid, which ought to be a novel property.[14]

Spencer-Smith's criterion for novelty can be improved by replacing *any* with *all*: the nonnovel properties of a whole object would be determinable properties, other determinates of which are had by all of its parts. An object's novel properties would be those determinable properties whose determinates are not had by all of the object's parts. Because not all of an object's parts are colored, and not all of a liquid's parts are wet, *color* and *wetness* are novel properties.

But is novelty – in this sense – sufficient for a property to be emergent? Not if emergent properties are meant to be distinguished from *reducible* properties. For even the most extreme reductionist can accept that there are novel properties in this sense. J.J.C. Smart, for example, emphasizes that "in saying that a complex thing is nothing but an arrangement of its parts, I do not deny that it can do things that a mere heap or jumble of its parts could not do."[15] Smart admits – as everyone should – that objects can have properties and powers that their parts do not have. But this doesn't mean that these powers or properties are not reducible to the powers of properties of the parts. The very most it means is that the properties need not be reducible in the "additive" sense.

So this definition of novelty fails to distinguish emergent properties from reducible properties. Perhaps the emergentist could say that we need a stronger notion of 'emergent property:' the notion of a property of a whole whose powers are unrelated to whatever the powers of its parts are. But how can we make sense of this idea? After all, if emergent properties are supposed to be properties of a thing which is *made out of* its parts, then how can it be that they are metaphysically unrelated to the parts in question? For instance, if affecting the parts can in many cases affect how the whole is – in other words, affect the *properties* of the whole – then the properties of the whole are, in these cases, related causally to the properties of the parts. And if putting the parts together in the same way guarantees that the whole will appear in the same way (*ceteris paribus*), then there is a metaphysical relation between the parts and the whole. But these apparently unproblematic part-whole relations would be denied by this strong conception of emergent properties.

This strong conception of emergence seems to require denying the plausible thesis that the emergent properties of a whole are supervenient upon the properties of its parts. This supervenience thesis will not be true for all properties of wholes – for instance, if there are relational properties, then truths about an object relational properties will not supervene upon truths about the object and its parts alone. But for someone who believes in Dependence, the idea that the truths about the *intrinsic* properties of wholes supervene on truths about the properties of their parts is surely a plausible thesis. For if they do not thus supervene, then it seems somewhat perverse to describe the properties as 'emergent.' Presumably part of the point of this label is to pick out the sense in which putting a thing's parts together gives you something new – but not because you have "added" something "from the outside." If emergentism is to be distinguished from dualism and vitalism (which do add something "from the outside") then it must reject this strong notion of emergence. The upshot is that a reasonable emergentist thesis is committed to the supervenience of a whole's properties on the properties of its parts. (Historically, this does seem to have been the case: drawing on important work by Brian McLaughlin, Terence Horgan argues some emergentists were explicitly committed to supervenience.)[16] .

This will seem strange to anyone who agrees with David Lewis that "a supervenience thesis is, in a broad sense, reductionist," or with D.M. Armstrong that "the supervenient is not a feature of the world distinct from the features it supervenes upon."[17] For on these views, the idea that X supervenes on Y is intended to express the idea that X is nothing "over and above" Y. The idea that everything supervenes on the physical, for instance, is intended to express the *necessary determination* of everything by the physical. The nonphysical is nothing "over and above" the physical because, given the physical facts in our world, any world with those facts (and no others) must contain the same nonphysical facts.[18] Yet if emergent properties are anything at all, they are precisely something "over and above" that from which they emerge. So how can an emergentist be committed to supervenience?

The solution to this apparent puzzle is to recognize that the mere idea of supervenience does not support the glosses that Lewis and Armstrong place upon it. For it is quite consistent to hold both that the physical facts determine all the facts, and also to hold that the nonphysical facts are distinct from the physical facts. In a word: determination of A by B does not imply that A and B are not distinct. Therefore, belief in a supervenience thesis does not require that one's ontological commitment to the supervenience base exhausts one's ontological commitments. One might, of course, have other reasons for requiring this. Consider, for instance, the reasons that led Lewis and Jackson to an identity theory.[19] But, the present point is that these reasons are independent of the supervenience thesis.

So an emergentist can hold that mental properties supervene on physical properties, yet they are something "over and above" those physical properties. This point can be explicitly spelled out by employing Kim's notion of *strong supervenience*. A family of properties A strongly supervenes on a family of properties B iff

(S) Necessarily, if anything has property F in A, then there is a property G in B such that that thing has G and necessarily everything that has G has F.[20]

This notion of supervenience does not say anything about whether the A-properties are "something over and above" the B-properties: S is consistent with the distinctness of the A- and B-properties, and also consistent with the identification of each A-property with a B-property. In addition, it is consistent with the A-properties having independent causal powers. So, the strong supervenience of the mental on the physical is consistent with emergentism.

Some philosophers have claimed that the supervenience claim is all that emergentism really amounts to. Kim, for example, claims that:

> According to emergentism, higher-level properties, notably consciousness and other mental properties, emerge when, and only when, an appropriate set of lower-level 'basal conditions' are present and this means that the occurrence of the higher properties is determined by, and dependent on, the instantiation of appropriate lower-level properties and relations. In spite of this, emergent properties were held to be 'genuinely novel' characteristics irreducible to the lower-level processes from which they emerge. Clearly, then, the concept of emergence combines the three components of supervenience, namely, property co-variance, dependence and non-reducibility. In fact, emergentism can be regarded as the first systematic formulation of non-reductive physicalism.[21]

But as I am understanding nonreductive physicalism, a nonreductive physicalist would disagree with Kim's description here, as it holds that mental properties are supervenient, but not emergent. So what extra feature distinguishes the idea of an emergent property from that of a supervenient property?

In the statements of many emergentists and their critics, we find the idea that an emergent property is one whose instantiation in an object is not predictable from knowledge of the instantiation of the properties of the object's parts. In discussing the emergence of organic properties, for instance, Broad says that

> No amount of knowledge about how the constituents of a living body behave in isolation or in other and non-living wholes might suffice to enable us to predict the characteristic behaviour of a living organism. This possibility is perfectly compatible with the view that the characteristic behaviour of a living body is completely determined by the nature and arrangement of the chemical compounds which compose it, in the sense that any whole which is composed of such compounds in such an arrangement will show vital behaviour and that nothing else will do so.[22]

Here Broad endorses the supervenience of the organic on the inorganic, but combines this with the view that facts about the organic cannot be predicted from knowledge of facts about the inorganic constituents alone. He would also say the same about mental and all other emergent properties.

But the fact that we cannot predict (or explain) the behavior of the higher-level properties from knowledge of the lower-level properties alone does not tell us whether these properties are emergent. For whether or not we can predict the higher-level phenomena will depend on our having a vocabulary with which to describe these phenomena. And it is a familiar fact that this vocabulary cannot be given solely by the science of the lower-level properties. Consider, for example, the case of intertheoretic reduction, where we may in certain cases identify a property at a lower level with a property picked out in the higher-level vocabulary. In order to derive truths expressed in the vocabulary of the higher-level science from truths expressed in the lower-level vocabulary, we need 'bridge laws:' sentences that tell us how to link the two vocabularies.[23] So in these cases (e.g., temperature in gases to mean molecular kinetic energy of constituent molecules) we cannot predict the macrophenomena from knowledge stated in the vocabulary of the science of the microphenomena alone, because we need bridge laws to link the vocabularies.

As I noted previously, reduction is not emergence. If the impossibility of predicting (from knowledge of the lower level alone) arises for reductionism, then it cannot be a distinguishing feature of emergentism. And in particular, it cannot distinguish emergent properties from other properties: for if prediction is impossible in the cases where we identify properties at different 'levels,' then its impossibility in the case of emergent properties does not help us in individuating those properties. The unpredictability arises because there are limits to what can be said in the lower-level vocabulary alone, not because of anything about the nature of the properties at the higher level.

Here I am understanding prediction and explanation as epistemic notions. An alternative is to take the notions more metaphysically, and talk of 'predictability in principle.' For the higher-level truths to be predictable from the lower-level truths in this sense is just for there to be some way of deriving one from the other, whether or not anyone will ever know it. We should not object to this as a way to talk – but what does it really amount to? As far as I can see, it is just another way of expressing the thought that fixing the lower level fixes the higher level. And this is simply the supervenience thesis to which we have already committed the emergentists.

It turns out, then, that neither predictability in principle nor unpredictability in practice can distinguish emergent properties from nonemergent properties. For insofar as emergentism is committed to the supervenience thesis – fix the base properties and the laws, and the emergent properties emerge – then emergent properties are as predictable "in principle" as nonemergent or reducible properties are. But insofar as bridge laws are required for prediction, then emergent properties are as unpredictable in practice as reducible properties are.[24]

So the notions of novelty, unpredictability, and supervenience as such do not distinguish emergent properties from the properties postulated by reductive physicalism. This does not mean that there is nothing to be said about emergent properties. For what does seem to be true is at least this: emergent properties are supervenient properties that are distinct from the properties on which they supervene. If we focus on what their distinctness consists of, we can begin to complete this story.

Why say emergent properties are distinct properties at all? Presumably because we think that they make a difference to an object that has them: the object is different from the way it would have been if it had just had (*per impossibile*) its nonemergent properties. Coming about through a purely natural process, this difference must be capable of manifesting itself in some way; and a theory of these properties will tell us how these manifestations are detectable. In other words, in picking out differences in natural properties, we are (at least) picking out the differences in an object's causal powers (whether or not we treat properties as identical to their causal powers). So an emergent property, on this conception, is one that has causal powers that are distinct from the causal powers of the lower level properties on which it supervenes. If you give a list of an object's causal powers, listing only the causal powers of the lower-level properties of the objects, then you will not have given a complete list of the object's powers. What is more, some of these properties are capable of affecting the motion of objects: emergent properties are responsible for 'downward causation' from the higher (e.g., mental) to the lower (e.g., microphysical) levels of nature. This, as Brian McLaughlin rightly observes, is one of the distinguishing features of emergent properties.[25] But if I am right that nonreductive physicalism and emergentism have the same metaphysical commitments, then nonreductive physicalists must be committed to downward causation too. Is this right?

Downward Causation

The idea of downward causation is a simple one: it is the idea of causal influence from the macroscopic to the microscopic levels of nature. How things are at a higher level of complexity affects what happens at a lower level. Take a mental case: I decide to take a drink from the glass in front of me. I move my arm. My arm moves and so do the molecules in the cells that make up my arm. A macroproperty of me – my decision – affects certain microproperties of my arm – the positions and velocities in the particles that make up my arm (and much more besides).

The British emergentists were explicitly committed to downward causation. C.L. Morgan is representative:

> when some new kind of relatedness is supervenient (say at the level of life), the way in which the physical events which are involved run their course is different in virtue of its presence – different from what it would have been if life had been absent.[26]

It is perhaps not so clear that the nonreductive physicalist, on the other hand, is committed to causation of this kind. But in fact it follows straightforwardly from the nonreductivist's denial of the identity theory plus their characteristic denial of epiphenomenalism. For the denial of the identity theory means that they cannot say that the molecules in my arm are only caused by some purely physical property of my arm; and the denial of epiphenomenalism just is the thesis that mental properties are causes.[27]

What are the consequences of this commitment to downward causation? Notice first that to believe in downward causation one does not have to believe that actions, such as moving my arm, are identical with bodily movements, or identical with aggregates of events described in the language of microphysics. Such identifications are implausible; but equally implausible is the idea that if my decision genuinely does move my arm, then this decision has nothing to do with the subsequent motion of the parts of my arm. There seem to be only two possibilities: either my decision does move my arm, in which case it has something to do with the simultaneous movement of the arm's parts; or all motion is determined by the microscopic properties of the parts, and the movement of my arm by my decision is an illusion. But this suggests a dilemma: in the first case, it seems that my mind acts immediately upon the molecules. But how? And in the second case, my mind makes nothing move at all.

It can seem that this dilemma – magic or epiphenomenalism – is spurious. For the fact that when I decide to move my arm, the molecules in my arm move with it might not, in itself, raise any metaphysical worries. The emergentist neuroscientist R.W. Sperry claims that to say that a mental event causes the motion of molecules is as innocuous as saying that "the molecules and atoms of a wheel are carried along when it rolls downhill."[28] Presumably, the idea here is that the motion of the wheel causes its atoms and molecules to move too. Or consider the case of a gas at constant temperature whose volume is suddenly halved:

> If the gas is ideal, Boyle's law entails that when its pressure settles down again it will be twice what it was. That law does not dictate all the interim behaviour of the sample's molecules – except that it must be such as will eventually double the sample's pressure.[29]

Again, we could cite this as an unproblematic example of downward causation. A macroscopic event – halving the volume of the gas – causes things to happen among the gas's molecules while also causing the sample to double in pressure. So why can't we say that the causation in question takes the same general form when my decision causes my arm to move, thus causing the molecules in my arm to move?

Peter Smith comments, of the gas case, that it "plainly doesn't cut against the notion that the microcausal interactions, this time of a gas, causally suffice to produce the macrobehavior (exemplified as pressure and temperature)."[30] This is true, but all it shows is that the downward causation so described is not inconsistent with the supervenience of the macrofacts on the microfacts. And because we have already assumed that both emergentism and nonreductive physicalism are committed to supervenience, this only goes to show that downward causation and supervenience are not inconsistent, without the addition of other assumptions.

What other assumptions must these be? It is sometimes said that such causation is incompatible with the laws of mechanics, the science of motion.[31] But, as McLaughlin points out, this is not so. Suppose for the sake of argument that what downward causation requires is what McLaughlin calls 'configurational forces:' forces that can only be exemplified by matter that has a certain complexity, or a certain kind of structure. Configurational forces are therefore unlike the gravitational force, which holds between any two particles. To illustrate McLaughlin's point, let's consider the case of the laws of classical mechanics: Newton's laws of motion.[32] When a body acts on another body to produce acceleration, it must conform to these laws. These laws are, in Broad's words, "general conditions which all motions, however produced, must conform to."[33] That is, they do not tell us everything about how motions are produced, or why things move. When a particular force is exerted on a given object, say the force exerted by a body's electric charge, then the acceleration of the body will be fixed by the laws governing electric charge – for example, Coloumb's law – and any other forces acting upon the body, in accordance with the general laws of motion, to produce the resultant acceleration. The laws of motion do not place any limit on what kinds of forces can operate on bodies. So if there are forces that can only come into being when matter achieves a certain level of complexity, all that classical mechanics requires is that the motion produced by these forces should conform to Newton's laws. So if we understand downward causation in terms of configurational forces, then the existence of downward causation is not incompatible with the laws of mechanics.

Where there might seem to be a conflict is between the existence of downward causation and a more general metaphysical principle, which has been called 'the completeness of physics.'[34] This principle has been stated in many ways, but essential to all its statements is the idea that any physical effect (that is, any effect describable in the language of physics) is completely fixed, deterministically or indeterministically, by purely physical causes. If the completeness of physics is true, then all physical effects are fixed (for example) by the behavior of atoms and their constituent electrons, protons, and neutrons. Yet according to both emergentism and nonreductive physicalism, there are physical effects – for example, movements of the molecules that make up the cells in my hand – which are the effects of mental properties. How is this compatible with the completeness of physics?

This is the problem of mental causation for nonreductive physicalists, which has recently generated much dispute about the causal character of the mind. Arguably, the acceptability of downward causation is the very issue that divides reductive from nonreductive views of mental properties. Now my aim here is not to resolve this dispute, but merely to point out that insofar as there is a problem here, it is the same problem that challenges emergentism and nonreductive physicalism. And it is the same problem for exactly the same reason: how should we reconcile Distinctness with the completeness of physics and the denial of epiphenomenalism?[35] If this is the problem, then emergentism and nonreductivism are in the same position. There is not a further problem that attaches to emergentism, as Horgan and McLaughlin claim.

The Epistemological Significance of Emergence

I have argued – with Kim and against Horgan – that the metaphysical commitments of the most plausible versions of nonreductive physicalism and emergentism are the same.[36] All possible worlds in which emergentism is true are worlds in which nonreductive physicalism is true. So it is a mistake to attempt to define nonreductive physicalism in terms of its denial of emergence. Why does this matter? I shall draw two morals: one about the cogency of nonreductive physicalism, the other about the current conception of the mind-body problem.

Let me begin with the relevance of my conclusion to nonreductive physicalism. McLaughlin describes the downfall of the British emergentist tradition as follows:

> In their quest to discover 'the connexion or lack of connexion of the various sciences' (Broad 1923 pp. 41–42) the Emergentists left the dry land of the a priori to brave the sea of empirical fortune. (The only route is by sea, of course.) They set off in a certain direction, and for awhile winds of evidence were in their sails; but the winds gradually diminished, and eventually ceased altogether to blow their way.[37]

McLaughlin's point is that British emergentism failed for empirical, rather than philosophical, reasons. With the advent of (for example) the quantum mechanical explanation of chemical bonding, there was no longer any need to postulate irreducible chemical forces, and the emergentists lost some of their most plausible examples (and consequently, lost their metaphysical nerve).

McLaughlin's claim about the failure of this particular version of emergentism is plausible. But what conclusions should contemporary nonreductive physicalists draw from this claim? Horgan argues that the failure of British emergentism gives the nonreductive physicalist a motive to look for an account of the mind-body relation, an explanatory relation stronger than supervenience, which he calls 'superdupervenience.' The appeal to the notion of superdupervenience is supposed to explain why supervenience claims are true, and therefore give us a satisfactory account of the relation between mind and body. Horgan's point is that without such an account, the nonreductive physicalist is left in the same position as the emergentist.

Now here we have finally located a difference between emergentists and nonreductive physicalists. For emergentists do not believe on a priori grounds that no explanation of the connection between the different levels of nature can be given. They believe it is the best conclusion to draw from their empirical investigations. What we find when we look at levels of nature are discontinuities and downwards causation. But although we should accept these facts with natural piety, this should not stop us from investigating the connections between levels, to see whether what we have is an emergent property or a 'resultant.' This was Morgan's view:

> Cognitive relatedness just emerges, as something genuinely new, at a critical stage of evolutionary advance. That, however, does not preclude

– nay, rather, it imperatively demands from us as evolutionists – a resolute attempt to analyse the situation and to trace, if possible, subsidiary stages of emergence, on the understanding that, in evolutionary progress, there is never any breach of continuity in the sense of a gap or hiatus.[38]

Perhaps when we investigate the relations between levels, all we will find are 'stages of emergence' but perhaps we will find resultants. Whether we do or not is an empirical matter (as McLaughlin says, the only way to go is by sea). It is for this reason that the emergentists should be considered 'naturalists.'

By contrast, the nonreductive physcialist's view can appear less naturalistic:

Resolutely shunning the supernatural, I think it is undeniable that it must be in virtue of *some* natural property of the brain that organisms are conscious. There just *has* to be some explanation of how brains subserve minds. If we are not to be eliminativists about consciousness, then some theory must exist which accounts for the psychophysical correlations we observe. It is implausible to take these correlations as ultimate and inexplicable facts.[39]

These remarks of Colin McGinn's express some of the assumptions that lie behind the recent debate about the problem of consciousness. In articulating the contemporary problem of consciousness, Joseph Levine says: "We want an explanation of why when we occupy certain physico-functional states we experience qualitative character of the sort we do."[40] Commenting on this passage, Spencer-Smith remarks that "we would like more than the neural correlate of an experience, an explanation which would ideally take the form "x is in pain iff . . ." – we want an explanation of how pains feel."[41]

It is here that we encounter the deep difference between emergentism and nonreductive physicalism. It is not a metaphysical difference, but a difference in the reactions of the two theories to limitations in our knowledge. Both emergentism and nonreductionism agree that we do not currently understand how the nonmental properties of the brain are related to its mental properties. But they react to this in different ways: the nonreductionists react by claiming that there must nonetheless be an account of *why* "we experience qualitiative character of the sort we do," an account that does not just state the complex correlations between the nonmental and the mental. The emergentists deny that this *must* be so. If it turns out that the relation between consciousness and the brain is inexplicable, this ends up being one of the facts that must be accepted with natural piety. As Morgan says, this does not preclude us from looking for levels of emergence, to ensure that there is no 'breach of continuity.' But levels of emergence are still levels of emergence, and at some point in our investigations we may have to accept that the most our scientific investigations will give us are correlations. The availability of the emergentist position encourages us to look with suspicion on the idea that there must nonetheless be a philosophical account of these correlations – the sort of account demanded (for various reasons) by Horgan, McGinn, Nagel, Levine, and others.[42]

So one possible approach to the mind-body problem, inspired by emergentism, is that the insistence that there must be a metaphysical 'explanation of how pains feel' is misplaced. This is not because consciousness and thought are mysterious properties, unrelated to prop-erties of the brain. On the contrary: anyone who takes a naturalistic approach to these issues is not going to find it surprising or illuminating to be told by John Searle that consciousness and thought are "higher-level features of the brain" (though they might find it more acceptable to say with Chomsky that "people think, not their brains, which do not, though their brains provide the mechanisms of thought"[43]). The mind-body problem from this emergentist perspective is not the mystery of how the brain can produce consciousness, because the existence of mental properties, and their dependence on the brain, are accepted with natural piety. Rather, it is what Chomsky calls a "unification problem:" to explain how the mind/brain works, given that "we have good and improving theories of some aspects of language and mind, but only rudi-mentary ideas about the relation of any of this to the brain."[44] This way of treating the mind-body problem does not assume that there is one explanatory gap, or one hard problem, any more than it assumes that one metaphysical notion such as superdupervenience should be usefully employed in bridging the gap or solving the problem. What it does assume is that we should not say a priori when we should take the facts of nature to require further explanation. Hence the need to be open to the attitude of natural piety.

The significance of emergentism, then, lies in the value of the episte-mological attitude it recommends to naturalism. Naturalistic nonreduc-tive approaches to the mind-body problem should look more favorably than they have done in recent years upon the attitude of natural piety. It may be that whether emergentism (in the sense explained in the second and third sections of this chapter) or reductionism is true is still an open question. But the contention of this chapter has been that emergentism is metaphysically indistinguishable from nonreductive physicalism, and perhaps a more authentic position for a genuine naturalist to adopt.[45]

NOTES

1. Nagel (1985, p. 51).
2. Similar ideas are found in Chalmers (1996); Levine (1993); and McGinn (1991), "Consciousness and content" and "Can we solve the mind-body problem?"
3. See, for example, the discussions by Shoemaker and Fodor (1994).
4. For discussion, see Nagel (1979); McGinn (1991a); Van Cleve (1990); McLaughlin (1992); Searle (1992); Horgan (1993).
5. See the valuable discussion in McLaughlin (1992). Despite my disagreement with some of the claims made in McLaughlin's paper, I am greatly indebted to it in what I write here. The central emergentist texts McLaughlin discusses are: Mill (1875); Alexander (1920); Morgan (1923); and Broad (1923).
6. Horgan (1993, pp. 557–8).
7. Horgan (1993, p. 560).
8. "A materialistic metaphysical position should assert that all supervenience facts are explainable – indeed, explainable in some materialistically acceptable way." Horgan (1993, p. 560).
9. For these physicalist commitments, see (for example) Lewis (1983); Papineau (1993a), ch. 1 – on the closure of the physical – and Horgan – on physical explicability.
10. The phrase, "the hard problem" is Chalmers's (1996, pp. xi–xii); for the "explanatory gap" see Levine (1983).
11. See Broad (1923, p. 55). The phrase "natural piety" derives from Alexander (1920, p. 47).
12. See Nagel (1963). For a recent discussion of the determinable/determinate relation, see Yablo (1992).
13. Spencer-Smith (1995, p. 117). Spencer-Smith does not think that novelty in this sense is sufficient for emergence.
14. Assuming that half of a sample of a liquid can be called a "constituent" of the sample. The contrast here between novel and nonnovel properties is called the contrast between 'Empedoclean' and 'Democritean' forms of explanation by Klee (1984, pp. 44–63), who follows Girill (1976, pp. 387–405). See also Searle (1992, pp. 111–12).
15. Smart (1987, p. 248). Alexander (1920, p. 47) does not help matters by arguing that accepting emergent properties is no more problematic than accepting colors. Compare Spencer-Smith (1995, p. 113).
16. Horgan (1993, pp. 558–9).
17. Lewis (1983, p. 358); Armstrong (1989, p. 7). My own sympathies are with Daly's discussion of this kind of point (1997, pp. 185–206).
18. See Jackson (1998, ch. 1).
19. See Jackson (1995).
20. See Kim (1993e).
21. Kim (1994, pp. 576–7).
22. Broad (1923a, pp. 67–8). The phrase "nothing else will do so" indicates that Broad will reject the possibility of variable/multiple realization of the emergent by the subvenient. But this can be safely regarded as inessential to the emergentist's picture.
23. See Nagel (1979, ch. 11).

24. In any case, there is something wrong with construing the notion of an emergent property in terms of epistemic notions such as predictability, because emergence is supposed to be a metaphysical category. See Spencer-Smith (1995, pp. 120–1).
25. The term *downward causation* derives from the biologist Campbell (1974). McLaughlin (1992) argues that downward causation, while not incoherent, presents emergentism with its biggest problems. The upshot of the next section is that if McLaughlin and I are both right, then these are problems for nonreductive physicalism too.
26. Morgan (1923, p. 16).
27. I am assuming here, with most participants in the debate, that properties are causes (rather then events in Davidson's sense). So by epiphenomenalism I mean the stronger thesis of what McLaughlin calls "type epiphenomenalism." See McLaughlin (1989). See also Jackson (1996). For a philosopher who embraces epiphenomenalism, see Chalmers (1996, p. 165).
28. Sperry (1996, p. 532).
29. Crane and Mellor (1990, pp. 190–1).
30. Smith (1992, p. 26).
31. The charge is implicit in Papineau (1990). See also Fodor (1994).
32. McLaughlin (1992, pp. 53–4 and 74–5), argues in addition that downward causation and configurational forces are not incompatible with quantum mechanics, nor with special and general relativity. But the essential point can be made in relation to classical mechanics.
33. Broad (1923b, p. 177).
34. See Papineau (1993a, p. 16.)
35. For a concise statement of the problem in this form, see Yablo (1992).
36. Though I am sympathetic to Kim's discussion in "The non-reductivist's trouble with mental causation" (1993e) I draw a somewhat different moral. It will also become apparent that I take a different view of the significance of emergence from that of Haldane (1996, esp. p. 267).
37. McLaughlin (1992, p. 90).
38. Morgan (1923, p. 9).
39. McGinn (1991b, p. 6).
40. Levine (1993, p. 128).
41. Spencer-Smith (1995, p. 127).
42. On this issue, see my debate with William Child in *Proceedings of the Aristotelian Society* 97, 1997.
43. See Searle (1992, ch. 1); Chomsky (1995, p. 8).
44. Chomsky (1995, p. 11).
45. For comments and advice I am especially grateful to Richard Holton and Rae Langton, and also to Chris Daly, André Gallois, Giovanna Hendel, Lloyd Humberstone, Neil Manson, Mike Martin, and Graham Oppy. This chapter was written while I was a visiting fellow at the Research School of the Social Sciences of the Australian National University, Canberra.

11

The Methodological Role of Physicalism: A Minimal Skepticism

CARL GILLETT

Substantial progress has been made working out the metaphysics under-lying physicalism (P) and its idea that everything is, in some sense, phys-ical. But its proponents have not confined themselves to metaphysical claims and have also argued that physicalism has an important method-ological role. Hartry Field, Jeffrey Poland, and W.V.O. Quine, among others, all defend what I will call *Methodological Physicalism* (MP), the position that we should use a *Physicalist Criterion* under which P is used to assess our theories.[1] Methodological Physicalism exerts con-siderable philosophical influence. Vindicatory 'naturalization' projects, for example, are apparently based upon implicit acceptance of MP. Theories that posit intentional states, moral properties such as goodness and the right, and mathematical entities such as sets and numbers, have all been argued to be in danger of abandonment, and in consequent need of naturalization, because they fail a Physicalist Criterion.[2]

The prescriptions of MP are clearly substantive and an obvious question is how use of a Physicalist Criterion is justified. Any such justification must be compatible with the broadly 'naturalistic' orienta-tion of defenders of MP who consequently look to the sciences.[3] For example, Harty Field (1972), and also Jeffrey Poland (1994), both offer what I will call the *Justification from Scientific Practice* (JSP) to defend their use of a Physicalist Criterion. This justification of MP has as its first premise some version of the normative position that we ought to use in all areas of empirical inquiry the methods that have been successfully used in sciences, and a second, descriptive premise that the Physicalist Criterion has been successfully used to appraise scientific theories in a variety of historical cases. If sound, a defense based upon these two premises offers a naturalistically acceptable justification of the central tenet of MP: that we ought to use a Physicalist Criterion in assessing our theories, scientific or otherwise.

One might fruitfully subject versions of either premise of JSP to crit-ical scrutiny. For example, should we really use scientific practices of inquiry, however successful, in all areas of empirical inquiry? Though such questions obviously merit critical attention, I will focus solely upon the descriptive historical claim underlying JSP. In my discussion I follow defenders of MP in analyzing a variety of historical cases toward which our present paucity of evidence necessitates a more abstract approach than has recently been common in the philosophy of science. Ultimately, one of the main points I hope to establish is that more detailed historical research is needed in order to settle the historical issues surrounding use of the Physicalist Criterion. Though proponents of MP have also endorsed the need for such research, they have argued that even without it they are still justified in their descriptive argue because they argue that the relevant historical cases are explained only by hypothesizing that scientists used a Physicalist Criterion to evaluate theories.

My primary goal will be to investigate whether Methodological Physicalists are correct that their descriptive claims are presently warranted. I will argue that they are not. I shall present a more modest interpretation of scientific theory appraisal that takes researchers to have assessed theories simply by their 'local' relationships to other scientific theories, rather than also by their relations to a physicalist cosmology. I will argue that, given our present evidence, such a 'locally' based account of scientific theory appraisal provides our best explanation of the relevant historical episodes, rather than an interpretation positing use of a Physicalist Criterion. However, Methodological Physicalists have often been unmoved by such conclusions, arguing that due to their similarities such mundane methodological canons actually justify the use of a Physicalist Criterion. After disentangling the physicalist methodology from my more modest methodological account, I will consequently attempt to sharpen my critique by posing the following dilemma for Methodological Physicalists. Either the prescriptions of MP are a subset of my more modest methodological account, or they are not. If the prescriptions of MP are a subset of those of my modest methodology, then MP can be given historical support. But the prescriptions sanctioned by this historical evidence amount to no more than the demand for a mundane kind of coherence among our theories. On this horn of the dilemma, the weakened form of MP would be such that it would not justify recent philosophical projects such as naturalizations. And there would be a real question why this position is distinctly 'physicalist,' because it apparently rests upon a simple demand for intertheoretic coherence. In contrast, if the prescriptions of MP conflict with those of my more modest methodological proposal, then I will argue that the historical claims of MP cannot presently be supported. On this second horn, Methodological Physicalism is unquestionably a full-blooded 'physicalist' methodology, but in this case its historical claims about scientific practice are unwarranted, and MP cannot be provided with its most common 'naturalistic' justification. Thus, on either horn, we will not have a methodology that is *both* full-bloodedly 'physicalist' in character *and* justified by scientific practice.

My skeptical arguments will ultimately be modest in being conditional, because they are predicated upon the present paucity of detailed historical research about the role of P in scientific theory assessment. I happily acknowledge that further research may well undermine my arguments, and I actively encourage defenders of MP to pursue the necessary type of historical investigation. However, although my arguments are modest in this respect, I will ultimately suggest that their wider implications are rather immodest. For, even if we grant the Methodological Physicalist all of their other assumptions, I will show that JSP is not successful, because its central descriptive premise about the historical use of a Physicalist Criterion is presently unwarranted. And the criteria of appraisal we are warranted in believing have been successfully used in the sciences do not sanction pursuit of a 'physicalist' methodology either in philosophy or the sciences. My final conclusion will consequently be that proponents of MP presently lack a justification for their use of a Physicalist Criterion that does not leave it 'physicalist' in name alone.

Methodological Physicalism and the Justification from Scientific Practice

In his famous paper "Tarski's Theory of Truth" (Field 1972), Hartry Field provided the seminal contemporary discussion of the methodological aspects of physicalism. Field's work thus provides a useful starting point in understanding MP, and in a recent paper he clearly outlines the type of scientific role he takes physicalism to play, telling us that:

> The methodological role of physicalism is double edged. On the positive side, the doctrine tells us that when we have some body of facts and causal explanations that we are quite convinced are basically correct, we need to find a physical foundation for them. . . . The other, negative, aspect of the doctrine of physicalism is that when faced with a body of doctrine . . . that we are convinced can have no physical foundation, we tend to reject that body of doctrine. . . . (Field [1992], p. 271)

Philosophers have made a number of closely related claims about the role of P in the sciences. For example, it has been claimed that P has played a positive role as some kind of heuristic, guiding scientific research by suggesting new, potentially fruitful theories or lines of inquiry, and this role may be implied by Field's first remarks. But a second role, which Field clearly endorses, has also been suggested. This is Field's claim that physicalism has been used in a potentially more negative manner, as part of a criterion of assessment whose use may lead to the abandonment of the hypotheses that fail it.[4]

The heuristic role would clearly lead to the formulation of potentially fruitful new accounts, but Field also argues that the second use of P also has this result. Field makes this point in "Tarski's Theory of Truth" when surveying the case of the concept of 'valence' in chemistry at the turn of the century. Field claims that at this time the chemical theories based on the notion of 'valence' failed a Physicalist Criterion. And Field explains how he believes researchers react to such a situation as follows:

> ... scientists would have eventually had to decide either (a) to give up valence theory, or else (b) to replace the hypothesis of physicalism by another hypothesis.... It is part of scientific methodology to resist doing (b); and I also think it is part of scientific methodology to resist doing (a) as long as the notion of valence is serving the purpose for which it was designed ... the methodology is to look for a real reduction. This is a methodology that has proved very fruitful in science.... (Field [1972], p. 363)

Here we see Field implying that a Physicalist Criterion was used to negatively assess certain chemical theories, but further arguing that in such a situation the first reactions of researchers is to try to vindicate the troubled theory by formulating what Field terms a "real reduction." The purpose of such accounts is to show that in fact there was merely the appearance of a conflict between the theory in question and P. It is the search for, and formulation of, such vindicatory theories that Field argues has been a fruitful a part of scientific methodology leading, for example, to quantum mechanical accounts of chemical phenomena such as valence, and also to biochemical accounts of genetic transmission.

Just this putative methodological role underpins both the perceived philosophical need for many naturalizations and also the implicit role such accounts are taken to play in philosophy. Where philosophers claim some theory must be naturalized there is a prima facie conflict with P and the theory is taken to be in danger of abandonment precisely because it fails some Physicalist Criterion. For example, Jerry Fodor has recently pursued a naturalization of intentionality because he believes this property underlies a conflict between physicalism and intentional psychology (Fodor [1987] and [1990c], among others). Fodor explains his concerns when he says:

If it turns out that the physicalization – naturalization – of intentional science . . . is impossible . . . then it seems to me that . . . we should stop doing intentional science and that counts for a lot more than some philosopher being worried. That's a matter of theoretical honesty. . . . The position we're in is, can we give a coherent account of this research project because, by Christ, if we can't we should stop spending the taxpayers' money. (Asher et al. [1990], pp. 202–3)

For Fodor a naturalization is an account that serves the role of Field's "real reduction." It is a vindicatory account offered to preserve a theory that apparently conflicts with P, because it is implied that failure to provide a naturalization would entail the abandonment of intentional psychology. Similar uses of a Physicalist Criterion, and resulting concerns, provide the implicit motivation for vindicatory naturalizations of mathematical entities such as sets and numbers, and moral properties such as goodness, among others.[5]

I suggest that it is no accident that these philosophical uses of a Physicalist Criterion in assessing our intentional psychology, moral discourse, mathematics etc., mirror the methodological role that Field claims working scientists have historically assigned to P. First, Field arguably inspired many of these philosophical projects by giving an exemplar of such a philosophical methodology in "Tarski's Theory of Truth." Field famously argued that the significance of Tarski's work is only properly appreciated as an instance of such a philosophical methodology, as an attempt to vindicate the concept of truth and show that it passed a Physicalist Criterion. And, second, Field also sketched a justification for philosophical applications of the Physicalist Criterion commonly used by naturalizers such as Fodor. For Field connects the appropriateness of philosophical application of a Physicalist Criterion, in a project such as Tarski's, with the putatively successful use of this criterion in the sciences. Later philosophical projects, I suggest, have appropriated both the philosophical methodology laid out by Field and also his naturalistic justification of it. Given its centrality to so many philosophical projects, I shall concentrate my discussion upon the putative role played by P as part of a criterion of theory assessment. However, later in the chapter, I will show that my skeptical arguments about the historical use of a Physicalist Criterion may also easily be applied to claims that physicalism has played the second heuristic role noted.

What is the precise form of this vaunted Physicalist Criterion? And how exactly is the use of this criterion justified? Critics of MP have recently emphasized the important connection between these two questions and the inadequacy of the Methodological Physicalist answers to them. For example, we find Stephen Stich stating that:

It is, I think, deeply irresponsible to suggest that research be stopped and
laboratories be closed because the work being carried on there fails to live
up to some vaguely stated ontological standard whose importance has not
been made clear. (Stich [1993a], p. 150)

Stich is concerned that we have not been either given the details of the
Physicalist Criterion, or a justification for its use. I believe such concerns
are reasonable, for only if one is clear about the precise nature of the
Physicalist Criterion can one evaluate whether one is plausibly justified
in using it. And unfortunately, as a quick consideration of a number of
points makes clear, Methodological Physicalists have rarely been explicit
about the details of their criterion.

Obviously the metaphysical version of physicalism one defends
becomes important in such a criterion, for different prescriptions
will result from criteria based on formulations using relations such as
constitution, realization, or type/token identity. However, though proponents of MP are usually clear about their stands on this metaphysical
issue, there are other important methodological and epistemic questions
that are generally left unanswered. For example, does the criterion
concern the acceptance or rejection of theories? Or just the investigation, pursuit, or some still further relation that we might bear to a theory?
We are generally never told, though this will greatly affect the nature
of the resulting criterion. Similarly, there is the question of what the
Physicalist Criterion assumes about the epistemic relation that must hold
between some theory and P. For example, must a theory be shown to be
plausible given the truth of P? Or must we simply lack any evidence that
the theory is incompatible with P? And exactly what types of evidence
will suffice to establish either such plausibility or incompatibility?
Criteria based upon different answers to these questions will make very
different prescriptions and this will again have serious implications
for any attempt to justify their use. To my knowledge, Methodological
Physicalists never clarify how they would answer such questions.

In order to begin to evaluate MP we do need some detailed version
of the Physicalist Criterion, though we should be careful to note that
there need not be only one version of the Physicalist Criterion that ought
to be used in all cases. As Richard Burian has recently suggested, when
assessing their theories scientists may use a 'reticulated' array of short-
and long-term norms that involve different sets of criteria of appraisal
(Burian [1993]). Scientists might thus use one version of the Physicalist
Criterion in the short term, or with regard to immature theories, while
reserving a different form for use in the longer term or with mature
theories. However, though one need not think that there is only one
Physicalist Criterion applicable in all cases, to assess MP we do need

some detailed formulation of this criterion. I shall, therefore, offer a version of the Physicalist Criterion that addresses the questions raised here and that I shall argue captures the intentions of Methodological Physicalists, while avoiding obvious, prima facie difficulties. I will call this criterion 'PC' and formulate it as follows (I use the term *entity* widely to refer to properties, individuals, states, and processes.):

> (PC) A theorist is justified in accepting a scientific theory T, all else being equal between this theory and its rivals, only if she lacks evidence that the entities of T cannot ultimately be realized, or constituted, by physical entities.

There are a number of important features of this criterion. First, PC uses a form of physicalism that claims all individuals are constituted by physical individuals and all properties are realized by physical properties. However, given the nature of the ontological relations concerned, if a criterion based upon realization/constitution cannot be shown to be have been used in the sciences, then it will also be implausible that an identity-based criterion has been used. Thus by considering PC we can also potentially resolve whether a metaphysically stronger criterion has been used.[6]

We should secondly note that PC is based around the acceptance of theories. A theorist cannot putatively bear the relation of acceptance to any theory that fails PC, but might nonetheless bear other relations such as those of mere pursuit or investigation. In addition, PC also implicitly assumes two features of scientific theory appraisal now familiar in the philosophy of science. For PC assumes the appraisal of a hypothesis is not done in isolation, but by comparison with rivals. And, furthermore, PC also allows that such assessment may involve a variety of different factors, thus taking the relation between T and physicalism to be one among many possible factors involved in the evaluative comparison made of T and its rivals.

Lastly, the epistemic relation at the heart of PC is basically the demand that one must lack evidence that the entities posited by the theory in question cannot be physically realized or constituted. And one should note the 'global' nature of this demand – PC places no constraint upon where the information used in assessing theories is drawn from. Presumably, the source of such information must be reliable, in a broad sense, but PC does not limit such sources, for example, to well-confirmed scientific theories. In addition, notice also that PC demands that we lack evidence of what I will call 'incompatibility' between T and P, in order to be justified in accepting T. I shall follow Larry Laudan in using the term *cognitive relationship* to describe such relations between theories, because they have an epistemic dimension and are not merely logical in nature. And also I shall roughly follow Laudan's characterizations of such relations.[7] I will take a cognitive relationship of 'incompatibility' to hold between a theory T and other theories when the implications of these other theories make one, or more, claims of T implausible. There are a variety of other cognitive relationships, but I will only be concerned with two. The relationship of 'reinforcement' holds between T and other theories when these theories provide a rationale for one or more claims of T. And what I shall call 'bare compatibility' holds between T and other theories when these theories imply nothing, or very little, about T.

Versions of physicalist criteria have been suggested that make stronger epistemic demands than PC, for example that T must be shown to bear a relationship of reinforcement to physicalism before T may be accepted. Such criteria would demand we positively show that T's entities are physically realized/constituted before we may accept T, rather than PC's negative demand that we must only lack evidence that these entities cannot be so realized/constituted. Stich and Laurence's (1994) has provided prima facie persuasive arguments that the stronger criteria are implausibly strong in their prescriptions, and I have argued at length elsewhere that PC does not fall prey to the arguments of these critics.[8] In addition, the truth of the stronger criteria would imply the truth of PC. Thus if one cannot justify the claim that PC has been used in the sciences, then it is plausible one will not be able to justify the claim that stronger criteria have been used. Given these points, I shall therefore take PC as my focus, rather than epistemically more demanding criteria.[9]

Can one charitably interpret Methodological Physicalists as accepting PC? I will argue that their philosophical activities support such an interpretation and that appreciating the character of PC even justifies some previously puzzling aspects of their projects. Let us again take Fodor's concerns with the naturalization of intentionality as our example, though other cases of naturalizations are also to be explained by similar interpretations. Fodor was concerned with the so-called 'problem of error' (Fodor 1987), and, putting it roughly, he argued that there was a prima facie problem in how intentional states with their property of having the potential to be erroneous could be physically realized/constituted. Fodor can therefore be interpreted as being concerned that intentional psychology failed PC, for he took the property of having the potential to be erroneous to provide evidence that intentional states could not be physically realized. What did Fodor try to establish with his naturalization of intentionality? He attempted to show that intentional states with the property of having the potential to be erroneous could be physically realized, which is all that needs to be shown for intentional psychology to pass PC (Fodor [1987] and [1990c]). It is often objected to Fodor that he does not provide, nor even seek to provide, any evidence about the actual existence of the type of physical state used in his naturalization, in other words states involved in laws bearing so-called relations of 'asymmetrical dependence' (Adams and Aizawa [1992]). But if Fodor is implicitly using PC, then he has no need to supply such further evidence. Under PC, Fodor only needs to show that intentional states could be physically realized/constituted, thus removing the evidence of an incompatibility with P and vindicating intentional psychology. Contrary to the critics' claims, to demand further positive evidence from Fodor misunderstands his project if he accepts PC and it thus appears that PC provides a rather plausible interpretation of the philosophical projects inspired by MP.

We have now begun to substantially address Stich's concerns about the vague formulation of a Physicalist Criterion. Let us therefore return to his second concern: How is use of the Physicalist Criterion justified? I have already suggested that the usual naturalistic answer, following Field, is based upon what I dubbed JSP. To recap, JSP's first premise is some version of the normative position that we ought to use in all areas of empirical inquiry those methods that have been successfully used in sciences. And its second premise is the historical claim that the Physicalist Criterion has been successfully used to appraise scientific theories. As I noted in my introduction, for argument's sake I shall accept the normative premise of JSP. The issue I want to explore is whether we should accept the Methodological Physicalist's descriptive claims about scientific theory appraisal.

As we have seen in the quotes from Field, Methodological Physicalists argue the history of the sciences justifies their belief that PC, or a similarly physicalistic criterion, has been successfully used in the sciences.[10] Using PC we can now clarify exactly what the Methodological Physicalist is claiming occurs in the relevant historical cases. In such episodes we have theories from two domains of inquiry, T_A and T_B, where the former is a well-confirmed theory. And a well-confirmed theory of the ontological relations of the entities posited by these theories, T_R, which postulates what I will call a '*vertical*' ontological relation, such as identity, realization, or constitution. Such vertical relations involve entities that are not wholly distinct and are thus vertically in the same ontological 'branch.' Let us take as our example a situation where T_R claims that the entities of T_A constitute and realize those posited by T_B. In such situations, scientists have often appraised theories using the following procedure. T_R is used in conjunction with information supplied by the other theories to produce the conclusion that the entities posited by T_B could not be realized/constituted by the entities of T_A. Consequently, researchers have often negatively appraised theories in the situation of the ontologically higher level theory T_B and I shall call these 'bottom-up' cases.[11]

The interpretation of such cases given by Methodological Physicalists is that the researchers in such episodes concluded that the ontologically higher level theory T_B fails PC, because in virtue of T_B's incompatibility with T_R and T_A we have evidence that its entities cannot be realized/constituted by those of T_A and hence by the entities of physics. This understanding of the assessment of theories made in such 'bottom-up' cases gives the broad outline of the Methodological Physicalist view of one important type of scientific theory appraisal and underpins JSP's descriptive premise. Though this view obviously needs to be qualified in a number of respects, the paucity of our present evidence about the relevant cases prevents us from pursuing such a detailed understanding. Rather strangely, proponents of MP such as Jeffrey Poland freely, and I believe rightly, acknowledge that we lack detailed historical studies of the relevant aspects of such cases (Poland [1994] pp. 265–6 and p. 339). Ultimately, the Methodological Physicalist thus accepts that she bases her interpretive claims only upon the gross features of the relevant cases, for she accepts that we lack detailed historical accounts of their relevant aspects. This is initially puzzling, for how can defenders of MP accept the paucity of our evidence and yet still argue that these cases justify their descriptive historical claims?

Poland suggests a characteristically clear answer to this question when he argues against critics of MP as follows:[12]

> I seriously question a description of current scientific practice that views science as broken down into fully autonomous, isolated, empirical inquiries concerned with specific local problems the solution to which is unconstrained by, for example, compatibility with models and theories in other domains. . . . So the critics who argue that it is unreasonable to be a [methodological] physicalist have, it seems to me, the burden of presenting an intelligible and appropriate alternative account of how various research programmes are (or are not) related. (Poland [1994], p. 338)

Poland frames the options as follows. Either accept that cognitive relationships between theories in different domains of inquiry have been important in theory assessment in the sciences, thus adopting the descriptive view of MP that a Physicalist Criterion has historically been used to assess theories. Or deny that cognitive relationships between theories in different scientific domains of inquiry have been used in scientific theory evaluation and accept a deeply implausible view of the practices, and history, of the sciences.

Poland thus runs an "only ball game in town"–style argument to defend the historical claims underlying JSP. Even given the present paucity of detailed historical accounts of the relevant cases, if we do indeed lack any alternative explanation of the relevant historical cases, then a Methodological Physicalist would be right to argue that we still ought to accept that scientists have used the Physicalist Criterion. In this manner, the crucial descriptive claim of JSP can thus be justified and so too can the use of a Physicalist Criterion. A great deal consequently rides upon the nature of available explanations of scientific theory appraisal, because it appears most Methodological Physicalists implicitly follow Field, and Poland, in relying upon just this type of naturalistic defense.

A Minimal Interpretation and a Skeptical Argument

Poland, and other defenders of MP, argue that interpretations based upon a Physicalist Criterion provide the only, and hence the best, explanation of scientific practice. But some troubling questions arise about this defense if one reflects upon the abstract structure of the relevant historical cases. Putting the worries most crudely, why should we think that anything more than a 'locally' driven concern with cognitive relationships between particular scientific theories explains these activities? For example, when theories from different domains of inquiry are incompatible is this not alone sufficient to explain why scientists reach a negative appraisal of such theories? Should we really assume that the significance of relationships of incompatibility is that they reveal some further fact about the cognitive relationship of the theory involved to physicalism in addition to such 'local' intertheoretic incoherence?

The intuition behind these questions is that a cognitive relationship of incompatibility between theories on its own has an obvious relevance to their assessment, because a triad of incompatible theories cannot all be true. Let us call the assessment of theories simply by their cognitive relationships to theories in other scientific domains '*minimal appraisal*,' to distinguish it from assessment using compatibility with physicalism. We can roughly capture the character of such appraisal in what I will call the 'Minimal Criterion' (MC):

> (MC) A theorist is justified in accepting a scientific theory T, all else being equal between T and its rivals, only if she lacks evidence that T is incompatible with well-confirmed scientific theories from other scientific domains of inquiry.

MC is similar to PC in a number of respects. Once again, MC acknowledges the multifaceted and comparative nature of scientific theory appraisal, and is also concerned with the acceptance of theories. Furthermore, MC basically demands the same epistemic relation be satisfied as PC, by concerning our lack of evidence of an incompatibility between theories. Crucially, however, the relata of this epistemic relation are different in the two criteria.

MC is not concerned with the implications of an incompatibility between a specific theory and P, but simply the 'local' issues of cognitive relationships between specific scientific theories from different domains. This difference manifests itself in a couple of respects. First, in order to ground a minimal appraisal, one needs two scientific theories from distinct domains of inquiry and a theory of the relations of their entities, where two of these theories must be well confirmed. Thus MC focuses solely upon scientific theories and does not have recourse to a physicalist cosmology. Second, as a result of this focus, MC is a 'local' criterion in the sense that it constrains the information it takes to be relevant in assessing scientific theories. This is in stark contrast to PC, which is 'global' in character and allows information from a variety of sources to be used in assessing theories.

With MC in hand, we can apparently provide an alternative explanation of the gross features of the historical examples emphasized by Field, Poland, and other defenders of MP. In such bottom-up cases, the ontologically higher level theory, T_B, bears a cognitive relationship of incompatibility to well-confirmed theories from other domains. Under MC, this state of affairs alone suffices to make acceptance of T_B illegitimate. In the minimal appraisal of theories it thus appears that we have a nonphysicalist explanation of scientific practice that meets Poland's challenge of showing how theories from different domains of inquiry can constrain each other without recourse to a Physicalist Criterion. Understanding the minimal appraisal of theories consequently makes questionable the success of the Methodological Physicalist's "only ball game in town" finesse of our paucity of historical evidence. We can explain the relevant historical episodes as instances of minimal appraisal as well as uses of the Physicalist Criterion.

However, undermining the descriptive claims of MP, and its deeper appeal, is unsurprisingly not this simple. The Methodological Physicalist's standard response at this point is to question whether minimal appraisal is really an alternative interpretation of the historical cases. The implication is that the minimal appraisal of theories is in some way connected to use of a Physicalist Criterion, and I believe this idea underlies much of the appeal of MP. Given its importance, I shall therefore return to this response in detail later in the chapter. First, however, it will be helpful to show that minimal appraisal actually grounds still greater problems for MP than simply undermining an "only ball game in town" argument for the truth of its historical claims.

The Minimal Criterion is broader in its interpretive scope than physicalist criteria such as PC, because MC is focused solely on intertheoretic relationships generally rather than cognitive relationships with P in particular. Two other kinds of historical cases serve to highlight these differences, and the first type I shall consider again involves a theory positing vertical ontological relations between entities. In this kind of case an incompatibility between theories is again generated, but this leads to the ontologically *lower-level* theory being called into question. Consider, for example, the 1960's rejection of connectionist accounts as a result of Papert and Minsky's results concerning 'exclusive-or.' (See Papert and Minsky [1969] for their results, and Papert [1988] for an informal account of this historical episode.) In this case, the connectionist networks, often also called *neural networks*, of the ontologically lower-level theory, T_{CON}, were taken to constitute psychological entities, such as beliefs, posited by the ontologically higher-level, psychological theory, T_{PSY}. Let us call this vertical relation theory, which was accepted by all sides, T_{RCP}. Crucially, systems involving beliefs, and other higher psychological states, are capable of performing operations involving exclusive-or. And scientists at this time took Papert and Minsky to have shown that connectionist networks could not perform this operation. In light of these findings, researchers concluded that the entities of T_{PSY} and T_{CON} could not bear the vertical relation posited by T_{RCP}. T_{PSY}, T_{CON}, and T_{RCP} were therefore taken to bear the cognitive relationship of incompatibility, and connectionist accounts thus were abandoned by most researchers.

Because the ontologically lower-level theory was negatively assessed I shall call such examples 'top-down' cases, and application of MC can explain the behavior of scientists in these episodes. Scientists apparently had evidence that the connectionist account T_{CON} was incompatible with two well-confirmed theories, in other words theories of higher human psychology and our account of the relation of psychological and neural states. Interpreting these scientists as using MC allows us to explain their behavior, because under MC they would be unjustified in continuing to accept T_{CON}, and this was apparently their actual reaction. But an interpretation based upon PC cannot easily make sense of such a case. Later I will discuss a common objection to this claim, but for now let us examine why it appears so plausible. The reason is that the incompatibility involved in this case does not obviously provide evidence that the entities of T_{CON} cannot be constituted/realized by physical entities, because T_{CON} is the ontologically lower-level theory. Problems about how connectionist entities might constitute, or realize, some other set of entities do not appear relevant to whether connectionist entities are themselves realized, or constituted, by physical entities. PC consequently has no obvious application in 'top-down' cases, and only MC clearly explains this type of assessment. We thus see that MC explains a wider range of cases involving vertical ontological relations than physicalist criteria such as PC.

Furthermore, scientific theories about the ontological relations of entities do not always posit vertical relations of realization, constitution or identity, because the "branches" of vertical relations divide at the higher ontological levels. For example, physical entities constitute meteorological entities such as clouds, geological entities such as continents, and biological entities such as primates. Yet none of the latter entities bear vertical ontological relations to each other, being in different ontological branches of constitution/realization. But the sciences do nonetheless take these higher-level entities to bear ontological relations to each other, often taking such entities to provide boundary-condition relations for each other, or simply to enter into causal relationships. Because the entities related in these cases are *wholly* distinct, and are in different ontological "branches," I shall call these '*horizontal*' ontological relations. And historical cases involving such relations, or 'horizontal' cases, further illuminate the differences in the scope of interpretive application of MC and PC.

At the beginning of the twentieth century, '*permanentism*', T_{PERM}, was a prominent theory about global geological phenomena, and its main thesis was that the continents and oceans have always been approximately in their present positions. Reginald Dana, and his followers, had effectively defended permanentism in the latter part of the nineteenth century (Dana 1873). But at the turn of the century, work in biogeography on the present and past distributions of life forms led to problems (see Frankel [1981], LeGrand [1988], and Stewart [1990] for historical surveys). Evidence began to accumulate supporting theories in biogeography, and paleobiogeography, which claimed that life forms, including both animals and plants, were to be found on continents presently separated by large bodies of water. Let us collectively call these theories T_{BIO}. To take one important example, many life forms were found to be common to both Africa and South America and were such that they could not plausibly have been distributed across these continents except by land connection. For instance, larger mammals cannot swim across great expanses of water.

An obvious relation theory concerning the entities of biogeography and geology forced its acceptance in this case. Past connection, or close contiguity, between two continents is a necessary condition for the life forms in question. For some larger mammals distributed over both of these continents, a land connection is the only means by which they could be so distributed given their natures. Thus a theory, T_{RB}, positing a horizontal relation, in this case a boundary condition, was accepted. But given both T_{RB} and T_{BIO}, which takes life forms that could not have been distributed except by a land connection to be on both Africa and South America, then we get the conclusion that Africa and South America must previously have been connected or contiguous. But Africa and South America are presently distant from each other, and T_{PERM} is committed to Africa and South America always having been where they now are. Thus T_{RB}, T_{BIO}, and T_{PERM} bore the cognitive relationship of incompatibility.

Once again, this cognitive relationship was found to be problematic by both critics and proponents of permanentism alike. Interpreting the scientists involved as having used MC provides a comfortable interpretation of the appraisals made in such a horizontal case, for T_{PERM} bore a relationship of incompatibility to well-confirmed theories. But, once again, the case cannot easily be interpreted as involving application of PC. (As noted earlier, I discuss a common objection to this assumption in the following text.) The incompatibility between T_{RB}, T_{BIO}, and T_{PERM} does not provide evidence that the entities of the latter two theories cannot be constituted/realized by physical entities, for T_{RB} does not concern a vertical ontological relation, such as those of realization or constitution, between the entities of T_{BIO} and T_{PERM}. Thus PC does not apply, because the incompatibility does not obviously illuminate anything about whether the entities of these theories can be realized/constituted by physical entities. In this and other horizontal cases, the cognitive relationship between theories is orthogonal to issues concerning compatibility or incompatibility with a physicalist cosmology. Once again, only application of MC clearly explains the assessment made by scientists in this type of historical case.

Reflecting upon this geological case also reveals some further interesting features of minimal appraisal. The behavior of its own supporters showed they negatively assessed permanentism, because they mounted various attempts to vindicate it. For example, the American geologist Bailey Willis (Willis [1932]) offered one of a number of different accounts formulated to overcome these problems. (Another vindicatory account of this type is offered in Simpson [1943]). Willis attempted to overcome the incompatibility between T_{BIO}, T_{PERM}, and T_{RB} by proposing that at some point in the past the relevant continents were connected by '*isthmian links*.' Willis suggested that a long, thin isthmus, similar to that presently connecting North and South America, had once connected the continents of South America and Africa allowing life forms to spread themselves over both of these continents. Willis further hypothesized that at some later time the isthmus had sunk into the ocean floor, leaving the continents unconnected as they are at present. Let us call this revised relation theory $T_{RB}*$: it asserts that common species distributions occur on continents that were previously contiguous or linked by an isthmus that since has disappeared. Unsurprisingly, given the ad hoc nature of the isthmian, or "land-bridge," hypothesis it was not widely accepted as vindicating permanentism. But for my purposes this is beside the point. For in this case we have seen that compatibility with physicalism clearly is not at issue, but that scientists may still be inspired to pursue vindicatory accounts as a result of their use of something like MC. Scientists such as Willis sought such vindicatory accounts to preserve an attractive theory that appeared to be incompatible with well-confirmed theories in other domains. This case consequently demonstrates that vindicatory accounts of the type emphasized by Field, and any explanatory benefits they may bring in their wake, may simply result from the desire to resolve 'local' intertheoretic incoherence, rather than attempts to establish compatibility with physicalism.

We have now examined two further cases of scientific theory assessment where MC has interpretive application, but PC has none. But MC has still further applications that PC lacks. I have only considered cases where a theory of the ontological relation between the entities posited by other theories generates such a cognitive relationship, since these are the cases focused on by the defenders of MP. But MC potentially explains the negative appraisals made by scientists in any situation where two or more theories are incompatible however this relationship is produced. In contrast PC only applies where theories positing vertical ontological relations are involved. Nonetheless, even just those cases involving ontological relations allow us to formulate a skeptical argument about the historical claims of MP. This is what I will dub the '*Third Wheel Argument*' and it is driven by the idea that the Physicalist Criterion is an interpretive "third wheel" forming no part of the best interpretation of scientific theory appraisal.

Roughly, the Third Wheel Argument goes as follows: (1) We need to posit the use of a Physicalist Criterion in explaining scientific theory appraisal only in order to explain cases in which accounts positing vertical relations between entities are used in appraising theories.[13] (2) Cases in which vertical relation accounts are used in appraising theories are wholly explained by positing the use of MC. Thus, from (1) and (2), we can conclude, (3), we need not posit the use of the Physicalist Criterion, in addition to positing use of MC, in explaining scientific theory appraisal. The Third Wheel Argument therefore reiterates that MC provides an alternative interpretation of the relevant cases that undermines the "only ball game in town" argument for the descriptive claims of MP. And we can extend the argument still further. Because it is true that, (4), we must accept that MC was used in scientific theory appraisal, regardless of whether we also accept this of the Physicalist Criterion. For, as I previously argued using the examples of connectionist theories and permanentism, only an interpretation based upon MC can explain top-down vertical cases and those involving horizontal relations. But it is a general methodological maxim that, (5), we should posit the use of no more methodological principles in explaining scientific practice than we need to. Therefore, from (4) and (5), given the dispensable nature of the Physicalist Criterion concluded in (3), the conclusion of the Third Wheel Argument is that we should not posit the use of the Physicalist Criterion in explaining scientific theory appraisal. If sound, the Third Wheel Argument undermines the crucial descriptive claim underlying JSP. And a similar argument can easily be constructed to undermine the claim that we are warranted in believing that a physicalist heuristic has guided scientific research.[14]

Given my juxtaposition of explanations ascribing the use of physicalist and minimal criteria, and heuristics, I want to note that these do not necessarily constitute mutually exclusive alternatives. There is again the possibility suggested by Burian (1993) that scientists use a 'reticulated' array of short- and long-term norms that involve different sets of criteria of appraisal. Scientists might use MC in the short term or with regard to immature theories, while reserving PC for use in the longer term or with mature theories. Consequently, there are potentially a variety of different sets of such norms in which both MC and PC may figure and I suggest that such a "mixed" account offers the supporter of MP their most promising descriptive account. However, putting these subtleties to one side, the possibility that scientists have minimally appraised their theories nonetheless undermines the crucial descriptive premise of JSP. The Third Wheel Argument establishes that we are not presently warranted in positing use of a Physicalist Criterion to provide even *part* of the most adequate historical explanation of the relevant scientific cases. Viewed through the lens of our present historical evidence I contend that qualified acceptance of the Third Wheel Argument is compelling. It may well turn out that further detailed investigation of the relevant cases, beyond their gross features, will show that we must interpret scientists as using a Physicalist Criterion. Nonetheless, the Third Wheel Argument presently shows that we are unwarranted in believing that a Physicalist Criterion has been used to successfully appraise theories in the sciences.

As I noted earlier, Methodological Physicalists are often unconvinced by objections such as the Third Wheel Argument, because they question whether such arguments, even if sound, really pose a difficulty for their descriptive claims. Such responses take a number of related forms.[15] First, even if the Third Wheel Argument were sound, it is asked, would our being justified only in using MC, rather than PC, really make any difference? Won't the philosophical projects undertaken by defenders of MP still be justified even if the practices of the sciences only justify us in using MC? Often underlying these points is a further idea: that the prescriptions of PC are just a *subset* of MC's prescriptions. Given this relationship, it is objected, even if the sciences only directly justify us in using MC, then the prescriptions made by Methodological Physicalists will be justified nonetheless.

Such responses clearly have deep roots that explain the persistent appeal of MP, and I therefore want to closely examine their basis. In particular, I shall try to disentangle minimal appraisal and physicalist methodologies so that we may precisely evaluate this type of defense of MP. I want to begin by considering the first question: Do PC and MC really justify the same philosophical projects? To investigate this issue let us take moral discourse as our primary example, though I will suggest similar points apply to intentional psychology. Under MC, a theory is assessed 'locally' as a result of its cognitive relationships to well-confirmed theories in scientific domains. The obvious question when applying MC is whether moral discourse bears cognitive relationships beyond bare compatibility with *any* scientific theories. At present it appears that moral discourse is marked by our lack of any developed theory of how its 'entities' or 'explanations' relate to those of scientific and other theories, and I use scare quotes because it is a question whether moral discourse even posits entities or offers explanations. Consequently, moral discourse apparently passes MC, because our understanding is presently too shallow to ground anything more than cognitive relationships of bare compatibility between moral discourse and scientific theories, from whatever domain. Though more controversial I believe that similar points hold with intentional psychology. We lack detailed scientific accounts of the neurophysiological states that realize/ constitute beliefs and desires, because our present understanding of them is at a very early stage. And again we are in a situation where intentional psychology plausibly bears nothing more than a cognitive relationship of bare compatibility to scientific theories in other domains, thus lacking the incompatibility needed to block acceptance under a 'local' criterion such as MC.

In contrast, PC does prescribe that we should not accept either moral discourse or intentional psychology. The reason for this difference is that PC is not limited in its application to information supplied by well-confirmed scientific theories, but instead casts a 'global' net for relevant information. In this respect, PC is in marked contrast to MC and, for example, under PC moral discourse is taken to have a problem simply because we cannot imagine any physical state that could, for instance, have the "queer" property of being normative (Mackie [1977b]). And, as we have seen, Fodor and others have negatively assessed intentional psychology because we had a prima facie problem imagining how any physical state could have the property of having the potential to be erroneous (Fodor [1987]). These facts, though not generated by evidence from well-confirmed scientific theories, plausibly do lead to cognitive relationships of incompatibility between P and moral discourse, and also intentional psychology, and hence to a negative appraisal under PC.

Under the 'global' PC, but not the 'local' MC, one becomes worried about general features of moral 'entities' such as their normativity, or mental states and their putative potential for being erroneous. Appreciating this difference may help us to understand recent critics of MP who have been concerned about what we might call its intellectually 'free-wheeling' approach. Critics such as Stich, and others, have emphasized that intentional psychology, for example, is highly successful in its own domain of inquiry and has no 'locally' based incompatibilities to other well-confirmed scientific theories (Baker [1995], Burge [1989] and [1992] and Stich [1993]). These critics are, I suggest, in large measure motivated by the fact that MP uses a 'global' criterion such as PC, when in fact the sciences only sanction the use of 'locally' driven criteria such as the MC. And such 'local' criteria, as I have just suggested, do not obviously prescribe that we should cease to accept moral discourse or intentional psychology.

In answer to the first response to the Third Wheel Argument we have found that only being justified in using a criterion of minimal appraisal such as MC would apparently leave Methodological Physicalists without any justification for their philosophical projects. But what of the second response to the Third Wheel Argument: that PC's, or some other

Physicalist Criterion's, prescriptions are just a *subset* of the prescriptions of the MC? The idea here is apparently that, although wider in its scope, application of MC tracks all the applications of physicalist criteria such as PC. We have already seen reasons to doubt this claim, but defenders of MP argue that our judgments about compatibility, or incompatibility, with physicalism are always mediated by our judgments about the compatibility, or incompatibility, of specific scientific theories from different domains. Consequently, proponents of MP often suggest, this mediating role entails that the prescriptions of a physicalist criterion must be a subset of a criterion of minimal appraisal such as MC. Let us call this the 'Subset Suggestion.' If this suggestion is correct, then it appears that if we are justified in using MC, then we are justified in using some Physicalist Criterion, and the Third Wheel Argument would again fail to undermine MP's most common naturalistic justification.

In evaluating the Subset Suggestion, we should first note that if the nature of a Physicalist Criterion is interpreted in this manner, then the criterion is very different from the criterion recently used in philosophy. As we have seen, naturalization projects can be justified by use of a 'global' criterion such as PC, as it allows a very wide body of information as relevant in assessing cognitive relationships to P. But if the Subset Suggestion is correct, then the only ground for naturalizations would be application of a 'local' form of a Physicalist Criterion under which the only relevant cognitive relationships to physicalism would be those mediated by 'local' cognitive relationships between well-confirmed scientific theories. But then recent philosophical projects would still not be justified, for we have seen that the 'local' cognitive relationships that moral discourse, or intentional psychology, bear to well-confirmed scientific theories are plausibly insufficient to generate incompatibilities.

Perhaps more importantly, under the Subset Suggestion we also need to ask why a Physicalist Criterion should be so named? Such a criterion would simply be a demand that we not accept theories involved in 'locally' based intertheoretic incoherence of just the type that the MC prescribes we should avoid. But in what way would the resulting criterion be 'physicalist' when construed in this manner? 'Local' intertheoretic relationships between specific theories are the engine of such appraisals and it again appears that physicalism is left as a 'third wheel.' This concern is further illuminated if we consider the common criticism of premise (1) of the Third Wheel Argument that I promised I would ultimately address.

Premise (1) assumes that physicalism is only relevant in scientific theory assessment when a vertical relation theory in involved. The common objection is that this premise embodies too narrow a construal of the role P may play in assessing theories (Field [1992] may favor this line of objection). For example, the objector argues that even in horizontal cases where a well-confirmed theory, T_{RBD}, posits a horizontal ontological relation between the entities of a well-confirmed theory T_D and a less well-confirmed theory T_B, then P may still be relevant to theory assessment. For, continues the objection, given the truth of physicalism, if T_D, T_{RBD}, and T_B bear a relationship of incompatibility, and T_D and T_{RBD} are well confirmed, then we have reason to believe that the entities of T_B cannot be physically realized or constituted. Consequently, the objector concludes, in this manner P does have application to the appraisal of theories even in horizontal cases. (Note that a similar objection holds about the role P might play in top-down cases.)

Once again, the important question to pose in response to this line of objection is why the relevant demand in such cases is at all 'physicalist'. The prescriptive demand at work here is apparently merely one for 'locally' grounded intertheoretic coherence, in other words the avoidance of relationships of incompatibility between our specific scientific hypotheses. The physicalist then apparently leverages the incompatibilities between scientific theories into a conclusion about incompatibility with physicalism. But why is the relevant assessment in such cases not *simply* that T_B is unlikely to be true given the truth of T_D and T_{RBD}, rather than that its entities cannot be physically realized/constituted? Before we accept the Methodological Physicalist's claim that premise (1) of the Third Wheel Argument is false, we need to be given a reason why the demand for coherence in such cases is specially 'physicalist' in character. Otherwise we will no longer apparently be discussing application of a *Physicalist* Criterion. Until such an answer is forthcoming, the second response of Methodological Physicalists to the Third Wheel Argument thus also fails to block its damaging conclusion.

The close similarity of mundane criteria, such as MC, and physicalist criteria lends a superficial plausibility to the Subset Suggestion, and such tangles of concepts are typical of many of the issues surrounding physicalism. Bas van Fraassen has argued that another of these conceptual tangles leaves physicalists in the grip of what he calls "false consciousness" with regard to possibility of defining the 'physical' and formulating a substantive version of physicalism.[16] Our work disentangling a physicalist methodology from the type of minimal appraisal often used in the sciences suggests that many philosophers may be in the grip of such "false consciousness" about the methodological role of physicalism. For the conclusions of our closer examination of the relevant issues can be sharpened into a dilemma for Methodological Physicalists as follows. Either the prescriptions of a Physicalist Criterion such as PC are simply a subset of those of minimal criteria such as MC, or they are not. If a Physicalist Criterion's prescriptions are a subset of those of a minimal criterion, then recent philosophical claims about the prescriptive implications of a Physicalist Criterion are incorrect, for example claims that intentional psychology, or moral discourse, fail this criterion. And, furthermore, there is the unanswered question about why the criterion taken to be a subset of MC is a 'physicalist' criterion at all. On the other hand, if a Physicalist Criterion and more minimal criteria differ in their prescriptions, then the Third Wheel Argument implies that we are presently unwarranted in taking working scientists to have used a Physicalist Criterion. Therefore, we are not presently justified in pursuing a 'physicalist' methodology and the types of recent philosophical projects inspired by such 'physicalist' methodologies, such as the plethora of naturalizing projects, are not justified either.[17] Let us call this the 'Methodological Dilemma,' as it frames serious questions about whether defenders of MP can save their methodological claims by using the Subset Suggestion, or related ideas, to respond to the Third Wheel Argument.

To conclude, we have now seen how the subtle similarities between a physicalist methodology, and more mundane methodological canons, such as MC, lead to the *appearance* that MP is justified by scientific practice. But I have argued that Methodological Physicalists are presently dangerously close to what van Fraassen calls "false consciousness." For on closer inspection of the relevant issues, I have argued that defenders of MP have not produced a criterion whose use is both justified by our present historical evidence and that is also distinctly 'physicalist' in nature. Although one can formulate criteria that would prescribe we must undertake vindicatory naturalizations of moral discourse, or intentional psychology, the problem is justifying the use of such a full-blooded Physicalist Criterion. For I have argued that such a criterion will fall prey to the Third Wheel Argument and will be not be naturalistically justified by scientific practice. On the other hand, one may also successfully formulate criteria of appraisal based around 'local' cognitive relationships between scientific theories that have clearly been historically used in the sciences. Yet such criteria, such as MC, are questionably 'physicalist' in character and do not justify the philosophical projects of MP. More detailed historical investigations may well show that these problems can be overcome. However, based upon the Third Wheel Argument and the Methodological Dilemma, my final conclusion is that it presently remains to be shown that MP, as critics have long suspected, is not either unjustified or 'physicalist' in name alone.[18]

NOTES

1. Methodological Physicalist positions are explicitly defended, for example, in Causey (1981); Field (1972) and (1992); Hellman and Thompson (1975); Poland (1994); Post (1987); Quine (1978, p. 25); and Railton (1985).
2. To note but a few examples of such naturalizations: Fodor's (1987) and (1990c) are both apparently instances of vindicatory naturalizations of intentionality; Maddy's (1990a) and (1990b) are examples of naturalizing accounts of mathematical entities such as sets and numbers; and Railton's (1986) is an instance of a naturalization of goodness. As I detail below in Note 17, naturalizations need not be important solely to Methodological Physicalists, but as I explain in the first section naturalizations will only usually have *vindicatory* significance for defenders of MP.
3. Thus although it might be possible to construct an a priori justification of MP this would be unacceptable because it offends against such naturalistic scruples. For unless a Physicalist Criterion has already been used in the sciences, then such a justification would imply a revision to existing scientific practice. Naturalists will be suspicious of such revisions, as their naturalism is partially motivated by the difficulty of predicting which methods of inquiry will be successful *prior* to their actual use.
4. The two roles correspond to those, (R1) and (R2), suggested and discussed by Poland (1994, pp. 245–6).
5. See Note 2 above for references.
6. To take another example, Field favors a still richer criterion based around the relations of the theory T's causal explanations to physical explanations, in addition to the relations of T's entities to physical entities (Field 1992). Again, my arguments about PC will apply equally to Field's richer criterion, and to avoid complicating my discussion I shall therefore focus upon the simpler criterion. In addition, Field (1992) also offers some plausible arguments that relations of supervenience will be insufficient as the basis of a Physicalist Criterion. I am sympathetic to his arguments, and I shall not therefore consider physicalist criteria based on supervenience relations in my discussion. However, I contend that my criticisms will ultimately apply to such criteria even if they can be successfully formulated.
7. Laudan's brief taxonomy of such relationships is my starting point (Laudan [1977], pp. 50–4). But Laudan couches his descriptions of these relationships in terms of entailment relations between pairs of theories, and I am both suspicious of the use of entailment and in the cases I consider triads of theories will be the focus.
8. See Gillett (1997, ch. 2), and (unpublished-a), for reasons why PC elides the critics' claims. Basically the defense is as follows. Stich and Laurence claim all versions of PC either (a) have implausible implications, such as that we are unjustified in accepting the theories that posit HIV or even pigs, or (b) are trivially satisfied by all theories. We can see that PC does not have these implications. Although we may not have established how, in every facet, pigs, for example, can be constituted by physical entities; we certainly do lack evidence that they cannot be so constituted, and hence also lack evidence that our pig theory is incompatible with physicalism. We are therefore justified under PC in accepting theories that posit pigs or HIV. On the other hand, PC is not trivially satisfied by all theories. With intentional psychology, or a

realistically construed moral discourse, it can plausibly be argued that there is 'global' evidence that the existence of the entities posited by these theories is incompatible with a physicalist cosmology.

9. Because I am ultimately skeptical that PC has actually been used in the sciences, it is reasonable for Methodological Physicalists to be concerned that I have foisted an overly strong, or otherwise flawed, criterion upon them. I therefore want to emphasize that with regard to each of the issues considered (metaphysical form of physicalism, epistemic relation, etc.) I have incorporated assumptions with weaker prescriptive implications into PC. In this manner, I have tried to 'lower the bar' for the Methodological Physicalist, for it should be easier to confirm that PC has been used in the sciences than criteria with stronger prescriptive implications.

10. Obviously in order to establish the historical claim relevant to JSP one needs to consider cases of successful scientific theory appraisal. Defenders of MP such as Field and Poland simply assume that the cases of theory appraisal they consider were successful, perhaps unsurprisingly given the complex and temporally extended nature of the historical issues involved. For the sake of argument, in my discussion I shall therefore assume that, unless we have strong evidence that an instance of theory appraisal was unsuccessful, then we may assume its success. Once again, I contend that ideally an extended examination of the historical evidence is needed to assess whether such an assumption is warranted.

11. An obvious example of such a situation would be that involving Alfred Wegener's theory of "continental drift," see LeGrand (1988, ch. 2) and Stewart (1990, ch. 2), for surveys.

12. I want to be careful to note that Poland believes that we are yet to provide a justification for MP, though he does claim it is "undeniable" that a Physicalist Criterion has been used in the sciences (Poland [1994], p. 265).

13. Both Field and Poland apparently implicitly assume the truth of this premise. Theories positing relations of constitution, realization or identity, are all vertical relation theories, and the cases Poland and Field consider are limited to cases involving such vertical accounts. We can also provide an obvious rationale for such an assumption. The cognitive relationship a theory bears to physicalism, given the very nature of this cosmology, is necessarily mediated by evidence about the vertical relations that can, or cannot, hold between entities. Lacking such a vertical relation account we therefore lack the basis for a generating a cognitive relationship of incompatibility between the theory and physicalism. However, see the following discussion for an obvious criticism of the premise.

14. Once again, I believe we can offer a Third Wheel Argument based around a simpler, minimal methodological account. In this case, the work of Lindley Darden and Nancy Maull (Darden and Maull [1977], Maull [1977], and Darden [1991]) provide a detailed treatment of this minimal alternative. Darden and Maul noted that it is very often the case that scientists investigate the relations holding between the entities of theories in two domains of inquiry in the search for explanatory insight through what they term '*interfield theories*.' The cases discussed by Darden and Maull thus provide us with a 'minimal heuristic': roughly, to search for theories of the ontological relations between the entities of theories in different domains of inquiry in order to increase explanatory efficacy.

The minimal heuristic account will potentially explain all the historical episodes involving searches for accounts of the ontological relations between entities. It explains the gross features of cases involving horizontal relations, for instance where entities serve as boundary conditions for each other, as well as those where the entities are related by vertical relations such as those of realization, constitution, or identity. In contrast, interpretations involving the use of P as a heuristic will only potentially explain cases involving vertical relations, and must be supplemented by the minimal heuristic account that is needed to explain the cases involving horizontal relations. Consequently, we are once again faced with a situation where one explanation interprets scientists as using both physicalist and minimal heuristics to guide their research, and the alternative simply interprets scientists as using a minimal heuristic. And we thus apparently ought to accept the simpler of the two hypotheses, that scientists only use a minimal heuristic.

15. Two rather different responses are less persuasive. Methodological physicalists such as Field and Poland both have noted that scientists may only implicitly use the Physicalist Criterion (Field [1992] and Poland [1994], p. 245). In the interpretation that underlies the Third Wheel Argument, however, no use has been made of what scientists explicitly say, and thus the interpretation is not obviously open to objection based upon implicit principles. In addition, it is often observed in response to the claim that scientists do not use a Physicalist Criterion that this is very odd, as most are physicalists. Would there not be many dualist scientists, it is objected, if the descriptive claims of MP were not true? Again, it should be obvious that evidence might be produced by the use of minimal appraisal that confirms physicalism. Thus there is nothing incongruous about the claim that scientists accept the truth of physicalism, given their evidence, but have not used physicalism as instrument in accumulating this evidence.

16. Van Fraassen (1996). See also Chomsky's (1968), and others, for a similar critique of the idea that physicalism can be successfully formulated. I am obviously sympathetic to what I take to be the deeper point of van Fraassen's and Chomsky's criticisms – namely, that we cannot formulate a substantive version of physicalism that ought to play a methodological role in the sciences. However, I have argued elsewhere (Crook and Gillett [forthcoming]) that these critics are wrong to conclude that no substantive version of physicalism can be formulated. When physicalism is once more properly located as a philosophical hypothesis, with no pretensions to a methodological role in the sciences, and is not based directly upon the concepts of the sciences, then I have argued that physicalism can be successfully formulated.

17. Have these philosophical projects thus been a dreadful waste of resources? Not necessarily. Naturalizing projects potentially significant under a minimal heuristic of the type I argued in Note 14 might be drawn from the work of Darden and Maull, and hence regardless of the fate of MP. If a naturalizing project were successful in showing how intentional states, for example, could be physically realized/constituted, then this would be an important achievement for the potential *explanatory* uses such an account might be put to. But far less hangs upon the success of these projects when viewed in this way. The "end of the world," to echo a famous phrase of Fodor's, would not follow the failure of naturalizing projects, for on this view of their import, though

potentially offering explanatory insight, naturalizing projects lack any urgent, *vindicatory* significance. For in the absence of a naturalistic justification for MP, neither intentional psychology, nor our moral discourse or mathematics, would be in danger of abandonment simply because it failed a Physicalist Criterion.

18. Thanks to Craig Callender, Lenny Clapp, Seth Crook, Jerry Fodor, Ernie Lepore, Barry Loewer, Paul Lodge, Steve Stich, and audiences at Rutgers University and the joint Illinois Wesleyan University/Illinois State University Philosophy colloquium, for their comments on earlier versions of this chapter.

12

Physicalism, Empiricism, and Positivism

GARY GATES

The word *physicalism*, when introduced into philosophical conversation by Neurath and Carnap, seemed theirs to define, much as a century earlier the word *positivism* had been Comte's to define. Not everyone is so lucky as to introduce a label by which they will later become known, and such was the lot of Locke who has been tossed with Hobbes and Hume into the catchall bin of Empiricism. Whether original with Locke or presaged in *Leviathan*, the idea that Ideas were all the mind could contemplate seems distinctive enough to deserve its own 'ism.' In any event, the marriage of Locke's internal Empiricism with Comte's cold Positivism produced the uneasy union that the Vienna Circle styled 'physicalism,' but that the world has since come to call by turns 'Logical Positivism' and 'Logical Empiricism.' That a philosophical position could be defined by conjoining two seemingly mismatched themes would itself be of at least historical interest. But it gains a more topical interest if we could show how antiphysicalist theses more recently bandied about were born of the same unhappy union. To that end we will begin in the middle.

Consistent with their antimetaphysical approach to philosophy, Neurath and Carnap cast their original definition of *physicalism* in linguistic terms. Roughly, *physicalism* was the name they gave to the thesis that every meaningful sentence, whether true or false, could be translated into physical language. Although both thought the thesis obviously true, neither thought it knowable a priori. That is, they were both convinced that physicalism was an empirical thesis. Moreover, neither supposed that the physical language was the language of that branch of science called *physics*, at least not at the level of precision and completeness physics had attained contemporaneous with their espousal of the thesis of physicalism. But if the physical language was not the language of physics, then it was incumbent upon them to characterize 'physical language' to make good their definition of 'physicalism.' On this they apparently reached an agreement, characterizing statements in the 'physical language' as statements in which an arrangement of objects or properties is "predicated of" some region or point of space-time (or its equivalent in a future science).

I say that they "apparently" reached an agreement because they quickly fell out over the nature of the physical language, or at least over the nature of those basic statements they called "protocol statements." Carnap envisioned protocol sentences playing some privileged role in what might be considered an egocentric process of justification. His talk of the "primitive protocol language" was continuous with what others had called the "language of direct experience" or "phenomenal language."[1] Neurath, on the other hand, saw in the physical language a way of subverting or avoiding altogether this epistemological project. He construed the protocol statements on a par with the rest of the physical language.[2] Thus Carnap's primitive protocol sentence, "Red at point x, y, z, t," became in Neurath's protocol the sentence, "Carnap says *sotto voce* the sentence-noise, 'Red at point x, y, z, t.'" That these two philosophers could come away from the definition of *physical language*, and hence the definition of *physicalism*, with such disparate views of the basic protocol into which all meaningful statements could be translated indicates that they came into the definition with very different expectations.

In order to understand their disagreement about protocol sentences, I think we might consider how positivism was grafted onto empiricist roots to create the peculiar hybrid philosophy Carnap and Neurath together espoused. To the contemporary American reader, that philosophy's empiricist roots are obvious, tracing back into well-known seventeenth-century British territory through perhaps less well-known nineteenth-century Kantian scholarship. Locke's bold epistemic conjecture,

> Since *the Mind*, in all its Thoughts and Reasonings, hath no other immediate Object but its own *Ideas*, which it alone can contemplate, it is evident, that our Knowledge is only conversant about them,[3]

had, by the time of Mach, become a commonplace of metaphysics: "That the world is our sensation, in this sense, cannot be questioned."[4] Carnap's nominal rejection of traditional epistemology and metaphysics notwithstanding, his claim that "protocols constitute the basis of the entire scientific edifice"[5] reflected this development in empiricist thought. The protocols, as reports of direct experience, were supposed to be both the evidential basis of any meaningful claim and were to provide such claims with any "content" they might have. In the final analysis, meaningful claims were to be both about and justified by sensations.

It is not immediately obvious how Positivism, at least as understood by its progenitor Auguste Comte, could be brought into line with the empiricist project. Comte was struck, as were many of his contemporaries, with the explosion in the natural sciences starting with Galileo. Comte attributed this explosion to the cooperative nature of the new science that he saw as relying on the importation of precise mathematical language and methodology into the natural sciences. In his *Cours de Philosophie Positive* he cited numerous instances where scientific advance came as a direct result of quantifying phenomena and establishing correlation between them and mathematical objects, so that predicting new phenomena was merely a matter of solving some equation of pure math. Universal agreement on mathematics made cooperative science possible as long as the phenomena in question could be intersubjectively identified and quantified. With the physical sciences as a model, Comte saw as the goal of a new social science the identification of intersubjectively quantifiable phenomena on which mathematical analysis could be brought to bear. He contrasted the projected agreement such a social science would allow with the chaos engendered by the subjective analysis of a single mind (what he called "psychology"):

> After two thousand years of psychological pursuit, no one proposition is established to the satisfaction of its followers. They are divided, to this day, into a multitude of schools, still disputing the very elements of this doctrine. This interior observation gives birth to almost as many theories as there are observers.[6]

For Comte, the success of a science was measured by the breadth of agreement it fostered. (Indeed that might have been the only measure of success Comte recognized.) By that standard, introspective empiricism was a manifest failure.

Neurath, more than any other member of the Vienna Circle, represented the Positivist branch of their collective tradition. Like the others, he aimed to make pseudoquestions of traditional epistemological and metaphysical concerns but, unlike the others, thought that Comte had shown the way. By denying "direct" experience any theoretical role at all, either evidential or ontological, he sought to eliminate the first-person perspective from psychology and thus from the rest of science. His criticisms of Carnap's "personal" and "primitive" protocols best illustrate this:

> In Carnap's writings we also encounter an emphasis on the "I" familiar to us from idealistic philosophy. In the universal-slang it is as meaningless to talk of a *personal* protocol as to talk of a *here* and *now*. In the physicalistic language personal nouns are simply replaced by co-ordinates and coefficients of physical states. One can distinguish an *Otto-protocol* from a *Karl-protocol*, but not a protocol of one's own from a protocol of others. The whole puzzle of *other minds* is thus resolved.[7]

Of course, Neurath realized that we accept and reject sentences or propositions for reasons and that those reasons correspond to psychological states. He simply rejected the idea of an epistemological 'ground zero' where a psychological reason obviously corresponded to something such as direct experience. All language is grounded in experience and hence was all equally objective or subjective:

> There are no sentences in the universal-slang which one may characterize as "more primitive" than any others. All are of equal primitiveness. Personal nouns, words denoting perceptions, and other words of little primitiveness occur in all factual sentences, or, at least, in the hypotheses from which they derive. All of which means that *there are neither primitive protocol sentences nor sentences which are not subject to verification.* (p. 205)

So we see that Neurath, as early as 1932, was urging the Vienna Circle toward the sort of epistemological holism Hempel, and later Quine, would eventually champion.

Epistemological holism, as a starting point, just makes good sense for the Positivist. Distrusting subjective analysis of experience (or single case induction), the Positivist seeks to discover and foster agreement. There is no telling beforehand whether a group of people will be more apt to agree on the color of a point in one's visual field, the presence of a duck in the room, or the valence of a particle passing through a bubble chamber. Nor is there any way of telling beforehand whether reaching the slightest agreement in one arena awaits unanimity elsewhere. Best to let "primitiveness" seek its own level as a psychological ("sociological" in Comte and Neurath's terminology) hypothesis. And because no two people ever reach any (verbal) agreement without at least enough background theory in common to share a natural language, complete holism seems the appropriate "*tabula rasa*" assumption for the linguistically oriented positivist. It was nothing more than a presumption in the face of evidence that, for instance, two people could achieve complete agreement in the language of psychology without sharing any 'physical language.' In any event, Neurath's criticisms and his steadfast adherence to the sociological point of view highlighted the solipsistic flavor of Carnap's Empiricism.

It is fair to say that Carnap was moved by Neurath's criticisms and attempted to reclaim the Positivist mantle by showing how personal protocols were either themselves subsets of the general intersubjective physicalistic language or translatable into such subsets. But as Quine pointed out in "Two Dogmas of Empiricism," as Carnap used it, the phrase "point in one's visual field" meant one thing from the first-person perspective and (quite possibly) another from the third-person perspective. Carnap offered no link between the two perspectives that could be justified in terms of (anyone's) direct experience.[8]

But if it is fair to say that Carnap suffered under Neurath's criticism it is also fair to say that Neurath faced a dilemma of his own. He was, after all, arguing for physicalism and so needed to justify the claim that all meaningful sentences could be translated into the physicalistic language. It was hardly an accident that Neurath's replacement for Carnap's protocol sentences ended up looking similar to reports of Carnap's sort of reports. However, calling such reports "physicalistic" seems completely arbitrary or at least not scientifically motivated. That is, Carnap's primitive protocol language, which was in some sense outside of or independent of any particular theory, was supposed to be the sum total of data for which a physical theory had to account. As such it could be used to identify a class of theories that Carnap was free to label "physical." Neurath's physicalism, without a primitive protocol and in the absence of a comprehensive psychological theory, either becomes something of a blank check, to be filled in if and when we ever hit upon a particular language that serves all of our theoretical needs, or the vacuous claim that all of our theories can be written in a natural language. Holism proved a two-edged sword, as likely to eviscerate 'physicalism' as lop off traditional metaphysics and epistemology. If Carnap had indeed hit upon a primitive protocol language, he could have been justified, at least by his own verificationistic standards, in rejecting some sentences as meaningless. It is not at all clear that Neurath could have done anything similar to that until our scientific theorizing was completed. Whereas Carnap might have said that all of our meaningful theorizing was about sensations, Neurath couldn't say that all of our meaningful theorizing was about anything in particular until we had finished theorizing.

I think that physicalism as an antimetaphysical movement disintegrated largely because of the incongruent Empiricist and Positivist aims with respect to protocol sentences. The Vienna Circle was unable to identify a set of sentences that would at one and the same time serve as the epistemological 'ground zero' of empirical justification and as the phenomena to be quantified and correlated by an intersubjective science. It is interesting, though, that antiphysicalistic reactions have suffered from the same ambiguities that beset the physicalists. Carnap and Neurath agreed on the physicalistic thesis for different reasons, reasons that in the end could not be reconciled with one another. Antiphysicalists reject the same thesis, but also for reasons that are, if not irreconcilable, at least divergent. There are those who seem to agree with Carnap and the Empiricist tradition that there is in fact a primitive protocol. They feel, though, that this protocol is, for some reason or other, logically or metaphysically independent from the language in which most of science is done. That is, they feel certain that there is some realm of discourse concerning consciousness, conscious states, qualia, or the 'raw feels' of direct experience that is manifestly or demonstrably distinct from any of the discourse belonging to the exact sciences.

These antiphysicalists have, in a sense, inherited Carnap's problem with a vengeance. Carnap only had to show that a language of direct experience could be an intersubjective language. These antiphysicalists not only have to make good on Carnap's promise, they have to do so while maintaining that none of the other intersubjective languages developed in pursuit of exact science fit the bill. They are not merely claiming that the languages of our present physical theories do not afford adequate descriptions of experience or of consciousness – something with which only a fool would disagree. They want to say that any continuous development of those languages would likewise prove inadequate. Hence they must think that our present talk of direct experience, although intersubjective enough to support meaningful conversation, differs fundamentally from any language in which we discuss something other than direct experience. In short, language must work differently from usual when the subject matter is direct experience.[9] This, of course, was Carnap's thesis as well; the only difference being that Carnap thought that the rest of language "logically" depended on talk of direct experience for its entire content. The sort of dependence at issue here is obviously not revealed by the surface structure of language, else how could the physicalist and the antiphysicalist so sharply disagree? Nor, it seems, could any amount of introspection settle the issue. Both Carnap and his detractors are introspectively convinced of a meaningful primitive protocol of subjective experience. Where they disagree is on the meanings of "objective" discourse. But that issue, encompassing as it does the question of how *two* people come to talk of a shared reality, must – for any but the solipsist – be settled by empirical investigation. Any introspective ability each of us might have extends at most to the nature of his or her own experience. That is, even if we stipulate meaningful talk of direct experience, we are left with unanswered "sociological" questions of how the rest of language works and of how it is related to talk of direct experience. Again, similar to Carnap, this sort of antiphysicalist has tied his hands, forgoing for introspective reasons epistemological or semantic holism, the most promising solution to the "sociological" question.

Oddly enough, this form of antiphysicalism is often considered compatible with physicalism about everything but what is "directly" experienced. Differing from Carnap's verificationist semantics, language on this view is usually characterized by an external/causal theory of reference, so that in general we might be referring to the same object or property with two different terms even though we have no subjective – or internal – means of determining this. Linguistic reference only becomes internal where consciousness or direct experience is concerned. This form of antiphysicalism must acknowledge two distinct ways in which language works, only one of which is anything close to well understood. Its most recent incarnation in David Chalmers' book, *The Conscious Mind*,[10] serves as a good example. In that voluminous defense of antiphysicalism, Chalmers devotes less than two pages to what he calls the "Argument from Reference." Responding to the criticism that we are presumably able to talk about our conscious experiences, Chalmers maintains that although referring to an entity usually requires a causal connection to it and although acquiring a complex, possibly nonreferring term usually requires causal connections to the referents of the basic terms from which it is composed, when it comes to consciousness these usual requirements are suspended – owing, perhaps, to our "knowledge of a more immediate variety" (p. 202). Chalmers gives no indication of how this more immediate knowledge could fix the reference of communal terms. Indeed, we are left with no option other than verificationism – that each conscious experience is precisely what it seems to be – to guarantee that a single person can successfully use a word to pick out various instances of the same experiential type. What parameters guide intersubjective talk of conscious experience on Chalmers's view is left completely mysterious. This view, just as Carnap's own, fits best if at all with solipsism, at least concerning direct experience.

There is another sort of antiphysicalist who, although an epistemological holist such as Neurath, seems to think that our theorizing wholly divides into two necessarily distinct realms. The supposed division in theorizing, however, does not reflect a division in subject matter – indeed this sort of antiphysicalism is reckoned compatible with "token physicalism." The division in theorizing purportedly reflects different attitudes we have toward that common subject matter, attitudes that could only be individually addressed by different methods of theorizing. This sort of antiphysicalist (Davidson and McDowell are convenient examples) inherits Neurath's dilemma: saying before our scientific theorizing is completed what the eventual shapes of our theories will be without the benefit of a topic-neutral or theory-neutral way of characterizing what our theories are meant to recover. This antiphysicalist claims that

although neither our present physical theory nor our present psychological theory is manifestly the best we can produce, the two theories are
such that we can now see that no better physical or psychological theory
could alleviate our need for its counterpart. As with Neurath it is difficult to see how they can make a principled distinction between types of
talk (their distinction between physical and mental talk here apposed
with Neurath's distinction between physical and metaphysical), when
they only have the example of presently held theories and the theories
that have, for one reason or another, been discarded. Surely our present
psychological and physical theories answer different practical needs.
However, given the present impoverished state of our knowledge it
seems no more warranted to say that our psychological theories and our
physical theories will forever diverge than it does to say that at some
point in the future they will likely converge.

Rather than engage in premature prognostication, I would like to call
attention to commonalities between the Carnapians and the Neurathi-
ans of both physicalist and antiphysicalist stripe. In particular, I wish to
identify two theses – one roughly Empiricist and the other roughly Positivist – that form a common platform for all four positions we have been
discussing, with hope of isolating a compromise solution that does justice
to all concerned parties. The Empiricist thesis can briefly be characterized as the unified nature of experience. The Positivist thesis can be somewhat less tersely characterized as follows: Agreement between two
people on a general claim requires agreement between them on how to
apply the terms from which the general claim is composed. In a way I
hope to make clear, the Empiricist thesis is what pulls us toward physicalism and the Positivist thesis attenuates that pull.

That Carnap saw experience as being unified goes without question.
He was, after all, arguing that all of science was unified and that the
content of science was experience. Perhaps less obviously, the unity
of experience is also a centerpiece of the Carnapian antiphysicalist's
thought. I say "less obviously" because it is not precisely clear why
these antiphysicalists often turn to *dualism*. It is certainly no easier to
understand how a thing that can see yellow could be the sort of thing
that could feel pain than it is to understand how a physical system could
do either. Yet these antiphysicalists don't talk of the difficult problem of
seeing yellow *and* the difficult problem of feeling pain. Instead they talk
of the general problem of consciousness that apparently encompasses
both. Their presumption that these various problems can be captured
under a single rubric bespeaks a commitment to the unified nature of
experience.

Neurath, despite his squeamishness about "introspection" and "subjective experience," felt this pull as well, as is revealed in his brief argument for the unity of science:

> The unified language of physicalism confronts us whenever we make a scientific prediction on the basis of laws. When someone says that if he sees a certain color he will hear a certain sound, or *vice versa*, or when he speaks of the "red patch" next to the "blue patch" which will appear under certain conditions, he is already operating within the framework of physicalism. As a percipient he is a physical structure: he must localize perception, e.g., in the central nervous system or in some other place. Only in this way can he make predictions and reach agreement with others and with himself at different times. Every temporal designation is already a physical formulation. (p. 287)

I think it is safe to say that the physicalism Neurath was announcing here was not a sociological thesis. That is, when Neurath claims that "*all types of laws must, under given conditions, be capable of being connected with one another*" (p. 284, emphasis added) he was not reporting the present state of science. Physics alone was and is, by this standard, in disarray. The inevitability of unified science in Neurath's sense is something we expect from science, not something we notice as the asymptote present scientific theorizing is approaching.

Even a Neurathian antiphysicalist such as Davidson could not resist the tug toward this sort of unity. Clearly he disagrees with Neurath concerning the necessary connection of all types of laws. Yet even while proposing that some of the very same pairs of events could be connected by different laws that themselves might not be connected, he maintains that there must be some unified set of laws that, in effect, connects all of the dots. Davidson champions the anomalous nature of the mental and its (nonstrict) laws, but only against the backdrop of the necessary subsumption of causally related events under a closed system of strict, physical law. The difficulty in understanding Davidson's position is not in grasping his thesis concerning the anomalous nature of the mental, which – as a sociological thesis – seems a far more accurate description of the present state of affairs than Neurath's thesis of reducibility. Rather, the difficulty lies in understanding his motivation for the strong physicalistic thesis enmeshed with his notion of causation. Why does Davidson presume that there must be a univocal sense of "event" in terms of which all the "causal" laws of every science may be written, and why does he assume that the "causal nexus provides for a 'comprehensive and continuously usable framework' for the identification and description of events"?[11]

The notion that the "principle elements of reality" might fit continuously into a single continuous framework (be it causal or spatiotemporal)
is hardly something one could glean from cursory examination
of the various sciences. Indeed, it is far from clear that there is a consistent way of linking the primitive vocabularies of statistical mechanics,
quantum mechanics, and general relativity. Standard quantum mechanics
alone divides the world into two distinct realms – the measured and
the unmeasured, each with it own basic physical systems and its own
distinct sorts of "events." Nor is this merely a feature of "new" physics.
Classical field theory and classical particle theory each developed without
any obvious ontological link to the other. We might suppose
that there is some notion of spatiotemporal relation primitive to all
physical theories, but it is not clear that even this could be considered
unique. Consider, for instance, Bohm's theory of particle motion that
posits both a configuration space of $3n$ dimensions for a system of n
particles in which the "wave-equation" develops and the 3-space through
which the particles trace trajectories. Physical theories taken as a whole
have defied ontological unification and continue to do so. This is not to
say that physicists have not sought a grand unified theory. Rather it is
to say that the notion of unification is a hope that physicists and philosophers have brought to the various theories they have developed, not
a lesson they have learned in developing those theories. I would suggest that it is a hope based in part at least on the presumed unity of
experience.

I have been arguing that all four positions are premised on something
similar to the unified nature of experience. How, though, is experience
unified? The unity of experience amounts to this: To identify an object
or event in our experience is to subjectively extract it, to recognize a
subjective relation between it and any other object or event we might
identify in our experience. To isolate a blue patch in my visual field is to
recognize its relation, in my experience, to anything in my visual field
that is not part of the patch. To identify it as blue is to recognize its relation to that which is not blue. To distinguish it as part of my visual field
is to recognize its relation to the auditory and tactile experiences that
temporally coincide with it. To identify it as occurring now is to recognize its relation to what I remember of the past and expect in the future.
To identify it as a nearby swatch of cloth is to recognize its relation
to those distant events or objects I am currently perceiving. That is, as
diverse as my experience may be, an object or event in my experience
that bears no relation whatsoever to the other objects or events in my
experience is simply inconceivable. A tactile experience of a fuzzy cloth
that occurs neither before, during, nor after my visual experience of a

blue patch is a tactile experience I cannot comprehend having. By isolating an object or event in my experience I recognize its relation to the other objects or events in my experience. I cannot imagine doing otherwise. Dualism is disquieting because it doesn't "fit" experience, not because it doesn't accord with scientific practice.

It is tempting to say that with this notion of "extraction" we also have a clear notion of successful scientific theorizing. When we extract objects and events from our experience they become fodder for scientific investigation. We generalize over them, explicitly relating them to other objects and events we have extracted. We construct models in which to fit them, and so on. Wouldn't a successful theory, then, be one that afforded us the ability to explicitly situate these objects in a model that included the whole of our extracted experience: past, present, and future? Wouldn't we, in effect, be replacing the object or event into the experience from which it had been extracted? Isn't that the notion at the heart of the physicalism we have been considering? How could we do justice to this notion of "replacement" with anything less than a unified theory, because what we would be modeling is itself recognizably unified?

While there is something intriguing about this idea, I think that this way of putting it suffers from incoherence. While it's true that in isolating an object or event from our experience we recognize its (at least subjective) relation to any other object or event that we might likewise extract from our experience, it is not true that we recognize its relation to the whole of what we might extract from our experience, merely because we have no clear notion of what such a totality might encompass. As we bumble through experience we learn new ways of isolating and identifying various aspects of it. Even words as mundane as *object*, *position*, and *separated* we have come to learn to use in ways that would have baffled our predecessors and our younger selves. In learning these new methods of extraction we develop an understanding of things we have previously missed – not that we missed experiencing, because we now remember experiencing them, but that we missed identifying or misidentified. We now know that much of what we experienced in the past we failed to identify at the time because we didn't have the theoretical apparatus now available to us. Experience teaches us modesty, and modesty prevents us from claiming any clear notion of what extracting the whole of experience for theoretical purposes would encompass. It was this modesty, I suppose, that kept Carnap from settling on any precise formulation of the primitive protocol.

Haven't we, though, identified an attenuated empiricist theme? Science could be the business of extracting aspects of our experience and reunifying them in an ever more detailed model. That would give us a predisposition toward Carnap's sort of physicalism. However, it seems that we should square this empiricist thesis with what is right about Neurath's positivism. Successful science depends on generalizing beyond our present personal experience. That is, science as a cooperative effort has succeeded where individual effort labored relatively fruitlessly. No recent scientist, however revolutionary, would disregard the benefits of reading and incorporating the work of her predecessors and contemporaries. We have learned not to expect anything revolutionary from someone who has not been trained in the rudiments of her chosen field of study. But generalizing beyond one's own present experience requires agreement with others, including one's own past and future self. To collectively test a hypothesis we must collectively agree on what would count as confirming or disconfirming that hypothesis. These are mere truisms by which we have come to identify good scientific practice.

When we speak generally of agreement such as this, what do we have in mind? Surely two people coming to agree that most of the Milky Way's mass is dark matter is very different from two people coming to agree that the Nile has eroded its outer bank, and both are different still from two people coming to agree that groundhogs are hairless at birth. The difference between these various acts of agreement is poorly masked by the locution, "In each case the two people have come to agree on the truth of a proposition." Is there really some generic sense of "to agree on the truth of a proposition" that encompasses each of these situations, one that we can recognize at work in each instance of cooperative scientific advance? The environmental, physiological, and psychological (not to mention, physical) details of these acts of agreement are such as to leave one wondering what "agreement on the truth of a proposition" could mean, or how we could hope to generally characterize cooperative scientific practice in terms of it. This point has nothing to do with verificationist psychology or antimentalism. One can be as realistic as one pleases about beliefs or about believing that snow is white without supposing that the science of doing science should find any use for generalizing over filmy abstract particulars such as propositions. They are, after all, merely the speculative brainchildren of philosophers, not entities presupposed by any psychological theory that has proved its worth in successful prediction.

It was the great good sense of the positivists to realize that, for the purposes of characterizing good science, a linguistic notion of agreement would be indispensable. Cooperative science results in the production of collectively accepted theories and methods of generating predictions in the form of sentences; sentences that, as they are accepted or rejected, are reckoned evidence for or against those theories. The eye of science is indiscriminate; galaxies fall as easily under its gaze as groundhogs. There is but one currency of science, though: the sentence. As sociologists, if we were to ignore the role of natural language in the scientific enterprise, we would be hard pressed to say much of interest concerning a notion of agreement common to the various subject matters of our scientific theorizing.[12] Once we turn our attention to the language of science, though, the problem appears much more tractable. If you want to know whether someone who speaks English agrees with the sentence, "Most of the mass in our galaxy is dark matter," you can ask her, "Is most of the mass in our galaxy dark matter?" If you want to know if she agrees with the sentence, "Groundhogs are hairless at birth," you can ask her, "Are groundhogs hairless at birth?" In either case, a *yes* in reply will indicate agreement with the original sentence and a *no* will indicate disagreement. Moreover, you need know nothing of her particular relationship to either groundhogs or galaxies to tell this. You only need to know how she treats sentences that she accepts.

Recognition of the centrality of linguistic agreement in theorizing about scientific theorizing is implicit in the philosophy of science as it has developed in the twentieth century. Reductionism, Eliminativism, Physicalism, and their negations are primarily linguistic notions. What is surprising is how little attention has been paid to the *linguistic* constraints on linguistic agreement. To be sure, linguistic constraints are dealt with obliquely in talk of "projection," "having a concept," "conceptual relativism," and the like. But such talk is usually so deeply enmeshed in ungrounded philosophical speculation about how language works that it clouds rather than clarifies the issue. This is not to say that there is a better, more scientific theory of how language works that is generally accepted.[13] In the absence of a generally accepted theory, though, it seems appropriate to let common sense be our guide. And what could be more commonsensical than the most basic constraint we impose on entry into scientific discussion: In order to be taken seriously as a contributor to a theoretical discussion in a certain realm of discourse one must display a certain amount of expertise in using the basic terminology of that realm. We would hardly have been convinced of the generalization, "Whales are not fish," had Linnaeus proved incapable of using the words *whales* and *fish* of whales and (other) fish respectively. If one wishes to be a contributing member of a scientific enterprise then one must be able to correctly (by communal standards) label intersubjectively observable phenomena using terminology basic to the enterprise. This not only serves to establish that all participants are "speaking the same language," it verifies that each has practical knowledge of the phenomena under consideration. Learning to label, the first basic step in learning language generally, enters anew with each major expansion of our theoretical repertoire. Labeling expertise thus presents an obvious initial constraint on achieving the sort of linguistic agreement characteristic of scientific discussion.

Labeling expertise also serves to distinguish realms of discourse. I would submit that one can satisfy current communal standards of expertise concerning psychology, for instance, without being able to correctly label an interference pattern produced by the famous two-slit experiment. One can likewise meet the current standards of expertise concerning microbiology without being able to correctly label an elm tree. And one could, I suppose, at least in principle become an expert in quantum mechanics without being able to correctly label dishonesty.[14] In this sense, at least, I take it that all are agreed that our current scientific theorizing decomposes into distinct realms of discourse and that there is not one single communal standard of expertise that one could satisfy in order to enter into every scientific discussion as a potential contributor. In fact, the number of distinct "protocols" in this sense is continually expanding as new enclaves of experts spring up around previously uncategorized phenomena. (Think, for instance, of chaos theory and all its shiny new jargon.)

As much as labeling expertise divides one scientific pursuit from others, it also serves to unify those engaged in that particular pursuit. That is, it gives them a common standard of success toward which to work. Thomas Kuhn recognized this as well as anyone has in *The Structure of Scientific Revolutions*.[15] A set of terms that one must become expert in applying in order to join a particular pursuit suggests a local standard of completeness: reaching consensus on *yes* or *no* answers to the entire "problem set" of general questions formed from those terms. This way of individuating collective scientific enterprises, then, brings with it a clear notion of successful completion of those enterprises.

Mightn't we use this notion of expertise to project to the positivistic thesis of physicalism envisaged by Neurath? What if we developed a primitive vocabulary that was agreed upon by all concerned to constitute the minimal and maximal criteria for entrance into scientific discussion generally; so that to be taken seriously as a potential contributor to scientific discussion one need only display expertise in using exactly those labels and so that inability at using any one of them called one's authority generally into question? Wouldn't this constitute the physicalistic basis Neurath hoped for as the end of science? Ideal completeness, then, would amount to reaching consensus on every generalization (or its negation) that could be formed from that basic vocabulary.

What guarantee would we have, though, that the vocabulary could not be augmented in some way in which we would all later agree was necessary to the advance of science? A communal standard of competence can establish a communally recognized standard of success. But that standard will always be restricted to the various labels we have so far been able to collectively apply to our experience.

What we have seen is that physicalism, as a general philosophical position, arises as an attempt to wed the extremely personal with the quintessentially social. The unity of experience with which each of us is faced offers a goal for scientific theorizing but no communicable standard of its success. We can individually look forward to an idealized future in which each new experience occurs exactly as expected, without getting too specific on the nature of the theory that produces those expectations. (Much as we might imagine meeting the queen without having any idea which particular woman is the queen.) But we can only communicate the specifics of those expectations in the terms that have been communally hammered out over intersubjectively observed phenomena. The communal notion of expertise that signals acceptance into scientific conversation offers a communicable standard of success but does not address our personal goal in scientific theorizing in the first place. We could, perhaps, reach agreement on every generalization that can be formed from the basic vocabulary currently available. But such concerted, monolithic behavior could, for all that, leave each of us wondering what the future might hold.

I think that we have done well to distinguish the positivist from the empiricist presuppositions interlaced by the Vienna Circle. We should not mistake a personal goal for a public standard of success. Carnap and Neurath's attempt to hang 'physicalism' somewhere between the two made it an untenable position. We might all have the same personal reason for doing science and yet be unwilling to confuse it with what can be precisely expressed in today's terminology. We might, for instance, think that it stays the same even as we change theories and today's terms go out of use. We should not then expect it to correspond to a publicly communicable standard for successful scientific practice (and thus serve, say, to separate science from pseudoscience or mind from matter). And if someone wishes to discuss some aspect of experience that "falls outside of" scientific inquiry, then we should ask if the terms she is using also fall outside of communal standards of labeling expertise. If so, then how does one distinguish meaningful discourse from sophisticated babbling?

On the other hand, we may identify from within any particular pursuit those who can and those who cannot use with authority the relevant labels. Those same terms thereby constitute a vocabulary from which we might construct questions meaningful for anyone properly engaged in that pursuit. But no particular vocabulary announces itself as "a sufficient basis" from which all of the important questions can be formed. We should be wary of elevating one realm of discourse to universal stature, even speculatively. A term hasn't been reductively eliminated until no productive realm of discourse requires mastery of its application.[16] For example, to be able to competently engage in psychological discourse one must be able to successfully distinguish, for example, assertion from denial. One displays this ability by using the labels "assertion" and "denial" discriminatively in accord with the general consensus of experts. Unless and until psychological talk becomes manifestly redundant, expert application of those labels will form part of the basis of our best scientific theorizing in at least one realm of discourse. The standards we can make explicit for the completeness of any science arise from within that science, even if our reasons for pursuing completeness do not.

NOTES

1. Carnap (1934, p. 44).
2. Neurath (1932/33).
3. Locke (1975, p. 525).
4. Mach (1986, p. 209).
5. *Ibid.*, p. 93.
6. Comte (1975).
7. Neurath (1932/33, p. 206).
8. It is far from clear how the holistic justification Quine proposes in that article is meant to solve this problem. Indeed, Quine seems to move freely from talk of accepting and rejecting sentences (the third-person perspective) to talk of believing (the first-person perspective) without explaining how a particular belief is supposed to be related to a particular accepted sentence. Given the holism of theoretical meaning, such one-to-one correspondence seems at best problematic.
9. The most extreme proponents of this sort of antiphysicalism – those that construe the subject matter of our direct experience talk as epiphenomenal – embrace this unlikely thesis with something approaching abandon. Everything we know about how language usually works points toward causal interaction with the subject matter under discussion as a primary basis of conversational agreement and disagreement. Agreeing about something, and recognizing that we agree about something, when the source of agreement is not a causal factor in our coming to agree, makes talk of direct experience as mysterious as talk of numbers – more so, because numbers don't change.
10. Chalmers (1996).
11. "The individuation of events," in Davidson (1980, p. 180).

12. Such is the state of our theory of psychology that we have little or no idea of what role the beliefs that underlie such agreement play in determining behavior that is not directly tied to linguistic interchanges.
13. I have attempted to spell out the rudiments of such a theory in an (as yet) unpublished manuscript entitled *Casual Words and Formal Objects*.
14. If, that is, one learned one's physics from scrupulously honest teachers.
15. Kuhn (1970).
16. AZ Gems of Redlands, California, despite the admonitions of mineralogists and philosophers of science, still offers jade beads at $22 a strand. They are hardly the exception.

Part III

Physicalism and Consciousness: A Continuing Dialectic

13

Mental Causation and Consciousness: The Two Mind-Body Problems for the Physicalist

JAEGWON KIM

Mental Causation and Consciousness

Schopenhauer famously called the mind-body problem a "world-knot," or "Weltknoten," and he was surely right. However, the mind-body problem is not really a single problem; it is a cluster of connected problems about the relationship between mind and matter. What these problems are depends, of course, on a broader framework of philosophical and scientific assumptions and presumptions in which the questions are posed and potential solutions are formulated. For the contemporary physicalist, I believe that there are two problems that truly make the mind-body problem a Weltknoten, an intractable and perhaps ultimately insoluble puzzle. These problems concern mental causation and consciousness. The problem of mental causation is to answer this question: How can the mind exert its causal powers in a world that is fundamentally material? The second problem, that of consciousness, is to answer the following question: How can there be such a thing as a mind, or consciousness, in a material world? Moreover, as I will argue, the two problems are interconnected – the two knots are intertwined, and this makes it all the more difficult to unsnarl either of them.

Giving an account of mental causation has been, for the past three decades, one of the main preoccupations of philosophers of mind who are committed to physicalism in one form or another. The problem, of course, is not new: As every student of western philosophy knows, Descartes, who arguably invented the mind-body problem, was confronted forcefully by his contemporaries on this issue.[1] But this does not mean that Descartes's problem is our problem. His problem, as his contemporaries saw, was to show how his all-too-commonsensical thesis of mind-body interaction was tenable within his ontology of two radically diverse substances, minds and bodies. In his replies, Descartes hemmed and hawed, but in the end was unable to produce an effective response. Some of his contemporaries, for example, Malébranche, chose to abandon mental causation but retain the dualism of two substances, and Leibniz is well known for denying causal relations between individual substances altogether, arguing that an illusion of causal transactions arises out of preestablished harmony among the monads. In defending mental causation to the bitter end, however, Descartes showed a commendable respect for philosophical common sense, and I believe we should remember him for this as well as for his much publicized failure to reconcile mental causation with his ontology.

In any case, substance dualism is not the source of our current worries about mental causation;[2] substantival minds are no longer a live philosophical option for most of us. What is new and surprising about the current problem of mental causation is the fact that it has arisen out of the very heart of our materialist commitments. This means that giving up Cartesian substantival minds and embracing a materialist ontology does not make the problem go away. On the contrary, our basic physicalist commitments, as I will argue, can be seen as the source of our current difficulties.

Let me begin with reasons for wanting to save mental causation – why it is important to us that mental causation is real. First, the possibility of human agency, and hence of our moral practice, evidently requires that our mental states have causal effects in the physical world. In voluntary actions our beliefs and desires, or intentions and decisions, must somehow cause our limbs to move in appropriate ways, thereby causing the objects around us to be rearranged. That is how we manage to cope with our surroundings, write philosophy papers, build bridges and cities, and destroy the rain forests. Second, the possibility of human knowledge presupposes the reality of mental causation: perception, our sole window on the world, requires the causation of perceptual experiences and beliefs by physical objects and events around us. Reasoning, by which we acquire new knowledge and belief from the existing fund of what we already know or believe, involves the causation of new belief by old belief. Memory is a causal process involving interactions between experiences, their physical storage, and retrieval in the form of belief. If you take away perception, memory, and reasoning, you pretty much take away all of human knowledge. To move on, it seems plain that the possibility of psychology as a science capable of generating law-based explanations of human behavior depends on the reality of mental causation: mental phenomena must be capable of functioning as indispensable links in causal chains leading to physical behavior. A science that invokes mental phenomena in its explanations is presumptively committed to their causal efficacy. If a phenomenon is to have an explanatory role, its presence or absence must make a difference – a causal difference.

Unsurprisingly, then, for most philosophers the causal efficacy of the mental is something that absolutely cannot be negotiated away. I believe Jerry Fodor is serious when he says:

> ... if it isn't literally true that my wanting is causally responsible for my reaching, and my itching is causally responsible for my scratching, and my believing is causally responsible for my saying ... , if none of that is literally true, then practically everything I believe about anything is false and it's the end of the world.[3]

Taking away mental causation will not put an end to the world, but it surely would be the end of a world that includes Fodor and the rest of us as agents and cognizers. The problem of determinism threatens human agency, and the challenge of skepticism threatens human knowledge. The stakes are even higher with mental causation, for this problem threatens to take away both agency and cognition.

Let us now briefly turn our attention to consciousness, an aspect of mentality that was strangely absent from both philosophy and systematic psychology for much of this century. As everyone knows, consciousness has now returned as a major problematic in philosophy and science, and the last decade of this century has seen an explosive growth and proliferation of research programs and publications on consciousness, not to mention symposia and conferences, all over the western world.

I won't try here to belabor the importance of consciousness to our conception of ourselves as creatures with minds. But I want to note the following paradoxical situation in philosophy. As we have seen, consciousness virtually disappeared from the philosophical and scientific scene for much of this century, and consciousness bashing still goes on in some quarters, with some reputable philosophers arguing that phenomenal consciousness, or 'qualia,' is a fiction of bad philosophy.[4] And even now there are philosophers and psychologists who, while they recognize phenomenal consciousness as something real, do not believe that a complete science of human behavior, including cognitive psychology, has a place for consciousness, that there is a need to invoke phenomenal consciousness in an explanatory/predictive theory of cognition and behavior. But consider the situation in moral philosophy and value theory: When philosophers discuss the nature of the intrinsic good, or what is worthy of our desire and volition for its own sake, the most prominently mentioned candidates include such things as pleasure, avoidance of pain, enjoyment, and happiness – states that are either states of phenomenal experience or states that are intimately tied to experience. To most of us, a fulfilling life, a life worth living, includes a life that is rich and full in phenomenal consciousness – rich in detail and variety and full of subtlety. We would regard a life as impoverished and unsatisfying if that life never included experiences such as the refreshing smell of the sea in a morning breeze, the brilliant colors of an autumn sunset, the fragrance of a bundle of roses, and the wonderfully layered soundscapes projected by a string quartet. In his speech accepting the Nobel Prize in 1904, Ivan Pavlov, whose experiments on animal behavior conditioning probably gave a critical impetus to the behaviorist movement, said, "In point of fact, only one thing in life is of actual interest for us – our psychical experience."[5] It is an ironic fact that consciousness, ultimately the only thing that matters to us, is often relegated in the rest of philosophy as "secondary qualities" or jettisoned outright as a piece of philosophical fiction.

What then is the philosophical problem of consciousness? In *The Principles of Psychology*, William James wrote:

> According to the assumptions of this book, thoughts accompany the brain's workings, and those thoughts are cognitive of realities. The whole relation is one which we can only write down empirically, confessing that no glimmer of explanation of it is yet in sight. That brains should give rise to a knowing consciousness at all, this is the one mystery which returns, no matter of what sort the consciousness and of what sort the knowledge may be. Sensations, aware of mere qualities, involve the mystery as much as thoughts, aware of complex systems, involve it.[6]

In this passage, James is recognizing, first of all, that thoughts and sensations, that is, various modes of consciousness, arise out of neural processes in the brain. But we can only record, or "write down" as he says, the observed de facto correlations that connect thoughts and sensations to types of neural processes. And "no glimmer of explanation" is "yet in sight" as to why these particular correlations hold, or why indeed the brain should give rise to consciousness at all.

Why does pain arise when there is electrical activity in the pyramidal cell layers, and not under another neural condition? Why doesn't itch or tickle arise from pyramidal cell activity? Why should any conscious sensation at all arise when pyramidal cell activity occurs? Why should there be consciousness in a world that is ultimately nothing but bits of matter scattered over space-time points? These questions are precisely the explanatory/predictive challenge posed by the emergentists, like Samuel Alexander, C. Lloyd Morgan, and C.D. Broad – a challenge that they despaired of meeting.

These, then, are the problem of mental causation and the problem of consciousness. Each of them poses a fundamental challenge to the physicalist worldview. How can the mind have a causal influence on the causally closed physical world? Why is there, and how can there be, such a thing as the mind, or consciousness, in a physical world? We will see that these two problems, mental causation and consciousness, are intimately intertwined, and that, in a sense, they make each other insoluble.[7]

I now want to set out in some detail how the problem of mental causation arises within a physicalist setting.

The Supervenience Argument

Mind-body supervenience can usefully be thought of as defining minimal physicalism – that it is the minimal commitment that anyone who calls herself a physicalist should be willing to accept. For present purposes we will not need an elaborate statement of exactly what mind-body supervenience amounts to. It will suffice to understand it as the claim that what happens in our mental life is wholly dependent on, and determined by, what happens with our bodily processes. In this sense, mind-body supervenience is a commitment of all forms of reductionist physicalism, such as the classic Smart-Feigl mind-brain identity thesis. Moreover, it is also a commitment of functionalism, arguably still the orthodoxy on the mind-body problem. For functionalism views mental properties as defined in terms of their causal roles in behavioral and physiological contexts, and it is plausible to assume that systems that are alike in physical constitution must be alike in their physiological and behavioral causal properties. It is noteworthy that emergentism, too, is committed to supervenience: If two systems are wholly alike physically, we should expect the same mental properties to emerge, or fail to emerge, in each.

Mind-body supervenience has seemed an attractive option to many philosophers because it seemed to them a possible way of safeguarding the autonomy of the mental domain without lapsing back into Cartesian substance dualism. Just as normative/moral properties are supervenient on, but irreducible to and autonomous from, factual/descriptive properties, the mental properties of a creature may supervene on, and yet remain distinct and autonomous from, its physical nature. In many ways, this is an attractive picture: while acknowledging the primacy and priority of the physical domain, it highlights the distinctiveness and specialness of creatures with mentality – consciousness, purposiveness, and rationality. It reaffirms our intuitive commonsense belief in our own specialness as beings with rich and complex mental natures and intelligent and creative capacities unseen in the rest of nature. Moreover, this view

276   J A E G W O N   K I M

provides the burgeoning science of psychology and cognition with a
philosophical rationale as an autonomous science in its own right: It
studies these irreducible psychological properties, functions, and capacities, discovering laws and regularities, and generating law-based explanations and predictions of behavior. It is a science with its own proper
domain not touched by other sciences, especially those at the lower
levels, such as biology and physics.

This seductive picture comes crashing down, however, when we consider the problem of mental causation – how it is possible, on such a
picture, for mentality to have causal powers, powers to influence the
course of natural events. There are several principles that conspire to
make trouble for mental causation. The first of these is the principle of
the Causal Closure of the Physical Domain. For our purposes we may
state it as follows:

> *The Causal Closure of the Physical Domain*: If a physical event has a cause
> at t, then it has a physical cause at t.

In terms of explanation we can put the principle as follows: If a physical
event has a causal explanation (in terms of an event occurring at t), it
has a physical causal explanation (in terms of a physical event at t).
According to this principle, physics is causally and explanatorily self-
sufficient: There is no need to go outside the physical domain to find a
cause, or a causal explanation, of a physical event. Note that physical
causal closure is entirely consistent with dualism. It does not say that
physical events and entities are all that there are, or that physical causal
explanations are all the causal explanations that there are. As far as
Physical Causal Closure goes, there may be entities and events outside
the physical domain, and causal relations may hold between these nonphysical events. The Causal Closure Principle, therefore, does not rule
out even substance dualism; for all it cares, there may be immaterial
Cartesian minds.

Moreover, Physical Causal Closure does not exclude nonphysical
causes, or causal explanations, of physical events. This possibility,
however, is ruled out by the exclusion principle:

> *Principle of Causal Exclusion:* If an event, e, has a sufficient cause, c, at t,
> no event at t distinct from c can be a cause of e (unless this is a genuine
> case of causal overdetermination).

There is also a companion principle regarding causal explanation, that
is, the principle of explanatory exclusion, but we will not need it for our
present purposes. However, it will be convenient to have a generalized
and slightly stronger version of the causal exclusion principle:

Principle of Determinative/Generative Exclusion: If the existence of an event e, or an instantiation of a property P, is determined/generated by an event c – causally or otherwise – then e's occurrence is not determined/ generated by any event wholly distinct from or independent of c (unless this is a genuine case of overdetermination).

The second principle broadens causation, or causal determination, to generation/determination simpliciter, whether causal or of another kind. The intuitive idea involved is that a given event, or property instantiation, owes its existence to another event, that the former is generated out of, or derives from, the latter. What I have in mind is very close to the basic notion of causation, or determination, that G.E.M. Anscombe was after in *Causality and Determination*.[8] I have extensively argued elsewhere for the causal/explanatory exclusion principle;[9] I think the fundamental rationale for the broader principle is essentially the same, and anyone who finds the former plausible should find the latter equally plausible. In any case, this is not the place to elaborate on the pros and cons regarding these principles.

It is quick and easy to see how these exclusion principles generate troubles for mental causation for anyone who accepts mind-body supervenience – that is, for anyone who is a minimal physicalist. Briefly, the argument goes like this:[10] Suppose a mental event, an instantiation of mental property M, causes another mental property M* to be instantiated. This is perfectly consistent with the doctrine of physical causal closure. But mind-body supervenience says that this instantiation of mental property M* is supervenient on a concurrent instantiation of a physical property P*. This means that given that P* is instantiated on this occasion, M* must of necessity be instantiated on this occasion. That is, the M* instance is wholly dependent on, and is generated by, the P* instance. At this point, the exclusion principle kicks in: Is the occurrence of the M* instance due to its supposed cause, the M instance, or its supervenient base event, P* instance? It must be one or the other, but which? Given that its physical supervenience base P* is instantiated on this occasion, M* must be instantiated as well on this occasion, regardless of what might have preceded this M* instance. In what sense, then, can the M instance be said to be a "cause," or a generative source, of the M* instance?

I believe that the only acceptable way of reconciling the two causal/generative claims and achieve a consistent picture of the situation is to say this: The M instance caused the M* instance by causing P* to be instantiated on this occasion. More generally, it seems like a plausible principle to say that in order to cause a supervenient property to be instantiated, you must cause one of its base properties to be instantiated.

At any rate, we now have it that the M instance causes a P* instance. This is a case of mental-to-physical causation, and this triggers the physical causal closure principle to kick in, yielding the proposition that there is also a physical cause, say P, of this P* instance. This means that the P* instance has both a physical cause P and a mental cause M, a situation that is inconsistent with the causal exclusion principle. One of these causes must go, and obviously it is the mental cause M that must go. The reason is simple: If P is let go and M stays, that violates the physical causal closure. Because M must cause P* in order to back up its claim to be a cause of M*, the conclusion is that M cannot be a cause of M*, or of anything else. And this, of course, holds for all mental properties, and we have the discouraging broader conclusion that, under mind-body supervenience, mental properties are causally impotent. We may summarize all this:

> The Problem of Mental Causation: Causal efficacy of mental properties is inconsistent with the joint acceptance of the following four claims: (1) physical causal closure, (2) exclusion, (3) mind-body supervenience, and (4) mental/physical property dualism.

Physical Causal Closure and mind-body supervenience are, or must be, among the inescapable commitments of all physicalists. The exclusion principle is a general metaphysical constraint, and I don't see how it can be successfully challenged. This leaves mind-body property dualism as the only negotiable item. But to negotiate it away is to embrace reductionism. This will cause a chill and a shudder in those physicalists who want to eat the cake and have it too – that is, those who want both the irreducibility and causal efficacy of the mental. I believe that the question no longer is whether or not those of us who want to protect mental causation find mind-body reductionism palatable. What has become abundantly clear after three decades of debate is that if we want mental causation, we had better be prepared to swallow reductionism whether we like it or not. But even if you are ready for reductionism, it doesn't necessarily mean that you can have it. For reductionism may be false. This is the point to which we now turn.

Can We Reduce Qualia?

Before reduction and reductionism can be usefully discussed, we need to be clear about the model of reduction appropriate to the issues on hand. I believe much of the philosophical debate during the past three decades concerning the reducibility of the mental has turned out to be a futile exercise because it was predicated on the wrong model of reduction. This is the derivational model of intertheoretic reduction developed by Ernest Nagel in the 1950s and 1960s. As many of you know, the heart of Nagel reduction is bridge laws, the lawlike principles that are supposed to connect properties of the domain to be reduced with the properties of the base domain. Specifically, the requirement, as popularly understood, is that each property up for reduction be connected by a bridge law with a nomically coextensive property in the base domain. All of the influential antireductionist arguments – most notably, Davidson's anomalist argument and the Putnam/Fodor multiple realization argument – have focused on showing that the bridge law requirement cannot be met for mental properties vis-à-vis physical/biological properties.

All this is by now a familiar story, and there is no need here to rehearse the arguments, counterarguments, and so forth. But the philosophical emptiness of Nagel reduction is quickly seen when we notice that a Nagel reduction of the mental to the physical is consistent with, and even entailed in some cases, by many all-out dualisms, such as the double-aspect theory, the doctrine of preestablished harmony, epiphenomenalism, and emergentism. The reason, of course, is that these doctrines are consistent with the mind-body bridge law requirement. In fact, some of them, such as the double-aspect theory, entail the satisfaction of this requirement.

What then is required to reduce mental properties, say pain? I believe that what has to be done is, first, to functionalize pain (or, more precisely, the property of being in pain): namely, to show that being in pain is definable as being in a state (or instantiating a property) that is caused by certain sensory inputs (i.e., tissue damage, trauma) and that in turn causes certain behavioral outputs (i.e., characteristic pain behaviors). More generally, to instantiate a mental property M, upon its functionalization, will turn out to be being in some state or other with such-and-such sensory causes and such-and-such behavior outputs. Next, once a mental property has been functionalized, we can look for its *realizers* – that is, states or properties that satisfy the causal specification that define the mental property. Thus, for pain, we look for an internal state in an organism that has the property of being caused by tissue damage and trauma and that in turn causes characteristic pain behavior. In case of humans and perhaps mammals, the state turns, or may turn, out to be an electrical activity in the pyramidal cell assemblies (pca). That is, pca is the realizer of pain for humans and mammals. Conventional wisdom has it that pain, and other mental states, have multiple diverse realizers across different species and structures, and even among members of the same species. This means that this second step in finding realizers of a given mental property is likely to be an ongoing affair with no clear end.

Obviously, we are not going to find, nor would we necessarily be interested in identifying, all actual and possible realizers of pain for all actual and possible species and pain-capable systems. Functional reduction, as I call it, can focus on the reduction of specific instances – that is, local reductions. We may be interested in finding the neural basis of human pain, or canine pain, or Martian pain. We may be interested in identifying the neural basis of your pain now or my pain yesterday. Neural bases may differ for different instances of pain, but individual pains do nonetheless reduce to their respective neural/physical realizers. Unlike in the case of Nagel "bridge-law" reduction, multiple realizability of pain is no barrier to instance-by-instance, or local, reduction by functionalization. Suppose that pain has physical realizers, P1, P2, . . . Then, any given instance of pain is an instance of either P1 or of P2 or. . . . If you are in pain in virtue of being in state P2, there is nothing more, or less, to your being in pain than your being in state P2. This particular pain is the very same state as this instance of P2. Each pain instance is a P1 instance or P2 instance or . . . ; that is, all pain instances reduce to the instances of its realizers.[11]

If pain can be functionalized in the foregoing sense, its instances will have the causal powers of pain's realizers. This solves the problem of their causal efficacy. What of pain? What would be the causal powers of pain as a mental kind? The answer is that as a kind, pain will be causally heterogeneous, as heterogeneous as the heterogeneity of its diverse realizers. Pain, as a kind, will not have the kind of causal/nomic unity we expect for true natural kinds, kinds in terms of which scientific theorizing is conducted. But that is what we must expect given that pain is a functional property with multiple, diverse physical realizers. If multiplicity means anything here, it must mean causal/nomic multiplicity; if two realizers of pain are not causally or nomologically diverse, there is no reason to count them as two, not one. On this reductive account, pain will not be causally impotent or epiphenomenal; it is only that pain is causally heterogeneous.

So the key question is this: Is pain functionally reducible? Are mental properties in general functionalizable and hence functionally reducible? Or are they "emergent" and irreducible? I believe that there is reason to think that intentional/cognitive properties are functionalizable. However, I am with those philosophers who believe that phenomenal properties of consciousness are not functional properties. To argue for this view of phenomenal properties, or qualia, we do not need anything as esoteric and controversial as the "zombie hypothesis" discussed by Ned Block, David Chalmers, and others – that is, the claim that zombies, creatures that are indiscernible from us behaviorally and physiologically but who lack consciousness, are metaphysically possible. All we need is something much more modest: the metaphysical possibility of qualia inversion. Perhaps the problem is still open, but I believe there is substantial and weighty reason, and a sufficiently robust consensus among the philosophers who work in this area,[12] to think that qualia are functionally irreducible.

If, however, intentional/cognitive properties are functionalizable and hence reducible, that removes a substantial amount of pressure from the mental causation problem. Recall Fodor's lament about the possible loss of mental causal efficacy: The mental phenomena he cites include both intentional states (wanting, believing) and sensory event (itching). This means that the functional reducibility of intentional properties should suffice to allay Fodor's worries about wanting and believing. That only leaves itching and other phenomenal/sensory mental properties.

The Two World-Knots

So this is where we now stand: The problem of mental causation is solvable for a given class of mental properties if and only if these properties are functionally reducible. But phenomenal mental properties are not functionally definable and hence functionally irreducible. Hence, the problem of mental causation is not solvable for phenomenal mental properties.

But, as we also saw, the problem of phenomenal consciousness, or "the mystery of consciousness," is solvable if and only if phenomenal consciousness is functionally reducible. So the nonfunctionalizability of phenomenal consciousness entails the unsolvability of the problem of consciousness, and hence the unsolvability of the problem of mental causation (for phenomenal consciousness). It is thus that the two problems, that of mental causation and that of consciousness, turn out to share an interlocking fate. What stands in the way of solving the problem of mental causation is phenomenal consciousness. And what stands in the way of solving the problem of phenomenal consciousness is the impossibility of construing it in terms of its causal relations to physical/biological properties. They are indeed Weltknoten, problems that have eluded our best intellectual efforts. They seem deeply entrenched in the way we conceptualize the world, and seem to arise from some of the fundamental assumptions we hold about it. Does that mean that there is some deeply hidden flaw somewhere in our system of concepts, and that we need to alter, in some basic way, our conceptual framework to solve these problems? Of course, if our scheme of concepts were radically altered, the problems themselves would radically be altered. Perhaps, the new scheme would not even allow the same or equivalent problems and puzzles to be formulated. Some philosophers would be willing to take this as a sufficient reason for abandoning our present system of concepts in favor of a "better" one, that the conundrum of mental causation and consciousness is a compelling reason for jettisoning our familiar scheme of intentional and phenomenal idioms and embracing a purely physical/biological framework. To me, this is the ostrich strategy – trying to avoid the problem by ignoring it. To motivate the discarding of a framework, independent reasons ought to be offered – we should be able to show it to be deficient, incomplete, or flawed in some fundamental way, independently of the fact that it generates puzzles and problems that we are unable to handle. It may well be that our mind-body problem, or something close to it, arises within any scheme that is rich enough to do justice to the world as we experience it. It could be that the problem is an inevitable consequence of the distinction between the objective world of physical existence and the subjective world of experience, and that such a distinction is unavoidable for self-reflective cognizers and agents of the kind that we are.

To conclude, then, the mind-body problem, for the physicalist, has boiled down to two problems, mental causation and consciousness, and these together represent the most profound and difficult challenge to physicalism. If physicalism is to survive as a worldview for us, it must show just where and how we belong in the physical world, and this means that it must give an account of our status as conscious creatures with powers to affect our surroundings, in virtue of our mentality and consciousness. I think there will be widely shared, if not unanimous, agreement among philosophers, physicalists, and nonphysicalists alike, that this has yet to be done.[13]

NOTES

1. For Gassendi's vigorous and powerful challenge to Descartes, see Cottingham (1985, p. 238).
2. To see why Descartes's difficulties with mental causation were genuine difficulties, and why it would not help one bit to reintroduce substantival minds, see my "Causality and Substance Dualism", Kim (forthcoming-b).
3. Fodor (1990a, p. 156).
4. See, for example, Dennett (1988).
5. Pavlov (1957, p. 148).
6. James (1981, p. 647).
7. I owe this way of putting it to David Chalmers.
8. Anscombe (1971).
9. See, for example (Kim 1993c).

10. This is the argument I first presented in Kim (1992). For more details see Kim (1998). I should note that my presentation here does not explicitly invoke the Principle of Physical Causal Closure.
11. See Kim (forthcoming-a) and Kim (1998) for more details, in particular concerning how reductions conforming to this model meet the basic methodological and metaphysical requirements of reduction.
12. To mention a few: Ned Block, Christopher Hill, Frank Jackson, Joseph Levine, Colin McGinn, and Brian McLaughlin.
13. No unanimous agreement because some philosophers apparently think that this has already been done, at least in outlines, or that doing more science, not philosophy, will solve the problems. Who some of these philosophers are should be obvious to those who have kept up with the field.

14

How Not to Solve the Mind-Body Problem

COLIN McGINN

I

The conclusion I aim to establish in this chapter is this: the solution to the mind-body problem cannot take the form of an empirical identity statement but must rather consist in an analytic identity statement. That is, to solve the problem we would need to provide a conceptual reduction of consciousness, not an a posteriori reduction. It is not that I know what this conceptual reduction would look like – far from it. My thesis is merely that there is a general argument that shows that the solution must take this form. I shall also be concerned to spell out the consequences of this thesis for the prospects of solving the mind-body problem, and to indicate how my conclusion bears upon certain arguments that have been given to undermine physicalism.

II

The logical analysis of identity statements has proved crucial in assessing the claims of physicalism, and so it will be in this chapter. Early identity theorists, notably J.J.C. Smart, observed that not all true identity statements are conceptual truths, following Frege's precedent. This opened the way to claiming that there might be true identity statements linking mental and physical properties that could not be certified to be true on conceptual grounds alone. It was thus not incumbent on a physicalist to provide any analysis of mental concepts in order to claim to possess a complete physical reduction of mental properties. This liberalization of the conditions of adequacy upon a physicalist theory brightened the prospects for that theory considerably, and it established a paradigm for what a solution to the mind-body problem might look like. We could say that pain is C-fiber stimulation in the same spirit in which we say that heat is molecular motion. The key is to recognize that true identities do not have to link synonyms. All at once a host of familiar objections, of a generally epistemic nature, fall away. In particular, the physicalist is under no obligation to say that I *know* my C-fibers are firing when I know I am in pain.

The next step came from Saul Kripke: although identity statements could be empirical and true, they could not be contingent and true. All identities are necessary, though some are a posteriori. So if we have good reason to think that psychophysical identity statements are not necessary then we have good reason to think they are not true. This spelled trouble for the identity theory, because such statements do appear contingent. The appearance of contingency has to be explained away if we are to accept the truth of the identity theory.

I want to focus on the informativeness of psychophysical identity statements. The argument I shall defend is not unfamiliar, but its power and ramifications have not been properly appreciated. In fact, the argument occurs quite plainly in Smart's original paper, and his response to it strikes me as basically correct, at least as to its general form. Smart writes:

> Even if objections 1 and 2 do not prove that sensations are something over and above brain processes, they do prove that the qualities of sensations are something over and above the qualities of brain processes. That is, it may be possible to get out of asserting the existence of irreducibly psychic processes, but not out of asserting the existence of irreducibly psychic *properties*. For suppose we identify the Morning Star with the Evening Star. Then there must be some properties which logically imply that of being the Morning Star, and quite distinct properties that entail that of being the Evening Star. Again, there must be some properties (for example, that of being a yellowish flash) which are logically distinct from those in the physicalist story. . . . Now how do I get over the objection that a sensation can be identified with a brain process only if it has some phenomenal property, not possessed by brain processes, whereby one-half of the identification may be, so to speak, pinned down.

In a footnote Smart says: "I think this objection was first put to me by Professor Max Black. I think it is the most subtle of any of those I have considered, and the one which I am least confident of having met." Smart's response to Black's objection is immediately to concede its force – the phenomenal property is indeed distinct from any brain property. He thus abandons the kind of type-identity theory based upon the usual scientific paradigms. But he works to retain a general materialism by offering a topic-neutral analysis of those residual mental properties – an analysis of basically functionalist cast. The result, though Smart does not have the apparatus to put it this way, is token identity materialism combined with analytic functionalism about mental properties. The processes that instantiate mental properties are brain processes, while the properties are analyzed in topic-neutral functional terms. Thus mental properties are *not* held to be identical with brain properties, but rather with topic-neutral functional properties. In effect, Smart in this paper introduces type-identity theory and then abandons it before the paper is finished. Some readers have been puzzled by his strategy: why not stick with type-identity theory and forgo the implausible topic-neutral analysis? But I think Smart's reasoning is impeccable, and the underlying predicament he uncovers is genuine. The point is that Black's objection refutes type-identity theory and the only way to go in saving materialism is to offer a conceptual reduction of the mental. What is absolutely crucial here is that any empirical identity theory will face the question of what makes its characteristic identity statements informative, and the only way out of this problem is to provide a nonempirical identity theory. Only conceptual reduction can block the resurgence of those "irreducibly psychic properties" Smart is so anxious to avoid. I shall now spell out the basic argument more rigorously than Smart does, so that its full force can be appreciated.

III

Everyone will agree that the informativeness of an identity statement depends upon there being two senses corresponding to a single reference. More controversial is the question of what distinguishes distinct senses – in particular, how epistemic or mentalistic the notion of sense should be. I shall put forward a schema intended to capture distinctness of sense and hence explain what identity informativeness consists in. If 'A' and 'B' are codenoting terms, then 'A = B' is informative if and only if 'A' connotes a property F that is numerically distinct from the property G that is connoted by 'B'. Connotation is not the same relation as denotation: 'A' and 'B' denote an entity that is not identical to either of the properties connoted by the terms; so there are three items at play here, two connoted, one denoted. This schema is intended to hold for any kinds of terms and any kinds of denotation. In effect, the idea is that when we learn the truth of an informative identity proposition we learn that two properties are coinstantiated: the connoted properties converge on a single object. According to this schema, we can say that an identity statement is never 'barely informative,' in the sense that there is no explanation of its informativeness in terms of coinstantiated connoted properties. Distinctness of sense is distinctness of connotation, and connotation consists in properties expressed. The fact that we come to know when we learn that A = B is the fact that F and G are coinstantiated. Let me now illustrate how the schema works in application to particular identity statements.

Take 'the evening star = the morning star,' where the flanking descriptions really are descriptive terms not disguised proper names. The denotation of both descriptions is Venus, so the statement is true. The connotations are, however, quite distinct: one description connotes the property of being (uniquely) an evening star, the other connotes the property of being (uniquely) a morning star. The statement tells us that these two properties are possessed by a single object: the proposition we come to know is that the property of being (uniquely) a morning star is coinstantiated with the property of being (uniquely) an evening star. (Ignore the fact that both descriptions are strictly improper. Think of them as short for 'the first star to appear in the morning/evening.') It seems entirely clear that exactly the same account should be given for all identity propositions involving descriptions; the predicates in the descriptions serve to express the connoted properties on the distinctness of which the informativeness turns.

I think the same is true of names, though it is a matter of controversy whether the properties involved belong to the senses of the names. The descriptions that express these properties may be merely reference-fixing descriptions, and they may vary from speaker to speaker. Still, what is learned by learning the truth of, say, 'Marilyn Monroe = Norma Jeane Baker' is that certain properties are coinstantiated – as it might be, that the property of being (uniquely) a platinum-haired actress in *Some Like it Hot* is coinstantiated with the property of having once been a rather plain brunette in such-and-such high school. What other kind of thing could make the identity statement informative? As we know from Frege, it certainly cannot be the denotation of the two names, because this is the same while the senses differ.

Similarly with demonstrative and indexical identity statements. Consider 'that elephant = that elephant' said while pointing successively to the tusks and tail of a partly occluded pachyderm. That could be informative, but only because the recipient learns that the property of being thus tusked is coinstantiated with the property of being so tailed, and these are quite distinct properties (tusks not being tails). We learn in effect that property diversity masks uniqueness of instantiating objects. Objects have many properties, and we sometimes discover that these distinct properties occur in the same entity. To be true, an identity statement must refer to a single entity, but to be informative it must express divergent properties. Or again, consider 'I am Colin McGinn,' learned after I wake from amnesia and discover that I wrote the book I am reading. Here again what I discover is something similar to this: the person with the property of having these mental states also has the property of having written this book. Two modes of presentation of me have been discovered to be such, as when my doctor remarks to me, "You know, you wrote that book." (I reply: "Oh, then it is a lot better than I thought.")

Same for natural kind identities. Following Kripke, we can say that 'heat = molecular motion' is informative because 'heat' connotes the property of causing the sensation of heat in people while 'molecular motion' does not, connoting instead the property of being molecules in motion. We accordingly learn that what has the former property also has the latter property, in other words what causes the sensation of heat is what has high molecular motion, where these are distinct properties of heat (which is why in some possible worlds molecular motion does not cause the sensation of heat). A single property or kind has two distinct properties, and we learn that these are coinstantiated, something that cannot be inferred from knowledge of the identity of the properties. Sometimes, as with 'heat', the connoted property involves the kind of mental state the natural kind in question produces in us.

Now we can move to putative psychophysical identities. Consider the double-aspect token-identity theory, which asserts such propositions as 'this pain is identical to that C-fiber firing.' Supposing such statements to be true, they fit our schema perfectly: a single token event is said to have two distinct properties, and this is informative because there is no a priori or analytic link between the concepts of the two properties. On another occasion, indeed, the property of pain might be coinstantiated with D-fiber firing or whatever. The case is, logically, exactly the same as the evening star and the morning star. But what of putative type-identities, the crucial case? Here we are saying that the properties are identical, so we cannot appeal to their distinctness to explain the informativeness of 'the property of pain = the property of C-fibers firing.' That statement is certainly informative – superinformative we might say – but it cannot be so in virtue of the denoted properties. So what else is there to explain the informativeness? On the face of it, the statement can be true only if uninformative, but it is informative, so it is not true. That is, this holds on the assumption that the properties connoted by the terms are those of pain and C-fiber firing. It begins to seem that we are mistaking a mere correlation of distinct properties for an identity, as is shown by the informativeness of bringing them together. That was

Black and Smart's original point: the two properties connoted have to be distinct, but they seem to be nothing other than the properties of pain and C-fiber firing, so the identity theory is false. Accordingly, we need an account of what pain is that does not lead to this proliferation problem; and because it cannot take the form of an empirical identity statement, it must be an uninformative analytic or a priori identity statement. This appears to spell a swift demise for empirical type-identity theory, and pointed out by someone widely believed to espouse that theory.

Let me make a couple of observations on what this argument establishes, if it is sound, before I turn to replying to objections to it. First, it is not specifically an argument against materialism; the same point would apply to an empirical identity statement linking mental terms with terms for the states of a Cartesian immaterial substance. What is shown is that no kind of solution to the mind-problem can take the form of an empirical identity statement, and substance dualism is no way out of that. The same point applies to versions of functionalism that offer empirical identity-based reductions. But the point does not apply to analytical functionalism, because that theory does not offer empirical identities but a priori or conceptual ones. Neither is the argument applicable solely to identity theories concerning the mind. It applies to any attempt to empirically identify one property with another. We always need to ask whether the connoted property needed to explain informativeness is actually just the denoted property, thus undermining the identity assertion. Thus, suppose we took a fancy to the idea of empirical phenomenalism, holding that material object properties such as squareness are really possibilities of sensation, this being an a posteriori claim. There would then be the objection that 'square' must denote something other than sensation possibilities, because the putative identity statement is held to be informative, and there is nothing but squareness to be the connotation of the term. (Actually, of course, phenomenalists have always been of the analytical persuasion, which shows some savvy on their part – ditto the logical behaviorists.) Or consider attempts to identify the Good with some naturalistic property on a posteriori grounds: the question arises whether the informativeness is consistent with the claimed identity, as 'good' will have to connote a property distinct from any property connoted by the naturalistic term in question. The challenge is always to find some extra property to be the connoted property, where this diverges from the denoted property. And the problem is that this seems none too easy a thing to do. Later I shall consider some ways to try to meet this challenge in the case of psychophysical identity theories and show why they fail. But first I want to bring to bear a cognate line of thought that casts doubt on the very structure of the standard type-identity picture that shows a deep internal tension in the position.

IV

Presumably all will agree that the appearance of pain is nothing like the appearance of C-fibers firing: the way pain seems from the inside (or indeed from the third-person point of view) is nothing like the way C-fibers appear when you look into a person's brain. It is precisely this fact that makes the identity theory surprising and informative – that these vastly different appearances are nevertheless appearances of a single property or kind. Who would have thought that one thing could give rise to such different appearances? And one's naive suspicion has always been that the appearances are actually too different to be consistent with the purported identity; hence the sense that one has to do some serious swallowing in order to accept the claim of identity. Now I want to argue that this natural response – so often dismissed as simply confused (can't you distinguish sense from reference?) – is actually soundly based. The point is that we cannot explain the distinction between the appearances in a way that is consistent with the identity claim. The way we explain distinctions of sense accompanied by sameness of reference in ordinary cases is to draw attention to the gap between the sense and the reference, because if there were no such gap, the unity of reference would give rise to a unity of sense; thus we need to show some distance between reference and sense – some degrees of freedom, some failure of determination. If we could not do that, then a distinction of sense would imply a distinction of reference.

Consider the appearances of pains and tickles. These appearances are totally distinct. But is it conceivable that they are nevertheless appearances of the same sensation? Someone might say that it is conceivable, because reference never determines sense. It is epistemically possible that only one sensation property underlies these admittedly divergent appearances. But this is crazy, and the reason is obvious: we cannot pull apart appearance and reality in this case. Given the relation between the appearance of pains/tickles and the actual pains/tickles, namely identity (or at least containment), and given the difference of the appearances, the realities *cannot* be the same. So sometimes it is valid to argue from appearance distinctions to reality distinctions, depending upon how intimately appearance and reality are related. I would argue that we can do this for perceptual appearances too – say, of colors and shapes. It is not conceivable that visual perceptions of red and green, or round and square, should correspond to one property that appears differently: the property represented can be inferred from its perceptual appearance and vice versa. (I don't mean that an object with one color or shape might not appear to have two such. I mean that the color or shape perceptually represented cannot admit of such divergent appearances, because that property determines the appearances.) So what now of pain and C-fiber firing?

Well, the appearance of pain clearly coincides with pain itself, so there is no exploitable gap there to play with. Given the identity between them, we can immediately infer that the (perceptual) appearance of C-fibers is not identical to pain, because it is not identical to the appearance of pain. But that in itself is nothing to worry about for the identity theorist, whose claim is not that the way C-fiber firing looks is identical to pain but that C-fiber firing itself is. If we could identify C-fiber firing with the way it looks, then we could indeed derive the nonidentity, just as we did with pains and tickles, but that hardly seems plausible. Yet there is still the question whether we can explain the distinction of appearances here given the slender materials available. For all we really have to go on is the gap between C-fibers and their appearance. Is this gap big enough to capture the difference between the appearance of pain (i.e., pain) and the appearance of C-fiber firing? I suggest that it is not. Intuitively, the problem is that the gap between C-fibers and their appearance is too small to be parlayed into the enormous gulf separating the appearance of pain and the appearance of C-fiber firing. Imagine staring at someone's firing C-fibers under a microscope: the content of your visual experience would be specified by saying that it is *C-fiber firing* that you are experiencing. The property enters into the very content of what you experience (or at least it could). But the appearance of pain is totally different from such an appearance of C-fibers. So how do we explain this difference, given that the gap between C-fibers and their appearance is so narrow? We simply don't have enough properties in play to explain the appearance distinctions that indubitably exist. If we started out agnostic on the question of identity, I think we would find it persuasive against identity that the appearances cannot be squared with the claim of identity. We would take it that there have to be two properties – pain and C-fiber firing – in order to account for the distinction of appearances. The problem, intuitively, is that we are driven to ascribe two aspects to a (putatively) single thing, but then we have given up the claim of property identity, because an aspect is just a property. Hence the internal tension: how can we have two appearance-fixing aspects of what is meant to be an indissoluble unity? The statement of property identity can be informative, again, only if it is not true. It is indeed highly informative to be told that these are appearances of the same thing, namely a brain state, but then we cannot find the resources with which to capture the conditions of the possibility of this informativeness, namely, the radical distinction of appearances. The question then is whether we can capture the needed distinction by appealing to something other than the distinctness of pain and C-fiber firing; to this I now turn.

V

The argument as presented so far relies on the assumption that the sense of 'pain' is the property of pain and the sense of 'C-fiber firing' is the property of C-fiber firing – that these properties are the proper connotations of the terms in question. Equivalently, the conceptual distinctness of the concepts *pain* and *C-fiber firing* consists in the ontological distinctness of the associated properties of pain and C-fiber firing. That is the overwhelmingly natural view to take, I think, but it is not the only conceivable view. As far as I can see, there are two alternative views that might be proposed to block the argument: one view accepts the requirement that some property be found that distinguishes the senses of the terms; the other view rejects this requirement and proposes that we can explain conceptual distinctness without invoking property distinctness. Let us consider these in turn. Is it possible to hold that the property that constitutes the sense of 'pain' is not pain but some other property? Well, we cannot say that this extra property is something like the appearance of pain, because that is not distinguishable from pain. We might try saying that it is the property of causing certain sorts of behavior, the kind that pain typically causes. That is certainly a distinct property from pain (unless you are a behaviorist), so that it has the potential to constitute the informativeness-generating concept we need. But the trouble is that it is implausible to suggest that this is really the sense of 'pain'. The reason is that 'pain = the cause of such-and-such behavior' is potentially informative, which it shouldn't be if the two terms have the same sense. Note that we cannot save the identity theory by identifying pain with such a behavioral property because then it will be false that pain = C-fiber firing, as the latter is not a behavioral property. No, we have to be saying that pain is a property distinct from the behavioral property that constitutes its mode of presentation, so that pain = C-fiber firing while the behavioral property does not. Logically that would do the trick in responding to the Smart-Black style of argument, but it is not just not credible that 'pain' means what it would have to for the response to succeed. I certainly do not think of my pains

under such a description when I self-ascribe 'pain', and it is entirely consistent to say 'it might turn out that pain does not cause such-and-such
behavior.'

It might be thought that I am here begging the question against the
thesis that 'pain' does just mean 'the cause of such-and-such behavior,'
but that is not what is going on. My point, remember, is that the Smart-
Black argument shows that in the end we have to give a conceptual
analysis in physical or topic-neutral terms of mental concepts if we are
to avoid the problem of residual mental properties. The behaviorist
response in question concedes this point. Now it is true that I have no
sympathy for this kind of behaviorist analysis for reasons not discussed
in this chapter, but the point I am making now is that such an approach
agrees with the upshot of the Smart-Black argument. Later I shall be discussing another way out and urging its merits.

On the other hand, if we suggest a mentalistic mode of presentation
for 'pain' – say, 'the sensation I dislike the most' – then we are still left
with a mental residue, which is what we are trying to avoid. It may be
analytic that pain is the sensation I dislike the most, but that is no help
if the new mode of presentation is a mental property, because the same
problem will arise for an empirical identity theory of it. So, although I
have not exhausted every possible property that might be suggested as
the mode of presentation of pain, I think it is pretty clear that this route
will not work: the plain fact is that it is pain itself that constitutes the
mode of presentation of pain – the connotation and denotation of 'pain'
coincide. And this is not meant to be a point solely about the first-person
perspective; 'pain' is univocal in first- and third-person uses, and its sense
is given by the property of pain in both uses. The sense of 'pain' is not
the place to look for that fugitive extra property over and above the
property of pain.

It might then be thought more promising to focus on the other term
of the identity statement. Thus it might be suggested that 'C-fiber firing'
connotes the property, not of C-fiber firing, but the property of looking
a certain way or the property of being responsible for such-and-such
observations. The idea might be that this is a theoretical term and that
such terms have modes of presentation that diverge from their denot-
ations. I think there are at least three problems with this. First, if we
allow ourselves mentalistic modes of presentation, as with how C-fibers
look, then we generate a vicious regress, because then we will have to
give an identity theory of these mental properties with the same problem
arising. Clearly we do not avoid the problem of the mental residue
by introducing a mental property in connection with the physical term
'C-fiber firing'! Second, the proposal is implausible for the same reason

the comparable move for 'pain' was, namely that it is informative to be told that C-fiber firing looks such-and-such a way. It is not analytic that C-fiber firing looks this way, and it might have turned out not to, so the sense of the term 'C-fiber firing' cannot consist in such a description. Nor is this a remotely plausible idea independently of trying to respond to the argument at issue. It sounds similar to one of those bad old positivist distortions, that theoretical terms have to be definable in terms of observations. Third, we surely do not want to generate an a priori proof that mental states cannot be identical to *observable* features of the brain on the grounds that if they were we would not be able to reply to the argument by invoking the alleged 'theoreticalness' of terms such as 'C-fiber firing'! In fact, I think it is quite clear that the way of thinking of C-fiber firing that is associated with 'C-fiber firing' is simply that of having the property of C-fiber firing – and not, say, the property expressed by 'the brain state most discussed by philosophers.' As it were, the term gives you the property it denotes – it connotes what it denotes. But if that is right then both terms connote what they denote, so that there is no room to capture informativeness by means of property connoted that is consistent with the claimed identity. The case is totally unlike those favored paradigms beloved of identity theorists – 'heat = molecular motion' and the like. For in these cases we always have a property such as 'cause of the sensation of heat' to invoke to capture informativeness, this description introducing a distinct property from any connoted by the term 'molecular motion'. The crucial disanalogy is that such identity assertions don't care if they invoke an unreduced mental property, because they are not in the business of trying to tell us what the sensation of heat is, only what heat is. But in the case of pain that is precisely what we are trying to do, which is why we cannot perform the analogous trick. So the analogy breaks down at exactly the point at which it needs to work most. The problem arises because we do think of heat under such a mental mode of presentation, and this is quite distinct from heat. In the case of pain the first part of this is true, but not the second (Kripke was tapping into the same point). Pain cannot be peeled off itself.

The second kind of response seeks to distinguish concepts by something other than property connoted. This response implicitly abandons externalism about meaning. It finds semantic distinctions that have no world-oriented counterpart. An externalist would say that two concepts C1 and C2 differ in their content if and only if there are properties P1 and P2 such that C1 connotes P1 and C2 connotes P2 and P1 is not identical to P2. One motivation for this is that a concept is a way of thinking of something, and a way of thinking of something is a way something is taken to *be*, in other words a property it is taken to have. Thus if two ways of thinking differ, then they differ in how the world is taken to be, in the properties that are taken to be instantiated. If I think of something as red, then I think of it precisely as having the property of redness – that is what this way of thinking consists in. To hold otherwise is to shift what belongs to the intentional object of the concept onto the mental vehicle of the concept. That is to psychologize sense in such a way as to detach it from how the world is taken to be. But, according to the line we are considering, there is no distinction in what properties the world is taken to have when one thinks of it as containing pain or C-fiber firing. Exactly the same state of affairs is represented when one thinks of propositions involving these two concepts. The concepts differ purely psychologically, purely "internally"; there is no difference in their intentional objects.

Now I have general misgivings about this approach to conceptual identity, because I am an externalist about content; but the point I want to make now is peculiar to the case at issue. The point is that this response to the Smart-Black argument leads to a vicious infinite regress. To see this, first consider an analogous proposal, namely that the identity theory applies to pain and not to the appearance of pain. Thus, pain is C-fiber firing but the appearance of pain is not – that is just the way pain presents itself to the subject. And we are not interested in an identity theory of appearances but only of realities. Now we are already familiar with the problem that pain and its appearance cannot be severed in this way, but there is another problem too: surely, even if we grant the distinction between pain and its appearance, the identity theorist needs an account of the appearance of pain also, because that itself is something mental. If we now propose an identity theory of this – say, that the appearance of pain is identical to D-fiber firing – then we face the question as to why this is not the way the appearance of pain appears. It is no use at this point to speak of the appearance of the appearance of pain because the same problem arises for that, with the same threat if we introduce a new physical property – say, E-fiber firing – to be identical with that higher-level appearance. We cannot keep peeling off the appearances at each new level in the hope of explaining the apparent distinction between the mental and physical property at the next level down. Put it this way: the way pain appears is the way pain really appears – it is an aspect of mental reality – so we need to give a materialist account of it if we are aiming to capture everything real. But then we always have a mental residue each time we identify an appearance with a physical property. This shows

that we cannot explain why pain does not seem similar to C-fiber stimulation by shifting the distinction onto the appearance of pain – on pain
of vicious regress (so to speak).

Now consider this: suppose the concepts of pain and C-fiber firing
are distinct, even though the denoted properties are identical; there is
still the property of satisfying one or other of these concepts. So consider
the property of satisfying the concept *pain*, or the property of applying
that concept to a subject, possibly oneself. That is a real property,
quite distinct from the property of satisfying the concept *C-fiber firing*;
and it is plainly a mental property. So I may have only one property when
I am in pain, because pain is identical to C-fiber firing, but I have two
properties in virtue of self-ascribing the concept *pain* and the concept *C-
fiber firing*, because these are admitted to be distinct concepts. (I could
have one of these properties without the other, as I might lack the
latter concept.) Then the question is what sort of property this is: is it
identical to some new physical property? If it is not, then there is a
mental property that is not physical, which abandons the identity theory.
If it is, then we can form a suitable identity statement for the property,
as it might be, 'the property of applying the concept *pain* = Z-fiber firing.'
But this is an informative empirical identity statement, so there has to
be a cognitive distinction between its two terms. If we explain the distinction by invoking distinct connoted properties, then again we have
a mental property left dangling, thus conceding the argument. Suppose
then that we explain the distinction by saying that the concepts differ
not in virtue of any distinct properties but in virtue of being irreducibly
distinct concepts. Then we can form a new property in turn – the
property of satisfying this new concept (the concept of the property of
satisfying the concept *pain*). But then again we need to find a physical
property for this mental property to be identical with, and the cycle
begins again. Each time we find a new concept to explain the informativeness we can form the property of satisfying this concept, and
this property needs its corresponding physical property. The regress
arises because concepts generate extra properties, the properties of
satisfying or applying them. If no new property came in the wake of
distinguishing the concepts, then there would be no regress, because all
the properties in the world would be accounted for at the first level. But
once we admit that there is a property of satisfying or applying the
concept *pain* then that property cries out for explanation, and the regress
is set to begin – for there is always a new property one step ahead of
the proposed explanation of informativeness. Logically, it is the same as
with the regress of appearances: distinguishing the appearance of pain
from pain to explain informativeness leaves the appearance dangling,

and once it is identified with a new physical property we have the same problem again. At bottom the difficulty is simple and predictable: we are trying to shove the apparent distinction between pain and C-fiber firing off onto a distinction in the concepts, but that in turn gives us a further mental property, and once this is identified with some physical property the cycle starts up again. The proposal only seemed as if it could work as an alternative to the property explanation of informativeness because we forgot to ask what the property of satisfying the concept consists in.

It may help if I put the point in terms of Frank Jackson's Mary thought experiment. In brief, Mary learns all of physics in a black-and-white room, then leaves it one day to be confronted with her first experience of red. She seems to learn a new fact thereby, while by hypothesis she knew all the physical facts already. Therefore experiencing red is not a physical fact. One popular reply to Jackson is that the same properties or facts are brought under new concepts when Mary emerges from the room, so that the argument fallaciously conflates facts and their conceptual representation. Mary knew all the facts; she simply didn't know all the *descriptions* of the facts. But, I reply to this reply, applying the concept *experience of red* to oneself is just another property one has. So if Mary knew all the properties before she left the room, she must have known this one; but she did not. If we try to say that she knew this property under another description, then there is the further property of applying that description, but this produces the same problem. The difficulty is that a mode of presentation of a fact is *itself a fact* – the fact that something has that mode of presentation. So if Mary knows all the facts in virtue of knowing all the physical facts, then she must already know that her internal states have every mode of presentation they actually have, so she must know that one of her brain states has the mode of presentation 'an experience of red' (she certainly must know that her brain state satisfies that linguistic string). If we now say that she knows about this mode of presentation but only under some other mode of presentation, then (a) this is crazy and (b) it just raises the same question again. She must know all the conceptual distinctions there are, because these are just one species of fact. So she must know the facts that constitute applying the concept *experience of red*. But how can she know this without knowing what it is like to see something red, which by hypothesis she does not know while still in the room? Compare the appearance version of this strategy again: she knows all the realities but not the way those realities appear – specifically, how her experience of red will appear. But that is just one more fact about the world, so she ought to know how experiences of red appear too. Yet she doesn't. If we say that she knows how experiences of red appear but not how these appearances appear, then (a) this is crazy and (b) it leads to an obvious regress. The problem is that the distinctions that are offered as alternatives to factual distinctions are really just another kind of factual distinction – only now at the level of appearances. Similarly, conceptual distinctions are just factual distinctions about how we represent the world, so we need to know what kinds of facts they are. In short, there isn't the kind of distinction between the ontological and the epistemological that the response we are considering relies on there being.

This problem is quite general and seems to me to undermine the second line of resistance to the Smart-Black argument. It also seems very peculiar and ad hoc that only psychophysical type identities should call for this kind of explanation of their informativeness, while every other identity statement (including token identity without type identity) should be explicable in the familiar property style. Is it that externalism about concept identity works in every case but this one? How surprising to find that type-identity theory is defensible only if externalism is (locally) false! Is that a consequence we envisaged when we found ourselves attracted to materialism?

I conclude, then, that neither line of resistance to the Smart-Black argument succeeds. It therefore looks as if either property dualism is true or that there is some kind of analytic version of the identity theory in the offing. Which of these is correct?

VI

It may seem at this point as if we have argued ourselves into a very nasty corner, because neither property dualism nor the standard sorts of analytical reduction are attractive options. I certainly find neither of these views palatable. But let us take stock: all we have really argued so far is that an account of mental properties must not take the form of an empirical identity statement. There is no argument yet for either of those unpalatable positions. Is there then a third option to consider here? I suggest that there is.

Someone could conclude from the argument so far that no *identity* statement can be made about mental properties of such a kind as to solve the mind-body problem; but I think this would be the wrong conclusion to draw. For any solution to the mind-body problem should tell us the nature of mental properties, and in such a way as to connect them explanatorily to the brain. The solution should not leave open what pain is. That is the problem with simple property dualism: in not telling us what mental properties are, it leaves them unconnected explanatorily to the brain. Thus it is hard to see how we can avoid couching our solution in the form of an identity statement. The right lesson, as I have already indicated, is that we need an account of mental properties that is conceptually true. The identity statement that solves the mind-body problem must be analytic. Only then do we have a genuine *reduction*, in contrast to empirical identity theories. An analytic identity statement is not empirically informative, so it does not force us to introduce or recognize an unreduced mental property. This is what Smart saw quite clearly, and he tried to offer a theory that would meet this condition of adequacy.

So should we embrace analytical functionalism, which is essentially what Smart does? Are we driven to embrace that theory by the argument so far, because there is nothing else left in logical space? I hope not, because I find analytical functionalism quite unacceptable, for reasons I cannot go into here. The threat then is that we have shown that there is no answer to the mind-body problem after all. What I want to suggest, however, is that there is a third type of position, which I shall describe as 'analytical central-state materialism.' According to analytical central-state materialism, mental properties are brain properties of some sort, and there are analytic identities linking mental terms and brain terms (these brain terms need not correspond to anything recognized in current neurophysiology). It is not a bit surprising that this position has been neglected, because it seems ruled out from the very start by the content of mental concepts – these concepts have no a priori links with concepts of the brain. The two principal theories have been varieties of analytical behaviorism that claim a priori connections between mental concepts and behavioral concepts, these connections being apparent to a master of mental concepts; and varieties of empirical materialism, which shun a priori connections between mind and brain, on the sensible ground that we know nothing about the brain just by having mastery of mental concepts. How can there be room for analytical materialism, granted that mental concepts contain nothing about the cerebral basis of mental states? At least in the case of analytical behaviorism ordinary masters of mental concepts are cognizant of the behavior that is apt to go with having a mental state; but the ordinary user of the concept *pain* has no idea what is going on in his brain when that concept applies to him.

The answer is that we need to introduce new concepts for mental properties, concepts that do provide the needed conceptual link to the brain. Thus suppose we introduce the new concept PAIN that refers to pain but does not have the sense of our word 'pain'; this concept reveals the essence of pain in such a way as to display analytic connections to concepts of the brain. The argument of this chapter so far can be construed as an existence proof with respect to this concept: there has to be such a concept as no other option is feasible. Because it is highly unlikely that our current concepts of the brain are sufficient to explain the mind, we will also need new concepts of the brain. On empirical grounds C-fibers look to be the correlates of pain, so we can assume that C-fibers have some property * such that * is what entails the presence of pain in the subject. Now we can form the identity statement 'PAIN = * (C-fibers).' This statement identifies pain (the property) with a property, namely*, that C-fibers have, and it does so by identifying these properties under descriptions that render the statement conceptually necessary. It will thus be possible to infer a priori from someone's having * that he is in pain and from his being in pain to infer a priori that he has *. Logically, this statement plays the role that analytical functionalists hoped that their psychofunctional identity statements would play, namely, to provide a conceptual reduction of mental properties. But, unlike that theory, our statement is central-state and conceptually innovative. The analytic links hold between concepts not in our current conceptual repertoire.

I suggest that this idea is not incoherent and, in the light of our earlier argument, is really the only way to think about the correct form of an identity theory. This is what the solution to the mind-body problem has to look like. What we have argued so far, in effect, is that there is no solution to the mind-body problem within the limits of our current concepts of mind and brain: for the solution must be a conceptual identity, by the Smart-Black argument. Yet our current concepts yield no such identities; therefore the correct solution requires new concepts. And because I believe it is independently plausible that major conceptual innovation is required, I take this to confirm the general argument we have been making so far.

What does the analytic status of 'PAIN = * (C-fibers)' imply? It clearly implies transparent necessary conceptual links between brain and mind. These generate epistemic consequences: that if we had the solution we could know that our brain had * just by knowing we were in pain; that I could deduce your mental states from your brain states, thus solving the problem of other minds; and that there is a sense in which we could *see* consciousness in the brain, assuming that we could see the brain to have * (but see the following text). Thus the upshot of possessing this form of solution is vastly more dramatic than what is envisaged under the empirical identity paradigm, where the whole

point of the exercise is to avoid commitment to these epistemic consequences (hence the great play made with the nonsynonymy of 'pain'
and 'C-fiber firing'). There is indeed no analytic link between 'pain' and
'PAIN', because otherwise we could infer * a priori from our present
concept of pain, which palpably we cannot do. That is why we need a
radically new concept, though one that is demonstrably a concept *of pain*
(there is no point in just inventing a concept that applies to the neural
correlates of pain and then merely declaring or stipulating that this
concept refers to pain). Clearly, possessing the concept PAIN would
transform our understanding of both mind and brain, by essentially unifying them. It would completely close any 'explanatory gap,' rid us of
puzzlement about how matter could give rise to consciousness in the
course of evolution, make dualism seem wildly unnatural, and turn psychophysical causation into regular science. Presumably too it would radically alter our conception of the physical world, by showing how matter
has the right properties to entail consciousness. The concept *PAIN*,
unlike our present concept *pain*, would connote precisely those properties of pain that render its connection to matter and the brain entirely
perspicuous.

All this may prompt the question: how distant are we from acquiring
such a marvelous concept? More pointedly, don't these utopian consequences show that this whole approach has to be wrong, because nothing
we might discover could have such revolutionary consequences? Well, I
do think an adequate solution to the mind-body problem would have to
have these strong consequences, but I also think we are unlikely to discover anything with such consequences. These are consistent beliefs: the
reconciling thought is that such a solution exists but is not discoverable
by us. I have not claimed to demonstrate the latter thesis in this chapter,
but the effect of what I have argued is to raise the bar for anyone trying
to solve the problem. If we think we need only seek empirical identities,
then we set the conditions of adequacy quite low, and we make it easy
to elevate mere empirical correlations into genuine theoretical reductions (which is exactly what I think has happened with the likes of 'pain
= C-fiber firing'). But if I am right, discovering empirical correlations
between mental and physical concepts is never enough to entitle us to
assert psychophysical identities; and the extra needed is not Occam's
razor but rather a set of convincing *conceptual* necessities linking mind
and brain. This sets the requirements on a solution much higher than we
have been taught to expect under the influence of the natural kind model
exemplified by 'heat = molecular motion' and the like. In fact, I think
that once it is appreciated how high the bar must be set it becomes difficult to see how we could clear the bar: where are we supposed to find

a concept PAIN that is analytically linked to concepts of C-fibers in such a way as to close the psychophysical gap? The very idea seems to boggle the mind.

The point I am making is that my pessimism about solving the mind-body problem might look unduly gloomy if we are fixated on the empirical identity paradigm, because that makes the demands on a solution look relatively minimal and permits empirical correlations to be promoted to the status of theoretical reductions. But once we see that any solution has to take the form of an analytically true psychoneural identity statement, where this calls for radical conceptual innovation of a kind of which we have not even an inkling, then my pessimism starts to look more reasonable. To be sure, these adequacy conditions do not entail such pessimism, but they do show how hard it would be to come up with what is necessary. To put it bluntly, how likely is it that we are going to come up with psychoneural identity statements with the semantic status of 'bachelors are unmarried males'?

VII

I now want to indicate briefly how this position bears upon some standard discussions of these matters. What I am suggesting, basically, is the existence of (humanly) unknowable conceptual connections between mind and brain. The implicated concepts are not ours, obviously. They belong in Frege's realm of sense, items that may or may not be grasped (or are graspable) by *human* minds. Heuristically, we can think of them as the contents of God's thoughts. So the idea is that God grasps the truth of 'PAIN = * (C-fibers)' and thus enjoys all the epistemic benefits thereof. God can see right into the conceptual necessities whose existence we can only gesture at. In his mind supervenience is a species of logical entailment.

This bears directly on all the modal arguments that have been given for dualism. These are all unsound because they assume that conceptual entailments should be epistemically transparent to us. When a psychophysical connection strikes us as contingent, that could be a reflection merely of our ignorance of the concepts and identity statements that secure the underlying conceptual entailments. Our modal faculty naturally goes haywire in the conceptual vacuum generated by our ignorance. If we had the concepts of PAIN and *, then we would not be tempted by these stampeding modal intuitions. But we are so cognitively distant from them (to the point of unreachability) that we cannot feel their necessity-conferring force. We certainly cannot argue for property dualism on the basis of these intuitions, because they can be otherwise explained as stemming from conceptual poverty. I am not saying that we know for sure that our present concepts of the brain form an adequate supervenience base that guarantees sameness of mental states across all possible worlds. What I am saying is that such a supervenience base exists, possibly in an extension of our present concepts, and that the supervenience holds as a matter of conceptual necessity. There is no conceptually possible world in which C-fibers have * and people are not in pain (i.e., PAIN applies to those people). Nor will multiple realization of mental states by (suitable) neural properties really be possible, though it will strike as possible in our epistemic predicament: there is no world in which someone is in pain and their C-fibers are not *. Analytic identity statements give us as tight a modal connection as could be wished.

Then there are the knowledge-based arguments. These turn out to be soundly based in terms of their argumentative strategy but not to lead to the conclusions commonly drawn from them. If Mary knows that John's C-fibers are *, then she knows a priori that he is in PAIN. So if she can know that * is instantiated before coming out of the room, then she knows all the facts about pain and will learn nothing new when she experiences her first pain. But can she know propositions involving the concept * before she comes out into a world of pain? Could she know propositions about the *-like property that entails experiencing red while living in a black-and-white room? I have no idea. Maybe the cognitive faculties necessary require more than this, maybe they require having experiences of red. The point is that Jackson sounded right when he claimed that all the physical facts can be known by Mary in her room if we assume that these facts are just the kind currently spoken of in physics. But if we allow for radically new kinds of properties, then it becomes quite unclear what the cognitive conditions for grasp of these properties might be. I have no idea what it would take to grasp the concept PAIN and hence whether Mary could in principle grasp that concept while still pain free. What I do know is that if she grasps that concept while in her room (and this may be impossible), *then* she will already know what property pain is. She will say when she first feels pain 'Ah, just the way I expected pain to feel!' Similarly for Nagel's bats: if we could grasp the concepts of the bat brain that analytically entail their experiences, *then* we would know what it is like to be a bat, but whether we could grasp these concepts as we are now constituted is another question. Maybe we need to have bat experiences ourselves in order to grasp the * property that entails those experiences. It is quite true that none of our present brain concepts gives us the entailments we would need, so those concepts do not enable us to know what it is like to be a bat. But of course it does not follow that no brain concepts could confer this kind of knowledge. I believe such concepts exist, though I don't believe we can grasp them; so the impossibility in question is entirely epistemic.

What I would especially emphasize here is that these kinds of epistemological arguments tacitly rely upon the kind of position I have defended in this chapter, notably the conception of concept identity I have argued for. For without that they are immediately vulnerable to the charge of trading illicitly upon an opaque context. The underlying issue about concept identity thus needs to be made explicit and brought to the fore in these arguments. Once it is, we see that it is doing all the heavy lifting in giving the arguments whatever plausibility they have. We can only derive a conclusion about property distinctness from premises about concept distinctness if we accept that concept distinctness ultimately depends upon property distinctness.

VIII

I need to say something finally about the relation between the two concepts expressed by 'pain' and 'PAIN'. Consider this objection: 'pain = PAIN' is informative, so the two concepts must connote distinct properties – which reinstates the dualism we are striving to avoid. We cannot say that this is an analytic statement, because clearly we cannot infer PAIN from our current concept *pain*. Yet we also want this identity statement to be truly assertible, or else we cannot claim to be giving an account of pain. So what is its status? I think this is quite a difficult question and I am not sure I have a complete answer to it. I know what one wants to say here, and I know that it is something we do say in other areas; but as to quite what the correct analysis of the statement comes to, that is trickier. The thought clearly is that PAIN is a kind of successor concept to *pain*, something that replaces it in a scientific picture of things. Analogies are the relation between *weight* and *mass* or our old earth-centered concept of motion and the relativistic notion now used in physics. What should we say about the analysis of 'weight = mass' and 'motion = MOTION'? These statements are not empirically discovered synthetic identities such as 'heat = molecular motion,' but neither are they analytic identities such as 'bachelors = unmarried males.' What they tell us, intuitively, is that an old concept has morphed into a new concept as our theory of the world has matured. They preserve the core of the concept while deepening it and shedding its erroneous associations. That is what I want to say about *pain* and *PAIN*: the latter concept will transform the former but will recognizably be a concept of the same thing. It will operate as a natural conceptual descendant of our present concept. This relation of descendancy fits neither the paradigm of two distinct senses of the same referent nor the paradigm of straight conceptual identity (analyticity). It belongs in a class of its own, and one that is not well understood. In any case, I do not think there is any sound objection to my final position that can be derived from reflection on 'pain = PAIN,' because this will not count as a case of same referent with two empirically associated senses, which is what threatened to resurrect the very objection we are trying to avoid.

IX

My conclusion then is twofold: the solution to the mind-body problem must take the form of a conceptually true identity statement, not an empirically true identity statement; and such an identity statement will contain concepts far removed from our current concepts of mind and body, calling for radical conceptual innovation. The overall thrust of the chapter is to make the conceptual innovation thesis mandatory. Whether we are capable of such innovation I have not discussed, though I believe the prospects are dim. The present point is that the conceptual and theoretical conservatism inherent in standard empirical identity theories is misguided.

NOTES

1. J.J.C. Smart, 'Sensations and Brain Processes.' In D. Rosenthal, ed., *The Nature of Mind* (Oxford University Press: 1991).
2. Saul Kripke, *Naming and Necessity* (Harvard University Press: 1980).
3. The only discussions I know of are Stephen White, 'Curse of the Qualia,' *Synthese* 68 (1986, pp. 333–68) and Christopher Hill, *Sensations* (Cambridge University Press: 1991, pp. 98–101).
4. Smart, p. 172.
5. Smart, n. 13.
6. Kripke, p. 131.
7. This is Hill's strategy (1991, p. 100).
8. This type of position is advocated by Brian Loar, 'Phenomenal States,' *Philosophical Perspectives* 4:81–108.
9. See my *Mental Content* (Basil Blackwell: 1989).
10. Frank Jackson, 'What Mary Didn't Know.' In Rosenthal, pp. 392–4.
11. See my *The Problem of Consciousness* (Basil Blackwell: 1991) and *Problems in Philosophy* (Basil Blackwell: 1993).
12. For example, Kripke (pp. 144–55); and David Chalmers, *The Conscious Mind* (Oxford University Press: 1996).

13. Thomas Nagel, 'What is it Like to be a Bat?,' *Mortal Questions* (Cambridge University Press: 1979). Jackson, cited in Note 10.
14. I am grateful to the following people for helpful discussions: Thomas Nagel, Michael Tye, Brian Loar, Brian McLaughlin, Ned Block, and Galen Strawson.

15

Deconstructing New Wave Materialism

TERENCE HORGAN AND JOHN TIENSON

In the first post World War II identity theories (e.g., Place [1956], Smart [1962]), mind-brain identities were held to be contingent. However, in work beginning in the late 1960s, Saul Kripke ([1971], [1980]) convinced the philosophical community that true identity statements involving names and natural kind terms are necessarily true and, furthermore, that many such necessary identities can only be known a posteriori. Kripke also offered an explanation of the a posteriori nature of ordinary theoretical identities such as that water = H_2O. We identify the kinds and substances involved in theoretical identities by certain of their contingent properties. What we discover when we discover a theoretical identity is the underlying nature of the kind that we identify by those contingent properties.

Now, of course, it was being a posteriori, not being contingent, that mattered to the identity theorists anyway, so the necessity of identity is not, in itself, damaging to mind-brain identity theories. However, Kripke also argued persuasively that the alleged mind-brain identities could not be treated in the same way as ordinary theoretical identities. We "identify" pain by feeling it, and surely how it feels is an essential property of pain, not a contingent property. Thus, a mind-body identity theory must provide a different explanation of why its identities are a posteriori.

A new wave of materialists has appeared on the scene with a new strategy for explaining the a posteriori nature of its alleged identities.[1] The strategy is to locate the explanation for the a posteriori nature of mind-body identities, not on the side of the world, but on the side of the mind – in different ways of thinking about or imagining, or in different concepts. Thus, on this new view, there is only one property, this brain process type, that is identical with this pain type, but we conceive of it under two different concepts, one phenomenal and one theoretical.[2] And these concepts are of such different types that it is not possible to know a priori that they are concepts that pick out the very same thing, and furthermore, it is not surprising that it is not possible to know this a priori.

We believe that this on-the-side-of-the-mind strategy is self-defeating. As far as we can see, differences on the side of the mind of the sort that the new wavers invoke imply different properties on the side of the world. At any rate, the new wavers have not given us an account of the intentional connection by virtue of which a concept or way of conceiving is of one property rather than another. Giving such an account in a way that avoids commitment to different properties is essential to their purposes.

We begin, in the first section, by briefly articulating the problem to which the new wave solution is directed. In the second section we lay out what we take to be the essentials of the solution the new wavers offer. In the third section we explain why, in our view, the new wavers have not given us an account of the intentionality of concepts that is sufficient for their purposes, and why it appears to us unlikely that such an account can be given. In the fourth section we illustrate the problem with reference to a representative version of new wave materialism, Loar (1997).

Conceivability Arguments

Various kinds of conceivability considerations, such as the conceivability of inverted spectra, have been urged against physicalism for a long time. In the post-Kripke era, conceivability arguments have taken a new form, particularly in the hands of David Chalmers ([1995], [1996], [in press]). However, Chalmers's formulations of the argument typically depend upon a fairly elaborate semantic apparatus. We offer here a minimalist formulation of the conceivability issue to which new wave identity theories are addressed. Let us use M for a particular mental state type (say a particular type of pain), and P/F for the physical or physical/functional state type to which M is allegedly identical. Consider the following argument.

(1) It is conceivable that P/F exist and M not exist (or vice versa).
∴ (2) It is possible that P/F exist and M not exist.
∴ (3) M is not (identical with) P/F.

Now, at one time a physicalist might have responded by bringing up the following, apparently parallel argument.

(1w) It is conceivable that water exist but H_2O not exist.
∴ (2w) It is possible that water exist but H_2O not exist.[3]
∴ (3w) Water is not H_2O.

But of course, water is H_2O. So, the response goes, (2w) does not imply (3w); the identity of water and H_2O is contingent. And thus, we can say that the identity of M and P/F is also contingent and that (2) does not imply (3).

However, Kripke convinced us that there are no contingent identities involving proper names or natural kind terms; (2w) does imply (3w). The trouble with the water argument is that (1w) and (2w) are false; you cannot really conceive of a world with water but without H_2O. At a certain level of reflection, it might seem that you can conceive such a world, but you cannot because anything that isn't H_2O would not be the same stuff, would not be water. The reason it may seem that you can conceive of a world with water but without H_2O is that we identify water by certain of its contingent properties: look, taste, feel, and behavior. It has turned out that the stuff we identify in this way is H_2O. If it seems that you conceive of a world with water but without H_2O, what you are really conceiving of is a world without water in which something other than water has the (contingent) properties by which we identify water in this world. To call that a possible situation with water but without H_2O would be to *misdescribe* the situation.

New wavers agree that the physicalist cannot respond to argument (1)–(3) in this way. They agree both that (2) implies (3), just as (2w) implies (3w), and that we should not deny (1). We do not identify our conscious states by their contingent properties. The basic way we have of identifying conscious states is by being in them, and the nature or essence of a conscious state is what it is like to be in it. Thus, we are not mistaken in thinking we conceive a world with P/F but lacking M (or vice versa). There are no contingent properties involved to confuse with the thing itself. A common alternative way to put the need to accept (1) is that we can conceive a world with P/F but lacking M because there is no a priori connection between phenomenal concepts and the theoretical concepts that would represent P/F as a physical/functional state type.

Thus, what the new wavers must say, and do say, is that (1) does not imply (2): conceivability does not imply possibility, at least in the special case where phenomenal concepts are involved. The heart of the position that we are calling new wave materialism is the account they offer of the a posteriori nature of (necessarily true) mind-brain identities, to which we now turn.

The Generic New Wave Position

Generically described, and apart from differences of detail and nuance among various specific versions, the new wave position goes as follows: phenomenal properties are identical to physical properties, in a broad sense of *physical* that includes, for example, functional properties.

(Following Loar [1997] we will speak of 'physical-functional' properties.) Phenomenal concepts, the concepts we apply to phenomenal properties on the basis of introspection, refer directly to those properties as they are in themselves. They do not refer via any contingent features of these referent properties. Nevertheless, phenomenal concepts are distinct from the physical-functional concepts that characterize the physical-functional nature of phenomenal properties. In fact, phenomenal concepts are conceptually independent of the coreferential physical-functional concepts, because the two kinds of concepts have such different conceptual roles in human thought. Because of this conceptual independence, identity statements reflecting the coreference of phenomenal and physical-functional concepts are a posteriori. Also because of this conceptual independence, "separability scenarios" involving phenomenal and coreferential physical-functional concepts are coherently conceivable. For instance, it is coherently conceivable that physical-functional property P/F is instantiated without phenomenal property M being instantiated (or vice versa), even though in fact, $P/F = M$. It is also coherently conceivable that creatures physically just like ourselves could exist, in an environment just like ours, whose internal states have phenomenal character that is systematically inverted relative the phenomenal character of our own experiences ('inverted qualia'). It is also conceivable that there could exist such duplicate creatures, in a duplicate environment, whose internal states have no phenomenal character at all ('absent qualia'). Nevertheless, both phenomenal concepts and the associated physical-functional concepts are rigid: they are coreferential not only in the actual world, but in all possible worlds. Thus, such separability scenarios are metaphysically impossible, despite being coherently conceivable and despite the fact that the relevant psychophysical identities are a posteriori. Conceivability does not imply possibility.

New wave materialists acknowledge three explanatory tasks that a credible version of materialism should simultaneously accomplish:

A: Explain the differences between phenomenal concepts and associated physical-functional concepts in a way that renders them conceptually independent, and thereby renders separability scenarios coherently conceivable.

B: Explain the differences between phenomenal concepts and associated physical-functional concepts in a way that fully respects the phenomenology of conscious experience.

C: Explain the differences between phenomenal concepts and associated physical-functional concepts in a way that is consistent with the claim that phenomenal properties are identical to physical-functional properties.

New wavers claim to be offering a philosophical position that does meet all three of these constraints. Separability scenarios, they say, are coherently conceivable because phenomenal concepts and coreferential physical-functional concepts are so different that they are conceptually independent. Phenomenology is fully respected by acknowledging that phenomenal concepts refer directly to phenomenal properties as they are in themselves, while also acknowledging that these concepts are not physical-functional concepts. And consistency with materialism is maintained because nothing in the proffered account of phenomenal concepts precludes the possibility that the properties to which they refer are physical-functional properties. So say the new wavers.

A Deconstructive Argument

But all is not well. Consider the following simple argument for dualism with respect to phenomenal properties:

Deconstructive Argument

1. When a phenomenal property is conceived under a phenomenal concept, this property is conceived otherwise than as a physical-functional property.
2. When a phenomenal property is conceived under a phenomenal concept, this property is conceived directly, as it is in itself.
3. If (i) a property P is conceived under a concept C, otherwise than as a physical-functional property, and (ii) P is conceived under C, as it is in itself, then P is not a physical-functional property.

Hence,

4. Phenomenal properties are not physical-functional properties.[4]

This argument is valid, and the new wave materialists are committed to premises 1 and 2. Yet premise 3 does not appear to be credibly deniable; on the contrary, it seems virtually tautologous. For, if indeed phenomenal properties, when conceived under phenomenal concepts, not only are conceived otherwise than as physical-functional properties but also are conceived as they are in themselves, then surely phenomenal properties must be otherwise than physical-functional properties. In other words, surely they must be properties that are not physical-functional.

So new wave materialism's doctrinal commitments, in combination with a tautologous-looking further claim that does not seem credibly deniable, lead inescapably to the conclusion that phenomenal properties are not physical-functional properties. This contradicts the new-wave claim that they are physical-functional properties. Thus, the argument evidently effects a deconstruction of the new wave position.

In order to fend off this deconstructive challenge, a new waver would need to articulate his or her account of phenomenal concepts in a way that makes credible the claim that premise 3, despite its initial air of tautologousness, is in fact false. So far the new wavers have not even recognized clearly that they face this dialectical burden, let alone shown how it might be met. We wish them well in trying to meet it, but we doubt that they can succeed.

We will now consider in more detail a version of new wave materialism due to Brian Loar, in order to see how it fares vis-à-vis the deconstructive argument.

Loar's Version

According to Loar (1997), phenomenal properties are physical-functional properties, whereas phenomenal concepts are a species of what he calls *recognitional* concepts. Concerning the notion of recognitional concepts, he says:

> Phenomenal concepts belong to a wide class of concepts that I call recognitional concepts. They have the form "x is one of *that* kind"; they are type-demonstratives. These type-demonstratives are grounded in dispositions to classify, by way of perceptual discriminations, certain objects, events, situations. These dispositions are typically linked with capacities to form images, whose conceptual role seems to be to focus thoughts about an identifiable kind in the absence of currently perceived instances. (pp. 600–1)

Concerning phenomenal concepts and phenomenal properties, he sketches his position as follows:

> Here is the view to be defended. Phenomenal concepts are recognitional concepts that pick out certain internal properties: these are physical-functional properties of the brain. They are the concepts we deploy in our phenomenological reflections; and there is no good philosophical reason to deny that, odd though it may sound, the properties these conceptions *phenomenologically reveal* are physical-functional properties, but not of course under physical-functional descriptions. [T]he property of *its being*

like this to have a certain experience is nothing over and above a certain physical-functional property of the brain. (pp. 601–2)

As regards the conceptual independence of phenomenal concepts and the corresponding physical-functional concepts, he says:

> What then accounts for the conceptual independence of phenomenal and physical-functional concepts? The simple answer is that recognitional concepts and theoretical concepts are in general conceptually independent. Concepts of the two sorts have quite different conceptual roles. It is hardly surprising that a recognitional conception of a physical property should discriminate it without analyzing it in scientific terms. (p. 602)

As so far articulated, Loar's account addresses two of the three above-noted constraints on a credible version of materialism, (A) and (C). It addresses (A) by explaining the differences between phenomenal concepts and physical-functional concepts in a way that is intended to render them conceptually independent, and it addresses (C) with the claim that phenomenal properties are identical to physical-functional properties. And as so far articulated, the account also evades the challenge posed by the deconstructive argument, because premise 2 of that argument has not so far been embraced.

However, not enough has yet been said to satisfy condition (B), which requires the explanation of phenomenal concepts to fully respect the phenomenology of conscious experience. One way to see this is to notice the conceptual possibility of creatures who have self-directed recognitional concepts that (i) refer to physical-functional properties, (ii) are conceptually independent of the physical-functional concepts that characterize the nature of these properties by virtue of their recognitional nature, and yet (iii) are phenomenally empty. Loar himself acknowledges this fact in the following passage:

> Not all self-directed recognitional concepts are phenomenal concepts. A fanciful self-directed nonphenomenal concept can be conceived. To begin with, consider blindsight. Some cortically damaged people are phenomenally blind in restricted retinal regions; and yet when a vertical or horizontal line (say) is presented to those regions, they can, when prompted, guess what is there with a somewhat high degree of correctness. We can extend the example by imagining a blindsight that is exercised spontaneously and accurately. At this point we shift the focus to internal properties and conceive of a self-directed recognitional ability, which is like the previous ability in being phenomenally blank and spontaneous but which discriminates an internal property of one's own. If this recognitional ability were suitably governed by the concept 'that state', the resulting concept

would be a self-directed recognitional concept that is phenomenally blank.
(p. 603)

So the account of phenomenal properties and phenomenal concepts
needs bolstering, in a way that distinguishes genuine phenomenal concepts from self-directed blindsight concepts. Loar addresses this issue in
two steps. First he considers what an antiphysicalist could be expected
to say about it:

> What might an antiphysicalist say about these various self-directed
> recognitional concepts? Let us make a good-faith attempt to present a
> reasonable version. We might say [says the antiphysicalist] that a phe-
> nomenal concept has as its mode of presentation the very phenomenal
> quality that it picks out. We might also say that phenomenal concepts
> have "token modes of presentation" that are noncontingently tied to the
> phenomenal qualities to which those concepts point: particular cramp
> feelings and images can focus one's conception of the phenomenal quality
> of cramp feeling. As for self-directed blindsight concepts, the antiphysi-
> calist then ought to say, they differ from phenomenal concepts in the
> obvious way, whether one puts it by saying that they lack the noncontin-
> gent phenomenal modes of presentation (types) that phenomenal quali-
> ties have, or that they lack their phenomenal "token modes of
> presentation." (p. 604)

Second, he claims that the physicalist can, and should, say such things too:

> Whatever the antiphysicalist has said about these cases the physicalist may
> say as well. The idea that one picks out the phenomenal quality of cramp
> feeling by way of a particular feeling of cramp (or image, etc.) is hardly
> incompatible with holding that that phenomenal quality is a physical prop-
> erty. The contrast between phenomenal concepts and self-directed blind-
> sight concepts finds physicalist and antiphysicalist equally able to say
> something sensible. (pp. 604–5)

Loar thus takes on board the claim that phenomenal concepts, unlike
self-directed blindsight concepts, have modes of presentation, and also
the claim that the mode of presentation of a phenomenal concept is
the very phenomenal property to which the concept refers. He thereby
embraces premise 2 of the deconstructive argument, as underscored by
the following further remarks:

> It is natural to regard our conceptions of phenomenal qualities as con-
> ceiving them as they are in themselves, that is, to suppose that we have
> direct grasp of their essence. Phenomenal concepts, as we have seen, do
> not conceive their reference via contingent modes of presentation. And so
> they can be counted as conceiving phenomenal qualities directly. Calling
> this a grasp of essence seems to me all right, for phenomenal concepts do

not conceive their references by way of their accidental properties.
(pp. 608–9)

So Loar's overall account of phenomenal concepts is now committed not
only to the claim that they are self-directed recognitional concepts, but
also to the claim that they differ from self-directed blindsight concepts
by conceiving their referents directly, as they are in themselves.

Where does this leave us, dialectically? Loar clearly thinks that this
further claim about phenomenal concepts can be added to the pot
without disrupting the erstwhile consistency between the account of phenomenal concepts and the physicalist claim that phenomenal properties
are identical to physical-functional properties. But it is just here that he
runs afoul of the deconstructive argument. For, insofar as a concept C is
characterized merely as a self-directed recognitional concept, the claim:

(a) C refers to a physical-functional property;

is consistent with the claim:

(b) C conceives its referent otherwise than as a physical-functional
     property;

because C could be a concept that picks out its referent in a nakedly
recognitional way, a purely demonstrative way, involving no mode of presentation at all. But once one adds that C directly picks out its referent
as it is in itself (rather than picking it out nakedly), this explanation for
the consistency of (a) and (b) is no longer available. So some different
account is needed for how (a) and (b) could be consistent. But Loar
offers no such account, and thus he fails to defuse the force of the deconstructive argument.[5]

In short: Loar's initial, partial, account of phenomenal concepts
addresses requirements (A) and (C) for an adequate version of materialism, by embracing premise 1 of the deconstructive argument
without premise 2. But the initial account does not adequately address
condition (B), which leads him to extend the account by embracing
premise 2 as well. This expanded account now perhaps satisfies conditions (A) and (B). But, given premise 3 of the deconstructive argument,
the expanded account evidently fails to satisfy condition (C). Loar has
failed to meet the dialectical burden of explaining how premise 3 could
be false.

We lack the space to consider in detail various other versions of new
wave materialism, such as Hill (1997) and Hill and McLaughlin (1999).
But in our view, these versions fail to address the crucial question of how
premise 3 could be false.

Conclusion

Let us summarize this discussion by formulating in a slightly different way the challenge we are posing for new wave materialism. Consider the following general principle about concepts and properties:

(i) If a concept C provides a direct grasp of the property P it refers to, in other words, if C conceives P directly as it is in itself (rather than conceiving P via a "mode of presentation" or "reference-fixing property" distinct from P itself), then P is as it is conceived by C.[6]

We fail to see how this principle could possibly be false. And as far as we can see, new wavers have said nothing that begins to explain how it could be false. Now consider these two claims about phenomenal concepts:

(ii) A phenomenal concept, by phenomenologically presenting the property to which it refers, provides a direct grasp of that property.

(iii) A phenomenal concept phenomenologically presents its referent property otherwise than as a physical-functional property.

Both of these claims seem clearly true, and new wave materialists affirm both of them.[7] But statements (i)–(iii) jointly entail that the properties referred to by phenomenal concepts are otherwise than physical-functional properties, in other words, that phenomenal properties are not physical-functional properties.[8]

New wavers tend to emphasize, correctly, that phenomenal concepts differ significantly from physical-functional concepts in their conceptual role, and in the conditions under which their application is epistemically warranted. They also tend to emphasize, again correctly, that these kinds of differences are sufficiently great to render phenomenal concepts conceptually independent of physical-functional concepts. But these kinds of observations, correct though they are, simply do not address the question of how principle (i) could be false, and specifically how it could be false for phenomenal concepts and properties. That question is what needs to be answered: otherwise, deconstruction.[9]

NOTES

1. Clear examples of what we are here counting as "new wave materialism" are Loar (1997), Hill (1997), and Hill and McLaughlin (1999). Versions of materialism that are somewhat similar in spirit, but do not clearly fall under this rubric, include Tye (1995), Levine (1998), and Melnyk (this volume). On the

problems faced by such recent views insofar as they might fall outside the rubric, see Note 5.

2. New wavers use various terminology, sometimes speaking of modes of presentation or modes of access. For the most part we will stick with *conceiving*, *concept of*, and the like.

3. Zombie worlds have become a common representative of conceivability arguments. So compare

> (1′)   A world that is physically identical to ours but lacking conscious states (a zombie world) is conceivable.
>
> ∴   (2′)   A world that is physically identical to ours but lacking in conscious states is possible.
>
> (1w′) A world with water but without H_2O is conceivable.
>
> ∴   (2w′) A world with water but without H_2O is possible.

(Again, the two arguments are now considered disanalogous. The intuition behind (1w) and (1w′) was, of course, that the stuff we identify as water could have turned out to have some other composition – to be an element, or homogeneous.)

4. This argument is similar in spirit to the "property dualism argument" presented in White (1986, pp. 351–3). Note well that premise 1 does not say that phenomenal properties are conceived, under phenomenal concepts, as non-physical-functional properties. Conceiving a property *otherwise than as a* physical-functional property is different from, and weaker than, conceiving it *as otherwise than* a physical-functional property.

5. A dilemma looms, for those materialists who acknowledge that phenomenal concepts do not pick out their referents via a contingent feature of the referent-property. On one hand they can avoid premise 2 of the deconstructive argument, by effectively treating phenomenal concepts as nakedly referential. The trouble with this option, as illustrated by Loar's discussion of generalized blindsight, is that it fails to respect the phenomenology of conscious experience. On the other hand, they can embrace premise 2, thereby falling prey to the deconstructive argument. (Our rubric "new wave materialism" covers positions that do embrace premise 2.) Graham and Horgan (forthcoming) argue, in effect, that the first horn of this dilemma impales certain current versions of materialism, notably Tye (1995).

6. Premise 3 of the deconstructive argument is essentially a special case of this principle. Note that principle (i) does not say that property P is, or is in its essence, only as it conceived to be under concept C. Likewise, premise 2 of the deconstructive argument does not say that when a phenomenal property is conceived under a phenomenal concept, this property is thereby conceived as it completely is in itself. The possibility is left open that there is more to a property P, as it is in its essence, than is revealed when P is directly grasped under a concept C.

7. Recall what Loar says in a passage quoted earlier: "Phenomenal concepts, as we have seen, do not conceive their reference via contingent modes of presentation. And so they can be counted as conceiving phenomenal qualities directly. Calling this a grasp of essence seems to me all right" (p. 609). Concerning the much-discussed problem of the "explanatory gap," Loar goes on to say this: "What generates the problem is not appreciating that there can be two conceptually independent 'direct grasps' of a single essence, that is,

grasping it demonstratively by experiencing it, and grasping it in theoretical terms" (p. 609). We are among those who fail to appreciate this contention. For, given that phenomenal concepts conceive phenomenal properties directly, the contention can be true only if principle (i) is false for phenomenal properties; yet Loar has failed to explain how it could be false.

8. Even if certain mental properties with phenomenal content (for instance, pain) are physical-functional properties, the point would still hold. Phenomenal properties (for instance, the hurtfulness of pain) then would be nonphysical properties that are possessed by the physical-functional properties. Moreover, even if it should turn out that phenomenal properties have a total essence that is partly physical-functional so that this aspect of their essence is not revealed when these properties are directly grasped under phenomenal concepts (see Note 6), nevertheless they still would be partly nonphysical (because they still would be as they are conceived under phenomenal concepts, and they are so conceived otherwise than as physical).

9. This chapter is entirely collaborative; order or authorship is alphabetical. We thank Ronald Endicott, Christopher Hill, Barry Loewer, and Brian McLaughlin for helpful discussion and/or comments.

16

In Defense of New Wave Materialism: A Response to Horgan and Tienson

BRIAN P. McLAUGHLIN

It is fairly widely believed that felt bodily sensations (aches, pains, itches, tickles, throbs, cramps, chills, and the like) have physical or at least functional correlates.[1] That is to say, the following thesis is fairly widely believed:

> *Correlation Thesis.* For every type of sensation state, S, there is a type of physical or functional state, P/F, such that it is nomologically necessary that for any being, x, x is in S if and only if x is in P/F.

The Correlation Thesis, if it is true, would not, of course, solve the mind-body problem for sensations. For the Correlation Thesis is compatible with virtually every theory of mind: not only with noneliminativist materialism and functionalism, but also with Cartesian Dualism, dual-aspect theory, neutral monism, and panpsychism.

Some philosophers, however, myself included, maintain that the following thesis would offer *the best explanation* of the correlation thesis:

> *Type Identity Thesis.* For every type of sensation state, S, there is a type of physical or functional state, P/F, such that S = P/F.[2]

This thesis implies the Correlation Thesis. For, as Saul Kripke (1971) demonstrated,

> *The Necessity of Identity.* For any A and B, if A = B, then necessarily A = B.[3]

The kind of necessity in question is the strongest sort: if A = B, then there is, unqualifiedly, no way the world could be such that A is not identical with B. Thus, given the necessity of identity, if the Type Identity Thesis is true, then the Correlation Thesis is true as well. We maintain, on grounds of overall coherence and theoretical simplicity, that the explanation of the Correlation Thesis that the Type Identity Thesis offers is superior to the explanations offered by other theories of mind.

We also believe that true sensory–physical/functional identity claims are only a posteriori knowable. The reason is that sensory concepts are distinct from both physical and functional concepts, and there is no a priori link between sensory concepts and physical/functional ones.[4] On our view, identity claims concerning sensations and their physical/functional correlates will be a posteriori justifiable on the grounds that they offer the best explanation of the relevant sensory physical-functional correlations.[5]

As Kripke (1980) pointed out, because a posteriori identity claims are necessary, to justify them, one must explain away their appearance of contingency. As he also pointed out, his own model for explaining away the appearance of contingency of a posteriori necessary identity claims, such as the claim that water = H_2O, is inapplicable to sensory physical-functional identity claims, such as, for instance, the claim that pain = C-fiber firing. The reason is well known: while ordinary natural kind concepts such as the concept of water have associated clusters of stereotypical observable properties that function as contingent modes of presentation for them, sensory concepts lack any associated clusters of properties that function as contingent modes of presentation for them. Something can look, smell, taste, feel, and observably behave like water yet not be water. Water is a natural kind with a hidden essence; and, so, something's having the stereotypical observable properties of water does not suffice to make it water. In contrast, whatever feels like pain is pain. Pain (i.c., the felt quality of pain) is a kind of feeling.

We propose an alternative model for explaining away the appearance of contingency of sensory physical-functional identity claims.[6] Such identity claims appear contingent because the concepts expressed by the terms flanking the identity sign have radically different conceptual roles.[7] It is because their conceptual roles are so different that we can both imagine and conceive of sensory states without their correlated physical-functional states, and conversely. We maintain that when one sees how such concepts differ in their conceptual roles, one will be in a position to see, as well, that there is no a priori reason to believe that such acts of imagining and conceiving are reliable guides to possibility in the cases in question. And we maintain, on broad empirical grounds, that acts of imagining and conceiving that involve the joint exercise of sensory and physical-functional concepts are not reliable guides to possibility.[8]

To convey at least the gist of the leading line of thought here about how to explain away the appearance of contingency of sensory and physical-functional identity claims, consider first imaginability, which in addition to involving the exercise of concepts also involves mental imagery. One can try to establish that a statement fails to be necessarily true by trying to imagine a possible situation in which the statement is false; that is, by trying to construct a qualitative or imagistic representation of such a situation. However, as Thomas Nagel (1974) has pointed out in a passage that warrants repeating, there is more than one form of imagination and that makes a difference in the cases in question. He writes:

> A theory that explained how the mind-body relation was necessary would still leave us with Kripke's problem of explaining why it nevertheless appears contingent. That difficulty seems to me to be surmountable, in the following way. We may imagine something by representing it to ourselves either perceptually [or] sympathetically.... To imagine something perceptually, we put ourselves in a conscious state resembling the state we would be in if we perceived it. To imagine something sympathetically, we put ourselves in a conscious state resembling the thing itself. (This method can be used to imagine mental events and states – our own or another's.) When we try to imagine a mental state occurring without its associated brain state, we first sympathetically imagine the occurrence of the mental state: that is, we put ourselves in a state that resembles it mentally. At the same time, we attempt to perceptually imagine the non-occurrence of the associated physical state, by putting ourselves into another state unconnected with the first: one resembling that which we would be in if we perceived the non-occurrence of the physical state. Where the imagination of physical features is perceptual and the imagination of mental features is sympathetic, it appears that we can imagine any experience occurring without its associated brain state, and vice versa. The relation between them will appear contingent even if it is in fact necessary, because of the independence of the disparate types of imagination. (Nagel [1974], fn. 11)

As Nagel indicates, imagining pain without its correlated brain state (a physical or functional state) or vice versa involves the joint exercise of the distinct faculties of sympathetic and perceptual imagination. Jointly exercising the faculties of sympathetic and perceptual imagination, one might, for instance, form an imagistic representation that "splices together" a sympathetic image of the felt quality of pain and a perceptual image of the nonoccurrence of C-fiber firing (e.g., a perceptual image of a certain electroencephalograph reading).[9] We hold that there is no a priori presumption in favor of dualist intuitions that are supported by acts of imagination involving the joint exercise of the sympathetic and perceptual imagination. For, as Nagel notes, due to the independence of these distinct faculties of imagination, acts of imagination involving their joint exercise would make it appear that an experience is only contingently related to its correlated brain state, even if the two were necessarily related.[10]

Let us turn to conceivability. One can try to establish that a statement fails to be necessarily true by trying to conceive of a situation in which it is false. One tries to construct a conceptual representation of such a situation – a representation that has a logical structure and that has concepts as its basic building blocks. Conceiving of a situation in which one is in a sensory state without being in its nomologically correlated brain state will involve the joint exercise of a sensory and a physical-functional concept. The epistemic constraints that govern our use of sensory concepts, however, are orthogonal to those that govern our use of physical-functional concepts. When one uses a sensory concept to classify one's own current experiences, the experiences that guide and justify one in applying the concept are always identical with the experiences to which the concept is applied. Sensory states are self-presenting states: we experience them, but we do not have sensory experiences of them. We experience them simply by virtue of being in them: for they are experiences. Sensory concepts are direct recognitional concepts: deploying such concepts, we can introspectively recognize when we are in a sensory state simply by focusing our attention directly on the state.[11] Moreover, our use of a sensory concept in an act of imagination is guided and justified, at least in part, by our having images that resemble *being in* the sensory state in question, rather than by our having images that resemble perceptual experiences caused by those states. The conceptual roles of perceptual, functional, and theoretical concepts are, of course, quite different. Our use of a perceptual concept, for instance, is guided and justified, at least in part, by experiences that are caused by the referent of the perceptual concept or by images that resemble experiences caused by the referent of the perceptual concept.

Now the acts of conceivability that are responsible for dualist intuitions involve the joint exercise of sensory and physical-functional concepts. Given the way in which the fundamental epistemic constraints on the use of sensory concepts differ from those on the use of physical and functional concepts, there is no a priori reason to trust intuitions arrived at by acts of conceiving that involve the joint exercise of such concepts. Given the differences between sensory concepts and physical-functional concepts, a sensory state and its nomologically correlated brain state would seem contingently related, even if they were necessarily related. Of course, this result does not entail that dualist intuitions based on such acts of imagining and conceiving are false. To repeat, the point is, rather, that there is no a priori presumption in favor of such intuitions.[12] But, of course, we argue on broadly empirical grounds that such intuitions are mistaken: for the Type Identity Thesis offers the best explanation of the Correlation Thesis. Even if the fact that one can imagine or conceive that

P is a prima facie reason for believing that P is possible, such a reason can be overridden by considerations of overall coherence and theoretical simplicity. And we maintain that *our prima facie* reasons are overridden in the cases in question.[13]

Much more can be said by way of elaboration and defense of the position that I have very briefly outlined. My aim here, however, is a modest one. I shall engage in a rear guard action. I shall respond to a line of objection that Terence Horgan and John Tienson (Chapter 15, this volume) raise to this position, a position they call "new wave materialism." (For stylistic convenience, I shall followed them in their use of "new wave materialism.")[14] Their line of objection is subtle, and so I shall examine it in considerable detail.

Framing the issue in terms of phenomenal properties and phenomenal concepts,[15] Horgan and Tienson offer the following argument, which they call "the deconstructive argument":[16]

1. When a phenomenal property is conceived under a phenomenal concept, this property is conceived otherwise than as a physical-functional property.
2. When a phenomenal property is conceived under a phenomenal concept, this property is conceived directly, as it is in itself.
3. If (i) a property P is conceived, under a concept C, otherwise than as a physical-functional property, and (ii) P is conceived, under C, as it is in itself, then P is not a physical-functional property.

Hence,

4. Phenomenal properties are not physical-functional properties. (p. 309)

As Horgan and Tienson note, the argument is valid. To resist the conclusion, new wave materialists must reject one of the premises. By way of clarification of premise 1, they say:

> Note well that premise 1 does not say that phenomenal properties are conceived, under phenomenal concepts, as non-physical-functional properties. Conceiving a property *otherwise than as* a physical-functional property is different from, and weaker than, conceiving it *as otherwise than* a physical-functional property. (p. 315)

New wave materialists will, of course, reject the claim that when a phenomenal property is conceived under a phenomenal concept it is conceived *as otherwise than* a physical-functional property. But, as Horgan and Tienson correctly note, premise 1 does not have that implication.[17] New wave materialists accept premise 1. Indeed, premise 1 is true in virtue of the fact that phenomenal concepts are not physical-functional concepts. For to conceive of a property otherwise than as a physical-functional property is just to conceive the property under a concept that is not a physical-functional concept.

New wave materialists also embrace premise 2: it is one of the central tenets of the view. New wave materialists hold that phenomenal concepts lack associated contingent modes of presentation that can serve as contingent a priori reference-fixing properties for them. Phenomenal properties are their own modes of presentation: they are self-presenting. Thus, when a phenomenal property is conceived under a phenomenal concept, the property is directly conceived as it is in itself, rather than as it stands in relation to something else that functions as a contingent mode of presentation of it. Horgan and Tienson say:

> Premise 2 of the deconstructive argument does not say that when a phenomenal property is conceived under a phenomenal concept, this property is thereby conceived as it completely is in itself. The possibility is left open that there is more to property P, as it is in its essence, than is revealed when P is directly grasped under a concept C. (p. 315)

Thus, they acknowledge that "direct grasp" does not imply "complete grasp." New wave materialists agree that in one sense this "direct grasp" does not imply a "complete grasp." From the fact that one "directly grasps" a phenomenal property when one exercises a phenomenal concept in introspection, it does not follow that one has a "complete grasp" of the property in the sense that the essential nature of the property is, thereby, conceptually revealed to one. For the property will have a neural essence or a functional essence, and that will not be revealed to one when one exercises a phenomenal concept in introspection. It will not be revealed to one for the simple reason that phenomenal concepts are neither neural nor functional concepts. Phenomenal concepts are of two sorts: nondescriptive name concepts and type-demonstrative concepts; as such, phenomenal concepts lack any descriptive content. They thus do not conceptually reveal anything about the essential nature of phenomenal properties: they simply name or demonstrate them. There is, however, a sense in which the direct grasp of a phenomenal property that a phenomenal concept provides is a "complete grasp": when one conceives a phenomenal property under a phenomenal concept, one does not conceive an aspect of the property, one conceives the property itself. One conceives the property directly. One conceives it, but not via conceiving either a wholly distinct property that is a contingent mode of presentation of it or via conceiving a property that is an aspect (essential or nonessential) of it. Phenomenal concepts refer directly to phenomenal properties.

We see, then, that new wave materialists accept both premise 1 and premise 2. Let us turn, then, to premise 3:

> 3. If (i) a property P is conceived, under a concept C, otherwise than as a physical-functional property, and (ii) P is conceived, under C, as it is in itself, then P is not a physical-functional property. (pp. 309, 321)

New wave materialists reject premise 3. Horgan and Tienson tell us, however, that:

> Premise 3 does not appear to be credibly deniable; on the contrary, it seems virtually tautologous. For, if indeed phenomenal properties, when conceived under phenomenal concepts, not only are conceived otherwise than as physical-functional properties but also are conceived as they are in themselves, then surely phenomenal properties must be otherwise than physical-functional properties. In other words, surely they must be properties that are not physical-functional properties. (p. 309)

This passage contains Horgan and Tienson's only defense of their claim that premise 3 is "virtually tautologous." So, let us examine it in detail.

Of course, if phenomenal properties must be otherwise than physical-functional properties, then they are not physical-functional properties. New wave materialists reject, however, Horgan and Tienson's claim that "if indeed phenomenal properties, when conceived under phenomenal concepts, not only are conceived otherwise than as physical-functional properties but also are conceived as they are in themselves, then surely phenomenal properties must be otherwise than physical-functional properties" (p. 309). When a phenomenal property is conceived under a phenomenal concept, it is indeed conceived otherwise than as a physical-functional property. The reason is simply this: to conceive a property as a physical-functional property, one must conceive it under a physical-functional concept. Phenomenal concepts are not physical-functional concepts: they differ from physical-functional concepts in their conceptual roles. Thus, to conceive a phenomenal property under a phenomenal concept is to conceive it otherwise than as a physical-functional property. To conceive a phenomenal property under a phenomenal concept is to conceive it otherwise than by conceiving it under a physical-functional concept. Moreover, when a phenomenal property is conceived under a phenomenal concept, it is conceived as it is in itself. That is to say, it is conceived as it is in itself, rather than conceived as it stands in relation to some wholly distinct property or as it stands in relation to some aspect of it. For, as we noted, phenomenal concepts directly refer to phenomenal properties. Phenomenal concepts do not refer to phenomenal properties via referring to wholly distinct properties that function as contingent modes of presentation of them or via referring to properties that are aspects of them. New wave materialists claim that phenomenal concepts are non-physical-functional concepts that directly refer to phenomenal properties. This claim is consistent with the claim that phenomenal properties are physical-functional properties. Horgan and Tienson say at one point that:

> the claim
>> (a) C refers to a physical-functional property;
> is consistent with the claim
>> (b) C conceives its referent otherwise than as a physical-functional property;
> because C could be a concept that picks out its referent in a nakedly recognitional way, a purely demonstrative way, involving no mode of presentation at all. But once one adds that C directly picks out its referent as it is in itself (rather than picking it out nakedly), this explanation for the consistency of (a) and (b) is no longer available. (p. 313)

Phenomenal concepts that are type-demonstratives indeed pick out phenomenal properties demonstratively. But they do not pick them out "nakedly"; that is, they do not pick them out in a way "involving no mode of presentation at all." For phenomenal concepts have associated modes of presentation. The mode of presentation associated with a phenomenal concept is the very phenomenal property to which the concept refers. The concept thus picks out its referent as it is in itself rather than picking it out "nakedly" or as it stands in relation to something else that functions as a mode of presentation of it. Furthermore, new wave materialists understand (b) as follows: a concept C conceives its referent otherwise than as a physical-functional property if and only if C is a referring concept and neither a physical nor a functional concept. It is in this sense, then, and only in this sense that new wave materialists maintain that (b) is satisfied by phenomenal concepts. When (b) is understood in the way that new wave materialists will grant that it is satisfied by phenomenal concepts, (a) and (b) can both be satisfied by phenomenal concepts. For there is no incoherence in the idea that a non-physical-functional concept can directly refer to a physical-functional property.

Horgan and Tienson offer a second argument against new wave materialism, one that they say puts their objection "in a slightly different way" than does the deconstructive argument. Let us turn, then, to the second argument:

(i) If a concept C provides a direct grasp of the property P it refers to, in other words, if C conceives P directly as it is in itself (rather than conceiving P via a "mode of presentation" or "reference-fixing property" distinct from P itself), then P is as it is conceived by C.

(ii) A phenomenal concept, by phenomenologically presenting the property to which it refers, provides a direct grasp of that property.

(iii) A phenomenal concept phenomenologically presents its referent-property otherwise than as a physical-functional property.

Both [(ii) and (iii)] seem clearly true, and new wave materialists affirm both of them. But statements (i)–(iii) jointly entail that the properties referred to by phenomenal concepts are otherwise than physical-functional properties, in other words, that phenomenal properties are not physical-functional properties. (p. 314)

As concerns premise (i), Horgan and Tienson tells us, "premise 3 of the deconstructive argument is essentially a special case of [principle (i)]." Of principle (i), Horgan and Tienson also say: "We fail to see how this principle could possibly be false" (p. 314). New wave materialists agree with this second claim but reject the first: they deny that premise (3) is a special case of (i). For principle (i) is true and premise (3) is false. Premise (3), in conjunction with a statement that its antecedent holds, falsely implies that the property P in question is a not a physical-functional property. Principle (i), however, has no such implication when conjoined with a statement that its antecedent holds. So, in rejecting premise (3) of the deconstructive argument, new wave materialists are not committed to rejecting principle (i) of the preceding argument. Indeed, as should be clear from our earlier discussion, new wave materialists embrace principle (i): it is a central tenet of their position.

Horgan and Tienson might acknowledge that principle (i), by itself, does not imply that the properties referred to by phenomenal concepts are not physical-functional properties. They claim, however, that principles (i)–(iii) jointly imply that phenomenal properties are not physical-functional properties. But notice first of all that principles (i)–(iii) do not imply that. There is a distinction between a phenomenal property being phenomenologically presented *otherwise than as* a physical-functional property and its being phenomenologically presented *as otherwise than* a physical-functional property. *If* phenomenal concepts phenomenologically present the phenomenal properties they refer to, then they present them otherwise than as physical-functional properties. For, once again, phenomenal concepts are not physical-functional concepts. However,

from the fact, *if* it were one, that phenomenal concepts phenomenologically present the phenomenal properties to which they refer and
present them otherwise than as physical-functional properties, it would
not follow that phenomenal concepts phenomenologically present
phenomenal properties as otherwise than physical-functional properties.
Thus, even if principles (i)–(iii) are all true, it does not follow that
phenomenal properties are not physical-functional properties.

Were this their only response to the second argument, however, new
wave materialists would face a formidable, perhaps insuperable, difficulty. For even *if* the phenomenal property that one conceives under a
phenomenal concept phenomenologically presents a physical-functional
property, the issue will arise as to whether the property of falling under
a phenomenal concept is a physical-functional property. And if one
appeals again to yet another phenomenal concept under which one conceives of the property of falling under the first phenomenal concept, then
the question will recur for the property of falling under that second-
order phenomenal concept. In other words, the mode of presentation
problem will recur for the phenomenal property of applying a higher-
order phenomenal concept.[18]

The response in question to the argument from principles (i)–(iii) is,
however, not the main response of new wave materialists. New wave
materialists deny that principles (ii) and (iii) "are clearly true" (p. 442),
and they do not affirm either of them; in fact, they maintain that (ii) and
(iii) are false. For principles (ii) and (iii) would be true only if phenomenal concepts *phenomenologically* present their referent properties. And
phenomenal concepts do *not* phenomenologically present their referent
properties. Phenomenal properties are, you will recall, phenomenologically *self-presenting*. They are not phenomenologically presented by
properties of any other sort, including the property of falling under a
phenomenal concept. Horgan and Tienson's basic mistake is to assume
that phenomenal concepts phenomenologically present phenomenal
properties, and thus stand to them as phenomenal modes of presentation.[19] Of course, in a sense, phenomenal concepts "present" their
referent properties; but they conceptually present them, rather than phenomenologically present them.[20] And phenomenal concepts conceptually present phenomenal properties only in the sense that they directly
refer to phenomenal properties.[21]

In summary, then, both of Horgan and Tienson's arguments against
new wave materialism are unsound. New wave materialists reject
premise (3) of the first argument. And they reject principles (ii) and
(iii) of the second. New wave materialists hold that (a) phenomenal
concepts directly refer to phenomenal properties, that (b) pheno-

menal concepts are not physical-functional concepts, and, that (c) phenomenal properties are identical with physical-functional properties. These three theses are consistent. And new wave materialists hold that they are all true.

NOTES

1. What I shall say about felt bodily sensations will apply as well to visual sensations, auditory sensations, olfactory sensations, and gustatory sensations if there are such. And it will apply as well to any kind of mental imagery. It will apply to any kind of sensory state.
2. See Papineau (1936); Loar (1997); Hill (1997); McLaughlin (1997); Balog (1998); Hill and McLaughlin (1999). See also Melnyk (Chapter 17, this volume).
3. Kripke (1971) derived this principle from the Indiscernibility of Identicals and the thesis that everything is such that it is necessarily identical with itself.
4. Of course, analytical functionalists would deny that there is no a priori link between sensory concepts and physical-functional concepts. We maintain that analytical functionalism is false, at least for sensations.
5. Of course, in addition to being empirical, this best-explanation argument for the Type Identity Thesis is also hypothetical: if the Correlation Thesis is true, then the Type Identity Thesis offers the best explanation of why it is true. Whether the Correlation Thesis is true is an empirical issue. No one has yet succeeded in identifying a physical or functional correlate of any type of sensation state. However, as I noted, it is fairly widely believed, on the evidence, that the Correlation Thesis is true or at least may well be true. The main concerns about the Identity Thesis are philosophical.
6. In proposing his model, Kripke (1980) was careful to note that he was not claiming that it was the only possible model for explaining away the appearance of contingency of an a posteriori identity claim.
7. We take concepts to be different from state types or properties. We thus reject the view of concepts as properties that figure predicatively in thoughts.
8. The model that I have alluded to here and shall describe directly is developed in Hill (1997), and discussed in Hill and McLaughlin (1999). While Loar (1997) is by no means committed to the specific model in question, he too holds that the appearance of contingency of a posteriori sensory and physical-functional identity claims is to be explained by appeal to the differences in the conceptual roles of sensory concepts and physical-functional concepts expressed by the terms flanking the identity sign in such claims. See, in this connection, his discussion of what he calls "the semantic premise."
9. Hill (1997) speaks of "image splicing."
10. For a different treatment of this passage from Nagel, see Papineau (1993b).
11. See Loar (1997) for a detailed discussion of sensory concepts as direct recognitional concepts. See also Price (1957) for earlier pioneer work on recognitional concepts.
12. There is thus no a priori route to possibility in the cases at issue. It should be noted that even on Kripke's alternative model for explaining away the appearance of contingency of a posteriori necessary identity claims there is

no a priori route to possibility. Unlike the model we favor, Kripke keeps the a priori tie between imaginability/conceivability and possibility. However, he rejects the idea that we can know a priori (i.e., in an empirically indefeasible way) what we are imagining or conceiving. Thus, he denies that we are really imagining that there is water but no H_2O when we seem to ourselves to be imagining that there is water but no H_2O. Our model is compatible with first-person authority in such case.

13. It should be noted that one can reject dualist intuitions while embracing other modal intuitions as trustworthy. Not all modal intuitions stand or fall together. A selective skepticism is a legitimate option. For further discussion, see Hill (1997) and Hill and McLaughlin (1999).

14. A more appropriate term would have been *new wave materialism/functionalism*. Hill and I, however, favor a strictly materialist version: we hold that sensory states have neural correlates and that they are identical with their neural correlates. See Hill and McLaughlin (1999).

15. The difference between *phenomenal property* and *sensory property* and between *phenomenal concepts* and *sensory concepts* is merely verbal.

16. Horgan and Tienson (p. 315) point out that the argument is "similar in spirit" to Stephen White's (1986) property dualism argument. (His argument was inspired by "objection five" in Smart [1962].) I respond to White's property dualism argument in McLaughlin (1997).

17. In general, from the fact that a representation R of something, X, does not represent X as F, it does not follow that R represents X as not-F.

18. Compare the objection that Colin McGinn (Chapter 14, this volume) raises to a certain way of trying to solve the mind-body problem, a way that looks on the surface (see Note 19) like the new wave materialist solution to the mind-body problem for phenomenal properties.

19. From the perspective of new wave materialism, McGinn (Chapter 14, this volume), or those who try to solve the mind-body problem in the way he criticizes, makes the mistake of assuming that phenomenal concepts phenomenologically present the properties to which they refer. (New wave materialists do not try to solve the mind-body problem in the way McGinn criticizes.)

20. Keep in mind here the point made in Note 7.

21. New wave materialists wish to be materialists across the board, so to speak, and so of course require an account of how concepts refer that is compatible with materialism.

17

Physicalism Unfalsified: Chalmers's Inconclusive Conceivability Argument

ANDREW MELNYK

Let a *conceivability argument* be any argument that aims to refute physicalism by showing that some claim that physicalism must treat as necessary is not in fact necessary because its negation is conceivable and hence genuinely possible. According to conceivability arguments in the recent tradition, it is conceivable that so-and-so iff the thought that so-and-so can be entertained without explicit contradiction or the sense of conceptual blockage one has (albeit to an unusually intense degree) in attempting to entertain the negation of the claim that two is a number. According to such arguments, the claim that it is assumed physicalism must treat as necessary is a certain more or less immediate consequence of any physicalist type-identity claim whereby some nonphysical property – some property expressible in nonphysical vocabulary – is identified with either a physical property or a physically realized functional property. So suppose the (nonphysical) property of being N is identified with the (physical or functional) property of being P. Then, on the assumption that the identity statement is formed using rigid designators and that such identity statements are necessary, it follows that, necessarily, an object is N iff it is P. But if, as the argument claims, it is conceivable, and hence possible, that something should be N but not P (or P but not N), then it is false that, necessarily, an object is N iff it is P, and hence false that being N just is being P.

But traditional conceivability arguments of this sort fail. Even though it is surely conceivable, in the sense specified, that something should be N but not P, the real possibility that something should be N but not P just does not follow. Someone competent with the concept of table salt could gain competence with the concept of NaCl in a chemistry class, which omitted to mention that NaCl is the same stuff as table salt. It would then be conceivable for this person, in the sense specified, that his food be sprinkled with salt but not with NaCl. He could entertain the thought that this is so without explicit contradiction or any sense of conceptual blockage. But it is not really possible that his food be sprinkled with salt but not with NaCl, because salt and NaCl are the very same stuff, and it is not possible that his food be both sprinkled and not sprinkled with the very same stuff. So the conceivability, in the sense specified, of a proposition does not in general entail its possibility.

The explanation for this failure of entailment is that the reference of our concepts is not an a priori matter. One does not know simply on the basis of one's competence with a concept what property that concept picks out. Accordingly, one might be competent with two concepts without realizing that in fact they pick out the very same property.[1] Someone might therefore entertain the formally consistent thought, "My food is sprinkled with salt but not with NaCl," and in doing so feel no sense of conceptual blockage, even though, given that 'salt' and 'NaCl' corefer, and that no food is both sprinkled and not sprinkled with the same stuff, this thought expresses no possible state of affairs. Similarly, someone might entertain the formally consistent thought, 'Something is N but not P,' and in doing so feel no sense of conceptual blockage, even if, because being N is the same property as being P, and it is impossible that something should both have and not have the very same property, it is impossible that something should be N but not P. So it is because the reference of our concepts is an a posteriori matter that conceivability (in the sense specified) does not entail possibility.[2] Someone can infer that her consistent and blockage-free thought that something is N but not P expresses a genuine possibility only if she makes an a posteriori assumption that conceptual competence alone does not guarantee: that 'being N' and 'being P' do not pick out the very same property. But this assumption begs the question against physicalism, because it is tantamount to assuming that being N is not the same property as being P.

Traditional conceivability arguments fail, therefore, because they rest on a false assumption in the philosophy of mind and language: that one knows, simply on the basis of one's competence with a concept, what property the concept picks out. Physicalism is safe from any traditional conceivability argument so long as whatever turns out to be the correct view of the determination of the reference of our concepts implies the falsity of this assumption.[3]

Now in his recent book, *The Conscious Mind*, David Chalmers offers a conceivability argument for the property-dualist conclusion that the property of having a red sensation, like all other phenomenal properties, is in no sense physical: it is neither type-identical with any physical property nor is it a functional property that is, as it happens, always realized physically.[4] But his argument is not of the traditional sort I have been discussing. It employs a different and proprietary notion of conceivability according to which the inference from conceivability to possibility is unproblematic; it is not targeted against the physicalist claim that each phenomenal property is necessarily coextensive with some physical property, and, most importantly, it is quite consistent with the very claim that undermines traditional conceivability arguments, namely that one can be competent with a concept and still not know what property it refers to.

My question is whether Chalmers's conceivability argument refutes physicalism. But because he introduces an elaborate technical machinery with which to express it, I cannot evaluate it either fairly or effectively while ignoring this machinery. In this chapter, then, I aim to reconstruct the argument as sympathetically as possible, taking his technical machinery as seriously as he does, but to argue that even so it is inconclusive, because it rests on a nonobvious psychosemantic assumption that we have been given no reason to believe. Having explained Chalmers's technical machinery in my first section, I use it in my second to reconstruct his antiphysicalist argument. In the next two sections, I identify the psychosemantic assumption on which the argument rests, and argue that it is in fact unsupported. Finally, I venture some conclusions about conceivability arguments in general.[5]

I

Chalmers claims (pp. 52–62) that an important part of the meaning of any concept is, or can be represented by, a pair of functions, which he calls the primary intension and the secondary intension of the concept. Each function is a mapping from possible worlds to referents in worlds, but not the same mapping. A concept's *primary* intension (henceforth, *1-intension*) is a mapping from each possible world, considered as *actual*, to the concept's referent in that world. It tells us not only what the concept actually refers to, given the way the actual world is, but also what it would have referred to, if the actual world had turned out to be different in various ways. "The [primary] intension," he says, "*specifies* how reference depends on the way the external world turns out" (p. 57). The 1-intension of 'water,' for example, which for expository purposes Chalmers suggests that we treat roughly as 'watery stuff,' maps each world onto whatever stuff in that world (if any) happens to be watery, regardless of whether the stuff that happens to be watery in that world is H_2O, or XYZ, or whatever. A concept's *secondary* intension (henceforth, *2-intension*), by contrast, is a mapping from each possible world, considered as *counterfactual*, to the concept's referent in that world. It tells us what the concept would refer to in each such world. If a concept is a rigid designator, its 2-intension maps each possible world onto the set of objects, in that world, which constitute the referent of the concept in the actual world (as determined by the 1-intension plus the way the actual world happens to be). So, given that 'water' is rigid, the 2-intension of 'water' maps each world onto H_2O in that world, because, given the way the actual world is, the 1-intension of 'water' maps the actual world onto H_2O.

Moreover, there is a crucial difference in epistemological status between 1- and 2-intensions. Every concept, Chalmers insists, is such that its 1-intension is accessible a priori to anyone who is competent with it (e.g., pp. 57–9). But the 2-intension of some concepts – those that are rigid designators – can only be known a posteriori, because to know them one needs to know not only their 1-intensions but also what the actual world happens to be like. Notice that, since knowing the 1-intension of a concept only tells you what the concept refers to in the actual world, if you also know – a posteriori, of course – what the actual world is like, Chalmers's view implies that one does not know, simply on the basis of one's competence with a concept, what property the concept picks out. He therefore rejects the assumption on which I diagnosed traditional conceivability arguments as relying.

A statement is necessary, according to Chalmers (pp. 62–6), iff it is true in all possible worlds, and possible iff true at some possible world. But because the truth of a statement at a world can be evaluated in light of either the 1- or the 2-intensions of its constituent concepts, we can distinguish between the necessity (i.e., truth in all possible worlds) of a statement according to 1-intensions (henceforth, *1-necessity*) and its necessity according to 2-intensions (henceforth, *2-necessity*); also between the possibility of a statement (i.e., truth at some possible world) according to 1-intensions (henceforth, *1-possibility*) and its possibility according to 2-intensions (henceforth, *2-possibility*). So, for example, to say that the conditional 'If P, then Q' is 1-necessary is to say that, when the truth value of P and Q is evaluated at each world by reference to the 1-intensions of the concepts deployed in P and Q, all the worlds at which P is true are worlds at which Q is true; and to say that 'P and not-Q' is 2-possible is to say that there is some possible world at which 'P and not-Q' is true when evaluated according to 2-intensions. And, according to Chalmers, 1- and 2-necessity and 1- and 2-possibility are the only kinds of necessity and possibility we need to postulate, even in order to handle Kripke-Putnam a posteriori necessities (see his critique of 'strong' metaphysical necessity on pp. 136–8).

The distinction between 1- and 2-intensions also generates a distinction between two kinds of conceivability, *1-conceivability* and *2-*

conceivability. "The conceivability of a statement," Chalmers says (p. 67), "involves two things: first, the conceivability of a relevant world, and second, the truth of the statement in that world." If the statement comes out as true at the conceived world when evaluated according to 1-intensions, then the statement is said to be 1-conceivable; but if the statement comes out as true at the conceived world when evaluated according to 2-intensions, then it is said to be 2-conceivable.

How, on Chalmers's account, is conceivability related to possibility? If a statement is 1-conceivable, then there is some conceivable world correctly describable as one in which the statement is true according to 1-intensions, from which it follows trivially that the statement is 1-possible (p. 67). And because 1-intensions are accessible a priori, the 1-conceivability of a statement is in principle an a priori affair, and so at least in principle the 1-possibility of any 1-possible statement can be determined a priori. In practice, however, judgments of conceivability can err, because although 1-intensions are accessible a priori, they may not actually have been accessed, because of insufficient reflection, and so a conceived world may be misdescribed (pp. 67 and 99). Similarly, the 2-conceivability of a statement entails its 2-possibility, though because 2-intensions are not in general accessible a priori, 2-conceivability is not even in principle an a priori affair, and so the 2-possibility of a 2-possible statement cannot in general be determined a priori. With this account, Chalmers can give a neat diagnosis of where traditional conceivability arguments fail. If being N just is being P, then what follows is that it is 2-necessary that something is N iff it is P. Now it is certainly 1-conceivable that something be N but not P. But because even the ideal 1-conceivability of a statement does not entail its 2-possibility, this does not entail that it is 2-possible that something should be N but not P, and so the 2-necessity that something is N iff it is P, and hence the claim that being N just is being P, is safe. According to Chalmers, however, the very same technical machinery that permits this diagnosis of the error in traditional conceivability arguments can still be used to refute physicalism.

II

But how, exactly? Surprisingly, in view of the poor track record of conceivability arguments, Chalmers presents nowhere in his book a formalized version of his argument sufficiently detailed to answer this question. But, for textual reasons I have no space to give, I offer the following reconstruction, where we let 'P' express every fact, past, present or future, including every nomic fact, expressible in the proprietary vocabulary of physics and let 'Q' be the (true) statement that sometimes people have red sensations:

(1) It is 1-conceivable that [P and not-Q].

∴ (2) It is 1-possible that [P and not-Q].

(3) All concepts in the proprietary vocabulary of physics are such that their 1-intensions map each possible world onto the same referents as do their 2-intensions.

∴ (4) There is a possible world in which 'P and not-Q' is true when 'P' is evaluated in light of 2-intensions and 'not-Q' is evaluated in light of 1-intensions.

(5) If physicalism is true, then there is no possible world in which 'P and not-Q' is true when 'P' is evaluated in light of 2-intensions and 'not-Q' is evaluated in light of 1-intensions.

∴ (6) Physicalism is false.

This argument can be seen at once to differ from a traditional conceivability argument. First, it employs a notion of conceivability that definitionally guarantees the validity of the step from (1) to (2), the inference from conceivability to (one sort of) genuine possibility. Secondly, what is claimed, by its first premise, to be 1-conceivable is not (a) that someone should be in physical or functional state B without actually having a red sensation (where B is whatever the physicalist identifies with having a red sensation), but (b) that the *totality* of physical facts, including but not limited to the tokening of B, should be exactly as they actually are and yet that no one should have a red sensation (p. 131). In fact, Chalmers holds that both (a) and (b) are 1-conceivable, but it is only the conceivability of (b) that generates an argument against physicalism. Contrast his position as regards water, where he holds that while the analog of (a) is 1-conceivable, the analog of (b) is not: it is 1-conceivable that my cup should contain H_2O but no water, but it is not 1-conceivable that the totality of physical facts, including but not limited to my cup's containing H_2O, should be exactly as they actually are and yet that there should be no water (see ch. 2, sect. 6). That is why Chalmers is not committed to an argument for the nonphysicality of water that parallels the one for the nonphysicality of phenomenal states.

The step from (2) and (3) to (4) is valid, given the definition of '1-possibility.' Premise (3) is defended on the grounds that denying it is tantamount to claiming that physical entities and properties have hidden essences of which we know nothing (pp. 134–6).[6] Premise (5) is obviously crucial, for it claims that physicalism is committed to the impossibility of precisely what conceivability has (allegedly) shown to be possible. It is equivalent to the claim that, given physicalism, 'If P, then Q' is true in all possible worlds when 'P' is evaluated in light of 2-intensions and 'Q' is evaluated in light of 1-intensions, in other words, that the physical facts in a certain sense necessitate a certain class of nonphysical facts. Now most physicalists will acknowledge that, given physicalism, the truth that P necessitates the truth that Q, but insist that this necessitation is entirely a posteriori, perhaps explainable (as I would explain it) by appeal to a posteriori necessary identities holding between each nonphysical property and some functional property whose associated role is specifiable in physical or topic-neutral terms. They will reject (5), only conceding that, given physicalism, 'If P, then Q' is 2-necessary. But physicalists should concede (5), according to Chalmers. If physicalism is true, then the way we have discovered the world to be physically should fix or determine all the (positive) nonphysical facts there are. And if 'Q' is true at all in the actual world, which by hypothesis it is, then it is true in the actual world when evaluated according to 1-intensions, because the 1-intension and 2-intension of any concept must map the actual world onto the same referent. So 'Q,' when evaluated in light of 1-intensions, expresses a fact, and hence one of those facts that should be necessitated by the physical facts, if physicalism is true (see pp. 132–3). From (5) and (4), the antiphysicalist conclusion obviously follows.

III

But why should we suppose that (1) is true, in other words, that it is 1-conceivable that P and not-Q? Let us first clarify the meaning of this premise. For Chalmers (p. 67), "The conceivability of a statement involves two things: first, the conceivability of a relevant world, and second, the truth of the statement in that world." So premise (1) is claiming that some possible world is conceivable at which 'P and not-Q' is true when evaluated according to 1-intensions. But what is it for a possible world to be conceivable? Chalmers surely does not intend the implausible and unmaterialist (hence question-beggingly) idea that conceiving a world is a matter of directing some alleged faculty of modal perception upon some segment of extramental modal reality. All that he can plausibly mean is that conceiving a possible world is somehow *mentally representing* a possible world, in other words, hosting mental representations of a possible world[7] – conscious or nonconscious, propositional or iconic – and doing so in a way functionally appropriate to conceiving. So what (1) is claiming is that some possible world is conceivable, in the sense of somehow mentally representable, at which 'P and not-Q' is true when evaluated according to 1-intensions.[8] And I shall be arguing that Chalmers has provided no good reason for supposing that this is true, which leaves the physicalist free to resist his argument by refusing to accept its first premise.

Chalmers's one and only reason for claiming that it is 1-conceivable that P and not-Q seems to be that it is conceivable in the *ordinary* sense that P and not-Q. He infers the 1-conceivability of 'P and not-Q' from the fact that, as revealed by thought-experiment, we can entertain the thought that P and not-Q without explicit contradiction or any sense of conceptual blockage.[9] But Chalmers is not just equivocating here on senses of 'conceivable'; he must be making a theoretical identification, that is, taking it that what is *in fact* going on in us when in the ordinary sense we conceive that P and not-Q is, often enough, that we are 1-conceiving that 'P and not-Q', in other words, that we are somehow mentally representing a possible world that we correctly describe as one at which 'P and not-Q' is true when evaluated according to 1-intensions.

But if conceiving in the ordinary sense does involve correctly describing a mentally represented possible world as one in which some statement is true when evaluated according to 1-intensions, then, when we are conceiving in the ordinary sense, we must evidently have at least potential access to the 1-intensions of the constituent concepts of the statement evaluated. And, according to Chalmers, so we do, because the 1-intensions of concepts we are competent with are allegedly accessible a priori to us. Perhaps experience was needed to acquire those concepts in the first place; but once they have been acquired, no further experience is needed for their 1-intensions to be accessible. So anyone who understands the claim that P and not-Q, and hence is competent with its constituent concepts, has potential access to their 1-intensions and is therefore potentially in a position correctly to describe a mentally represented possible world as one in which it is true, according to 1-intensions, that P and not-Q. Of course, as noted, Chalmers allows that potential access is not always turned into actual access; but in principle, anyway, 1-intensions are always accessible a priori to those competent with the corresponding concepts.

Would it suffice for Chalmers's argument if the 1-intensions of concepts we are competent with were indeed accessible to us, but only a posteriori? Chalmers does insist that the accessibility is a priori, but yes, so long as we do in fact have potential access of some sort to the 1-intensions of the relevant concepts, even if it is a posteriori, Chalmers may still identify conceiving in the ordinary sense that P and not-Q with 1-conceiving that P and not-Q. But taking ordinary conceivers' accessibility to 1-intensions to be a posteriori presents problems. First of

all, Chalmers would need to supply some empirical evidence for thinking that we do in fact enjoy the alleged a posteriori accessibility. For
if the accessibility is not understood as a priori, a consequence of our
competence with the relevant concepts, then its presence cannot simply
be inferred from our conceptual competence. And this empirical evidence is bound to be contested by physicalists, who will contend that,
assuming the soundness of the rest of Chalmers's argument, the evidence
for the physical character of phenomenal states is automatically evidence
against thinking that we actually enjoy the a posteriori accessibility in
question. Secondly, if the alleged accessibility to 1-intensions is a posteriori, then physicalists will rightly demand to know the evidence for so
taking the 1-intensions of the constituent concepts of 'P and not-Q' that
its 1-possibility is a consequence. And, as before, physicalists will insist
that the evidence for physicalism is automatically evidence against so
taking the 1-intensions of the constituent concepts of 'P and not-Q.' So
an appeal to a posteriori accessibility opens more than one can of very
messy worms. It is a priori accessibility to 1-intensions on which, in fact,
Chalmers bases his conceivability argument, and it is the adequacy of
this basis that I shall discuss.

The dialectical situation, then, is this: unless the 1-intensions of
concepts we are competent with are accessible to us a priori, Chalmers
cannot construe conceiving in the ordinary sense that P and not-Q as
1-conceiving that P and not-Q; and unless he can construe conceiving
that P and not-Q in the ordinary sense as 1-conceiving that P and not-
Q, he has provided no reason to think that it really is 1-conceivable that
P and not-Q, in other words, no reason to think that the first premise of
his argument against physicalism is true.

IV

So the key assumption on which the first premise of Chalmers's
conceivability argument rests is that the 1-intensions of the concepts with
which ordinary conceivers are competent are accessible to them a priori.
Chalmers's idea, however, is not that, in applying concepts to hypothetical worlds considered as actual, we ordinary conceivers draw upon
some previously existing database of explicitly represented knowledge
of 1-intensions, for example, discursive definitions, on the pattern of
'watery stuff' for 'water.' Rather, the a priori accessibility to us of 1-
intensions is embodied in a certain capacity he says we possess: the
capacity to consider a possible way the world might have turned out to
be, and then to say what the concepts we are competent with would have
referred to, if the world had turned out to be that way (see pp. 57–60).

Using this capacity, we can say, for example, that 'water' would have referred to XYZ had the actual world turned out to be one in which the watery stuff was XYZ. Our knowledge of a concept's 1-intension is therefore merely implicit, implicit in our capacity to consider various ways the actual world might have turned out to be, and to say what the concept would have referred to, had the world turned out in those ways; and this knowledge becomes explicit only to the extent that we exercise this capacity and take note of its deliverances (see p. 59, on Kripke's apparent methodology). So we can now say with more precision what exactly Chalmers takes to be going on when we 1-conceive (and hence when we conceive in the ordinary sense) that P and not-Q: we are somehow mentally representing a possible world, and, by exercising the 1-intension–respecting capacity just described, we are able to say that the possible world we have mentally represented is one at which, according to 1-intensions, 'P and not-Q' is true.

The crucial question, therefore, becomes whether we ordinary con-ceivers do in fact possess the 1-intension–respecting capacity. I cannot prove that we do not, but it is remarkably difficult to come up with a good reason for thinking that we do.[10] Notice, first, that our possession of such a capacity does not follow simply from the definition of the 1-intension of a concept. For the 1-intension of a concept is officially defined as what *in fact* the concept would have referred to, had the world turned out to be different in various ways. It is not defined as what com-petent concept-users *say* the concept would have referred to, had the world turned out to be different in various ways. Whether we can say what our concepts would have referred to had the actual world turned out to be different in various ways is what is at issue. Secondly, our possession of the 1-intension–respecting capacity does not follow from the undisputed fact that, when presented with a description of how the world might have turned out, we make confident pronouncements about what various concepts would then have referred to. For our confident pronouncements might nevertheless be wrong. Many people pronounce confidently but wrongly when asked in what direction a ball would move, if it were gently released from the back of a vehicle moving rapidly forward.[11] Similarly, one could pronounce confidently but wrongly about what a concept would refer to, if the world were discovered to have been different in a certain way.

The obvious suggestion at this point is that possessing a 1-intension–respecting capacity with respect to a concept is an inevitable consequence of being competent with the concept. But there is at least one influential way of understanding concepts that implies that although concepts definitely have 1-intensions, one can be competent with them without possessing a 1-intension–respecting capacity to consider possible ways the world might have turned out to be, and then say what those concepts would have referred to, had the actual world turned out in those ways.

On the (Fodorian) view I have in mind, then, a (primitive) concept, 'F,' perhaps to be understood as a word in the language of thought, refers to Fs (rather than Gs, say) in virtue of the fact that it stands in a certain complex causal or nomological relation – call it 'R' – to Fs (though not to Gs).[12] But then, because it is contingent that 'F' stands in this reference-constituting relation to Fs, there will be possible worlds in which it stands in R to nothing, or to Gs, or to Hs, and so on. Accordingly, 'F' will certainly have a (contingent) 1-intension: had the actual world turned out to be one in which 'F' stood in R to Gs, it would have referred to Gs; had the actual world turned out to be one in which 'F' stood in R to Hs, it would have referred to Hs, and so on. However, in order to be competent with this concept, the only capacity one needs is the capacity to host a symbol which *in fact* stands in R to Fs. In order to exercise this capacity, in other words to think an 'F'-thought, one needs only to host a token of a type that *in fact* stands in R to Fs. One does not need any awareness at all that 'F' refers to Fs in virtue of standing in R to Fs, or that any particular token of 'F' stands in R to Fs. Neither does one need to host the token, even in part, *because* one in any way represents to oneself that it is of a type that stands in R to Fs.[13] Consequently, one could be presented with a description of a possible way the actual world might have turned out, a description that could even state explicitly that 'F' stands in R to Gs, and yet be quite unable to say what 'F' would have referred to, had that description turned out to be true of the actual world (unable to say, that is, that it would in that case have referred in fact to Gs). And, quite generally, if a concept is similar to 'F' one could be competent with it, and it could have a 1-intension, but one could still be unable to say what it would have referred to, had the actual world turned out differently in various ways.

Moreover, phenomenal concepts – certain concepts, picking out phenomenal states, that we deploy when, in higher-order introspective thoughts about phenomenal states, we ascribe phenomenal states to ourselves; concepts, that is, of the same sort as the one that is a constituent of 'P and not-Q' – are as good candidates as any to be primitive Fodorian concepts, in other words to refer to phenomenal states in virtue of standing in some complex causal or nomological relation to those states, and to be such that their exercise requires no response to a representation. And if they are, then one could be given a complete description of the physical and functional state one is in while one has a

red sensation, and yet simply lack any capacity to say what 'is having
a red sensation' would apply to were the situation described to turn
out to be actual, even though, were you actually in that physical and
functional state, you would apply to yourself the concept, 'is having a
red sensation.' So if phenomenal concepts are primitive Fodorian concepts, competence with them does not guarantee that one possesses the
relevant 1-intension–respecting capacity. But Chalmers offers nothing to
show that they are not Fodorian. So, for all he says, we might not possess
the 1-intension–respecting capacity he must suppose we possess in order
to be able to construe the ordinary conceivability of 'P and not-Q' as
evidence for its 1-conceivability.

But the difficulty in finding reason to think that we possess the
relevant 1-intension–respecting capacity does not arise solely from
the neglected possibility that phenomenal concepts might be primitive
Fodorian concepts. Consider the following, more promising-looking view
of concepts, one that forges a very close link between competence with
a concept and its 1-intension: to be competent with a concept is to possess
a certain *disposition to apply it* under various circumstances, actual and
counterfactual; and the 1-intension of a concept – what it would *in fact*
have referred to, had the world turned out to be different in various
ways – is to be identified with what people possessing the competence-
constituting disposition *would in fact have applied the concept to*, had the
world turned out to be different in various ways.

But this alternative, dispositionalist view of concepts, even if true,[14]
does not help. Even if, to be competent with a given concept, I must have
a disposition to apply it in certain ways, a disposition constitutive of its 1-
intension, it just does not follow that I possess a 1-intension–respecting
capacity with regard to it, in other words, that I can consider possible ways
the world might have turned out to be and then say what the concept
would have referred to had the world turned out in those ways. For I might
have a disposition to apply a concept in a certain way, depending on
circumstances, and yet simply not know how I would have applied it, had
the world turned out in various ways. How I would in fact have applied
the concept and how I say I would in fact have applied the concept clearly
need not be the same. Nor is there any guarantee, or even presumption,
that, in general, if I have a disposition, I know enough about it to enable
me to say what I would have done had circumstances turned out to be
different. Suppose I have a food allergy, that is, a disposition to react in
various unpleasant ways to various foodstuffs; then (without consulting
an allergist) I know only as much about it as I can infer from self-
observation of actual reactions, and I might be quite wrong about whether
I would have broken out in hives if the mystery dish I ate last night had

turned out to be sea slugs. Similarly, even on the alternative view of concepts, I might be quite wrong about what I would have called 'water' had the world turned out to be one in which XYZ is the colorless, odorless liquid that falls from the sky as rain, and so forth. One simply need have no special epistemic access to one's dispositions.

An advocate of the dispositionalist view of concepts might reply, however, that one's 1-intension–respecting capacity results from a sort of simulation, in particular, from allowing the dispositions that constitute one's conceptual competence to be triggered by *counterfactual* situations, 'off-line,' rather than by the *actual* situations that trigger them when, 'on-line,' one applies concepts in real life. So in the special case of dispositions that constitute conceptual competence, we have more to go on than inferences from self-observation of actual reactions. But if one could be enabled in this way to say what a given concept would have referred to had some counterfactual situation between actual, then one could not be doing it by literally allowing one's competence-constituting dispositions to be triggered by counterfactual situations, because counterfactual situations, being merely counterfactual, cannot literally trigger anything. One would have to be doing it by allowing one's dispositions to be triggered by *mental representations* of counterfactual situations. In that case, however, competence-constituting dispositions must have mental representations as their triggers. (Otherwise, why should exercising the disposition off-line in response to mere *representations* of counterfactual situations that you are not actually in cause any manifestation of the disposition at all?) So if one is to argue that we possess a 1-intension–respecting capacity in regard to phenomenal concepts by arguing from a dispositionalist account of conceptual competence, then one must argue that competence with phenomenal concepts is not merely a disposition to apply them, but a disposition to apply them that is triggered by mental representations. But nowhere does Chalmers attempt to do so. Nor, on the face of it, do phenomenal concepts seem very strong candidates to be concepts applied in reaction to mental representations. All the introspective considerations that have traditionally made knowledge of one's own phenomenal states seem peculiarly direct and unmediated seem to count against the idea. So, for all Chalmers says, competence with phenomenal concepts might be the possession of a disposition that is nonrepresentationally triggered, in which case, once again, competence with phenomenal concepts will not guarantee possession of the relevant 1-intension–respecting capacity.

Chalmers provides no reason at all to think that we actually possess the required 1-intension–respecting capacity, and it is not easy to think one up. But if we lack the capacity, as I suggest we might, then how can we explain the fact that, when presented with a hypothetical situation nonphenomenally described, we make confident pronouncements about what *nonphenomenal* concepts would have referred to, had that situation turned out to be actual; whereas when presented with a hypothetical situation nonphenomenally described, we feel no inclination to make any pronouncements at all about what *phenomenal* concepts would have referred to, had that situation turned out to be actual? Why do we respond in these different ways to representations of hypothetical situations? An obvious possibility is that we are exercising off-line an *epistemological* capacity, a capacity to judge that a concept applies to the world – that the property it refers to is actually instantiated. However, whereas our application to the world of nonphenomenal concepts is always based on representations (possibly sensory) of the world, representations that constitute our evidence, our application to ourselves of phenomenal concepts is, as I just mentioned, notoriously direct and not based on any evidencing representations at all. We do not judge that a sensation feels *like this* on the basis of any evidence that we represent to ourselves, and we are at a loss if asked *how* we know we are in pain.[15] Because our epistemological capacity to apply phenomenal concepts, when exercised in regard to the actual world, does not take representations as input,[16] we should not expect it to produce any output when exercised in regard to representations of merely counterfactual situations. But if we nevertheless try so to exercise it, we will note its lack of output and find ourselves, by a natural movement of thought, with the sense that fixing the physical and functional facts leaves it wide open as to what the phenomenal facts are, at least when these are thought of via the deployment of phenomenal concepts.[17]

Similarly, if we do lack the 1-intension–respecting capacity with regard to certain concepts, then how, if at all, can we determine what the 1-intensions of those concepts are? By the usual methods of science, a posteriori. Consider for a moment the representational systems of nonhuman animals. The dances of honeybees, we think, represent the locations of pollen sources. Because these dances possess a sort of rudimentary compositional structure, the elements of these dances can be seen as strongly analogous to concepts (or terms). Now these elements presumably get to refer to features of the locations of pollen sources in virtue of meeting some naturalistically specifiable condition, a condition that would determine a 1-intension. But because we are not honeybees, there is no question of our knowing a priori what that condition is; yet we can hope nevertheless to find out what it is – by a posteriori means. And what we can do for honeybees we can presumably do for ourselves.[18]

My conclusion, then, is that, for all that Chalmers has shown, it may be conceivable in the ordinary sense that P and not-Q, even though it is not 1-conceivable that P and not-Q, the explanation for this being simply that conceiving in the ordinary sense lacks even the potential access to relevant 1-intensions (via a 1-intension–respecting capacity) that would be required for it to constitute 1-conceiving and hence provide information about 1-possibility. But in that case no reason to believe the first premise of Chalmers's conceivability argument – the 1-conceivability of 'P and not-Q' – is provided by the (undisputed) conceivability in the ordinary sense of 'P and not-Q.' And because the conceivability in the ordinary sense of 'P and not-Q' is the only reason offered for believing this first premise, we are left with no reason at all to believe it. Chalmers's conceivability argument, as it currently stands, is therefore inconclusive.

Traditional conceivability arguments fail, it will be recalled, because we do not know a priori, simply on the basis of our competence with a concept, what that concept refers to. Now Chalmers explicitly allows that we do not know this a priori, but he still claims that we have a sort of implicit a priori knowledge – embodied in a 1-intension–respecting capacity – of what the concepts we are competent with would have referred to had the actual world turned out to be different in various ways, of "how reference depends on the way the external world turns out" (p. 57). But Chalmers has not shown, and there is no obvious reason to think, that even this much of the semantics of our concepts is a priori. Nor, in consequence, has he shown that there is any sort of modal truth that is accessible a priori, even though, as he insists and I agree, all (nonnomological) modal truths are, in a broad but still worthwhile sense, conceptual.[19]

V

Any adequately presented conceivability argument must address these questions:

(1) How does physicalism's commitment to some allegedly necessary truth arise?
(2) How are we to understand the conceivability of something?
(3) Why does the conceivability of something, understood in line with the answer to (2), entail, or even defeasibly support, its possibility?

Traditional conceivability arguments are clear on (1), clear enough, at least by implication, on (2), and deplorably silent on the all-important (3). It is a signal merit of Chalmers's conceivability argument that it is tolerably clear on (1), and quite explicit on (2) and (3). But answering these questions opens up the possibility that adequate answers to one question may preclude adequate answers to others; and this possibility, or so I have claimed, is actual in the cases I have discussed. Traditional conceivability arguments respond to (2) by construing conceivability in such a way that their conceivability premises are very plausible; but then their implicit answer to (3) must rely on the implausible psychosemantic assumption that one knows, simply on the basis of one's competence with a concept, what property the concept picks out. Chalmers's argument addresses (3) by understanding conceivability in such a way that the conceivability of something evidently entails its possibility; but then it must answer (2) in such a way that the resulting conceivability premise is in fact groundless unless one makes the unsupported and nonobvious psychosemantic assumption that the 1-intensions of concepts they are competent with are accessible a priori to ordinary, flesh-and-blood conceivers. A good question to ask about any conceivability argument is whether it can simultaneously return adequate answers to (2) and (3).

The psychosemantic assumptions on which traditional conceivability arguments and Chalmers's nontraditional argument rest certainly appear to be a posteriori. On the face of it, at least, it is a matter for empirical discovery what human conceptual competence is and hence what it requires. If it turns out that all conceivability arguments rely on a posteriori assumptions, then conceivability arguments can *at best* be as strong as the evidence supporting those assumptions; but then into the other pan of the scales must be thrown such evidence as supports physicalism, and even good conceivability arguments (if such exist) will lose the apodictic character I suspect they have often been thought to possess. Moreover, these assumptions are certainly no less controversial than physicalism. If that too is typical of the assumptions on which conceivability arguments rest, then conceivability arguments offer little promise of assisting any movement to rational consensus on the issue of physicalism, and those interested in physicalism would better spend their time discussing the bearing of actual scientific findings upon the prospects for physicalism. However, it has been altogether too common for the presenters of conceivability arguments – and not only their advocates – to proceed as if such arguments, especially when they move from conceivability to possibility, do not depend on any nontrivial assumptions at all. I hope that Chalmers's example encourages the view that launching a conceivability argument with any hope of success requires embedding it within ambitious positions in metaphysics and the philosophy of mind and language.[20]

NOTES

1. Sophisticated thinkers obviously do know simply on the basis of their competence with the relevant concepts that 'salt' refers to salt, that 'NaCl' refers to NaCl, and so on; but these metalinguistic platitudes evidently provide no hint that 'salt' and 'NaCl' pick out the very same stuff.

2. Might conceivability nevertheless provide prima facie support for possibility? Only if, and to the extent that, it is reasonable to make the empirical presumption about our minds that distinct concepts generally pick out distinct properties. I cannot recall ever having seen any evidence offered for such a presumption.

3. Adopting a descriptivist theory of predicative concepts, incidentally, does not make knowledge of the coreferentiality of two concepts a priori in every case. Suppose competence with a concept requires associating it with some description uniquely satisfied by the referent. Then if two concepts have different, but consistent, associated definite descriptions, it is not a priori whether or not the two concepts corefer. For the very same referent might satisfy both unique descriptions. This point applies with especial force if a descriptivist, such as Frank Jackson in his "Reference And Description Revisited" (forthcoming), allows such descriptions as 'is the appropriate (actual) causal origin of uses of term T.' Who knows – a priori – what other terms' uses the object that meets this description might also be the appropriate (actual) causal origin of?

4. Chalmers (1996). All subsequent page references in the text are to this book.

5. I might add that I consider the representationalist theory of phenomenal states to provide an entirely satisfactory physicalist treatment of them; see, for instance, Dretske (1995) and Lycan (1996). I understand physicalism along the lines sketched in Melnyk (1994, pp. 221–41).

6. In fact, (3), which seems equivalent to denying that physical terms are rigid designators, strikes me as false: surely the 1-intension of (say) 'electron' is something similar to 'particle causally responsible for that sort of track on the cloud chamber's screen,' whereas its 2-intension is as specified by physical theory, something similar to 'negatively-charged particle with so-and-so mass, spin, and so forth.' But Chalmers can easily reformulate his argument to avoid this objection. Given that we have in fact determined the essences of physical properties, which a physicalist opponent should probably concede, we can in fact conceive in accordance with the 2-intensions of physical terms. So Chalmers can replace (1) with the claim that 'P and not-Q' is conceivable when 'P' is evaluated in light of 2-intensions and 'not-Q' is evaluated in light of 1-intensions. This claim makes a large a posteriori assumption about the world, but it is not one that his physicalist opponent need treat as question begging. Because it immediately entails (4), premises (2) and (3) are not required in this reformulation.

7. Or, better, of part of a world, else no work is left for the second component in conceiving a statement, namely, correctly describing the conceived world in light of the relevant intensions.

8. It might be objected to this account of 1-conceivability that it now begs the question to claim that 1-conceivability entails 1-possibility; for this entailment will hold only if the originally conceived world is 1-possible, in other words, only if the representation of a possible world hosted by a conceiver

before she starts evaluating statements at that world in light of 1-intensions describes a genuinely 1-possible world. But Chalmers can avoid this difficulty in practice by letting the hosted representations be such as are thought to describe the actual world, so that their expressing a genuine 1-possibility will not be contested by any of his opponents.

9. Actually, Chalmers's appeal to conceivability in the ordinary sense (pp. 94–9) is not his only support. He also invokes other considerations (pp. 99–106). But they all depend on the basic consideration of conceivability in the ordinary sense. For example, Mary would know the phenomenal facts on the basis of just the physical facts if it were inconceivable that P and not-Q.

10. In private correspondence, Chalmers concedes that in his book he does not say much about the warrant for assuming the a priori accessibility of 1-intensions, but he adds that "it seems to hold in just about every case we can think of." But this just assumes that we possess the 1-intension–respecting capacity, in other words, that, when we consider a possible way the world might have turned out to be, and then say what a concept would have referred to had the world turned out that way, we get it right, as defined by the concept's 1-intension. Why think a priori accessibility holds in even one case?

11. It turns out that many people say that the ball would fall vertically, or even backward; in fact it would briefly travel forward. See McCloskey (1983, pp. 122–30).

12. See Fodor (1990).

13. Concepts of this sort are concepts that have what Joe Levine calls "non-ascriptive modes of presentation"; see his "Conceivability and the Metaphysics of Mind" (1998).

14. On the face of it, the view seems to confuse semantics with epistemology, what it is to think an F-thought with what it is to judge that something is F, the latter reflecting not just conceptual competence but also substantive beliefs about the world.

15. Phenomenal concepts may not be quite unique in this respect. Perhaps there is a singular term, in "mentalese," for referring to oneself, whose application to the world (i.e., to oneself) is also not based, epistemologically, on representations. If so, then its existence would predict that fixing all the physical facts would seem to leave undetermined whether some object is oneself.

16. Except, of course, for those special representations that just are phenomenal states, on the representationalist view I endorse.

17. In private correspondence, Chalmers asks how I can explain, on this account, our apparent ability to conceive *also* of a world physically *and phenomenally* just like ours. The answer is that representations of phenomenal states can be included *by stipulation* in the set of mental representations we host (in our conceiving boxes) when we conceive a possible situation. That is, they can be part of the mentally represented situation we allow our epistemological capacity to take as *input*.

18. Jerry Fodor, in particular, has told me that he regards as a posteriori the task of discovering the reference-constituting relation for concepts. However, such views as Fodor's are inspired by those of Kripke, and Chalmers points out (p. 59) that Kripke, in arguing for his causal theory of reference, routinely appeals to what we say a term would refer to were a certain counterfactual situation actual, apparently assuming thereby the a priori accessi-

bility of 1-intensions to competent concept-users. But if he does, then we have to say that Kripke's methodology is just wrong. In fact, it is not obvious why Kripke cannot be understood as construing the deliverances of intuition about counterfactual situations as feasible empirical evidence (which would, of course, open the cans of worms mentioned earlier in connection with the possibility of Chalmers's allowing 1-intensions to be accessible a posteriori only).

19. The only necessities and possibilities I am committed to are those that are logical or conceptual in Chalmers's sense – necessities and possibilities induced by 1- and 2-intensions. So I am not committed to what Chalmers calls "strong" metaphysical necessity. I am simply suggesting that, because not all 1-intensions are accessible a priori, certain 1-necessary claims, though conceptual, are not a priori. Latham (forthcoming), assumes that any a posteriori necessity would have to be strong, in this same sense, and hence also overlooks the possibility of a necessity that is conceptual but not a priori.

20. Thanks to Terry Horgan, Michael Levin, Peter Markie, Jamie Phillips, Paul Weirich, and especially David Chalmers for comments on earlier drafts.

References

Adam, C. and Tannery, P., eds. 1964. *Oeuvres de Descartes*. Paris: Vrin.

Adams, F. and Aizawa, K. 1992. " 'X' Means X: Semantics Fodor-Style." *Minds and Machines* 2:175–83.

Albert, D. 1996. "Elementary Quantum Metaphysics." In Cushing, J., Fine, A., and Goldstein, S., ed. *Bohmian Mechanics and Quantum Theory*. Dordrect: Kluwer.

Alexander, H., ed. 1956. *The Leibniz-Clarke Correspondence*. Manchester: Manchester University Press.

Alexander, S. 1920. *Space, Time and Deity*. London: Macmillan.

Anscombe, G.E.M. 1971. *Causality and Determination*. Cambridge: Cambridge University Press. Reprinted in Sosa, E. and Tooley, M., ed. (1993). *Causation*. Oxford: Oxford University Press.

Anthony, L. and Levine, J. 1997. "Reduction with Autonomy." In *Philosophical Perspectives*, v. 11.

Armstrong, D. 1968. *A Materialist Theory of the Mind*. London: Routledge and Kegan Paul.

Armstrong, D. 1978. *A Theory of Universals*. Cambridge: Cambridge University Press.

Armstrong, D. 1989. *A Combinatorial Theory of Possibility*. Cambridge: Cambridge University Press.

Asher, N., Brooks, L., Dretske, F., Fodor, J.A., et al. 1990. "Round Table Discussion." In Hanson, P., ed. (1990). *Information, Language and Cognition*. Vancouver: University of British Columbia Press.

Ayer, A.J. 1969. "Man as a Subject for Science." In Laslett, P. and Runciman, W., eds. *Philosophy, Politics and Society 3rd Series*. Oxford: Basil Blackwell.

Bach, K. 1978. "A Representational Theory of Action." *Philosophical Studies* 34:361–79.

Baker, L. 1995. *Explaining the Attitudes*. Cambridge: Cambridge University Press.

Balog, K. 1998. *Conceivability Arguments*. Ph.D. Dissertation, Rutgers University.

Balog, K. 2000. "The New Conceivability Arguments." *Philosophical Review*.

Bealer, G. 1984. "Mind and Anti-Mind." *Midwest Studies in Philosophy* IX:283–328.

Bealer, G. 1997. "Self Consciousness." *Philosophical Review* 106(1):69–117.

Beckerman, A., Flohr, H., and Kim, J., eds. 1992. *Emergence or Reduction.* New York and Berlin: De Gruyter.

Block, N. 1980a. *Readings in Philosophy of Psychology.* Cambridge, MA: Harvard University Press.

Block, N. 1980b. "What is Functionalism?" In Block (1980a), v. 1, pp. 171–84.

Block, N. 1990. "Can the Mind Change the World?" In Boolos (1990).

Block, N. 1995. "On a Confusion About a Function of Consciousness." *Behavioral and Brain Sciences* 18:227–87.

Block, N. 1997. "The Anti-reductionist Slaps Back." In Tomberlin, J., ed. *Philosophical Perspectives*, v. 11. Oxford: Blackwell.

Block, N., Flanagan, O., and Guzeldere, G., eds. 1997. *The Nature of Consciousness.* Cambridge, MA: MIT Press.

Boghossian, P.A. 1990. "The Status of Content." *Philosophical Review* 99: 157–84.

Boolos, G. ed. 1990. *Meaning and Method: Essays in Honor of Hilary Putnam.* Cambridge: Cambridge University Press.

Brandt, R. and Kim, J. 1967. "The Logic of the Identity Theory." *Journal of Philosophy* 64:515–37.

Broad, C.D. 1923a. *Mind and its Place in Nature.* London: Routledge and Kegan Paul.

Broad, C.D. 1923b. *Scientific Thought.* London: Kegan Paul, Trench, and Trisner.

Burchfield, J. 1975. *Lord Kelvin and the Age of the Earth.* New York: Macmillan.

Burge, T. 1986. "Individualism and Psychology." *Philosophical Review* XCV(1):3–46.

Burge, T. 1989. "Causation and Individuation in Psychology." *Pacific Philosophical Quarterly* 70:303–22.

Burge, T. 1991. "Vision and Intentional Content." In *John Searle and His Critics*, LePore, E. and van Gulick, R., eds. Oxford: Blackwell, pp. 195–213.

Burge, T. 1992. "Philosophy of Language and Mind 1950–1990." *Philosophical Review* 101:1–51.

Burge, T. 1993. "Mind-Body Causation and Explanatory Practice." In Heil, J. and Mele, A., eds. (1993), pp. 97–120.

Burian, R. 1993. "Unification and Coherence as Methodological Objectives in the Biological Sciences." *Biology and Philosophy* 8:301–18.

Byrne, A. 1993. *The Emergent Mind.* Ph.D. Dissertation. Princeton University.

Campbell, D.T. 1974. " 'Downward Causation' in Hierarchically Organized Biological Systems." In *Studies in the Philosophy of Biology*, Ayala, F.J. and Dobzhansky, T., eds. (1974). Berkeley: University of California Press.

Carnap, R. 1934. *The Unity of Science.* London: Kegan, Paul, Trench, Trubner & Co. Ltd.

Carnap, R. 1955. "The Logical Foundations of the Unity of Science." In Neurath, O., Carnap, B., and Morris, C. (1955).

Cartwright, N. 1999. *The Dappled World.* Cambridge: Cambridge University Press.

Chalmers, D. 1995. "The Puzzle of Conscious Experience." *Scientific American* 273:80–6.

Chalmers, D. 1996. *The Conscious Mind: In Search of a Fundamental Theory.* Oxford: Oxford University Press.

Chalmers, D. Forthcoming. "Materialism and the Metaphysics of Modality." In *Philosophy and Phenomenological Research.*

Charles, D. 1992. "Supervenience, Composition, and Physicalism." In Charles, D. and Lennon, K. (1992), pp. 265–96.

Charles, D. and Lennon, K., eds. 1992. *Reduction, Explanation and Realism.* Oxford: Clarendon Press.

Child, W. 1997. "Crane on Mental Causation." *Proceedings of the Aristotelian Society* 97:97–102.

Chomsky, N. 1968. *Language and Mind.* New York: Harcourt Brace & World.

Chomsky, N. 1993. *Language and Thought.* London: Moyer Bell.

Chomsky, N. 1994. "Entry on Chomsky." In *Blackwell Companion to Philosophy*, Bunnin, N. and Tsui-James, E.P., eds. Oxford: Blackwell, pp. 153–67.

Chomsky, N. 1995. "Language and Nature." *Mind*, v. 104.

Chomsky, N. 1996. *Powers and Prospects.* Boston: South End Press.

Churchland, P. and Sejnowski, T. 1992. *The Computational Brain.* Cambridge, MA: MIT Press.

Clapp, L. 2001. "Disjunctive Properties." *Journal of Philosophy* XCVIII:111–36.

Clarke, S. 1996. Review of C. Taliaferro, "*Consciousness and the Mind of God.*" *Times Literary Supplement*, Feb. 23.

Coleman, W. 1971. *Biology in the Nineteenth Century.* New York: John Wiley and Sons.

Comte, A. 1975. *The First System*, trans. Harriet Martineau and reprinted in Lenzer, G., ed. (1975). *Auguste Comte and Positivism.* New York: Harper & Row, p. 80.

Cottingham, J., Stoothoff, R., and Murdoch, D., eds. 1985. *The Philosophical Writings of Descartes*, v. 2. Cambridge: Cambridge University Press.

Crane, T. 1991. "All God Has to Do." *Analysis* 51:235–44.

Crane, T. ed. 1992. *The Contents of Experience*. Cambridge: Cambridge University Press.

Crane, T. 1995. "The Mental Causation Debate." *Aristotelian Society Supplementary*, v. 69.

Crane, T. 1997. "Reply to Child." *Proceedings of Aristotelian Society* 97:103–8.

Crane, T. and Mellor, D.H. 1990. "There is No Question of Physicalism." *Mind* 99:185–206.

Crook, S. and Gillett, C. Forthcoming. "Why Physics Alone Cannot Define the 'Physical': Materialism and the Formulation of Physicalism." *Canadian Journal of Philosophy*.

Cussins, A. 1992. "The Limitations of Pluralism." In Charles, D. and Lennon, K., eds. (1992), pp. 179–223.

Daly, C. 1997. "Pluralist Metaphysics." *Philosophical Studies* 87:185–206.

Dana, J. 1873. "On Some Results of the Earth's Contraction from Cooling: Part V." *American Journal of Science*, 3rd Series 6:161–72.

Darden, L. 1991. *Theory Change in Science: Strategies from Mendelian Genetics*. Oxford: Oxford University Press.

Darden, L. and Maull, N. 1977. "Interfield Theories." *Philosophy of Science* 44:43–64.

Davidson, D. 1963. "Actions, Reasons and Causes." *Journal of Philosophy*, v. 60.

Davidson, D. 1970. "Mental Events." In Foster, L. and Swanson, J.W., eds. *Experience and Theory*. Amherst: University of Massachusetts Press. Reprinted in Davidson, D. (1980).

Davidson, D. 1980. *Essays on Actions and Events*. Oxford: Clarendon Press.

Davidson, D. 1987. "Problems in the Explanation of Action." In Pettit, P., Sylvan, B., and Norman, J., eds. (1987), pp. 35–49.

Davidson, D. 1993. "Thinking Causes." In Heil, J. and Mele, A., eds. (1993), pp. 3–17.

Davies, M. 1991. "Individualism and Perceptual Content." *Mind* C(4):461–84.

Davies, M. and Humphreys, G., eds. 1992. *Consciousness*. Oxford: Blackwell.

Dell, G. 1995. "Speaking and Misspeaking." In Osherson, D. (1995–8), v. 1, pp. 183–208.

Dennett, D. 1978. *Brainstorms*. Cambridge, MA: MIT (Bradford) Press.

Dennett, D. 1987. *The Intentional Stance*. Cambridge, MA: MIT Press.

Dennett, D. 1988. "Quining Qualia." In Marcel, A.J. and Bisiach, E., eds. *Consciousness in Contemporary Science*. Oxford: Clarendon.

Dennett, D. 1991. *Consciousness Explained*. New York: Little Brown.

Dray, W. 1957. *Laws and Explanation in History*. Oxford: Oxford University Press.

Dretske, F. 1993. "Mental Events as Structuring Causes of Behavior." In Heil, J. and Mele, A. (1993).

Dretske, F. 1995. *Naturalizing The Mind*. Cambridge, MA: MIT Press.

Dwyer, S. and Pietroski, P. 1996. "Believing in Language." *Philosophy of Science* 63:338–73.

Elkana, Y. 1974. *The Discovery of the Conservation of Energy*. London: Hutchinson.

Faraday, M. 1857. "On the Conservation of Force." *Proceedings of the Royal Society*.

Feigl, H. 1958. "The 'Mental' and the 'Physical.' " In Feigl, H., Scriven, M., and Maxwell, G., eds. (1958). *Minnesota Studies in the Philosophy of Science vol. II*. Minneapolis: University of Minnesota Press.

Field, H. 1972. "Tarski's Theory of Truth." *Journal of Philosophy* 69:347–75.

Field, H. 1992. "Physicalism." In Earman, J., ed. *Inference, Explanation and other Frustrations*. Berkeley: University of California Press.

Fodor, J. 1974. "Special Sciences, or the Disunity of Science as a Working Hypothesis." *Synthese* 28:77–115.

Fodor, J. 1975. *The Language of Thought*. New York: Thomas Crowell.

Fodor, J. 1981. *RePresentations*. Cambridge, MA: MIT Press.

Fodor, J. 1983. *The Modularity of Mind*. Cambridge, MA: MIT Press.

Fodor, J. 1987. *Psychosemantics*. Cambridge, MA: MIT Press.

Fodor, J. 1990a. "Making Mind Matter More." Reprinted in Fodor (1990b).

Fodor, J. 1990b. *A Theory of Content and Other Essays*. Cambridge, MA: MIT Press.

Fodor, J. 1990c. "A Theory of Content I & II." In Fodor (1990b).

Fodor, J. 1994. "The Mind-Body Problem." In Szubka and Warner (1994).

Fodor, J. 1997. "Special Sciences; Still Autonomous After All These Years." In Tomberlin, J., ed. *Philosophical Perspectives*, v. 11. Oxford: Blackwell.

Fodor, J. 1998. *Concepts: Where Cognitive Science Went Wrong*. Oxford: Oxford University Press.

Fodor, J. Forthcoming. *The Mind Doesn't Work That Way: The Scope and Limits of Cognitive Science*.

Foster, J. 1968. "Psychophysical Causal Relations." *American Philosophical Quarterly* 5:64–70.

Foster, J. 1991. *The Immaterial Self: A Defense of the Cartesian Dualist Conception of the Mind*. London: Routledge.

Foster, L. and Swanson, J., eds. 1970. *Experience and Theory*. London: Duckworth.

Frankel, H. 1981. "The Paleobiogeographical Debate over the Problem of Disjunctively Distributed Life Forms." *Studies in the History and Philosophy of Science* 12:211–59.

Gates, G. 1996. "The Price of Information." *Synthese* 107(3):325–47.

Gillett, C. 1997. *Naturalization: Scientific Theory Appraisal and the Warrant of Physicalism.* Ph.D Thesis. New Brunswick: Rutgers, State University of New Jersey.

Gillett, C. Unpublished. "Naturalization for Physicalists."

Girill, T.R. 1976. "Evaluating Micro-Explanation." *Erkenntnis* 10:387–405.

Goldstein, H. 1964. *Classical Mechanics,* 2nd ed. Reading, MA: Addison-Wesley.

Goodman, N. 1979. *Fact, Fiction, and Forecast.* Cambridge, MA: Harvard University Press.

Graham, G. and Horgan, T. Forthcoming. "Mary Mary, Quite Contrary."

Haldane, J. 1996. "The Mystery of Emergence." *Proceedings of the Aristotelian Society* 96:267.

Harman, G. 1972. *Thought.* Princeton: Princeton University Press.

Hawking, S. 1980. *Is the End in Sight for Theoretical Physics: An Inaugural Lecture.* New York: Cambridge University Press.

Heil, J. 1992. *The Nature of True Minds.* Cambridge: Cambridge University Press.

Heil, J. 1998. *Philosophy of Mind: A Contemporary Introduction.* London: Routledge.

Heil, J. and Mele, A., eds. 1993. *Mental Causation.* Oxford: Clarendon Press.

Hellman, G. 1989. *Mathematics Without Numbers.* Oxford: The Clarendon Press.

Hellman, G. and Thompson, F. 1975. "Physicalism: Ontology, Determination, Reduction." *Journal of Philosophy* 72(1):551–64.

Hellman, G. and Thompson, F. 1977. "Physicalist Materialism."*Nous* 11:310.

Hempel, C. 1942. "The Function of General Laws in History." *Journal of Philosophy*, v. 39.

Hill, C. 1991. *Sensations.* Cambridge: Cambridge University Press.

Hill, C. 1997. "Imaginability, Conceivability, Possibility and the Mind-Body Problem." *Philosophical Studies* 87:61–85.

Hill, C. and McLaughlin, B. 1999. "There are Fewer Things than are Dreamt of in Chalmers's Philosophy." *Philosophy and Phenomenological Research* LIX:445–54.

Horgan, T. 1993. "From Supervenience to Superdupervenience: Meeting the Demands of a Material World." *Mind* 102:555–86.

Hornsby, J. 1993. "Agency and Causal Explanation." In Heil, J. and Mele, A. (1993).

Hornsby, J. 1997. *Simple Mindedness: In Defense of Naive Naturalism in Philosophy of Mind.* Cambridge, MA: Harvard University Press.

Horwich, P. 1998. *Meaning.* Oxford: Oxford University Press.

Hursthouse, R. 1991. "Arational Actions." *Journal of Philosophy* 88(2):57–68.

Jack, A. 1994. "Materialism and Supervenience." *Australasian Journal of Philosophy* 72:426–44.

Jackendoff, R. 1990. *Semantic Structure.* Cambridge, MA: MIT Press.

Jackson, F. 1986. "What Mary Didn't Know." *Journal of Philosophy* 83:291–5.

Jackson, F. 1993. "Armchair Metaphysics." In O'Leary-Hawthorne, J. and Michael, M. eds. *Philosophy in Mind.* Dordrecht: Kluwer, pp. 23–42.

Jackson, F. 1995. "Essentialism, Mental Properties and Causation." *Proceedings of the Aristotelian Society,* v. 95.

Jackson, F. 1996. "Mental causation." *Mind* 105:377–413.

Jackson, F. 1998. *From Metaphysics to Ethics: A Defence of Conceptual Analysis.* Oxford: Oxford University Press.

Jackson, F. Forthcoming. "Reference and Description Revisited."

Jackson, F. and Pettit, P. 1993. "Folk Belief and Commonplace Belief." *Mind and Language* 8:298–305.

James, W. 1981. *The Principles of Psychology.* Cambridge, MA: Harvard University Press. First published in 1890.

Kane, R. 1996. *The Significance of Free Will.* Oxford: Oxford University Press.

Kemeny, J. and Oppenheim, P. 1956. "On Reduction." *Philosophical Studies* 7:6–19.

Kim, J. 1984. "Concepts of Supervenience." *Philosophy and Phenomenological Research* 45:153–76. Reprinted in Kim, J. (1993e).

Kim, J. 1990. "Supervenience as a Philosophical Concept." *Metaphilosophy* 21:1–27. Reprinted in Kim, J. (1993e).

Kim, J. 1992. "'Downward Causation' in Emergentism and Nonreductive Materialism." In Beckermann, A., Flohr, H., and Kim, J., eds. (1992).

Kim, J. 1993a. "Can Supervenience and 'Non-Strict Laws' Save Anomolous Monism?" In Heil, J. and Mele, A., eds. (1993), pp. 19–26.

Kim, J. 1993b. "Multiple Realizability and the Metaphysics of Reduction." In Kim, J. (1993e), pp. 309–35.

Kim, J. 1993c. "Mechanism, Purpose, and Explanatory Exclusion." Reprinted in Kim, J. (1993e).

Kim, J. 1993d. "The Non-Reductivist's Troubles with Mental Causation." In Heil, J. and Mele, A., eds. (1993), pp. 189–210.

Kim, J. 1993e. *Supervenience and Mind: Selected Essays.* Cambridge: Cambridge University Press.

Kim, J. 1994. "Supervenience." In Guttenplan, S. ed. *A Companion to the Philosophy of Mind.* Oxford: Blackwell.

Kim, J. 1998. *Mind in a Physical World.* Cambridge: Cambridge University Press.

Kim, J. Forthcoming-a. "Making Sense of Emergence." In *Philosophical Studies.*

Kim, J. Forthcoming-b. "Causality and Dualism."

Kirk, R. 1994. *Raw Feels.* Oxford: Clarendon Press.

Klee, R. 1984. "Micro-Determinism and Concepts of Emergence." *Philosophy of Science* 51(4):44–63.

Kripke, S. 1971. "Identity and Necessity." In Muntiz, M., ed. *Identity and Individuation*, pp. 135–64. New York: NYU Press.

Kripke, S. 1972. "Naming and Necessity." In Davidson, D. and Harman, G., eds. *Semantics of Natural Language.* Dordrecht: Reidel, pp. 235–355.

Kripke, S. 1980. *Naming and Necessity.* Cambridge, MA: Harvard University Press.

Kripke, S. 1982. *Wittgenstein on Rules and Private Language.* Cambridge, MA: Harvard University Press.

Kuhn, T. 1970. *The Structure of Scientific Revolutions*, 2nd ed. Chicago: University of Chicago Press.

Larson, R. and Segal, G. 1995. *Knowledge of Meaning.* Cambridge, MA: MIT Press.

Latham, N. Forthcoming. "Chalmers On The Addition Of Consciousness To The Physical World." *Philosophical Studies.*

Latham, N. Unpublished. "What is Token Physicalism?"

Laudan, L. 1977. *Progress and its Problems.* Berkeley: University of California Press.

LeGrand, H. 1988. *Drifting Continents and Shifting Theories.* Cambridge: Cambridge University Press.

Leibniz, G. 1696. *The Monadology.* Trans. Latta, R., 1898: Oxford.

LePore, E. and Loewer, B. 1987. "Mind Matters." *Journal of Philosophy* 84:630–42.

LePore, E., and Loewer, B. 1989. "More on Making Mind Matter." *Philosophical Topics* 17:175–92.

Levi, I. 1980. *The Enterprise of Knowledge.* Cambridge, MA: MIT Press.

Levine, J. 1983. "Materialism and Qualia: The Explanatory Gap." *Pacific Philosophical Quarterly* 64:354–61.

Levine, J. 1993. "On Leaving Out What It's Like." In Davies, M. and Humphreys, G., eds. (1992).

Levine, J. 1998. "Conceivability and the Metaphysics of Mind." *Nous* 32:449–80.

Lewis, D. 1966. "An Argument for the Identity Theory." *Journal of Philosophy*, v. 63.

Lewis, D. 1972. "Psychophysical and Theoretical Identifications." *Australasian Journal of Philosophy* 50:249–58.

Lewis, D. 1980. "Mad Pain and Martian Pain." In Block, N., ed. (1980a).

Lewis, D. 1983. "New Work for a Theory of Universals." *Australasian Journal of Philosophy* 61:343–77.

Lewis, D. 1990. "What Experience Teaches." In Block, N., Flanagan, O., and Gulzeldere, G., eds. (1997), pp. 579–95.

Lewis, D. 1994. "Lewis, David: Reduction of Mind." In Guttenplan, S., ed. (1994). *A Companion to the Philosophy of Mind*. Oxford: Blackwell.

Libet, B. 1985. "Unconscious Cerebral Initiative and the Role of Conscious Will in Voluntary Action." *Behavioral and Brain Sciences* 8:529–66.

Loar, B. 1997. "Phenomenal states." In Block, N., Flanagan, O., and Guzeldere, G., eds. (1997), pp. 597–616.

Locke, J. 1975. *An Essay concerning Human Understanding*. Oxford: Oxford University Press.

Loewer, B. 1995. "An Argument for Strong Supervenience." In Savellos, E. and Yalcin, U. (1995).

Loewer, B. 1996. "Humean Supervenience." *Philosophical Topics* 24(1):101.

Loewer, B. 1997. "A Guide to Naturalized Semantics." In Hale, R. and Wright, C., eds. *Blackwell Companion to the Philosophy of Language*. Oxford: Blackwell.

Loewer, B. Forthcoming. "Review of Nancy Cartwright's *The Dappled World*." *British Journal for the Philosophy of Science*.

Lowe, E.J. Forthcoming. "Self, Agency, and Mental Causation."

Lycan, W.G. 1987. *Consciousness*. Cambridge, MA: MIT Press.

Lycan, W.G. 1996. *Consciousness and Experience*. Cambridge, MA: MIT Press.

MacDonald, C.M. and MacDonald, G. 1986. "Mental Causes and the Explanation of Action." *Philosophical Quarterly* 36:145–58.

MacDonald, C.M. and MacDonald, G. 1995. "How to be Psychologically Relevant." In MacDonald, C.M. and MacDonald, G., eds. *Philosophy of Psychology*. Oxford: Blackwell.

Mach, E. 1986. "The Economical Nature of Physical Inquiry." In *Popular Scientific Lectures*, trans. McCormack, T. La Salle, IL: Open Court Publishing Company.

Mackie, J.L. 1977a. "The Subjectivity of Values." Originally Ch. 1 of Mackie (1977b). Reprinted in Sayre-McCord, G., ed. (1988). *Essays on Moral Realism*. Ithaca: Cornell University Press.

Mackie, J.L. 1977b. *Inventing Right and Wrong*. London: Penguin.

Maddy, P. 1990a. "Physicalistic Platonism." In Irvine, ed. *Physicalism in Mathematics*. Dordrecht: Kluwer.

Maddy, P. 1990b. *Realism in Mathematics*. Oxford: Oxford University Press, The Clarendon Press.

Malcolm, N. 1959. *Dreaming.* London: Routledge and Kegan Paul.

Malcolm, N. 1977. *Thought and Knowledge.* Ithaca: Cornell University Press.

Marr, D. 1982. *Vision:* San Francisco: Freeman & Co.

Martin, C.B. 1980. "Substance Substantiated." *Australasian Journal of Philosophy* 58:3–10.

Martin, C.B. 1992. "Power for Realists." In Bacon, J., Campbell, K., and Reinhardt, L., eds. (1992). *Ontology, Causality, and Mind.* Cambridge: Cambridge University Press.

Martin, C.B. 1993. "The Need for Ontology: Some Choices." *Philosophy* 68:505–22.

Martin, C.B. 1994. "Dispositions and Conditionals." *Philosophical Quarterly* 44:1–8.

Martin, C.B. 1997. "On the Need for Properties: The Road to Pythagoreanism and Back." *Synthese* 112:193–231.

Maull, N. 1977. "Unifying Science without Reduction." *Studies in the History and Philosophy of Science* 8:143–62.

McCloskey, M. 1983. "Intuitive Physics." *Scientific American* 248:122–30.

McDowell, J. 1985. "Functionalism and Anomalous Monism." In LePore, E. and McLaughlin, B., eds. *Actions and Events: Perspectives on the Philosophy of Donald Davidson.* Oxford: Blackwell, pp. 387–98.

McGinn, C. 1982. *The Character of Mind.* Oxford: Oxford University Press.

McGinn, C. 1989. *Mental Content.* Oxford: Blackwell.

McGinn, C. 1991a. "Consciousness and Content." In McGinn, C. (1991c).

McGinn, C. 1991b. "Can We Solve the Mind-Body Problem?" In McGinn, C. (1991c).

McGinn, C. 1991c. *The Problem of Consciousness.* Oxford: Blackwell.

McGinn, C. 1996. *Problems of Philosophy.* Oxford: Blackwell.

McGinn, C. 1999. "Can We Ever Understand Consciousness?." *New York Review of Books* 46(10):44–8.

McLaughlin, B. 1989. "Type Epiphenomenalism, Type Dualism and the Causal Priority of the Physical." *Philosophical Perspectives*, v. 3.

McLaughlin, B. 1992. "The Rise and Fall of British Emergentism." In Beckerman, A., Flohr, H., and Kim, J., eds. (1992).

McLaughlin, B. 1993. "Davidson's Response to Epiphenomenalism." In Heil, J. and Mele, A., eds. (1993), pp. 27–40.

McLaughlin, B. 1995. "Varieties of Supervenience." In Savellos, E. and Yalcin, U., eds. *Supervenience: New Essays.* Cambridge: Cambridge University Press.

McLaughlin, B. 1997. "Review of Stephen White's *The Unity of the Self.*" *Journal of Philosophy* 97:638–44.

Mellor, D.H. 1995. *The Facts of Causation.* London: Routledge.

Melnyk, A. 1994. "Being A Physicalist: How And (More Importantly) Why." *Philosophical Studies* 74:221–41.

Mill, J.S. 1875. *A System of Logic.* London: Longmans.

Moore, G.E. 1903. *Principia Ethica.* Cambridge: Cambridge University Press.

Morgan, C.L. 1923. *Emergent Evolution.* London: Williams and Norgate.

Nagel, E. 1961. *The Structure of Science.* London: Routledge and Kegan Paul.

Nagel, E. 1963. "Wholes, Sums and Organic Unities." In Lerner, D., ed. (1963). *Parts and Wholes.* New York: Free Press.

Nagel, T. 1974. "What is it Like to Be a Bat?" *Philosophical Review* 83:435–50.

Nagel, T. 1979. "Panpsychism." *Mortal Questions.* Cambridge: Cambridge University Press.

Nagel, T. 1985. *The View From Nowhere.* Oxford: Clarendon Press.

Nemirow, L. 1990. "Physicalism and the Cognitive Role of Acquaintance." In Lycan, W., ed. *Mind and Cognition.* Oxford University Press, pp. 490–9.

Neurath, O. 1932–3. "Protocol Sentences." *Erkenntnis*, v. III. Reprinted in Ayer, A.J., ed. (1959). *Logical Positivism.* New York: Free Press.

Neurath, O., Carnap, R., and Morris, C. 1955. *International Encyclopedia of Unified Science.* Chicago: University of Chicago Press.

Newton, I. 1686 (Cajori, F., ed. [1960]). *Mathematical Principles of Natural Philosophy.* Berkeley: University of California Press.

Newton, I. 1704. *Opticks.* New York: Dover, 1952.

Nisbett, R. and Wilson, T. 1977. "On Telling More Than We Can Know." *Psychological Review* 84(3):231–59.

Noordhof, P. 1999. "Reply to Sturgeon." *Mind*, v. 111.

O'Connor, T., ed. 1995. *Agents, Causes, and Events.* Oxford: Oxford University Press.

Oppenheim, P., and Putnam, H. 1958. "Unity of Science as a Working Hypothesis." In Feigl, H., Scriven, M., and Maxwell, G., eds. *Minnesota Studies in the Philosophy of Science vol II.* Minneapolis: University of Minnesota Press.

Osherson, D. 1995–8. *An Invitation to Cognitive Science.* Four volumes, Cambridge, MA: MIT Press.

Palmer, S. 1999. "Color, Consciousness, and the Isomorphism Constraint." *Behavioral and Brain Sciences* 22(6):923.

Papert, S. 1988. "One AI or Many?" *Daedalus* 117:1–14.

Papert, S. and Minsky, M. 1969. *Perceptions.* Cambridge, MA: MIT Press.

Papineau, D. 1977. "The *Vis Viva* Controversy: Do Meanings Matter?" *Studies in History and Philosophy of Science*, v. 8.

Papineau, D. 1990. "Why supervenience?" *Analysis*, v. 50.

Papineau, D. 1993a. *Philosophical Naturalism.* Oxford: Basil Blackwell.

Papineau, D. 1993b. "Physicalism, Consciousness, and the Anti-Pathetic Fallacy." *Australasian Journal of Philosophy* 71:169–83.

Papineau, D. 1998. "Mind the Gap." In Tomberlin, J., ed. *Philosophical Perspectives*, v. 12.

Paull, R.C. and Sider, T. 1992. "In Defense of Global Supervenience." *Philosophy and Phenomenological Research* 52:833–54.

Pavlov, I. 1957. *Experimental Psychology and Other Essays*. New York: Philosophical Library.

Peacocke, C. 1979. *Holistic Explanation*. Oxford: Clarendon Press.

Pettit, P. 1993. "A Definition of Physicalism." *Analysis* 53:213–23.

Pettit, P., Sylvan, R., and Norman, J., eds. 1987. *Metaphysics and Morality*. Oxford: Blackwell.

Pietroski, P. Forthcoming. "Small Verbs, Complex Events." In Antony, L. and Hornstein, N. *Chomsky and his Critics*. Oxford: Blackwell.

Pietroski, P. and Rey, G. 1995. "When Other Things Aren't Equal: Saving *Ceteris Paribus* from Vacuity." *British Journal for the Philosophy of Science* 46:81–110.

Place, U.T. 1956. "Sensations and Brain Processes." *British Journal of Psychology* 47:44–50.

Poland, J. 1994. *Physicalism: The Philosophical Foundations*. Oxford: Oxford University Press.

Post, J. 1987. *The Faces of Existence*. Ithaca: Cornell University Press.

Post, J. 1995. "'Global' Supervenient Determination: Too Permissive?" In Savellos, E. and Yalcin, U., eds. (1995).

Price, H.H. 1957. *Thinking and Experience*. Cambridge, MA: Harvard University Press.

Prior, E., Pargetter, R., and Jackson, F. 1982. "Three Theses about Dispositions." *American Philosophical Quarterly* 19:251–7.

Putnam, H. 1960. "Minds and Machines." In Hook, S., ed. *Dimensions of Mind*. New York: New York University Press.

Putnam, H. 1967. "Psychological Predicates." In Capitan, W.H. and Merrill, D.D., eds. (1967). *Art, Mind, and Religion*. Pittsburgh: University of Pittsburgh Press.

Putnam, H. 1975a. *Mind, Language and Reality: Philosophical Papers, Volume 2*. Cambridge: Cambridge University Press.

Putnam, H. 1975b. "Minds and Machines." In Putnam, H. (1975a), pp. 362–85.

Putnam, H. 1975c. "The Nature of Mental States." In Putnam, H. (1975a).

Putnam, H. 1983. "Why There isn't a Ready Made World." In *Realism and Reason*, v. 3. Cambridge: Cambridge University Press.

Putnam, H. 1992. "Is it Necessary that Water is H_2O?" In Hahn, L., ed. *The Philosophy of A.J. Ayer*. Open Court: La Salle.

Pylyshyn, Z. 1999. "Is Vision Continuous With Cognition? The Case for Cognitive Impenetrability of Visual Perception." *Behavioral and Brain Sciences* 22(3):341–423.

Quine, W. 1953a. "Two Dogmas of Empiricism." In Quine, W. (1953c), pp. 20–46.

Quine, W. 1953b. "Notes on the Theory of Reference." In Quine, W. (1953c), pp. 130–9.

Quine, W. 1953c. *From a Logical Point of View*. New York: Harper & Row.

Quine, W. 1960. *Word and Object*. Cambridge, MA: MIT Press.

Railton, P. 1985. "Moral Realism." *Philosophical Review* 95:163–207.

Railton, P. 1986. "Facts and Values." *Philosophical Topics* 14:5–31.

Rey, G. 1982. "A Reason for Doubting the Existence of Consciousness." In Davidson, D., Schwartz, G., and Shapiro, D., eds. (1982). *Consciousness and Self-Regulation*, v. III. New York: Plenum Press, pp. 1–40.

Rey, G. 1988. "Toward a Computational Account of *Akrasia* and Self-Deception." In McLaughlin, B. and Rorty, A. *Perspectives on Self-Deception*. Berkeley: University of California Press, pp. 264–96.

Rey, G. 1992. "Sensational Sentences." In Davies, M. and Humphreys, G., eds. (1992).

Rey, G. 1993. "Review of Colin McGinn's *The Problem of Consciousness*." *Philosophical Review* 102(2) April:274–8.

Rey, G. 1995a. "Dennett's Unrealistic Psychology." In Hill, C., ed. (1994). *Philosophical Topics* 22(1–2):259–89.

Rey, G. 1995b. "Wittgenstein, Computationalism and Qualia." In Casati, R., Smith, B., and White, G. (1995). *Philosophy and the Cognitive Sciences*. Vienna: Hölder-Pichler-Tempsky, pp. 61–74.

Rey, G. 1997. *Contemporary Philosophy of Mind: a Contentiously Classical Approach*. Oxford: Blackwell.

Rey, G. 1998a. "A Naturalistic *A Priori*." *Philosophical Studies* 92:25–43.

Rey, G. 1998b. "A Narrow Representational Account of Qualitative Experience." Tomberlin, J. ed. (1998). *Philosophical Perspectives*, v. 11.

Rey, G. Forthcoming-a. "Chomsky, Intentionality and a CRTT." In Antony, L. and Hornstein, N. *Chomsky and his Critics*. Oxford: Blackwell.

Rey, G. Forthcoming-b. "Searle's Misunderstandings of Functionalism and Strong AI."

Robb, D. 1997. "The Properties of Mental Causation." *Philosophical Quarterly* 47(187):178–94.

Robinson, H. 1982. *Matter and Sense*. Cambridge: Cambridge University Press.

Robinson, H. ed. 1993. *Objections to Physicalism*. Oxford: Clarendon Press.

Robinson, H. 1994. *Perception*. London: Routledge.

Rosenberg, A. 1985. "Davidson's Unintended Attack on Psychology." In LePore, E. and McLaughlin, B. *Actions and Events: Perspectives on the Philosophy of Donald Davidson*. Oxford: Blackwell, pp. 399–407.

Russell, B. 1927. *The Analysis of Mind*. London: Kegan Paul.

Ryle, G. 1963. *The Concept of Mind*. Harmondsworth: Penguin Books.

Savellos, E. and Yalcin, U., eds. 1995. *Supervenience: New Essays*. Cambridge: Cambridge University Press.

Schein, B. 1993. *Plurals and Events*. Cambridge, MA: MIT Press.

Searle, J.R. 1983. *Intentionality*. Cambridge: Cambridge University Press.

Searle, J.R. 1992. *The Rediscovery of the Mind*. Cambridge, MA: MIT Press.

Segal, G. 1989. "Seeing What Is Not There." *Philosophical Review* 98(2) April:189–214.

Segal, G. 1991. "Defence of a Reasonable Individualism." *Mind* C(4) October: 485–94.

Segal, G. and Sober, E. 1991. "The Causal Efficacy of Content." *Philosophical Studies*, v. 63.

Shoemaker, S. 1975. "Functionalism and Qualia." *Philosophical Studies* 27:291–315. Reprinted in Block, N. (1980a).

Shoemaker, S. 1980. "Causality and Properties." In Van Inwagen, P., ed. (1980).

Shoemaker, S. 1981. "Some Varieties of Functionalism." *Philosophical Topics* 12:83–118.

Shoemaker, S. 1994. "The Mind-Body Problem." In Warner, R. and Szubka, T., eds. (1994), pp. 55–60.

Shoemaker, S. 1998. "Causal and Metaphysical Necessity." *Pacific Philosophical Quarterly* 79(1):59–77.

Simpson, G. 1943. "Mammals and the Nature of the Continents." *American Journal of Science* 241:1–31.

Smart, J.J.C. 1959. "Sensations and Brain Processes." *Philosophical Review* 68:141–56. Reprinted in Chappell, V.C., ed. (1962). *The Philosophy of Mind*. Englewood Cliffs: Prentice Hall, pp. 160–72.

Smart, J.J.C. 1987. "Physicalism and Emergence." *Essays Metaphysical and Moral*. Oxford: Blackwell.

Smith, A.D. 1993. "Non-Reductive Physicalism?" In Robinson, H. (1993), pp. 225–50.

Smith, P. 1992. "Modest Reductions and the Unity of Science." In Charles, D. and Lennon, K., eds. *Reduction, Explanation and Realism*. Oxford: Oxford University Press.

Sosa, E. 1993. "Davidson's Thinking Causes." In Heil, J. and Mele, A., eds. (1993), pp. 41–50.

Spelke, E. 1991. "Physical Knowledge in Infancy: Reflection on Piaget's Theory." In Carey, S. and Gelman, R., eds. *The Epigenesis of Mind*. Hillsdale: Erlbaum Associates, pp. 133–70.

Spencer-Smith, R. 1995. "Reductionism and Emergent Properties." *Proceedings of the Aristotelian Society*, v. 117.

Sperry, R.W. 1969. "A Modified Concept of Consciousness." *Psychological Review*, v. 76.

Spurrett, D. and Papineau, D. 1999. "A Note on the Completeness of 'Physics.'" *Analysis*, v. 58.

Stairs, A. 1998. "Parapsychology." *Routledge Encyclopedia of Philosophy*, Oxford: Routledge.

Steigerwald, J. 1998. *Lebenskraft in Reflection*. Ph.D. Dissertation. London: University of London.

Stewart, J. 1990. *Drifting Continents and Colliding Paradigms*. Bloomington: Indiana University Press.

Stich, S. 1984. "Relativism, Rationality and the Limits of Intentional Description." *Pacific Philosophical Quarterly* 65:211–35.

Stich, S. 1993. "Puritanical Naturalism." In Neander, K. and Ravenscroft, I., eds. *Prospects for Intentionality*, Working Papers in Philosophy 3. Canberra: Research School of Social Sciences, Australian National University. Reprinted in Stich (1996).

Stich, S.P. 1996. *Deconstructing the Mind*. Cambridge, MA: MIT Press.

Stich, S.P. and Laurence, S. 1994. "Intentionality and Naturalism." In French, P., Uehling, T., and Wettstein, H., eds. *Midwest Studies in Philosophy*. Minneapolis: University of Minnesota Press. Reprinted in Stich (1996).

Strawson, G. 1987. *Freedom and Belief*. Oxford: Oxford University Press.

Strawson, G. 1994. *Mental Reality*. Cambridge, MA: MIT Press.

Strawson, P.F. 1949. "Ethical Intuitionism." *Philosophy* 24:23–33.

Strawson, P. 1974. "Freedom and Resentment." In *Freedom and Resentment and Other Essays*. London: Methuen.

Sturgeon, S. 1994. "The Epistemic View of Subjectivity." *Journal of Philosophy*, v. 91.

Sturgeon, S. 1998. "Physicalism and Overdetermination." *Mind*, v. 110.

Swoyer, C. 1982. "The Nature of Natural Laws." *Australasian Journal of Philosophy* 60:203–23.

Szubka, T. and Warner, R., eds. 1994. *The Mind-Body Problem*. Oxford: Blackwell.

Teller, P. 1989. "Relativity, Relational Holism, and the Bell Inequalities." In Cushing, J.T. and McMullin, E., eds. (1989). *Philosophical Consequences of Quantum Theory*. South Bend: University of Notre Dame Press.

Tversky, A. 1975. "A Critique of Expected Utility Theory." *Erkenntnis* 3:163–73.

Tye, M. 1995. *Ten Problems of Consciousness: A Representational Theory of the Phenomenal Mind.* Cambridge, MA: The MIT Press.

Van Cleve, J. 1990. "Emergence or Panpsychism: Magic or Mind-Dust?" In Tomberlin, J., ed. *Philosophical Perspectives Vol. 4.* Atascadero: Ridgeview.

Van Fraassen, B. 1996. "Science, Materialism and False Consciousness." In Kvanvig, J., ed. *Warrant In Contemporary Epistemology: Essays in Honor of Plantinga's Theory of Knowledge.* Lanham, MD: Rowman and Littlefield.

Van Inwagen, P. ed. 1980. *Time and Cause.* Dordrecht: D. Reidel Publishing.

Von Haller. 1751. "A Dissertation on the Sensible and Irritable Parts of Animals." Trans. Temkin, O. (1936). *Bulletin of the History of Medicine*, v. 4.

Von Helmholtz, H. 1847. *Uber die Erhaltung die Kraft.* Berlin.

Walker, R. 1993. "Transcendental Arguments against Physicalism." In Robinson, H., ed. (1993), pp. 61–80.

Warner, R. and Szuba, T., eds, 1994. *The Mind-Body Problem.* Oxford: Blackwell.

Watkins, M. Forthcoming. *Discovering Colors.*

Weinberg, S. 1992. *Dreams of a Final Theory.* New York: Pantheon.

Weiskrantz, L. 1986. *Blindsight.* Oxford: Clarendon Press.

White, S. 1986. "Curse of the Qualia." *Synthese* 68:333–68.

Whytt, R. 1755. *Physiological Essays.* Edinburgh.

Wiggins, D. 1973. "Towards a Reasonable Libertarianism." In Honderich, T., ed. *Essays on Freedom and Action.* London: Routledge and Kegan Paul.

Williams, B. 1978. *Descartes: The Project of Pure Enquiry.* London: Penguin Books.

Willis, B. 1932. "Isthmian Links." *Bulletin of the Geological Society of America* 43:917–52.

Winch, P. 1958. *The Idea of a Social Science.* London: Routledge and Kegan Paul.

Witmer, D.G. 1997. *Demanding Physicalism.* Ph.D. Dissertation. Rutgers University.

Witmer, D.G. 1999. "Supervenience Physicalism and the Problem of Extras." *Southern Journal of Philosophy* 37:315–31.

Witmer, D.G. Forthcoming. "Causal Overdetermination and the Macro-Micro Gap."

Wittgenstein, L. 1953. *Philosophical Investigations.* Trans. Anscombe, G.E.M. New York: Macmillan.

Wittgenstein, L. 1975. *Philosophical Remarks.* Rhees, R., ed. Oxford: Blackwell.

Wittgenstein, L. 1977. *Remarks on Colour.* Anscombe, G.E.M., ed. Oxford: Blackwell.

Wittgenstein, L. 1978. *Lectures and Conversations on Aesthetics, Psychology and Religious Belief.* Barrett, C., ed. Oxford: Blackwell.

Wittgenstein, L. 1980. *Remarks on the Philosophy of Psychology, II*. Anscombe, G.E.M. and von Wright, G.H., eds. Oxford: Blackwell.

Wittgenstein, L. 1981. *Zettel*. Anscombe, G.E.M. and von Wright, G.H., eds. Oxford: Blackwell.

Wittgenstein, L. 1988. *Wittgenstein's Lectures on Philosophical Psychology 1946–47*. Notes by Geach, P.T., Shah, K.J., and Jackson, A.C. Geach, P., ed. London: Harvester.

Woolhouse, R. 1985. "Leibniz's Reaction to Cartesian Interaction." *Proceedings of the Aristotelian Society*, 86.

Yablo, S. 1992. "Mental Causation." *Philosophical Review* 101(2):245–80.

Yablo, S. 1993. "Is Conceivability a Guide to Possibility?" *Philosophy and Phenomenological Research* 53:1–42.

Zangwill, N. 1998. "Direction of Fit and Normative Functionalism." *Philosophical Studies* 91:172–203.

Index

anomalous monism, 111–12, 138

Baker, Lynne, 99
Bealer, George, 74–6, 83–5, 96 n.19, 150 n.8
behaviorism, 132–3
Broad, C.D., 36 n.18, 214–15, 223 n.23
Burge, Tyler, 99–100, 146

Carnap, Rudolf, 255–6, 258
Cartwright, Nancy, 52–3
causal closure of physical. *See* completeness of physics
Chalmers, David, 257, 308, 332–46
Charles, David, 131
Chomsky, Noam, 116, 222
Clapp, Lenny, 93 n.3
Clark, Stephen, 5, 6, 33
completeness of physics, 7, 27–32, 38, 50, 116, 168, 219, 276–7
Comte, Auguste, 252–3
conceivability, 173, 186, 322–3, 331–3, 337–40
concepts, 337–42
conceptualism, 179, 181–2
consciousness, 273–5
conservation of energy, 20–6, 34 n.12, 34 n.17
Cussins, Adrian, 145–6

Darden, Lindley, 248 n.14, 249 n.17
Davidson, Donald, 5, 80, 111–14, 130–41, 136–9, 144–5, 259
Dennett, Daniel, 111–14

Descartes, Rene, 13–18, 154–8, 273–4
determinates and determinables, 77–9, 85–6
downward causation, 216–19, 224 n.25
dualism, 302–3
  substance, 156–61, 162–3, 165–7, 272

emergence, 142–3, 166, 208, 211–16, 224 n.24
emergentism, 30–2, 36 n.20, 50–2, 207, 210–16, 222, 274
epiphenomenalism, 10–11, 119–20
externalism, 294–5

Field, Hartry, 227–9
Fodor, Jerry, 228–9, 232–3, 349 n.19
folk psychology, 4, 75, 102–14
Foster, John, 115
free will, libertarian, 159–60
functionalism, 10–11, 83, 132–3, 285–6

Hellman, Geoffrey, 154, 192 n.5
Hill, Chris, 315
Horgan, Terry, 32–7, 209, 321–7
Hornsby, Jennifer, 104–6, 108–9
Hursthouse, Rosalind, 107–8

identity, 284–5, 289, 294
intension, 333–5

Jackson, Frank, 39, 41, 297–8, 347 n.3
James, William, 274
Joule, James, 22–3

Printed in the United States
115687LV00004B/51/A